ALDHELM

THE POETIC WORKS

ALDHELM
THE POETIC WORKS

TRANSLATED BY MICHAEL LAPIDGE
AND JAMES L. ROSIER

WITH AN APPENDIX BY
NEIL WRIGHT

D. S. BREWER

First published 1985
D. S. Brewer, Cambridge
Reprinted in paperback 2009

Transferred to digital printing

ISBN 978 1 84384 198 2

D. S. Brewer is an imprint of Boydell & Brewer Ltd
PO Box 9, Woodbridge, Suffolk IP12 3DF, UK
and of Boydell & Brewer Inc.
668 Mount Hope Avenue, Rochester, NY 14620, USA
website: www.boydellandbrewer.com

A catalogue record for this book is available
from the British Library

Library of Congress Catalog Card Number 84-29781

This publication is printed on acid-free paper

Printed in Great Britain

TABLE OF CONTENTS

PREFACE

The present volume is intended as a companion to the earlier *Aldhelm: The Prose Works*, by Michael Lapidge and Michael Herren (Ipswich: D. S. Brewer Ltd., 1979). Like its predecessor, which gave English translations of Aldhelm's major prose writings (the *Epistola ad Acircium*, prose *De Virginitate* and *Epistolae*) the present book provides translations of Aldhelm's poetic corpus: the *Carmina Ecclesiastica, Enigmata, Carmen de Virginitate* and *Carmen Rhythmicum*. (Of these, only the *Enigmata* have ever before been translated.) *Aldhelm: The Poetic Works*, then, is complementary to *Aldhelm: The Prose Works*: together they provide translations of all of Aldhelm's surviving Latin writings. In order that the two books may be used independently, however, each has been provided with introductory accounts of Aldhelm's life and writings as well as a full bibliography of writings on Aldhelm.

When *Aldhelm: The Prose Works* was in preparation, its authors became aware of Professor Rosier's independent but parallel work of translation on the *Carmen de Virginitate*, and the decision was subsequently taken to incorporate that translation into a collaborative volume of Aldhelm's poetic works. Accordingly, in the present volume, the translation of the *Carmen de Virginitate* is by James Rosier; translations of the remaining poems (*Carmina Ecclesiastica, Enigmata* and *Carmen Rhythmicum*) are by Michael Lapidge. The introductory chapters (pp. 1–33) as well as the Introductions and Notes to all the various poems are by Michael Lapidge.

We are grateful to many colleagues for advice on various points, but one colleague deserves special mention. Neil Wright's engaging enthusiasm for Aldhelm's Latin verse has been a source of inspiration throughout the preparation of the volume, and he has kindly read through our translations with painstaking attention. Furthermore, because it was felt that some parts of Aldhelm's prose treatises on metre (the *De Metris* and *De Pedum Regulis*) help to throw light on Aldhelm's poetic practice, he readily agreed to our suggestion that he translate the passages which are printed in the Appendix (below, pp. 181–219). It needs hardly to be added that we ourselves are responsible for any errors that remain in the translations.

M.L.
J.R.

July, 1984

GENERAL INTRODUCTION

Aldhelm was the first English man of letters. He was also perhaps the most widely learned man produced in Anglo-Saxon England during its first four centuries of Latin Christendom. Even the learning of Bede, whose knowledge of patristic literature was impressively wide, will not bear comparison with that of Aldhelm who, in addition to patristic and hagiographical literature of many kinds, had an enviable knowledge of Latin poetry, both Classical and Christian: indeed, his knowledge of Classical Latin poetry included familiarity with poems which have not come down to us. His learning and literary enterprise appear to us all the more extraordinary because we know so little of his education and background. He springs fully learned, a sort of latterday Athena, from a country which only in the previous generation had been converted from heathenism to Christianity. We know that Aldhelm studied in Canterbury with Theodore and Hadrian, and we know from Bede that theirs was the most brilliant school in early England. Bede names the most distinguished alumni of this school (all of whom are now little more than names to us): but — for reasons difficult to estimate — does not include Aldhelm among them. Similarly, we can deduce from one of Aldhelm's Letters that he spent some two or three years studying with Hadrian; but this is manifestly too brief a period for Aldhelm to have acquired his prodigious knowledge of Classical and patristic literature. In this respect, as in so many others, Aldhelm is a tantalizing enigma.

Wherever or however he acquired his prodigious learning, Aldhelm's Latin writings very quickly gained him universal prestige. As soon as they were published, it would seem, his extensive corpus of writings found admirers and imitators. The Latin writings of the missionary Boniface (*ob.* 754) and his circle of

1

English correspondents, for example, betray close familiarity with Aldhelm's Latin prose and poetry, a familiarity which must have been acquired in the early years of the eighth century, before Boniface departed for missionary work in Germany in 716. Bede, writing his *Historia Ecclesiastica* in 731, knew of Aldhelm's writings by reputation (if not necessarily at first hand), and could report that Aldhelm was a man 'most learned in every respect' who was 'both resplendent in his style and also noteworthy for his erudition in classical as well as patristic writings'.[1] Aldhelm's reputation had reached the Continent by the early eighth century at latest, for an Irish monk — one Cellanus (or Coelán) — of Péronne in Picardy wrote to Aldhelm before his death in 709 to say that 'the encomiastic report of [Aldhelm's] Latinity had reached his ears' and that 'although he had not had the privilege of hearing [Aldhelm] in the flesh, nonetheless he had read [Aldhelm's] books'.[2] We do not know if Aldhelm sent to Cellanus the books he had requested; but there is sound evidence that the writings of Aldhelm were soon carried to the Continent, not least by Boniface and his followers.[3] And, just as Boniface and his followers had evidently studied Aldhelm's writings closely before leaving England, so in the schools they established in Germany — especially at Fulda, Würzburg and Mainz — the study of Aldhelm came to occupy an important place in the curriculum.[4] The importance of Aldhelm as a curriculum author[5] can be gauged from the frequent appearances of his works in booklists and library catalogues from continental libraries. For example, a booklist from Reichenau dated 822 includes four volumes of Aldhelm; a list from Saint-Riquier of 831 includes a composite volume of his writings; a ninth-century catalogue from St Gallen includes four volumes of Aldhelm; and so on.[6]

Aldhelm was also studied in his native England. Alcuin, for example, listed Aldhelm among the authors to be found in Archbishop Ælberht's library at York (c. 778), and Alcuin's own Latin verse betrays intimate familiarity with Aldhelm.[7] But it is a curious irony that during the ninth century, when (principally as a result of Viking incursions) monastic life and Latin learning declined, manuscripts of Aldhelm's writings became scarce. Accordingly, when during the reigns of Alfred and his successors Edward and Athelstan ecclesiastical schools were re-established in England, manuscripts of Aldhelm's writings had to be imported from the Continent: none, it would seem, was to be found in England.[8] Thereafter, however, Aldhelm's writings became a staple of the school curriculum in England. The attentiveness with which all his writings were studied may easily be seen in surviving manuscripts. Nearly all the manuscripts of Aldhelm written in England in the tenth and eleventh centuries have been densely glossed in both Latin and Old English; the glossing is both lexical,[9] to help readers with Aldhelm's unusual vocabulary, and syntactical,[10] to help them unravel the complexities of Aldhelm's syntax. And given this close attention to Aldhelm's Latin writings, it is hardly surprising that his difficult Latin style should have found its imitators, or that the majority of Anglo-Latin authors of the tenth and eleventh centuries should have practised the so-called 'hermeneutic' style — a style, that is, which affected the use of abstruse and apparently learned vocabulary, drawn most often from glossaries of the 'hermeneumata' sort (hence the name) and including archaisms, grecisms and neologisms of all kinds — for the later practice of this style was grounded principally in the study and imitation of Aldhelm.[11]

Virtually every aspect of Aldhelm's literary activity found its imitators among Anglo-Saxon writers. The *Carmina Ecclesiastica* (dedicatory verses for various churches and altars) were imitated by the Northumbrian poets Alcuin and Æthilwulf.[12] The *Enigmata* inspired imitations by the Anglo-Latin poets Tatwine (archbishop of Canterbury, 731–4), 'Eusebius' (allegedly the Hwætberht who became abbot of Wearmouth/Jarrow in 716) and Boniface, as well as by the continental poets of the Lorsch and Bern riddle collections.[13] In addition, several of Aldhelm's *enigmata* were translated into Old English (both Northumbrian and West Saxon dialects), and it is probable that Aldhelm's collection of one hundred *Enigmata* served as the model for the collection of nearly one hundred Old English riddles which are preserved in the Exeter Book. By the same token, Aldhelm's prose writings — especially the *De Virginitate* and the Letter to Heahfrith (no. V) — were a stylistic model for later generations of Anglo-Latin prose writers. The Latin prose of Boniface and his circle of English correspondents — Eadburg, Ecgburg, Daniel, Leofgyth, and others — reveals close familiarity with Aldhelmian vocabulary and syntax.[14] Similar familiarity is seen in the Latin of two English writers active in Germany, in the wake of the Bonifatian mission, in the second half of the eighth century: Willibald, author of the *Vita S. Bonifatii*,[15] composed shortly after Boniface's martyrdom in 754; and the nun Hygeburg, who composed at Heidenheim a *Vita SS. Willibaldi et Wynnebaldi*[16] to commemorate two English brothers who were prominent in the mission in Germany. So too in the later Anglo-Saxon period, after

3

the efforts of King Alfred and his successors to re-establish ecclesiastical education, the influence of Aldhelm's prose was pervasive. For example, many Anglo-Saxon charters issued by kings from Athelstan (924–39) onwards are little more than Aldhelmian centos.[17] At the end of the tenth century and beginning of the eleventh, the Latin prose of Byrhtferth of Ramsey — particularly in his *Vita S. Oswaldi* and *Vita S. Ecgwini* — is studded with reminiscences of and quotations from Aldhelm's prose.[18] Only with the Norman Conquest, when native English educational traditions were replaced by Norman practices, does Aldhelm's influence begin to wane.[19]

From what has been said, it will be clear that Aldhelm is a cardinal figure in Anglo-Saxon literature, both in Latin and Old English. Indeed, in view of Aldhelm's profound influence on later English writers, it might well be argued that the study of Anglo-Saxon literature should properly begin with Aldhelm. But Aldhelm is not an easy author to study: his Latin is often fiercely difficult, and even scholars with years' training in Classical Latin may find themselves lost in Aldhelm's *densa Latinitatis silva*. It is not surprising, therefore, that until very recently Aldhelm has largely been ignored by students of Anglo-Saxon England, and that he has never been the subject of a full-scale monograph. Yet in one important respect the student of Aldhelm is well served: the edition of his writings by Rudolf Ehwald[20] is as fine an edition as exists for any early Medieval Latin author, being a rich treasury of information on Aldhelm's sources, life, Latinity and manuscripts as well as a thoroughly reliable critical edition. It is perhaps the very comprehensiveness of its treatment of Aldhelm that makes it a somewhat daunting tool of research for the would-be student of Aldhelm. The present book, like *Aldhelm: The Prose Works* before it, is intended primarily as a propaedeutic to Ehwald's monumental edition, in the hope that Aldhelm may become more accessible to students of Anglo-Saxon England. After too many years (and centuries) of neglect, Aldhelm deserves fresh attention, for he has much of precious value to tell us about Anglo-Saxon civilization.

ALDHELM'S LIFE

It is an unfortunate paradox that, whereas in Anglo-Saxon times Aldhelm's writings were perhaps the best known of any Anglo-Saxon author, the details of his personal life are virtually unknown. Unlike Bede, Aldhelm left us no *curriculum vitae*; and no loving disciple recorded an account of Aldhelm's last hours. Sources contemporary with Aldhelm provide us with a mere skeleton of facts: Bede, for example, tells us that Aldhelm became bishop of the westernmost part of the West Saxon diocese on the death of Bishop Hædddi in 705, and that he held that bishopric until his death four years later.[1] In an attempt to flesh out this bare skeleton, we turn not unnaturally to the biographies of two later Malmesbury writers: Faricius (*ob.* 1117) of Arezzo, who was at Malmesbury between *c.* 1080 and 1100, when he was appointed abbot of Abingdon,[2] and William of Malmesbury (*c.* 1090–1143).[3] These two authors had access to some sources (among them the *Handboc* of King Alfred) which have not come down to us, but we on the other hand have writings of Aldhelm which they apparently did not possess. They, like us, responded to the impulse to flesh out the bare skeleton of facts with inferences drawn sometimes from Aldhelm's writings, sometimes from fantasy. We must always bear in mind that Faricius and William were writing some four hundred years after Aldhelm's death. Their inferences, in other words, cannot be accepted uncritically. It is safer to proceed with utmost caution, eking out the bare skeleton of facts where possible with inferences legitimately drawn from Aldhelm's own writings, but declaring our ignorance where it is necessitated by the absence of evidence.[4]

We do not know where or when Aldhelm was born. His writings contain no indication of his age at any point. We may perhaps infer that he was born in Wessex, since his entire career

5

was apparently spent in that kingdom; but Aldhelm tells us nothing of his family, save that he was related by 'family bonds of kinship' to one Osburg (otherwise unknown).[5] But from his dealings with various members of the nobility, and especially with kings, it is a fair inference that Aldhelm himself was of noble, and perhaps royal, blood. Aldhelm stood as sponsor at the baptism of Aldfrith, king of Northumbria;[6] he addressed his De Virginitate among others to Cuthburg, quondam queen of King Aldfrith and sister of King Ine of Wessex.[7] In his role as bishop of Wessex he was evidently a member of King Ine's witan,[8] and William of Malmesbury reports — but gives no source for his report — that Aldhelm acted as spiritual adviser to King Ine.[9] Even setting aside William's report, there is no need to doubt these royal connections, and they perhaps lend credence to the story, told by both Faricius and William, that Aldhelm was the son of one Kenten, who was a brother (otherwise unknown) of King Ine.[10]

Concerning the date of Aldhelm's birth, William of Malmesbury tells us that Aldhelm was 'not less than a septuagenarian when he died'.[11] If this report were true, Aldhelm — who died in 709 or 710 (see below, p. 8) — would have been born no later than 639 or 640; and these are the dates which are usually given for his birth. However, William's statement is manifestly a conjecture, based on the psalmist's allotted 'threescore years and ten' (Ps.LXXXIX.10), for elsewhere he states openly that he had no accurate information concerning Aldhelm's age.[12] We must therefore confess to ignorance about the date of Aldhelm's birth. It is enough to remark that Wessex was converted to Christianity c. 635,[13] and that, if Aldhelm was born in Wessex c. 640, his parents would almost certainly have been pagans by birth and may have been numbered among the earliest West Saxon converts.

Aldhelm's probable pagan ancestry appears all the more remarkable when we consider the vast extent of his Christian learning and make some attempt to appreciate how and where he acquired that learning. Unfortunately we have no sound evidence on this subject. In a letter addressed to Aldhelm by an anonymous student (no. VI), the writer remarks that Aldhelm was 'nourished by a certain holy man of our race'.[14] But since the writer does not declare which race he himself belongs to, the information is impossible to interpret. The writer also mentions that Aldhelm had travelled to Rome; in this context it might appear that the writer was of Italian origin, in which case the 'man of our race' who instructed Aldhelm would presumably be Hadrian, an African by origin who had lived most of his life in Italy.[15] On the other hand,

William of Malmesbury reports — on the basis of no known evidence — that Aldhelm's early training took place at Malmesbury with one Máelduib.[16] This information has led modern students, including Ehwald, to deduce that the 'man of our race' was in fact Máelduib, and hence that the author of the letter was an unknown Irishman. But this is by no means a necessary deduction, and in the present state of our knowledge it is more prudent to declare *nescimus* on the subject of Aldhelm's early training.[17]

The subsequent stage of Aldhelm's education, however, is better documented. In a fragmentary letter preserved by William of Malmesbury (no. II), Aldhelm addresses Hadrian as 'the venerable teacher of my rough ineloquence', and recalls that he had left Hadrian's tuition three years previously and had been unable to return for various reasons, illness among them.[18] We know from Bede that Hadrian arrived in England shortly after Archbishop Theodore, hence in late 669 or 670. Bede further reports that Theodore and Hadrian 'attracted a crowd of students into whose minds they daily poured the streams of wholesome learning' and that 'they gave their hearers instruction not only in the books of Holy Scripture but also in the art of metre, astronomy and ecclesiastical computation'.[19] Bede adds that some of the students in question were still living in his own day (i.e. 731) and elsewhere he names Tobias (bishop of Rochester) and Albinus (abbot of SS. Peter and Paul in Canterbury) among them. Yet it is remarkable that Bede does not mention Aldhelm, who by any reckoning must have been one of the most learned men of his time, in the context of the Canterbury school. The answer may be that Aldhelm spent so brief a period at Canterbury — as little as two years (see below, p. 8)? — that he was not universally known as a Canterbury alumnus. The problem remains that, wherever he studied, Aldhelm acquired an astonishing breadth of learning, and even several years' study at Canterbury will scarcely account for this breadth.

Whatever the case, Aldhelm's advanced studies with Theodore and Hadrian seem to have been interrupted (terminated?) by ecclesiastical duties. Aldhelm attended an episcopal synod convened by Archbishop Theodore at Hertford in September, 672; at this synod Aldhelm was apparently instructed to write to King Geraint and the bishops of *Domnonia* concerning the synod's decisions, particularly on matters such as paschal reckoning. In the letter which resulted (no. IV), Aldhelm refers to himself as one 'performing the office of abbot without distinction of merits'. Since the letter must have been written soon after the synod,

Aldhelm will have been abbot — presumably at Malmesbury[20] — by late 672 or 673 (or 674 at the latest).[21]

We do not know whether he was the first abbot of Malmesbury; certainly there is no contemporary evidence for the existence of the abbey before Aldhelm's abbacy. Given Aldhelm's royal connections, one may suspect that the abbey originated as an *Eigenkirche*[22] on an estate belonging to Aldhelm's family.[23] In any case it is clear from Aldhelm's writings that as abbot of Malmesbury he was actively involved in the ecclesiastical affairs of Wessex (and beyond). On several occasions he writes that he has been 'weighed down with the burden of pastoral care' (prose *De Virginitate*, c. LIX); his royal connections ensured that he was equally weighed down by 'great tumultuous uproars in secular affairs' (*Epistola ad Acircium*, c. CXLII). He travelled to Rome on at least one occasion (Letter no. VI), and perhaps it was his experience at Rome which led him to sympathize with the abbots of the romanizing Bishop Wilfrid — and by implication to oppose the decrees of Archbishop Theodore — on one of the occasions when Wilfrid was expelled from his see (Letter no. XII). Aldhelm was vigorously active in establishing the Church in Wessex: he is known to have built churches at Bradford on Avon, Bruton, Wareham, and on the river Frome (possibly at the town of Frome itself), in addition to the two churches he built or rebuilt at Malmesbury.[24]

When Bishop Hæddi died in 705, the decision was taken to split the vast diocese of Wessex into two smaller, more manageable, sees, one having its centre in Winchester, the other in Sherborne. In spite of his advancing years, Aldhelm was an inevitable choice as bishop of the westernmost see, for he had conducted ecclesiastical business with neighbouring *Domnonia* (Letter no. IV), had travelled through Devon and Cornwall on at least one occasion (*Carmen Rhythmicum*) and had been instrumental in establishing the Church in Wessex. Aldhelm was consecrated in 705 or 706.[25] We know little of his episcopal activities, but Bede tells us that he presided very energetically (*strenuissime*) over his bishopric,[26] and (according at least to William of Malmesbury)[27] he built in Sherborne a cathedral of marvellous construction (*mirifice construxit*) which was still visible in William's day, but of which little or nothing remains today.[28] We may note that the diocese of Sherborne, once established by Aldhelm's efforts, remained intact until after the Norman Conquest, when it was moved to Salisbury (in 1078).

According to Bede, Aldhelm presided over his bishopric for

four years until his death in 709 (or possibly 710). William of Malmesbury reports[29] that he died at Doulting in Somerset, at a church which he as bishop had granted to the monks of Glastonbury. Again, according to William,[30] Aldhelm's remains were transported with due ceremony back to Malmesbury by Ecgwine, bishop of Worcester, who had learned of Aldhelm's death in a vision; but it is doubtful if any reliance can be placed on this report.[31]

THE WRITINGS OF ALDHELM

The following Latin writings of Aldhelm are extant (they are listed in the order in which they are printed by Ehwald, without prejudice to the question of their relative chronology):

(a) the *Carmina Ecclesiastica*. This is the title given by Ehwald to a collection of five *tituli* (dedicatory poems for churches or altars) which have been transmitted under Aldhelm's name in several continental manuscripts. The poems vary considerably in length and purpose; some, but not all, may have been composed for actual dedications. It is possible to make reasoned conjectures about the identification of some of the churches in question (nos. I–III). Dating of the *Carmina Ecclesiastica* is highly problematic, but two of them (nos. I and IV) may well be reckoned among Aldhelm's earliest compositions; the remainder are not precisely datable. The *Carmina Ecclesiastica* are discussed and translated below, pp. 35–58.

(b) the *Epistola ad Acircium*. An immense and composite work addressed to one 'Acircius', who can be identified with some confidence as Aldfrith, king of Northumbria (685–705). Aldfrith was an enlightened monarch who had studied at Iona with Adomnán and who could speak Irish; Bede tells us of his deep interest in books and learning.[1] According to some (slightly ambiguous) words in the introduction to the work, Aldhelm had stood as Aldfrith's godfather on an occasion twenty years earlier (presumably the occasion was Aldfrith's baptism); but we have no further evidence for the relationship between the two men.

The *Epistola ad Acircium* consists of several parts. After some prefatory remarks to Aldfrith (c. I), Aldhelm enters into a lengthy discussion of the allegorical and symbolical significance of the number 7 (cc. II–IV).[2] This disquisition is then followed by the first of two treatises on metre (which for convenience may be entitled *De Metris* and *De Pedum Regulis*). *De Metris*[3] is concerned principally with the various combinations of metrical feet (dactyls, spondees, etc.) which go to make up an hexameter line. This treatise is translated in the Appendix, below, pp. 191–211.

At the end of the treatise *De Metris*, and ostensibly to illustrate the various metrical principles which he had been enunciating, Aldhelm inserted his collection of one hundred hexametrical *Enigmata*, usually translated as 'Riddles', but better understood as 'Mysteries'. The *Enigmata* are only loosely connected with the preceding and following metrical treatises, and one is left with the impression that they were an earlier composition inserted in the *Epistola ad Acircium* to give it greater ballast; they frequently circulated independently of the metrical treatises in medieval manuscripts. The *Enigmata* are discussed and translated below, pp. 61–94.

Following the *Enigmata* is a second metrical treatise, the *De Pedum Regulis*.[4] This work consists of a catalogue of various metrical feet (for example, iamb, trochee, spondee, anapest, amphibrach, and so on); for each type of metrical foot Aldhelm includes a lengthy list of Latin words which naturally have the quantity of the foot in question. Thus, for example, as natural spondees Aldhelm gives *felix, pernix, perdix, index, inlex, cortex, remex, cornix, bombix, cervix, audax, forfex, forceps*, and so on for several pages. *De Pedum Regulis* is not a work which can ever have been read with ease or pleasure, but it would have provided a useful resource for a student attempting to master the complexities of quantitative verse-composition. As a sample of its method, one chapter (that on the pyrrhic) is translated in the Appendix, below, pp. 213–9.

Finally, the *Epistola ad Acircium* concludes with an apologetic *Allocutio excusativa* addressed to King Aldfrith, in which Aldhelm compares his role as poet among the Anglo-Saxons with that of Vergil among the Romans.[5]

The date of the *Epistola ad Acircium* cannot be established precisely. The outer dating *termini* are the dates of Aldfrith's reign, 685 x 705. Aldhelm relates in c. I of the *Epistola* that he had stood as Aldfrith's godfather on an occasion twenty years earlier; he then goes on to say, 'In the era of our young manhood (*pubertatis nostrae*) . . . I acquired the name of "father" . . . you received the appellations of your adoptive station'. However it be interpreted, *pubertas* would seem best to refer to an age from the late teens to the early thirties. If we begin with the dates traditionally assigned to Aldhelm's birth (630 x 640; see above, p. 6), then add the highest possible age to which *pubertas* could refer — say, 35 — and add finally the twenty years of which Aldhelm speaks, we arrive at a date of approximately 685 x 695, where 695 must represent the outer possible limit. That is to say, the composition of the *Epistola ad Acircium* probably fell within the earlier rather than the later part of Aldfrith's reign; but this is at best a guess, based on two unverifiable assumptions: that the date of Aldhelm's birth can even approximately be known, and that the word *pubertas* can safely be interpreted.

(c) the *De Virginitate*. This massive work is made up of two parts, one in prose consisting of sixty chapters of varying length (occupying some 100 pages in Ehwald's edition), the other a verse counterpart consisting of 2904 hexameters. The prose work[6] is addressed to Abbess Hildelith and a number of her nuns in a monastery at Barking (Essex). Barking was probably founded after the conversion of the East Saxons, possibly during the years 665 x 675; Hildelith, its second abbess, ruled the monastery for a very long period, from *c.* 675 to a time after 716. The prose *De Virginitate* consists of an elaborate theoretical introduction to the problem of virginity (cc. III–XIX), a catalogue of exemplary male virgins (cc. XX–XXXVIII) in roughly chronological order — Old Testament, New Testament, martyrs and Church Fathers — and then a catalogue of exemplary female virgins (cc. XL–LII) similarly ordered, then more accounts of some Old Testament patriarchs (Joseph, David, Abel, Melchisedech) (cc. LIII–LIV); then follows a diatribe against ostentatious dress worn by members of the Church (c. LVIII) and finally a conclusion (cc. LIX–LX) in which Aldhelm promises to send Hildelith and her nuns a poem on the same subject of virginity.

The poem on the subject, the *Carmen de Virginitate*, is discussed and translated below (pp. 97–167). In broad outline it follows the structure of the prose *De Virginitate*, in that it consists principally of a lengthy catalogue of exemplary virgins; but there are also significant structural differences, notably in the fact that the *Carmen de Virginitate* ends with a long section describing allegorically the confrontation of the vices and virtues (the section is entitled *De Octo Vitiis Principalibus* in some manuscripts) that has no correlate in the prose work.

The composite *De Virginitate* is the most difficult of Aldhelm's works to date. In its very first chapter Aldhelm remarks that he had received letters from the nuns at Barking while he was 'proceeding to an episcopal convention'.[7] This might suggest at once that the work dated from the period of Aldhelm's episcopacy (705/6 x 709/10); however, he need not have been a bishop to attend an episcopal synod. In fact we know that he attended at least one such synod — possibly that at Hertford in 672 — at a much earlier stage in his career (see above, p. 7). If the synod mentioned in c. I is indeed that held at Hertford in 672, an approximate date could be assigned to the *De Virginitate*: Aldhelm states that he had attended the synod 'some time ago' (*iamdudum*), and we could therefore date the *De Virginitate* after 675, perhaps after 680, depending on how we might wish to interpret *iamdudum*.

However, an active abbot and a disciple of the archbishop might well have attended many such synods; and Theodore, at the same synod at Hertford, made some attempt to ensure that synods would be convoked each subsequent year on 1 August at a place called *Clofeshoh*. One is therefore obliged to seek some other control for dating the *De Virginitate*. In a letter to Aldhelm from Cellanus of Péronne (no. IX), Aldhelm is addressed as 'abbot' (*archimandrita*); and Cellanus notes that he has read Aldhelm's 'books (*fastos*) which were painted with the charms of various flowers'. Now Aldhelm himself describes the composition of his prose *De Virginitate* as 'plucking crimson flowers of modesty from the meadow of holy books' (c. XIX). Furthermore, Aldhelm describes the prose part of his *De Virginitate* by the glossary word *fastus* (= 'book') in the later poetic part of the same work (line 21), and this is the same word which Cellanus used in the plural to describe the works of Aldhelm which he had read; it is probable, therefore, that the *fasti* which Cellanus had read were the two parts of Aldhelm's *De Virginitate*. Unfortunately — once again — it is impossible to date the letter of Cellanus exactly. But we know that Cellanus wrote before 706 (since Aldhelm was still abbot), and we must allow some lapse of time — how much is difficult to say — for the works to have been circulated and read in northern France. All that Cellanus's reference to the two books of the *De Virginitate* can safely establish is that they were written somewhat before the period of Aldhelm's bishopric.

One other fact needs to be considered. In his letter to Heahfrith (no. V), Aldhelm quotes four lines which are also found in the poetic *De Virginitate* (although they do not occur consecutively there).[8] If these lines were indeed repeated from the poetic *De Virginitate*, the date of the letter could be used to establish a *terminus ante quem* for both parts of the *De Virginitate*. The letter to Heahfrith describes Theodore as alive and as actively engaged in teaching. The letter must therefore have been written before 690 at the latest (the date of Theodore's death), and it was probably written a good deal earlier, perhaps by about 675.[9] The citation of lines from the poetic *De Virginitate* would thus appear to confirm an early date for the composite work. The problem is that Aldhelm may well have re-cycled in his *Carmen de Virginitate* four lines which he had earlier composed for inclusion in his letter to Heahfrith. In that case, the date of the letter could not be a reliable *terminus ante quem* for the composition of the *De Virginitate*.

Attempts by earlier scholars to establish a date for the *De Virginitate* are not trustworthy. Ehwald's arguments for a date after 685 are not acceptable. Ehwald argued[10] that, since Cuthburg was the queen of Aldfrith of Northumbria, and since she was already installed at Barking when Aldhelm was writing the *De Virginitate*, the date of the work must be later than 685. Unfortunately, we have no contemporary evidence concerning Cuthburg, and no source of any date tells us when she married Aldfrith or when she left him. It must remain at least a possibility that she had married and left him before he acceded to the Northumbrian throne. In these difficulties, perhaps a passage from the epilogue to the *Epistola ad Acircium* (c. CXLII) may be of avail. Aldhelm there would appear to be comparing Aldfrith to the emperor Theodosius, whom Aldhelm describes as married (*maritabatur*), and this may well suggest that Aldfrith was married (to Cuthburg?) at the time he was writing the *Epistola ad Acircium*. And this in turn might suggest that Cuthburg abandoned Aldfrith after the *Epistola ad Acircium* was written, and therefore that the *De Virginitate* was later than the *Epistola ad Acircium*. But in view of the insubstantial nature of all this evidence, it is impossible to ascertain a date for the *De Virginitate*.

(d) *Epistolae*. A number of letters to and by Aldhelm survives, either separately in manuscripts or in excerpts quoted by William of Malmesbury.[11] The genuine letters of Aldhelm include the following: Letter no. I, addressed (probably) to Leuthere, bishop of the West Saxons (670–6), in which Aldhelm, apparently writing from Canterbury, expresses his apologies that he will be unable to visit the bishop after Christmas, but takes the opportunity of giving a detailed account of the subjects he is currently studying; Letter no. II, addressed to Hadrian (c. 675), in which Aldhelm apologizes for the fact that, after leaving Hadrian's company in

14

Kent nearly three years ago, he has been prevented by illness from rejoining Hadrian; Letter no. III, dating from Aldhelm's abbacy and addressed to one Wihtfrith, an otherwise unknown student of Aldhelm, in which Aldhelm counsels Wihtfrith — who was proposing to journey to Ireland — about the vices and perils of that country; Letter no. IV, addressed to Geraint, king of *Domnonia*, and datable probably to 673, in which Aldhelm expounds at length the (Roman) views of the Council of Hertford (September 672) concerning church unity and the problem of reckoning Easter; Letter no. V, datable to *c*. 675 and addressed to one Heahfrith (otherwise unknown), who had studied in Ireland for some six years and was apparently seeking to become a student of Aldhelm, in which Aldhelm stresses the benefits of undertaking higher education in England; Letter no. VIII, addressed to one Sigegyth (otherwise unknown) and dating from Aldhelm's abbacy, in which he reports the outcome of a personal appeal to an unnamed bishop concerning the baptism (or re-baptism?) of a certain nun; Letter no. X, a fragment of a reply to Cellanus of Péronne, who had written to Aldhelm requesting copies of his books; Letter no. XI, a letter of moral exhortation addressed to Æthilwald, one of Aldhelm's students; and Letter no. XII, addressed to the abbots of the notorious Bishop Wilfrid on one of the occasions (probably that of 677) when he was expelled from his see, in which Aldhelm expresses solidarity with Wilfrid's cause. Another letter, no. XIII, addressed to Wynberht, is probably but not certainly genuine as well.

Three letters addressed to Aldhelm survive: by an anonymous student (no. VI), by his student Æthilwald (no. VII) and by Cellanus of Péronne (no. IX).

(e) *Carmen Rhythmicum.* A poem of 200 octosyllables addressed to one Helmgils (otherwise unknown), in which Aldhelm describes the cataclysmic effects of a violent storm on a small church and congregation somewhere in the southwest, on the occasion of a trip by Aldhelm through Devon and Cornwall. The *Carmen Rhythmicum* is discussed and translated below, pp. 171–9

(f) Other works possibly by Aldhelm. During the nineteenth century and earlier this century there was much scholarly concern with the canon of Aldhelm's writings. Giles, for example, suggested that Aldhelm was the author of a long biblical epic on the Heptateuch; but this work was subsequently recognized as the *Heptateuchos* of the Late Latin poet Cyprianus Gallus.[12] Similarly,

Lehmann proposed Aldhelm as the author of a letter addressed to an unknown Sigeberht on the study of grammar;[13] but this letter was later shown to be none other than the dedicatory preface of Boniface's *Ars Grammatica*.[14] In more recent times the canon of Aldhelm's writings has been fixed more or less on what is printed between the covers of Ehwald's edition. In certain (minor) respects this canon deserves continuing attention; in particular three works possibly by Aldhelm deserve mention.

First, Aldhelm in his *Epistola ad Acircium* quotes on three occasions[15] from a poem attributed to the Sibyl and concerning the Day of Judgement.[16] On the third occasion, Aldhelm follows the Sibylline verse with the statement *et alibi poeta dicit*, and then proceeds to quote a line from his own *Carmen de Virginitate* (line 530). There is some implication here that the author of the Sibylline verse and the *poeta* are one and the same, and we know that Aldhelm frequently quotes his own verse under a similar pretext of anonymity.[17] The complete Sibylline poem from which Aldhelm quotes is an acrostic poem of thirty-four lines (inc. 'Iudicio tellus sudabit maesta propinquo')[18] preserved uniquely in a manuscript from Leipzig (Stadtbibl., Rep. I.74 [Loire region, s. ix[1]], ff. 24r–25r), a manuscript which also contains Aldhelm's *Enigmata* (ff. 1r–13r). The poem itself is a (fairly loose) translation of a Greek acrostic poem beginning ΙΗΣΟΥΣ ΧΡΕΙΣΤΟΣ ΘΕΟΥ ΥΙΟΣ ΣΩΤΗΡ ΣΤΑΥΡΟΣ. We have insufficient evidence from elsewhere in Aldhelm's writings to establish beyond doubt that he knew Greek well enough to translate such a poem.[19] However, it is noteworthy that on two occasions Aldhelm employed the acrostic form himself (the metrical prefaces to his *Enigmata* and *Carmen de Virginitate*); furthermore, there are certain similarities of diction between the Sibylline poem and Aldhelm's other Latin verse.[20] There is good reason, therefore, to suppose that the Latin Sibylline poem originated in the school of Theodore and Hadrian; but whether it is the work of Aldhelm requires further investigation.

Another poem which bears the imprint of Aldhelmian diction, and which is conceivably by Aldhelm himself, is a metrical epitaph for Archbishop Theodore (*ob.* 690), which is quoted in part by Bede in his *Historia Ecclesiastica*,[21] and was reportedly inscribed as a *titulus* on Theodore's tomb. According to Bede, the epitaph consisted of thirty-four verses, and began as follows:

> Hic sacer in tumba pausat cum corpore praesul
> Quem nunc Theodorum lingua Pelasga uocat.
> Princeps pontificum, felix summusque sacerdos
> Limpida discipulis dogmata disseruit.[22]

Similarly, Bede gives the conclusion of the epitaph:

> Namque diem nonam decimam September habebat,
> Cum carnis claustra spiritus egreditur,
> Alma nouae scandens felix consortia uitae,
> Ciuibus angelicis iunctus in arce poli.[23]

It is unfortunate that Bede did not quote the entire poem, for even in the short compass of these two excerpts there are several distinctively Aldhelmian phrases, such as *lingua Pelasga* (*Enigm.* lx.10), *consortia uitae* (*CdV* 155, 739, 1980 and 2378) and *arce poli* (*Enigm.* prol. 35 and viii.3); and compare *ciuibus angelicis* with Aldhelm's *coetibus angelicis* (*CE* IV.ii.36). Aldhelm had known Theodore, and was an accomplished occasional poet, as may be seen from his *Carmina Ecclesiastica*; but without further evidence it is not possible to press Aldhelm's claim for authorship of the epitaph.

Finally, it is worth mentioning that in a number of manuscripts either of English origin or from continental centres with English connections, there occurs a lunar table with the rubric *Ciclus Aldhelmi de cursu lunae per signa .xii. secundum grecos.*[24] We know from Bede that the curriculum studied at Canterbury under Theodore and Hadrian included the computus, and in Aldhelm's letter to Leuthere (no. I) he explained that, although he previously thought he had mastered computistical studies, he now realized that he was merely a beginner in that difficult subject.[25] It is conceivable, therefore, that Aldhelm devised the lunar table in question; but the matter requires investigation by experts in the field of medieval computus.[26]

(g) Lost works of Aldhelm. Aldhelm's works were copied and circulated enthusiastically as soon as they were composed, and the wide manuscript circulation has ensured that most, if not all, of his writings have survived. But some writings may not have come down to us. For example, Cellanus of Péronne wrote to Aldhelm before 706 to request a copy of Aldhelm's *sermones*. The term *sermones* could conceivably describe a collection of homilies,[27] but it is equally possible that Cellanus was using the term in the vague sense of 'writings', and hence that he was not requesting a specific work now lost to us.

More interesting, perhaps, is the question of verse composed by Aldhelm in Old English. William of Malmesbury[28] reports the testimony of King Alfred's *Handboc* to the effect that Aldhelm had no equal as a poet in his native language. It is a matter of great regret that Alfred's *Handboc* has not survived, and we are obliged to accept William's account of it. According to William, King Alfred attested that one of the best-known Old English poems — which was still being sung in Alfred's time — had been composed by Aldhelm, and Alfred then proceeded to relate the now famous anecdote about Aldhelm chanting profane poetry interspersed with biblical phrases at the bridge in Malmesbury for the benefit of his congregation. Aldhelm's Old English verse has apparently not survived, and there have been no successful attempts to discover it among the body of surviving Old English poetry. In any case, Aldhelm's attempts to combine biblical narrative with traditional native verse mark him as a pioneer in this endeavour, since he is at least contemporary with if not earlier than Cædmon, whose similar attempts to combine biblical and traditional verse are recorded at some length by Bede.[29]

(h) Spuria. Among Aldhelm's writings Ehwald printed five Anglo-Saxon charters[30] which, in his opinion, deserved to be included among the genuine writings of Aldhelm,[31] principally because they exhibited Aldhelmian diction. However, as mentioned above (p. 4), Aldhelm's Latin prose frequently served as a quarry for the draftsmen of Anglo-Saxon charters, particularly from the reign of King Athelstan (924–39) onwards. Aldhelmian diction is not, therefore, an argument in favour of Aldhelmian authorship or draftsmanship.[32] Accordingly, none of the charters in question can be accepted as a genuine work of Aldhelm.

Another work which has often been associated with Aldhelm,[33] and which was transmitted under his name in at least one (lost) medieval manuscript,[34] is the *Liber Monstrorum*.[35] However, although this fascinating work shares certain features — including the use of extremely rare sources — with Aldhelm's writings, close study of its syntax and prose style indicates that it is a work by a colleague or disciple of Aldhelm rather than one by Aldhelm himself.[36]

Finally, two ghosts (of nineteenth-century fabrication) must be laid: that Aldhelm was the author of a (now lost) treatise of *De Laude Sanctorum*, parts of which were quoted by Aimoin of Fleury,[37] and that Aldhelm composed a six-book grammatical treatise *De Nomine*.[38]

ALDHELM AS LATIN POET

Aldhelm occupies a unique and cardinal position in the history of Medieval Latin poetry. He was the first Latin poet of the Middle Ages who composed quantitative Latin verse extensively and who was not a native speaker of Latin. In this respect, as in so many others, Aldhelm was a pioneer, as he himself rightly recognized. Towards the end of his *Epistola ad Acircium* he observes 'that no one born of the offspring of [the English] race and nourished in the cradles of a Germanic people has toiled so mightily in a pursuit of this sort before [his] humble self',[1] and he goes on to compare his efforts in this sphere with those of Vergil in another, in that Vergil in his *Georgics* was the first Roman poet to treat of agriculture in verse. Aldhelm's pioneering efforts deserve study in their own right, but they are especially important for the influence which they had on later Medieval Latin — and particularly Anglo-Latin — poets.

Quantitative verse consists of combinations of metrical feet, and a metrical foot consists of the alteration of long and short syllables. For example, a dactyl consists of one long followed by two short syllables (- ⌣ ⌣) and a spondee in two long syllables (- -); and a hexameter in turn — to choose only one example of a metrical verse — consists of six dactyls or spondees in combination. The composition of quantitative verse entails the knowledge of what constitutes a long or short syllable. In Latin, each of the vowels may be either long or short. A native speaker of Latin would know naturally (even unconsciously) whether a particular vowel was long or short; but a would-be Latin poet who was not a native speaker of Latin would be obliged to learn painstakingly the quantities of the vowels in all the Latin words which he might wish to employ in a verse before he could begin the process of fitting the words into the various metrical feet.

Nor was guidance in the matter of quantitative verse-composition easily obtained. The various treatises on Latin metre which were compiled in late antiquity — for example, those of Audax, Diomedes, Servius, Mallius Theodorus and the rest — were written as reference works for the consultation of grammarians and professional teachers; no consideration is ever given in them to elementary matters such as the quantity of vowels and syllables, for such matters would be second nature to the intended readership. These treatises, in other words, provided minimal help for the beginner in Latin verse-composition who was not a native speaker of Latin.[2]

Given these circumstances, it is not surprising that early medieval poets should have experienced immense difficulties in composing quantitative verse. In Ireland, for example, which had been converted to Latin Christianity in the fifth century and had by the seventh century produced a number of competent Latin authors, no attempt seems to have been made to master the difficulties of quantitative verse-composition before the ninth century; there, such verse as was composed was entirely rhythmical (based, that is, on the stress-patterns of individual words, rather than on the quantity of their syllables), not quantitative.[3] It may be thought that the difficulties of mastering the scansion and composition of quantitative verse were so severe for non-Latin speakers that they could best (and perhaps only) be mastered through instruction by a native Latin speaker; and one might wonder if quantitative verse was not mastered in early Ireland because Ireland had not enjoyed the benefit of foreign teachers who were native speakers of Latin. Seen from this perspective, the advent of Hadrian in England assumes new importance, for Hadrian was a native of Africa who had lived his life in Italy and who was (presumably) a Latin speaker. Bede[4] tells us that among the subjects taught by Hadrian (and Theodore) in the school at Canterbury was the 'art of metre' (*metricae artis . . . disciplina*); and Aldhelm, writing (from Canterbury?) to Bishop Leuthere (Letter no. I) reports that he is in the process of learning 'to distinguish among the hundred types of metres according to their divisions of feet and to survey the musical modulations of song along the straight path of syllables'. He adds, revealingly, that 'the more the inextricable obscurity of this subject is put forward to studious readers, the smaller the number of scholars becomes'.[5] It is a valuable testimony to Aldhelm's prodigious achievement that he not only acquired competence in Latin verse-composition, but that he took the trouble to compose two elementary treatises on metrics — the *De Metris* and *De Pedum Regulis* — to help his students over obstacles which he had surmounted only with difficulty himself.

Let us now consider briefly Aldhelm's metrical practice.[6] An hexameter[7] consists of six metrical feet; of these, each of the first four may be either a dactyl or a spondee; the fifth foot is normally a dactyl (although classical poets admitted fifth-foot spondees on rare occasions) and the sixth foot either a spondee or trochee. Since Aldhelm never admitted a fifth-foot spondee, the last two feet, or cadence, of the hexameter were for him an invariable unit of dactyl + spondee/trochee. Only in the first four feet, then, did Aldhelm have any potential for metrical variation. In theory, there are sixteen possible combinations of dactyl and spondee in the first four feet ($2^4 = 16$); in practice Aldhelm used an extremely limited range of combinations. Aldhelm's practice in the first four feet may be illustrated by reference to the opening eight lines of his *Carmen de Virginitate* (let D = dactyl and S = spondee in accordance with normal convention):

1 Ōmnĭpŏ+tēns gĕnĭ+tōr mūn+dūm dĭcĭ+ōne gubernans: DDSD
2 Lūcĭdă | stēllĭgĕr+ĭ qui | cŏndĭs | culmina caeli: DDSS
3 Nēcnŏn | tēllūr+ĭs fŏr+mans fūnd+ămĭna verbo: SSSS
4 Pāllĭdă | pūrpŭrĕ+ŏ pĭn+gĭs qui | flore virecta: DDSS
5 Sīc quŏquĕ | flūctĭvă+gĭ rĕ+frĕnans | caerula ponti: DDSS
6 Mērgĕrĕ | nĕ uălĕ+ănt tĕr+rārŭm | litora limphis: DDSS
7 Sēd tŭmĭ+dŏs frăn+gănt flŭc+tŭs ŏb+stacula rupis: DSSS
8 Ārvŏr+ŭm gĕlĭ+dŏ qui | cultus | fonte rigabis: SDSS

Several salient features of Aldhelm's verse technique may be seen in these lines. First, Aldhelm very frequently treats the cadence (that is, the final two feet) of the hexameter as a detachable unit. Thus in lines 2, 4, 5, 6 and 8 the final two feet are made up of words of 3 + 2 syllables (e.g. *culmina caeli*) or of 2 + 3 (e.g. *fonte rigabis*).[8] Classical poets avoided the repeated use of such cadences, and sought to achieve variety by employing longer words which would span the fourth and fifth feet and so bind the cadence more tightly to the hexameter. Aldhelm does this in lines 1, 3 and 7; but his normal practice is to treat the cadence as a free-standing, detachable unit. Secondly, out of the sixteen possible combinations of dactyl and spondee which may be employed in the first four feet, Aldhelm in fact employs very few. Classical poets sought to achieve variety by avoiding the repeated use of particular combinations; thus Vergil allowed himself to repeat one combination about once every twelve lines, Lucan once every eleven lines.[9] Aldhelm, by contrast, uses a very few combinations over and over again: thus, in the sample given above, he uses the combination DDSS three times in a row and four times in the eight lines. It will also be noticed that in the eight lines quoted, the third and fourth feet on every occasion but one (line 1) consist of two spondees. What variation he does attempt is limited in effect to the first two feet of the hexameter, leaving the final four feet as a sort of fixed, invariable block (spondee + spondee + dactyl + spondee/ trochee). By any standard, then, Aldhelm's hexameters are rhythmically monotonous.

Classical Latin poets employed many devices in order to avoid monotony in their verse, and it is an interesting index of Aldhelm's craftsmanship to ask how he handled such devices. Three in particular may be mentioned. First, elision. Elision occurred when a word ending with a vowel or diphthong, or with a vowel plus *m*, came before a word beginning with another vowel or diphthong; in such cases the final syllable of the first word was slurred into the initial syllable of the following word so as to make one syllable out of two. Elision may be seen in two consecutive lines of the *Carmen de Virginitate* (62–3):

> Et brut(um) inspiras vitali flamine pectus
> Qui cord(a) ingeniis ornas et labra loquelis.

Classical poets used elision deftly and frequently in order to vary the flow of syllables within their hexameters. Vergil allows on average one elision every two lines, Ovid one every three or four, Lucan one every six. Aldhelm, however, in spite of the impression conveyed by the two quoted lines, rarely employs elision. Elision is found on average once every twenty lines in his verse (and usually in the second foot of an hexameter, as in the quoted lines); when it does occur in his verse, it tends to occur in clusters, as if he occasionally reminded himself of the need to employ it. We may surmise that the concept of elision would have seemed foreign to anyone who had not spoken Latin from birth, and that its practice would have entailed severe difficulty.

Secondly, Classical Latin poets often achieved variety by employing one or two monosyllables in the final foot of the hexameter, to give the sense of an abrupt and emphatic ending; or, alternatively, by filling the fifth and sixth feet at one stroke with a pentasyllabic word, which can impart a sense of grandiloquence. On extremely rare occasions Aldhelm uses two monosyllables in the sixth foot, such as *CE* II.26 = *CdV* 1704, 'spiritus e caelo veniet sanctissimus in te', or *Enigm.* prol. 12, 'Cynthi sic numquam perlustro cacumina sed nec'.[10] On even rarer occasions

22

he ends an hexameter with a single monosyllable (*Enigm.* prol. 19: 'late per populos illustria qua nitidus sol'). There are very few examples in Aldhelm of an hexameter ending with a pentasyllabic word.[11]

Finally, in order to achieve variety of pace Classical Latin poets sometimes used end-stopped lines (lines, that is, in which the end of the hexameter and the end of a sentence or clause or sense-unit coincide) and sometimes lines which contained internal pauses. In Aldhelm, however, nearly every single hexameter is end-stopped. Thus in the example from *CdV* 1–8 quoted above (p. 21), there is no example of an internal pause: all eight lines are end-stopped. This may be taken as a typical sample of Aldhelmian verse. Only rarely does Aldhelm employ an internal pause, as in the third line of the following *enigma*:

> Sum mihi dissimilis vultu membrisque biformis:
> Cornibus armatus, horrendum cetera fingunt
> Membra virum; fama clarus per Gnossia rura . . .
> [*Enigm.* xxviii.1–3]

Here the sense-unit in line 2 continues past *fingunt* and concludes at *virum* in the middle of line 3; but such internal pauses are rare in Aldhelm. In fact more than ninety per cent of Aldhelm's hexameters are end-stopped. The implication is that Aldhelm conceived his poetry one line at a time rather than in longer and more complex sense-units (it is this feature of his verse, one may note in passing, that makes it somewhat less difficult to understand than his prose).

The many and various subtle devices employed by Classical Latin poets to achieve variety of rhythm and pace were, by and large, ignored or avoided by Aldhelm. He seems to have been fully occupied in mastering the quantities of syllables and the combinations of metrical feet without having the leisure to concern himself with embellishments and refinements. Some sense of the difficulties he faced may be glimpsed through the measures he devised to cope with them. One such measure is the use of what one might call 'formulas', that is, groups of words which are regularly employed under similar metrical conditions to express a given idea.[12] Consider the following examples from the *Carmen de Virginitate*, in which Aldhelm expresses in various ways the given idea of 'the realms/regions of the heavenly skies':

> Aurea tum propere penetrarat *regna polorum* (2160)
> *Summa supernorum* conquirens *regna polorum* (755)
> *Alta supernorum* patuerunt *claustra polorum* (428)

> *Alta supernorum* qui scandunt *arva polorum* (2862)
> *Cuncta supernorum* convincens *astra polorum* (182)

There is minor variation each time, but it is clear that each line is a reworking of the one metrical formula. So too with various reworkings of a formula describing 'the clear summits of the starry sky':

> *Lucida stelligeri* qui condis *culmina caeli* (2)
> *Lucida stelligeri* scandentes *culmina caeli* (1445)
> *Limpida stelligeri* conscendens *culmina caeli* (2816)

From examples such as these — and the list could be extended almost indefinitely — it can be seen that Aldhelm's technique of hexameter-composition involved the use of a number of metrically measured, but slightly and easily variable, formulas, which could be adapted at will to local grammatical circumstances whenever the given idea arose. The use of such a technique makes Aldhelm's poetry exceedingly repetitious, but one can see that the technique was designed by Aldhelm as a sort of helpmeet, to help him master the difficulties which hexameter-composition entailed. It is a reasonable inference that hexameter-composition for Aldhelm's students involved the elaboration and memorization of such metrically prefabricated formulas.[13]

Aldhelm's Latin poetry, then, is rhythmically monotonous and verbally repetitious. Yet it is no less remarkable for all that. Aldhelm was a pioneer, and he forged a language and a poetic diction which was to influence Latin poets in England and on the Continent for four centuries. The technique which he devised to facilitate metrical composition was adopted by his own students and then by generations of Medieval Latin poets. It would not be misleading to describe Aldhelm as the father of Anglo-Latin poetry. His comparison of himself with Vergil is overwrought, yet in retrospect we may see that it has a certain aptness.

TRANSLATORS' NOTES

The present translations, like those in *Aldhelm: The Prose Works*, are intended primarily to introduce the interested student to Aldhelm's Latin poetry, and hence they are designed to serve as a 'crib' to Ehwald's edition of Aldhelm. We have therefore attempted to provide literal translations, so that the reader may follow the Latin text with some ease. To this end we have given references to pages of Ehwald's edition (in slant brackets) throughout, and have arranged the separate works in the same order as that followed by Ehwald. Line references to the individual poems are also given in square brackets. Words in ordinary parentheses are not present in the Latin but have been added in English for the sake of clarity or coherency. On occasions when Aldhelm quotes from the Bible, we give the biblical source in square brackets; and note that all biblical quotations in English are taken from the Douay-Rheims translation of the Vulgate of 1582–1609. In general we have kept our annotation to a minimum, thus hoping to encourage readers to consult the more extensive documentation to be found in Ehwald's edition. Note that in references to Aldhelm's poetry the following abbreviations are used: *CE* = *Carmina Ecclesiastica*; *Enigm.* = *Enigmata*; and *CdV* = *Carmen de Virginitate*.

ALDHELM BIBLIOGRAPHY

A. EDITIONS OF ALDHELM'S WORKS

R. Ehwald, *Aldhelmi Opera Omnia*. Monumenta Germaniae Historica. Auctores Antiquissimi XV (Berlin, 1919).
[a veritably monumental edition which entirely supersedes earlier editions]

J. A. Giles, *Sancti Aldhelmi Opera* (Oxford, 1844), reprinted by Migne, *Patrologia Latina*, vol. LXXXIX, cols. 87–314.
[even by Giles's deplorable standards, his edition of Aldhelm is poor. It should not be consulted.]

J. H. Pitman, *The Riddles of Aldhelm*. Yale Studies in English LXVII (New Haven, 1925; repr. Hamden, Conn.: Archon Books, 1970).
[Ehwald's text of the *Enigmata* with facing English translation]

F. Glorie, *Collectiones Aenigmatum Merovingicae Aetatis*. Corpus Christianorum, Series Latina CXXXIII–CXXXIII A. 2 vols. (Turnhout, 1968), I, 359–540.
[reprints Ehwald's text of the *Enigmata* together with Pitman's translation]

G. van Langenhove, *Aldhelm's de Laudibus Virginitatis* (Bruges, 1941)
[a facsimile edition of Brussels, Royal Library, MS. 1650]

Sancti Bonifacii Epistolae. Codex Vindobonensis 751 der österreichischen Nationalbibliothek, ed. F. Unterkircher. Codices selecti phototypice iɩ ɔressi XXIV (Graz, 1971).
[facsimile of the manuscript ɩich contains some of Aldhelm's letters and rhythmical poemʂ]

B. GLOSSARIES AND GLOSSES IN ALDHELM MANUSCRIPTS

C. W. Bouterwek, 'Angelsächsische Glossen. (1) Die Ags. Glossen in dem Brüsseler Codex von Aldhelms Schrift *De Virginitate*', *Zeitschrift für deutsches Altertum* IX (1853), 401–530.

R. Derolez, 'Zu den Brüsseler Aldhelmglossen', *Anglia* LXXIV (1957), 153–80.

———, 'Aldhelmus Glosatus III', *English Studies* XL (1959), 129–34.

———, 'Aldhelmus Glosatus IV', *Studia Germanica Gandensia* II (1960), 81–95.

C. E. Fell, 'A Note on Old English Wine Terminology: The Problem of *Cæren*', *Nottingham Medieval Studies* XXV (1981), 1–12.

[on the meaning of *carenum*]

L. Goossens, *The Old English Glosses of MS. Brussels, Royal Library 1650 (Aldhelm's De Laudibus Virginitatis)* (Brussels, 1974).

[an important new edition, with valuable introduction on glossing in Aldhelm manuscripts]

J. H. Hessels, *A Late Eighth-Century Latin-Anglo-Saxon Glossary Preserved in Leiden* (Cambridge, 1906).

W. M. Lindsay, *The Corpus Glossary* (Cambridge, 1921).

———, *The Corpus, Epinal, Erfurt and Leyden Glossaries* (Oxford, 1921).

[on Aldhelm's use of glossaries, see pp. 97–105]

H. Logeman, 'New Aldhelm Glosses', *Anglia* XIII (1891), 27–41.

H. D. Meritt, *Old English Glosses* (New York, 1945).

———, 'Old English Aldhelm Glosses', *Modern Language Notes* LXVIII (1952), 553–4.

H. Mettke, *Die althochdeutschen Aldhelmglossen* (Jena, 1957).

T. F. Mustanoja, 'Notes on Some Old English Glosses in Aldhelm's *De Laudibus Virginitatis*', *Neuphilologische Mitteilungen* LI (1950), 49–61.

A. S. Napier, 'Collation der altenglischen Aldhelmglossen des Codex 38 der Kathedralbibliothek zu Salisbury', *Anglia* XV (1893), 204–9.

———, *Old English Glosses, Chiefly Unpublished* (Oxford, 1900).

[prints glosses from many Aldhelm manuscripts, including those from Oxford, Bodleian Library, MS. Digby 146]

R. T. Oliphant, *The Harley Latin–Old English Glossary* (The Hague, 1966).
[see review by R. Derolez, *English Studies* LI (1970), 149–51]
R. I. Page, 'More Aldhelm Glosses from CCCC 326', *English Studies* LVI (1975), 481–90.
_____, 'OE. "fealh", "harrow",' *Notes & Queries* XXVI (1979), 389–93.
[on the meaning of *occa*]
_____, 'Four Rare Old English Words', *Notes & Queries* XXX (1983), 2–8.
J. D. Pheifer, *Old English Glosses in the Epinal-Erfurt Glossary* (Oxford, 1974).
[the suggestion (p. lvii) that the ancestor of the Epinal-Erfurt glossary was compiled in the school of Aldhelm at Malmesbury]
K. Schiebel, *Die Sprache der altenglischen Glossen zu Aldhelms Schrift De Laude Virginitatis* (Halle, 1907).
T. Wright and R. P. Wülcker, *Anglo-Saxon and Old English Vocabularies*. 2 vols. (London, 1884).

C. MEDIEVAL LIVES OF ALDHELM

Faricius, *Vita Aldhelmi*, ed. J. A. Giles, in his *Sancti Aldhelmi Opera* (Oxford, 1844), 354–82, and repr. in his *Vita Quorundum Anglo-Saxonum*. Publications of the Caxton Society (London, 1854), 119–56.
[Giles's edition of Faricius is reprinted by Migne, *Patrologia Latina* LXXXIX, cols. 63–84. Another edition of Faricius is printed by the Bollandists, *Acta Sanctorum, Maii*, vol. VI, 84–93]
William of Malmesbury, *Gesta Pontificum*, ed. N. E. S. A. Hamilton. Rolls Series (London, 1870).
[William's *vita* of Aldhelm constitutes Book V of his *Gesta Pontificum*, ed. Hamilton, 330–443. The *Gesta Pontificum* are also printed in Migne's *Patrologia Latina*, CLXXIX; the life of Aldhelm occupies cols. 1617–80]
[Thomas of Malmesbury], *Eulogium Historiarum*, ed. F. Haydon, 3 vols., Rolls Series (London, 1858–63), I, 224–6.
[the account of Aldhelm is based principally on William of Malmesbury, interpolated with Geoffrey of Monmouth]
John Capgrave, *Vita Aldhelmi*, in *Nova Legenda Anglie*, ed. C. Horstman. 2 vols. (Oxford, 1901), I, pp. 38–40.
[based entirely on William of Malmesbury, but that it borrows the story of St Ecgwine's vision of Aldhelm's death directly from Dominic of Evesham's *Vita S. Ecgwini*]

D. WORKS WHICH CONTAIN SOME DISCUSSION OF ALDHELM

T. Allison, *English Religious Life in the Eighth Century* (London, 1929), 86–9.

W. F. Bolton, *A History of Anglo-Latin Literature I: 597–740* (Princeton, 1967), 68–100.
[general treatment containing much error; useful bibliography]

B. B. Boyer, 'Insular Contribution to Medieval Literary Tradition on the Continent', *Classical Philology* XLII (1947), 209–22.
[on Aldhelm manuscripts]

T. J. Brown, 'An Historical Introduction to the Use of Classical Latin Authors in the British Isles from the Fifth to the Eleventh Century', *Settimane di studio del Centro italiano di studi sull' alto medioevo* XXII (1975), 237–93.

F. Brunhölzl, *Geschichte der lateinischen Literatur des Mittelalters* (Munich, 1975), I, 200–6, 208–9.

W. Bulst, 'Eine anglo-lateinische Übersetzung aus dem Griechischen um 700', *Zeitschrift für deutsches Altertum* LXXV (1938), 105–11.

M. Byrne, *The Tradition of the Nun in Medieval England* (Washington, 1932), 25–43.
[on the prose *De Virginitate*]

G. T. Dempsey, 'Legal Terminology in Anglo-Saxon England: The "Trimoda Necessitas" Charter', *Speculum* LVII (1982), 843–9.

E. S. Duckett, *Anglo-Saxon Saints and Scholars* (New York, 1947), 3–97.
[a popular biography of Aldhelm which is filled with error and is totally unreliable]

E. von Erhardt-Siebold, *Die lateinischen Rätsel der Angelsachsen.* Anglistische Forschungen LXI (Heidelberg, 1925).

———, 'An Archaeological Find in a Latin Riddle of the Anglo-Saxons', *Speculum* VII (1932), 252–5.
[on *Enigma* liv]

———, 'The Hellebore in Anglo-Saxon Pharmacy', *Englische Studien* LXXI (1936), 161–70.
[on *Enigma* xcviii]

E. Faral, 'La queue de poisson des sirènes', *Romania* LXXIV (1953), 433–506.
[Aldhelm as author of the *Liber Monstrorum*: pp. 466–70]

J. Godfrey, *The Church in Anglo-Saxon England* (Cambridge, 1962), 201–6.

P. Godman, 'The Anglo-Latin *Opus Geminatum*: From Aldhelm to Alcuin', *Medium Ævum* L (1981), 215–29.

P. Grosjean, 'Confusa Caligo. Remarques sur les *Hisperica Famina*', *Celtica* III (1956), 35–85.
[Aldhelm's alleged knowledge of the *Hisperica Famina*: pp. 64–7]

H. Hahn, *Bonifaz und Lul* (Leipzig, 1883).
[much interesting discussion of Aldhelm scattered throughout]

M. Herren, *Hisperica Famina I* (Toronto, 1974).

––––––, 'Some Conjectures on the Origins and Tradition of the Hisperic Poem *Rubisca*', *Ériu* XXV (1974), 70–87.

P. Hunter Blair, *An Introduction to Anglo-Saxon England*. 2nd edn. (Cambridge, 1977), 314–15, 326–7.

C. W. Jones, *Bedae Opera de Temporibus* (Cambridge, Mass., 1943), 100–1.
[Aldhelm's Letter to Geraint on the Easter-question]

M. L. W. Laistner, *Thought and Letters in Western Europe 500–900* (Ithaca, N.Y., 1957), 153–6.

M. Lapidge, 'The Hermeneutic Style in Tenth-Century Anglo-Latin Literature', *Anglo-Saxon England* IV (1975), 67–111.

––––––, 'The Present State of Anglo-Latin Studies', in *Insular Latin Studies*, ed. M. W. Herren (Toronto, 1981), 45–82.
[Aldhelm at pp. 48–50]

V. Law, *The Insular Latin Grammarians* (Woodbridge, 1982).

––––––, 'The Study of Latin Grammar in Eighth-Century Southumbria', *Anglo-Saxon England* XII (1983), 43–71.
[detailed discussion of the grammatical sources used by Aldhelm, pp. 46–57]

A. F. Leach, *The Schools of Medieval England* (London, 1915), 31–45.
[sceptical treatment of Aldhelm's debt to Irish learning; much error]

H. R. Loyn, *Anglo-Saxon England and the Norman Conquest* (London, 1962), 269–74.

M. Manitius, *Geschichte der lateinischen Literatur des Mittelalters*. 3 vols. (Munich, 1911–31), I, 134–41.

H. Mayr-Harting, *The Coming of Christianity to Anglo-Saxon England* (London, 1972), 192–219.

J. D. A. Ogilvy, *Books Known to the English, 597–1066* (Cambridge, Mass., 1967).
[Aldhelm mentioned *passim*; but the book contains so many errors that it cannot be used with confidence]

J. Peter, *Complaint and Satire in Early English Literature* (Oxford, 1956).

C. Plummer, ed., *Venerabilis Baedae Opera Historica*. 2 vols. (Oxford, 1896), II, 308–13.

F. J. E. Raby, *Christian-Latin Poetry* (Oxford, 1953), 142–5.
[a tissue of errors and wrong-headed opinions]

P. Riché, *Education et culture dans l'occident barbare, VIe–VIIIe siècles.* 3rd edn. (Paris, 1962), 419–26.

M. Roger, *L'enseignement des lettres classiques d'Ausone à Alcuin* (Paris, 1905), 288–303.
[still the most detailed and reliable study of Insular Latin culture of Aldhelm's time, though out-dated in some respects]

F. M. Stenton, *Anglo-Saxon England.* 3rd edn. (Oxford, 1971), 180–3.

W. Stubbs, in *A Dictionary of Christian Biography*, ed. W. Smith and H. Wace. 4 vols. (London, 1877–87), I, 78–9 (s.v. 'Aldhelm').

G. Wieland, '*Geminus Stilus*: Studies in Anglo-Latin Hagiography', in *Insular Latin Studies*, ed. M. W. Herren (Toronto, 1981), 113–33.

L. G. Whitbread, 'The *Liber Monstrorum* and *Beowulf*', *Mediaeval Studies* XXXVI (1974), 434–71.
[Aldhelm possibly the author of *Liber Monstrorum*: pp. 455–8]

T. Wright, *Biographia Britannica Litteraria.* 2 vols. (London, 1842–6), I, 209–22.

E. WORKS DEVOTED TO ALDHELM

G. K. Anderson, 'Aldhelm and the Leiden Riddle', in *Old English Poetry*, ed. R. P. Creed (Providence, 1967), 167–76.

L. Bönhoff, *Aldhelm von Malmesbury* (Dresden, 1894).
[a standard work, now in need of considerable revision]

L. N. Braswell, 'The "Dream of the Rood" and Aldhelm on Sacred Prosopopoeia', *Mediaeval Studies* XL (1978), 461–7.

G. F. Browne, *St Aldhelm* (London, 1903).
[out-dated in many respects, and containing many inaccuracies, but also contains many fascinating conjectures, particularly with regard to archaeological evidence]

A. S. Cook, 'Aldhelm's Legal Studies', *Journal of English and Germanic Philology* XXIII (1924), 105–13.

———, 'Sources for the Biography of Aldhelm', *Transactions of the Connecticut Academy of Arts and Sciences* XXVIII (1927), 273–93.

A. S. Cook, 'Aldhelm at the Hands of Sharon Turner', *Speculum* II (1927), 201–3.

_____, 'Who was the Ehfrid of Aldhelm's Letter?', *Speculum* II (1927), 363–73.

_____, 'Aldhelm's Rude Infancy', *Philological Quarterly* VII (1928), 115–9.

_____, 'A Putative Charter to Aldhelm', in *Studies in English Philology: A Miscellany in Honor of Frederick Klaeber*, ed. K. Malone and M. B. Ruud (Minneapolis, 1929), 254–7.

R. Ehwald, *Aldhelms Gedicht De Virginitate. Programm des herzögliches Gymnasium . . . von Gotha* (Gotha, 1904).

_____, 'De aenigmatibus Aldhelmi et acrostichis', in *Festschrift für Albert von Bamberg* (Gotha, 1905), 1–26.

_____, 'Aldhelm von Malmesbury', *Jahrbuch der königlichen Akademie gemeinnütziger Wissenschaften in Erfurt* XXXIII (1907), 91–116.

E. von Erhardt-Siebold, 'Aldhelm in Possession of the Secrets of Sericulture', *Anglia* LX (1936), 384–9.

_____, 'Aldhelm's Chrismal', *Speculum* X (1935), 276–80.

J. Fowler, *St Aldhelm* (Sherborne, 1947).
[a brief commemorative lecture]

N. Howe, 'Aldhelm's *Enigmata* and Isidorian Etymology', *Anglo-Saxon England* XIV (1985), 37–59.

M. R. James, *Two Ancient English Scholars* (Glasgow, 1931).
[a lecture; brief but interesting comments on manuscripts which Aldhelm may have seen at Malmesbury and which William saw after him]

P. F. Jones, 'Aldhelm and the Comitatus-Ideal', *Modern Language Notes* XLVII (1932), 378.

F. Kerlouégan, 'Une liste de mots communs à Gildas et à Aldhelm', *Études celtiques* XV (1976–8), 553–67.

M. Lapidge, 'Aldhelm's Latin Poetry and Old English Verse', *Comparative Literature* XXXI (1979), 209–31.

_____, '*Beowulf*, Aldhelm, the *Liber Monstrorum* and Wessex', *Studi Medievali* 3rd ser. XXIII (1982), 151–92.

_____, and M. Herren, *Aldhelm: The Prose Works* (Ipswich, 1979).

R. Leotta, 'Considerazioni sulla tradizione manoscritta del *De Pedum Regulis* di Aldelmo', *Giornale italiano di filologia* XXXII (1980), 119–34.

_____, 'Una classificazione aldelmiana', *Giornale italiano di filologia* XXXII (1980), 245–50.

Z. Mády, 'An VIIIth Century Aldhelm Fragment in Hungary',

Acta Antiqua Academiae Scientiarum Hungaricae XIII (1965), 441–53.
[a fragment of what may be the earliest surviving Aldhelm manuscript]

F. P. Magoun, 'Aldhelm's Diocese of Sherborne *be westan wuda*', *Harvard Theological Review* XXXII (1939), 103–14.

M. Manitius, 'Zu Aldhelm und Beda', *Sitzungsberichte der österreichischen Akademie der Wissenschaften*, phil.-hist. Kl., CXII (Vienna, 1886), 535–634.
[pp. 535–614 deal with Aldhelm; in need of revision, but still a standard work on the sources of Aldhelm]

J. Marenbon, 'Les sources du vocabulaire d'Aldhelm', *Archivum Latinitatis Medii Aevi (Bulletin du Cange)* XLI (1979), 75–90.

A. Manser, 'Le témoignage d'Aldhelm de Sherborne sur un particularité du canon grégorien de la messe romaine', *Revue Bénédictine* XXVIII (1911), 90–5.

D. Mazzoni, 'Aldhelmiana: studio critico letterario su Aldhelmo di Sherborne', *Rivista storica benedettina* X (1915), 93–114, 245–50, 402–47.

K. O'B. O'Keefe, 'The Text of Aldhelm's *Enigma* no. c in Oxford, Bodleian Library, Rawlinson C. 697 and Exeter Riddle 40', *Anglo-Saxon England* XIV (1985), 61–73.

H. M. Porter, 'Saint Aldhelm and Wareham', *Notes and Queries from Somerset and Dorset* XXX (1975), 142–5.
[Aldhelm born at Wareham; the church at Wareham built by him]

_____, 'Frome and a Bull of Sergius I', *Notes and Queries from Somerset and Dorset* XXX (1977), 249–52.

G. Prago, 'La legenda di S. Ilarione a Epidauro in Adelmo scrittore anglosassone', *Archivio storico di Dalmazia* XXV (1938), 83–91.

P. D. Scott, 'Rhetorical and Symbolic Ambiguity: The Riddles of Symphosius and Aldhelm', in *Saints, Scholars and Heroes: Studies in Honour of Charles W. Jones*, ed. M. H. King and W. Stevens, 2 vols. (Collegeville, Minn., 1979), I, 117–44.

W. B. Wildman, *The Life of St Ealdhelm* (London, 1905).
[an honest and thoughtful biography, but very much out of date]

M. Winterbottom, 'Aldhelm's Prose Style and its Origins', *Anglo-Saxon England* VI (1977), 39–76.
[an extremely important study of Aldhelm and his intellectual heritage]

THE CARMINA ECCLESIASTICA

TRANSLATED BY MICHAEL LAPIDGE

INTRODUCTION TO THE
CARMINA ECCLESIASTICA

The term 'Carmina Ecclesiastica' is an editorial title confected by
Ehwald to describe a number of *tituli* or dedicatory inscriptions
composed by Aldhelm to commemorate various churches and
altars. The poems are transmitted in random groups in continental
manuscripts, and were apparently not issued by Aldhelm as a
single collection (see below, p. 44). Nevertheless, Ehwald's title is
sanctioned by general use and may be retained here.[1]
  During the early centuries of Anglo-Saxon Christendom, when
the Church was expanding into pagan territories and new churches
were continually being built and consecrated, it was an important
function of the literate ecclesiastic to compose metrical *tituli* to be
inscribed in these churches. Bede, for example, is known to have
composed a number of such *tituli*, and it is probable that they
were contained in his (lost) *Liber Epigrammatum*.[2] Among the
surviving remnants of this book of epigrams is one such dedicatory
poem intended for a church built at Lincoln by Bishop
Cyneberht.[3] Alcuin, too, was active in this sphere. During his
busy career on the Continent as master of the palace school and
adviser to Charlemagne, Alcuin had occasion to compose dozens
of *tituli* for churches within the ambit of his influence.[4] And
Cellanus of Péronne (in Picardy), who was a correspondent of
Aldhelm (Letters nos. IX and X), composed a *titulus* for an
oratory dedicated to St Patrick at Péronne.[5] It is not surprising
that Aldhelm should have engaged in similar literary activity.
  The earliest Latin *tituli* date from late antiquity.[6] Thus the
Epigrammata of Pope Damasus (*ob.* 384) include a number of
tituli.[7] Paulinus of Nola (*ob.* 431) composed *tituli*,[8] as at a later
period did Venantius Fortunatus, an indefatigable author of
occasional verse.[9] The *tituli* of these Late Latin poets were used in

turn as models by poets of the early Middle Ages. And in order
further to facilitate the composition of *tituli*, they were frequently
collected — together with large numbers of anonymous *tituli*
taken from various churches, principally in Rome — into what are
called *syllogae* ('collections') which served in effect as pattern-
books for composers of *tituli*. A number of such *syllogae* survive
from the early medieval period.[10] It is clear that various
continental *syllogae* circulated in Anglo-Saxon England, and that
these were used in turn as sources for English collections. For
example, Milred, bishop of Worcester (*ob.* 775) is known to have
made such a collection, for a fragmentary manuscript of Milred's
collection now survives as Urbana, University of Illinois Library
128 (unknown English origin, s. x^med).[11] In compiling his
collection Milred drew on various earlier, seventh-century,
syllogae, such as the *Anthologia Isidoriana* and the *Sylloge
Laureshamensis Secunda*.[12] There can be no doubt, therefore, that
various continental *syllogae* circulated in Anglo-Saxon England.
Aldhelm was certainly familiar with such collections, for at one
point of his *Epistola ad Acircium* he quotes the following
hexameter:

Virgo Maria, tibi Sixtus noua templa dicaui.[13]

This line is found only in the so-called *Sylloge Turonensis*,[14] which
suggests that it or a congener was available to Aldhelm in the late
seventh century. On *tituli* in such collections, then, Aldhelm will
have modelled his own *Carmina Ecclesiastica*.

As abbot of Malmesbury and later as bishop of Sherborne,
Aldhelm was an active builder of churches. As we have seen, he
built two churches at Malmesbury and a cathedral at Sherborne,
and minsters at Bruton, Bradford on Avon, Wareham, and next to
the river Frome (above, p. 8). It is a reasonable surmise that
Aldhelm will have composed *tituli* for each of these churches; but,
of the churches in question, only that at Bradford is thought to be
be extant, and it bears no dedicatory inscription. We can form
some notion of the form and size such an inscription might have
from two contemporary pieces of evidence. First, there is the
dedication-stone of the church of Jarrow, consecrated by Abbot
Ceolfrith in 685, and still to be seen *in situ*.[15] This inscription is
incised in two stones each measuring about 65 x 25 cm. and
consists of a single, brief sentence:

DEDICATIO BASILICAE SANCTI PAVLI .VIIII. KALENDAS
MAIAS ANNO .XV. ECFRIDI REGIS CEOLFRIDI ABBATIS

EIVSDEMQVE ECCLESIAE DEO AVCTORE CONDITORIS
ANNO .IIII..[16]

The second piece of evidence is an inscription which does not
survive, but which is more directly relevant to Aldhelm's Wessex.
William of Malmesbury, in his *De Antiquitate Glastonie Ecclesie*,
reports that King Ine (688–726) constructed a church in
Glastonbury dedicated to SS. Peter and Paul, and that he had the
following inscription incised in it:

Siderei montes, speciosa cacumina Syon,
    A Libano, gemine, flore comante, cedri,
Celorum porte, lati duo lumina mundi,
    Ore tonat Paulus, fulgurat arce Petrus.
Inter apostolicas radianti luce coronas,
    Celsior ille gradu, doctior hic monitis.
Corda per hunc hominum reserantur, et astra per illum.
    Quos docet iste stilo, suscipit ille polo.
Pandit iter celi hic dogmata, clauibus alter.
    Est uia cui Paulus, ianua fida Petrus.
Hic petra firma manens, ille architectus habetur.
    Surgit in hiis templum quo placet ara Deo.
Anglia plaude libens, mittit tibi Roma salutem.
    Fulgor apostolicus Glastoniam irradiat.
A facie hostili duo propugnacula surgunt,
    Quos fidei turres urbs, capud orbis, habet.
Hec pius egregio rex Ina refertus amore
    Dona suo populo non moritura dedit.
Totus in affectu diue pietatis inherens,
    Ecclesie iuges amplificauit opes.
Melchisedec noster, merito rex <atque> sacerdos,
    Conpleuit uere religionis opus.
Publica iura regens et celsa palacia seruans,
    Unica pontificum gloria norma fuit.
Hinc abiens, illic meritorum uiuet honore.
    Hic quoque gestorum laude perennis erit.[17]

This poem is not an entirely original composition: it was confected
from two *tituli* of Venantius Fortunatus (lines 1–16 are from his
Carm. III.vii.1–12 and 17–20, and lines 17–26 are from *Carm.*
II.x.17–26, with the necessary alterations of (say) *Gallia* into
Anglia having been made). Whether original or not, Ine's *titulus*
gives some clear notion of the length of a poem which could be
incised in a church (it is twenty-six lines long).[18] It is worth
bearing this length approximately in mind when considering
Aldhelm's various *tituli*.

Of the five *Carmina Ecclesiastica*, nos. I–III are *tituli* for churches and nos. IV–V are *tituli* for altars.

Carmen Ecclesiasticum I: On the Church of SS. Peter and Paul

The length of this poem (21 lines) suggests that it may in fact have been inscribed in a church. According to Faricius, Aldhelm composed the poem one day in Rome while he was visiting the 'Apostolorum ecclesiam'.[19] It was presumably the church's joint dedication to the two principal apostles which led Faricius to think of Rome.[20] However, Faricius's assumption was unnecessary: there were several churches in early Anglo-Saxon England dedicated to SS. Peter and Paul — for example, at Canterbury and Winchester — as well as the church at Glastonbury whose *titulus* was quoted above.[21] In fact William of Malmesbury reports that Aldhelm rebuilt the pre-existing church at Malmesbury and dedicated it to SS. Peter and Paul,[22] and it was this church, in William's opinion, for which Aldhelm composed his *Carmen Ecclesiasticum* I. William does not say when the poem was composed. Because one line of the poem ('Claviger aetherius portam qui pandis in aethra') is quoted by Aldhelm in his Letter to Geraint (no. IV) — a letter which was probably composed in 672 or 673 — it is arguable that the poem predates the letter, which would make it one of Aldhelm's earliest works; however, the very same line is used by Aldhelm on various occasions,[23] and this makes it difficult to establish a relative chronology. Alternatively, if we should wish to accept the evidence of William, we might assume that Aldhelm rebuilt the church at Malmesbury soon after he became abbot there (673 or 674), and hence date the poem to *c.* 675. But there can be no certainty, since either dating relies on unverifiable conjectures.

Carmen Ecclesiasticum I has not been preserved entire in any medieval manuscript. It was apparently contained in Milred of Worcester's *sylloge* of epigrams, however. Milred's *sylloge*, as mentioned above (p. 36) is now preserved only in a fragmentary tenth-century manuscript. In the sixteenth century, however, before this manuscript was broken up, it was seen by the antiquary John Leland, and Leland noted among its contents some 'versus Aldhelmi ... de ecclesia Petri et Pauli'.[24] Leland saw the manuscript at Malmesbury. There is reason for thinking that the manuscript was at Malmesbury four centuries earlier. Faricius and William of Malmesbury both quote *Carmen Ecclesiasticum* I in full, and although there are minor variants between the versions they quote, it would seem that they were quoting from the same manuscript. William of Malmesbury is known to have quoted other poems from the Malmesbury manuscript, and the simplest explanation of his and Faricius's knowledge of *CE* I is that they knew it from the now lost part of the manuscript of Milred's *sylloge* which survives in Urbana 128. The poem was also known on the Continent. A number of its lines were excerpted by the continental scribe of Berlin, Deutsche Staatsbibl. Phillipps 167 (Saint-Aubin of Angers, s. ix), who used them to confect a new dedicatory poem *in basilica sanctorum Petri et Paul* (f. 29r–v).[25] From various orthographical errors it is clear that the Angers scribe was copying from a manuscript of Insular origin, but this has not survived.

Carmen Ecclesiasticum II: On the Church of St Mary the Perpetual Virgin

A poem of 31 lines, which — to judge only from its length — could conceivably have been inscribed in a church. We know from William of Malmesbury that Aldhelm built a second church within the monastic precincts at Malmesbury, and that this second church was dedicated to the Virgin Mary;[26] the *titulus* may have been intended for this church. However, dedications to the Virgin Mary were common at that time,[27] and Aldhelm is known to have built at least one other church in her honour, at Bruton (Somerset),[28] so certainty is not possible. A curious feature of the poem is that it is concluded (lines 13–31) by some 19 lines which appear to have been lifted whole from the *Carmen de Virginitate* (lines 1691–1709).[29] If so, *CE* II must presumably post-date the *Carmen de Virginitate*; but — unfortunately — it is impossible to assign even an approximate date to that poem (see above, pp. 12–14). Another possibility may be mentioned: that it was not Aldhelm himself but a later scribe who added the 19 lines from *CdV* to *CE* II. In support of this supposition one may note that the ninth-century Angers scribe of Berlin Phillipps 167 — who was, as noted above, following an Insular exemplar — did not, in transcribing *CE* II, transcribe any of the final 19 lines from *CdV*, but added in their stead the following two hexameters:

> Hic quoque apostolicis ditantur templa triumphis
> Qua fulgent arae bis seno nomine sacrae.[30]

This might suggest that the Insular exemplar used by the Angers scribe lacked the interpolated lines from *CdV*, and hence that the interpolation was not made by Aldhelm himself. But the matter is far from clear.

Carmen Ecclesiasticum III: On a Church of St Mary built by Bugga

This poem consists of 85 lines — far too long, one would think, to have been inscribed in a church. But in other respects it is an extremely valuable source for the early Church in Wessex.

The identity of Bugga (and hence the location of the church in question) cannot be precisely established. The name *Bugga* is presumably an hypocoristic form based on a name with the final theme -*burg*, such as Æthelburg, Cuthburg, Cwenburg, Heahburg, Osburg, and so on. It is interesting that among the Bonifatian correspondence is a letter (datable 719 x 722) addressed to Boniface from one Abbess Eangyth and her only daughter *Haeaburg cognomento Bugge*;[31] however, it is unlikely for various reasons that Boniface's correspondent is identical with the subject of Aldhelm's poem.[32] It has also been thought that the Bugga of Aldhelm's poem is identical with a Bugga who is mentioned in some early Mercian charters[33] and to whom King Æthelred of Mercia (675–704) and his *subregulus* Oshere (680–93) granted land for a monastery on the river Colne, probably near the present-day village of Withington (Gloucs.).[34] Withington is only some twenty miles from Malmesbury, and the dates of the *subregulus* Oshere (680 x 693) square roughly with what can be deduced of the monastery's foundation from Aldhelm's poem (see below), but the identification cannot be pressed. The only other surviving evidence for the Bugga of Aldhelm's poem is an epitaph of her which was preserved in Milred's aforementioned *sylloge* of inscriptions.[35] This epitaph is verbally indebted to Aldhelm's poem (*CE* III), but it does supply the additional detail that Bugga presided as abbess of her minster for thirty-four years.[36]

One other possibility should be mentioned, although it too is incapable of proof. According to line 2 of the poem, Bugga was the daughter of King Centwine of Wessex (676–85). According to Faricius — not always a reliable source[37] — Aldhelm was of *regia stirpe* and was the son of one Kenten,[38] apparently a misspelling of the name Centwine. If Faricius's information could be believed, Aldhelm could have been the brother of Bugga. We may recall in this connection that Aldhelm's prose *De Virginitate* was addressed *inter alias* to one Osburg, who was said by Aldhelm to be related to him *contribulibus necessitudinum nexibus*. These words could describe a sister-brother relationship, but could equally well describe one that was less close. If the relationship *were* that of brother and sister — and there is nothing in the poem to prove or disprove it — then Bugga could be taken as an hypocoristic form of Osburg. Students of Aldhelm would be left to puzzle out the implications of making Aldhelm a son of King Centwine of Wessex.

The date of the poem cannot be established precisely. It was composed after the death of King Cædwalla in 689 and during the reign of his successor, Ine — 'qui *nunc* imperium Saxonum iure gubernat' (line 37). Ine died in 726. The dating could be more narrowly limited to the years 689 x 693 if the identification of Bugga with the recipient of the grant by King Æthelred and his *subregulus* Oshere could be accepted. Given that Bugga presided over the minster as abbess for thirty-four years, such an identification would have the further implication that Bugga died in the years 723 x 727.

It is unfortunate that the identity of Bugga and her church and the dating of the poem are matters of such uncertainty, for the poem is a valuable source of information for early West Saxon history. It tells us of three important battles fought by King Centwine. It provides details of the structure and furnishings of an early Anglo-Saxon minster. It provides evidence for the liturgy of the early Anglo-Saxon church, and gives a fascinating glimpse of the performance of the Divine Office in a double monastery. For all these reasons the poem deserves closer study than it has hitherto received.

Carmen Ecclesiasticum IV: On the Altars of the Twelve Apostles

Unlike the three previous *tituli*, CE IV is ostensibly intended to commemorate twelve altars within a church rather than the church itself. It is interesting to note that the church built by Bugga had twelve altars (CE . III.40: 'Qua fulgent arae bis seno nomine sacrae'). However, it is unlikely that CE IV refers to altars in Bugga's church, for there the altar in the apse (*absida*) was dedicated to the Virgin Mary (line 41), whereas in CE IV the apse is dedicated to St Peter (CE IV.i.1). This may imply that it was conventional in early Anglo-Saxon England to dedicate altars within a church to the twelve apostles. But whether the separate poems which make up Aldhelm's CE IV were ever intended to be inscribed in a church is another matter. None of them is longer than 36 lines. However, they are accompanied by a brief poem (no. xiii) which is manifestly literary in intent and is utterly unsuitable as a *titulus* intended to be inscribed: 'I have now set out the twelve names of the (apostolic) fathers ...' In the collection of *tituli* which make up *CE* IV, therefore, Aldhelm was attempting something other than the composition of church dedications.

In each of the poems in *CE* IV Aldhelm provides a brief biography of the apostle in question: the apostle's origin (and relationship to other apostles, if any) and the place of his apostolic activity is followed in each case by an account of how the apostle died. In this respect *CE* IV may be seen to belong to a literary tradition which stretches back to late antiquity and includes the *Breviarium Apostolorum*,[39] and forward to the Old English poem 'Fates of the Apostles' by the (probably ninth-century) Mercian poet Cynewulf.[40] Using the framework of the *titulus*, Aldhelm created an extended poem on the lives and fates of the apostles, and it is possible to regard the lives of the apostles in *CE* IV as a miniature version of (and a preparatory exercise towards?) the collection of saints' lives which constitutes the *De Virginitate*.

Two questions deserve consideration: the order in which Aldhelm presents the apostles, and the sources on which he drew in compiling them. First, the order. There are various lists of the apostles given in the Bible (the most complete being that in Mt. X. 2–4), and various sequences of the apostles' names are found in early Insular litanies of the saints;[41] any of these sources could have provided Aldhelm with a sequence to be followed. There is no doubt, however, about what sequence Aldhelm did adopt: he follows precisely that of the prayer *Communicantes* from the Canon of the Mass:

> Communicantes, et memoriam uenerantes, in primis gloriosae semper Virginis Mariae, genitricis Dei et Domini nostri Iesu Christi: sed et beatorum Apostolorum ac Martyrum tuorum, Petri et Pauli, Andreae, Iacobi, Iohannis, Thomae, Iacobi, Philippi, Bartholomaei, Matthaei, Simonis et Thaddaei.[42]

Hence Aldhelm's sequence in *CE* IV: St Peter (no. i), St Paul (no. ii), St Andrew (no. iii), St James 'the Great' (no. iv), St John the Apostle and Evangelist (no. v), St Thomas (no. vi), St James 'the Less' (no. vii), St Philip (no. viii), St Bartholomew (no. ix), St Matthew (no. x), St Simon the Zealot (no. xi) and St Thaddeus or Jude (no. xii). In his adherence to this sequence, Aldhelm reveals his Roman orthodoxy.

The principal source of Aldhelm's various accounts of the

apostles is also readily identifiable: Isidore's treatise *De ortu et obitu patrum*.[43] In this work Isidore (*ob*. 636) presented brief biographies of some 64 principal Old Testament figures, followed by 21 from the New Testament, including particularly the apostles. In compiling his biographies Isidore culled the Bible carefully, but also supplemented biblical accounts with information drawn from various sources including works by Jerome, Epiphanius and pseudo-Dorotheus.[44] Isidore's work was widely known throughout the Middle Ages, and was known in the British Isles in particular at a very early date.[45] Aldhelm's dependence on cc. lxviii–lxxx of Isidore's work can readily be seen by placing one of the poems in *CE* IV alongside the corresponding chapter of Isidore.[46] Thus, of the many details which might have been related concerning St Paul, Aldhelm chooses precisely those which are recorded in Isidore (c. lxix) and gives them in the same order.[47] Similarly, *CE* IV.iv (on St James 'the Great') may be compared with c. lxxi of Isidore's treatise:

Iacobus filius Zebedaei frater Ioannis, quartus in ordine, duodecim tribubus quae sunt in dispersione gentium scripsit, atque Hispaniae et occidentalium locorum gentibus Euangelium praedicauit, et in occasu mundi lucem praedicationis infudit. Hic ab Herode tetrarcha gladio caesus occubuit. Sepultus in Marmorica.[48]

From this brief account Aldhelm selected three details (see below, p. 52): that James was sired by his aging father Zebedee, that he converted Spain, and that Herod the tetrarch killed him with a sword. From comparisons such as these it will be seen that Isidore's treatise was Aldhelm's principal source for the biographies of apostles in *CE* IV.

However, Aldhelm occasionally amplified the accounts he found in Isidore with information drawn from various other sources. For example, details of the story of Peter's defeat of Simon Magus are probably drawn from the apocryphal *Acta Petri*. The account of St James 'the Less' is much amplified by recourse to the account of the fall of Jerusalem in Eusebius's *Historia Ecclesiastica*, which Aldhelm knew in the Latin translation of Rufinus. Other sources were laid under contribution for various minor points of detail (see below, pp. 239–42).

Carmen Ecclesiasticum IV is of especial interest because it represents a miniature version of the full-scale treatment of exemplary saints that was to constitute Aldhelm's *De Virginitate*; it is therefore a matter of some importance to establish their relative chronology. Unfortunately, the *De Virginitate* cannot be dated precisely (see above, pp. 12–14), and there is apparently no means of dating *CE* IV. One of its lines (*CE* IV.i.2: 'Claviger aetherius qui portam pandit in aethra') is quoted in Aldhelm's Letter to Geraint (no. IV), but we have already seen that this is a line which was frequently recycled by Aldhelm; it cannot therefore be used as a dating criterion. In these circumstances, there is no way of assigning even an approximate date to *CE* IV.

Carmen Ecclesiasticum V: On St Matthias the Apostle

After the fall and death of Judas, the apostles were instructed by Jesus to choose a replacement in order to make their number up to twelve; and the lot fell on Matthias (Act. I.24–6). Matthias is not numbered among the apostles in the *Communicantes*-prayer of the Canon of the Mass, but he is often added to lists of the apostles in early Insular litanies,[49] and in any case Aldhelm will have known him from the biblical Acts. It is evident that Aldhelm wished to complete the list of apostles commemorated in *CE* IV, and that the poem on Matthias was composed as a sort of appendix. It is unlikely, therefore, to have been intended as a *titulus* for an actual church or altar.[50] It is also worth noting that in two of the three principal surviving manuscripts of *CE* IV the poem on Matthias is found interpolated into the sequence of poems that is *CE* IV (see Ehwald's apparatus), so that it follows the poem on Thaddeus (IV.xii) and precedes the verse epilogue (IV.xiii); it is possible that this order reflects Aldhelm's original intentions.

To judge from the evidence of surviving manuscripts, the *Carmina Ecclesiastica* were not transmitted as a collection, and one may suspect that they were issued separately on various occasions. The poems are preserved now only in continental manuscripts, although it is clear that they circulated in England as well, to some extent at least. In Southumbria, the early eighth-century author of the aforementioned metrical epitaph of Bugga was certainly familiar with *CE* III, for he pillaged a number of its verses.[51] As we have seen, Milred of Worcester included *CE* I in his *sylloge* of inscriptions, whence it was known to Faricius and William of Malmesbury. Of Northumbrian authors Bede does not appear to have known any of the *Carmina Ecclesiastica*, but Alcuin knew and drew on all Aldhelm's verse, including the *CE*.[52] *CE* III was known to Æthilwulf, who borrowed freely from it in his poem *De Abbatibus* (written 803 x 821),[53] as did the anonymous Northumbrian poet of the *Miracula S. Nyniae*.[54] Manuscript evidence establishes that the *CE* were known on the Continent in the ninth and tenth centuries,[55] where they were used as models for the composition of *tituli*. During his continental sojourn Alcuin composed a number of *tituli* (see above, p. 35), a task in which he had the *CE* (especially *CE* I and IV) constantly at hand. The compiler of the famous *Codex Bertinianus*, printed in the seventeenth century from a manuscript then at Saint-Bertin and now lost, incorporated *CE* II–V into a collection of some 272 poems mostly by Alcuin; it has been thought that the *Codex Bertinianus* represents Alcuin's poetic *Nachlass* and that it was compiled soon after his death in 804 by a disciple or colleague.[56] If so, the inclusion of Aldhelm's *CE* probably reflects Alcuin's personal interest in the verse of his earlier compatriot. The ninth-century Angers scribe of Berlin Phillipps 167 used the *CE* as a quarry for the composition of two *tituli* which are in effect centos of Aldhelm.[57] *CE* IV.ii (on St Paul) served as the principal quarry for a cento of Aldhelmian verses on St Paul which is transmitted in some manuscripts of the *Enigmata* of Boniface; it is possibly an Anglo-Latin composition from the circle of Boniface.[58]

The evidence listed above indicates that Aldhelm's *Carmina Ecclesiastica* were well known in England in the eighth and ninth centuries, and on the Continent in the ninth century and later. One curious feature of the transmission of the *CE* should perhaps be mentioned. Unlike his other writings (the *Enigmata*, both parts of the *De Virginitate*, certain *Epistolae*), manuscripts of the *CE* do not seem to have been imported into England in the tenth century (cf. above, p. 2). There is consequently no evidence, as far as I am aware, that the *CE* were known or studied in late Anglo-Saxon England; but the matter deserves further consideration.

CARMINA ECCLESIASTICA

I. ON THE CHURCH OF SS. PETER AND PAUL[1]

/p. 11/ Here flowers the renowned glory of a new church,[2] (glory) which emblazons bright banners of a holy victory; here Peter and Paul, the lights of a darkened world, excellent Fathers who control the reins of their people, are venerated in this holy church with continual prayers [5].

(To St Peter): Ethereal key-bearer, you who open the gateway to the skies,[3] unlocking the shining realms of God's heavens: listen mercifully to the petitions of these peoples praying, who moisten their withered faces with streams of tears; /p. 12/ acknowledge the lamentations of those who bewail the sins they have committed, who with their burning prayers are cauterizing the evils of this life [11]!

(To St Paul): And you, great doctor, who, at the time when you were inclined to prefer pagan mysteries to Christ, were summoned from on high; (and), who previously were called Saul, with your name changed to Paul you began to see the clear light after the shadows [Act.XXII.3–13] [15]: now open your kindly ears to the voices of those praying (to you) and, kindly guardian, in company with St Peter, extend your right hand to the fearful (crowds) who in multitudes seek the holy threshold of this church, so that eternal forgiveness, flowing from bountiful kindness and the heavenly font — which shall never grow still for those who deserve — may here be given for their sins [21].

II. ON THE CHURCH OF ST MARY THE PERPETUAL VIRGIN[4]

[p. 12] Mary's protection keeps this house of the Lord: to her the venerable heights of this new church[5] are consecrated, and new banners with their holy victories stand forth. In this church is proclaimed the glory of the Holy Mother, who bore the True Light from the light of the Father, *[p. 13]* Whom prophets with divine inspiration acclaim as Titan[6] [i.e. the sun] [6]!

Excellent lady and holy virgin mother: listen mercifully to the petitions of these peoples praying, who moisten their withered faces with streams of tears[7] and, on bended leg, strike the earth with their knees, seeing that they deserve forgiveness from the flowing fountain of their tears and obliterate the sins of their life with their continual prayers [12].

This Virgin, I tell you, pregnant with heavenly offspring, produced from her womb the King Who redeems all ages, Who alone rightly controls the government of the world — just as this young maiden had previously learned from an angelic announcement, when the high-throned Father sent Gabriel (down) from the stars [17].

It was she whom the excellent prophet [i.e. Solomon], who once ruled as a wealthy man over the fields of Jerusalem, revealed in his song: '(My sister, my spouse) is a garden closed up, verdant on the flowering summit [*scil.* of Libanus], a fountain sealed up, welling from the heavenly pool [cf. Cant.IV.2], a quivering dove [Cant.II.14, V.2 and VI.8]. To her the prescient angel began to speak [23]: 'Behold, you shall beget an immortal offspring and you, a mother about to give birth, shall bring forth an infant; let this Son of the high-throned (God) be called blessed for all eternity! The Holy Spirit shall come unto you from heaven: behold, its might provides a (shady) bower for your heart; the heavenly power of the Father, holy maiden, shall protect you' [28]. When this had been said the mother's womb swelled with the child Who, when He had been born, delivered the world from its lamentable defect (of sin) and, when He had been crucified, wiped away its foul wickedness.[8]

III. ON A CHURCH OF ST MARY BUILT BY BUGGA[9]

[p. 14] The renowned daughter[10] of King Centwine built this church: it was erected through the excellent effort of Bugga.[11]

Centwine[12] formerly wielded justly the government[13] of the (West) Saxons, until, rejecting the summits of this temporal realm, he abandoned his worldly wealth and the reins of power by granting many estates[14] to recently-established churches[15] in which Christian worshippers now keep their monastic vows [7]. /p. 15/ Thereupon he set out to seek the holy way of life as he abandoned his hereditary kingdom in the name of Christ; nevertheless, he had previously waged war in three battles,[16] and had likewise brought them to a conclusion with three victories. Thus he ruled his kingdom happily for several years until, having been converted, he retired to a holy (monastic) cell.[17] Thereafter he sought the heavenly citadels by virtue of his resplendent merits, and was led by angelic throngs to the summits of heaven; united with the citizens of heaven he now rejoices in his celestial deserts [16].

After him King Cædwalla,[18] renowned in war and arms, succeeded to the kingdom, a powerful occupant of the throne and its rightful heir. But, abandoning soon afterwards the sceptre and government of this world, he furrowed the swelling waters [*scil.* of the English Channel] with the curved keel (of his boat) and traversed the briny expanses of the sea by oar. The frozen sails crackled in the windy blasts until the ship touched the shore with its untried prow; thereafter he crossed on foot the stormy Alps, closed in by massed glaciers and mountain peaks [25]. The clemency[19] of Rome [*scil.* the papacy] rejoiced in Cædwalla's arrival; and at the same time the clergy of the church in Rome rejoiced as the blessed man was found worthy to be immersed in the waters of baptism. Consumed with illness, then, he began to sicken after he had taken the baptismal chrism, until at last he ceased to draw breath in this mortal life[20] — seeking the lofty realms of the celestial kingdom, ascending to the shining summit of starry heaven [32].

/p. 16/ But as these kings — whose two names I have just disclosed — made their way to heaven on high, a third ruler here took up the noble sceptre, whom all peoples acclaim by the specific name of Ine;[21] he is now duly reigning over the kingdom of the (West) Saxons [37]. During his reign Bugga, a humble servant of Christ, built (this) new church with its lofty structure,[22] in which holy altars gleam in twelve-fold dedication; moreover, she dedicates the apse to the Virgin. Therefore let us all rejoicing celebrate this present day and let us chant hymns in turn to Christ the Lord! The months revolve with their successive feast-days, and cycles of years shall pass with the feasts in fixed order[23] [45]: (on this day each year) may antiphons strike the ear with their pleasing harmonies and the singing of psalms reverberate from twin choirs;[24] may the trained voice of the precentor resound repeatedly and shake the summit of heaven with its sonorous chant [49]!

Brothers, let us praise God in harmonious voice, and let the throng of nuns also burst forth in continual psalmody! /p. 17/ On these feast-days let us all chant hymns[25] and psalms and appropriate responds beneath the roof of the church, intoning the melodies with the continuous accompaniment of the psaltery;[26] and let us strive to tune the lyre with its ten strings — just as the psalmist urges us to 'praise (the Lord) with ten strings' [cf. Ps.XXXII.2]. Let each one of us adorn the new church with his singing, and let each lector[27] — whether male or female — read the lessons from Holy Scripture [58].

With her own birth the Virgin Mary consecrated this very day,[28] on which the dedication of Bugga's church gleams brightly — the day which the month of August perpetually renews, when torrid Sextilis [i.e. the Roman month of August] is divided in the midst of its rotation [i.e. on 15 or 16 August]. It restores once again the joys in our minds when the feast of St Mary returns at its accustomed time, and the holy altars are redolent with the holy gifts (of incense) [65].

This church glows within with gentle light on occasions when the sun shines through the glass windows,[29] diffusing /p. 18/ its clear light throughout the rectangular[30] church. The new church has many ornaments: a golden cloth glistens with its twisted threads and forms a beautiful covering for the sacred altar.[31] And a golden chalice[32] covered with jewels gleams so that it seems to reflect the heavens with their bright stars; and there is a large paten[33] made from silver. These [scil. the chalice and the paten] bear the holy medication for our life — for we are nourished by the body and blood of Christ [76]. Here glistens the metal of the Cross[34] made from burnished gold and adorned at the same time with silver and jewels. Here too a thurible[35] embossed on all sides hangs suspended from on high, having vaporous openings from which the Sabaean[36] frankincense emits ambrosia when the priests are asked[37] to perform mass [82].

Now let bright glory be to the unbegotten Father, and let glory no less be offered to the begotten Son, and may the Holy Ghost receive equivalent praise!

IV. ON THE ALTARS OF THE TWELVE APOSTLES[38]

i. *On St Peter*

[p. 19] St Peter crowns this apse[39] with the blessedness of the saints — the celestial key-bearer, who opens the gateway to heaven, the doorman who throws open the doors of eternal life. He made clear his two-fold doctrine to all (peoples) throughout the world — (two-fold), in that it is duly written down in two books [*scil.* the two Epistles of Peter] which contain the teachings of Christ in clear conscience [6]. Just as he had formerly caught fishy shoals in his net, stretching out flaxen fetters for the scaly tribes, so now in his heavenly ship he takes the throngs of men (which he has) snatched from the whirlpool of this world to the eternal realm — exactly as the Saviour promised to him in true words when He called from the curved boat to Peter[40] (who was) fishing [12]. Peter (also) walked by foot on the blue waters of the sparkling sea: but the sea did not swallow up the sinking man in its swelling surge since the right hand of Christ calmed the raging waters. Peter's shadow[41] used to provide a remedy for those who had died, since, having been healed, they returned once again to the light of this life even though they formerly had entered the gates of black death [18]. Peter also, aided by the divine power of God, restored a man who was lame in his knees and in both thighs; Peter immediately ordered him — *[p. 20]* whom neighbours had previously happened to carry to the temple — to walk on both his newly-healed feet [Act.III.2–9]. He also punished with death two evil people [i.e. Ananias and his wife Saphira] who had by fraud concealed (part of) the unspeakable price (for a piece) of land [Act.V.1–10] [24]. What is more, he completely banished the magical practices of the false Simon Magus, driving them off into dark shadows (and thus) freeing the Roman populace from ancient superstition. For Simon[42] had climbed the lofty summits of a new tower and, crowned with a branch of laurel, he set off flying; but the greedy crook fell face-down on the ground, expelling at once his vital breath, with all his bones shattered; and victory in this battle went to St Peter [32]. (In the end) Peter, fixed rejoicing on the cross, underwent torture, suffering the horrendous wounds (inflicted by) the cruel sword.[43] God, the omnipotent Judge, took Peter, duly adorned with his heavenly triumphs, to the summits of heaven.

ii. *On St Paul*

Saul, who punished holy crowds (of Christians) with prison sentences, is made a believer with the altered name of Paul, sowing many seeds through his fruit-bearing words: from Paul the holy crop grew in the ploughed field[45] of the world [4]. /p. 21/ God called down to him, (while he was still) an unbeliever, from the summit of heaven: 'Why do you persecute me, kicking (against me) with a hard boot?' [cf. Act.IX.4–5]. Accordingly, when he was submerged by day and night under the waters of the sea [II Cor.XI.25], he was found worthy (to behold) mighty visions of heavenly occurrences;[46] transported, he ascended to the third summit of heaven, and in his mind he gazed on the excellent companies of the heavenly host [10]. The insolent priestess of Delphi called out to Paul in a vehement voice; Paul purified the girl (and) the spirit departed — fleeing far off it disappeared into the empty air [Act.XVI.16–18]. Paul resuscitated an adolescent boy [i.e. Eutychus] who was entering the abodes of death, so that his spirit quickened the boy's own limbs [Act.XX.9–12] [15]. And did he not — rightly — deprive the sorcerer [i.e. Elymas] of (the sight of) his two eyes, so that he could never again see the sun with its radiant light [Act.XIII.8–11]? He restored a sick man who was lame in the shins and calves, whom fate had previously deprived of the ability to walk [Act.XIV.7–9]. Likewise, with the Lord granting a remedy, he quickly cured the father of Publius, whom a gasping fever was torturing: an excessively high temperature was roasting him and (alternating with periods of) icy coldness and an embarrassing pain was afflicting his intestines (with dysentery) [Act.XXVIII.8] [23]. As St Paul was piling a bundle of brushwood on the fire so that its heat might drive away the chill of the wintry fog, a poisonous viper fastened on his hand with its deadly fangs; but Paul did not feel the cold poison in the wound, nor was the fierce venom able to harm the saint; thereupon he cast the viper, with its covering of scaly skin, straight into the fire, to be consumed in the black flames [Act.XXVIII.3–6] [30]. /p. 22/ After he had completed the course of this transient life, he sought a holy martyrdom with his red blood, and the purple gore flowed from the fountain of his veins. Although the earth heaped up in a tomb now covered his bones, his spirit nevertheless ascended the high citadels (of heaven), guided through the cloudy reaches of the upper sky by angelic hosts [36].

iii. *On St Andrew*

Here too the church shall be protected by the altar of St Andrew, the brother of Peter, who once joyfully suffered a terrible death, hanged by his holy flesh. Christ, walking along the shore of the Sea (of Galilee), accepted Andrew by divine prescience, as he was traversing the waves of that sea in a skiff [Mt.IV.18] [5]. Straightway Andrew, moved by the voice of God, put his belief in the Eternal King Who redeems the world; scorning his dangling nets and rejecting their catch, he implemented Christ's commands more quickly than the telling of it [9]. Who would be able to enumerate the many towns with their populous crowds which, as a result of Andrew's teaching, demolished their unholy holies and opened their believing hearts to Christ the King? Indeed he recompensed his Lord with his bloody end /p. 23/ when he was hanged as a martyr from the broad tree of the cross;[47] he breathed the last breath of this mortal life, taking on a purple crown in Christ's kingdom [16].

iv. *On St James 'the Great'*

Here also St James, who was sired by an aging father [i.e. Zebedee], defends the lofty church with its holy roof.[48] When Christ was calling him from the shore of the sea, he left his own father behind in the curved boat [Mt.IV.21–2]. St James was the first to convert the Spanish peoples[49] with his teaching [5], converting the barbaric multitudes with his holy words; deceived by falsehood, they formerly worshipped the ancient mysteries and ghastly shrines of the dreadful demon. Here the marvellous apostle performed a number of miracles, which are now duly recorded in books[50] [10]. The savage tyrant Herod (Agrippa), a tetrarch of the (eastern) empire, murdered St James, striking him (down) with a sword in cruel death.[51] But the heavenly Father, Who justly makes His saints to triumph, transported him to the celestial citadels, his merits resplendent.

v. *On St John the Apostle and Evangelist*[52]

No less was the virgin John recruited at that time, whom brotherly love [*scil.* for his brother St James] joined to Christ, when John too abandoned his aging father in the curved boat, /p. 24/ which contained in its nets the watery catch (taken) from the sea [Mt.IV.21-2]. John formerly used to sweep along the blue waters with oars dripping sea-weed [5], weaving snares for fish beneath the water's surface; but when Christ called to him, he left the waves beating against the shore and the net-filled boat and, together with his dear brother, followed the Lord Who reigns in the citadel of Heaven [9].

John was the outstanding disciple of Christ the King, coming before all the others, beloved (by Christ) with great affection. The Emperor [i.e. Domitian] who ruled the Roman empire forced John as an outcast into exile,[53] transporting him by boat across the seas (to Patmos). Stationed there as an exile, he saw in a trance — aided by the heavenly will [15] — many visions of things, which are now written on parchment and read throughout the world [scil. in the biblical Apocalypse]. This aforementioned apostle lies buried in Ephesus,[54] ready to receive his rewards when the battle-trumpet resounds as the last days (of the world) pass away with former ages.

vi. *On St Thomas*[55]

Here St Thomas, who was given the Greek name Didymus, protects the holy church with its repaired roof.[56] Thomas, when he touched the wounds made by the cruel spear [Ioan.XX.24-5], *[p. 25]* believed at once in (the resurrection of) the King Who redeems the world — even though he had previously been distrustful of his kindly colleagues [5] and had nourished an improper belief in his doubtful heart as the Redeemer, arising from death, left the murky chaos of hell accompanied by a vast multitude. But the red scar immediately resolved the doubt when the disciple touched the wounds left by the savage blade, as Christ the peace-bringing Saviour entered the room where the fearful crowd (of disciples) was hiding behind closed doors [Ioan.XX.26] [12].

Christ, therefore, the holy offspring of God, sent this man, who was performing many miracles with magnificent success, to convert the peoples of the orient with holy books. India[57] at that time worshipped icons with unspeakable rites, having been indoctrinated by the stupid teaching of its forefathers; but it confessed the true faith when Thomas won its salvation and (henceforth) believed in Christ, Who controls the sceptres of heaven [19].

Accordingly, when his time in this present life had been spent,

Thomas straightway sought the ethereal heaven. A temple-priest, the officiant of an ancient shrine, transfixed (Thomas) with a hard blade so that he was dripping with blood[58] (but) he is to receive his rewards when the earth of its own accord shall gape open and all corpses shall arise from their ancient tombs.

vii. On St James 'the Less'

So too St James, who was born the son of Christ's aunt and who enjoyed the happy distinction of being Christ's cousin,[59] *[p. 26]* protects from the highest heaven this house of God. The Jews,[60] raging in insane fury, pushed him from the battlements of the church and he was killed by a laundryman's club — all because, after climbing to the roof of the temple, the priest [i.e. James] (had) preached Christ to the people with insistent words [7]. He is said to have had callous skin on his knees because on so many occasions he used to pray aloud to God, pounding the pavement of the church with his bended knees. He scorned the woollen covering of a shaggy cloak, adopting a linen mantel (to face the) wintry blasts. Similarly, he scorned perfumed oil for his body, and completely avoided the splendour of the public baths for his soul's sake. He did not cut off the locks of his hair with steel scissors, nor did any knife shave the down of his beard from his cheeks [16].

The reputation of his powers was so great that as punishment for his murder — which he underwent through a cruel death — the destruction of Jerusalem and the fall of the Jews took[61] place, when Titus Caesar — together with his father (Vespasian) who was born in a Roman citadel — accompanied by a massive army, deployed his armed soldiers to lay siege to the great city, until at length a terrible famine wasted with death and destruction the crowds contained by the ramparts and enclosed within the prison of the city walls [24]. It was at this time that a woman butchered her young child;[63] what is more, she transfixed him with sharp spits in order to be roasted; when he was cooked by the flames, the cruel mother ate him, *[p. 27]* destroying utterly the bonds of human nature: I recoil in horror from describing the boy's violent death [29]. Thus did the vengeance of the Cross punish the impious with destruction; so too did the martyrdom of St James punish the guilty! Eleven times 100,000 are said to have died at that time in the wretched city [i.e. Jerusalem] with its doomed inhabitants; moreover, another 100,000 were sold into slavery everywhere — those whom the rigid blade of the steel sword spared and who (only) escaped from death by starvation on miserable rations [36].

viii. *On St Philip*

Here too the measure of my verses commemorates St Philip, whom the holy Christ enriched with heavenly grace. With his holy teaching Philip taught the barbarous multitudes throughout Scythia[64] to believe in Christ Who is the Saviour throughout all ages. Until then the Scythians were lying listless in the dark shadow of death [5], denying the Creator of Light in their blackened hearts and perversely worshipping His creation, until (at length) their ears took in the preaching of the apostle. Gazing now on the clear light of the Perpetual Sun [i.e. Christ], they are all eagerly immersed in holy water, thereby cleansing the shame of their sin in the fountain of baptism [11].

Thereupon Philip hastens with holy books to convert Asia, a continent which, misled by deception, formerly worshipped idols; but it quickly opened its believing hearts to Christ as it took in the glorious words of the disciple's preaching. Thus did the blessed man convert the realm of Asia with his teaching [16]. /p. 28/ He was laid to rest in Asia after his death through fatal destiny.[65] The altar dedicated in his name shall protect this church.

ix. *On St Bartholomew*

Mighty India stands as the last of the lands of the earth, which the writings in books divide up into three parts.[66] Given over to pagan rites, India used to worship idols. But Bartholomew[67] destroyed the pagan shrines, duly smashing the images of the ancient gods [5]. A dialect of the Hebrew language [i.e. Syrian] names him 'the offspring of one suspending the waters in black clouds'[68] — inasmuch as humid skies drip with swelling drops[69] — which refers to the exalted doctrine concerning the 'vast heaven', as the poet of the Psalms once sang in verse [10]: 'Behold, the dark water drips from the clouds of the sky' [cf. Ps.XVII.12].

After these events (Bartholomew) purchased martyrdom with a bloody garland and, marked with the stigma of Christ, he follows his Lord. This church shall be protected by the venerable altar in his name.

x. *On St Matthew*

Matthew, in setting down the excellent doctrine of salvation, produced his account in Hebrew[70] in (the form of) a simple book, narrating many miracles in these holy pages *[p. 29]* which scripture now makes known throughout the tripartite world. The River Fison, emanating from the fountainhead of Paradise and opening the hidden mysteries of things, symbolizes Matthew[71] in wondrous fashion [6]. The symbol of the fountainhead itself properly signifies the Saviour from Whom the rivers flow in four channels since, in the beginning of the world, four clear rivers once flowed through the wide world and irrigated with their pure streams and crystal-clear waters the red flowers and the meadows growing green in the land: thus did the teaching of God flow from the four-fold fountainhead, irrigating parched hearts with its holy streams [14].

Matthew, the trustworthy narrator, was represented by that (symbol). The prophet of God [i.e. Ezechiel], filled with the Holy Spirit, once saw him to be symbolized by human likeness,[72] because he [i.e. Matthew] had enumerated the (human) forebears of Christ and the forefathers of their forefathers, from whom the Saviour in this world had entered the cradle of our flesh,[73] (thereby) removing the guilt of our sins [20].

xi. *On St Simon the Zealot*

[p. 30] Simon the Zealot, the same who was a Chanaanite [Mt.X.4], was known among the apostles by the name of Peter.[74] He taught pagan multitudes the divine doctrine so that they might seek the heavenly kingdom along a celestial path. In this church his holy altar shall be preserved [5] until the sky and the earth and the waters of the sea fade away, up till the moment when all ages burn in the final conflagration, and the mass of the earth, hills and mountains melts, and the structure of creation dissolves like a flux of wax, with fire crackling throughout the world.

xii. *On St Thaddeus (Jude)*

The last (apostle), Thaddeus, concludes the holy number (twelve); his name had formerly been Libbeus [Mt.X.3]. They say that he brought a letter in Christ's own handwriting to Abgar,[75] who once ruled the sceptres of the realm, (written) after Christ had condemned the tyrant of hell to death and emerged rejoicing from the dark abyss of hell; He thereupon ascended the starry heavens. This man is commonly known by the name of Jude; his praise is celebrated in the present church [9].

Jude produced for us one book in eloquent writing [*scil.* the biblical Epistle of Jude], bringing forth from his mouth the ancient words which the prophet Enoch had written down in days of yore, before the all-engulfing Flood had punished the world with its waters, /p. 31/ saying: 'Behold, the Lord comes with his holy thousands to impose judgement on all those who inhabit the earth' [Iud.14] [15]. He describes these (sinners) as clouds devoid of dripping rainwater which freezing winds disperse with impetuous blasts [cf. Iud.12]; he also compares them to trees sprung from a sterile trunk which lose their fruit in the autumn; he likens them as well to the foaming surge of waves, referring to these guilty (sinners) as the wandering stars of the heavens [Iud.13] for whom a punishment in (the realms of) shadowy tempests is reserved (in the hereafter) [22].

To be sure, Jude, with his holy teaching, converted the savage races and barbarous realms of the Pontus to the Lord.[76] His body lies in Armenia,[77] released through death, to be resurrected at the end of allotted time; but his spirit nevertheless traverses the heavenly citadels.

xiii. Conclusion[78]

I have now set out the twelve names of the (apostolic) fathers through whom the world was converted to belief in the High-throned God. I, (their abject) servant, humbly beseech them in my heart with frequent prayers that they may mercifully remit the burden of my sins and, offering forgiveness, may absolve the iniquities I have committed so that, sustained by divine grace, I may enter as the last into (eternal) peace, with Christ reigning in heaven.

V. ON ST MATTHIAS THE APOSTLE[79]

/p. 32/ St Matthias watches over this holy shrine. He is said to have been one of the Lord's seventy[80] disciples who taught His holy doctrine. God marked him out as elect by divine lot

[Act.I.24–6] when Judas Iscariot, deceived by evil malice [5], lost the lofty glory of his apostolic calling and poured out his stinking guts together with his blackened bowels when he burst open as he hung from the lofty noose [Mt.XXVII.5]: he had sold the Lord of Light Who redeems all ages with His blood, so that he could greedily acquire a burnished coin [Mt.XXVI.14–16]. Accordingly Matthias, trusting in the Lord and having spurned the evil thief, made up the same number (of twelve apostles): he duly rejoices in being associated with the apostolic victories.

THE ENIGMATA

TRANSLATED BY MICHAEL LAPIDGE

INTRODUCTION TO THE ENIGMATA

Aldhelm's collection of one hundred *Enigmata* — 'Riddles', or better perhaps, 'Mysteries'[1] — form part of his vast *Epistola ad Acircium*, and were inserted in that work ostensibly to demonstrate the properties of hexametrical verse expounded in the treatise on metre.[2] Aldhelm implies that he had composed the *Enigmata* on an earlier occasion, and he describes himself as having composed them 'in order to exercise the first beginnings of his intelligence';[3] similarly, in the metrical preface to the *Enigmata* he describes himself as 'unskilled' (line 7: *rudis*). These words imply that the *Enigmata* are one of Aldhelm's earliest compositions, perhaps the earliest. Yet even in so early a work, Aldhelm's genius is fully apparent.

Riddles are an ancient and ubiquitous form of expression.[4] As an oral form of expression among primitive peoples, popular riddles have been widely studied by anthropologists.[5] The popular riddle has usefully been defined as 'a traditional verbal expression which contains one or more descriptive elements, a pair of which may be in opposition; the referent of the elements is to be guessed'.[6] The riddle thus always implies a question (whether or not it is syntactically interrogative), and the juxtaposition of the elements usually constitutes a metaphor.[7] For example: What has eyes and cannot see? — Potato. Here the leaf-buds of the potato are described metaphorically as eyes. The point of this and any riddle is to evoke recognition of the metaphor and hence appreciation of the congruence between elements which may be in opposition (as here: potatoes do not have real eyes) and may even be antithetical. The ambivalent element in the riddle is the key to its solution.[8] The human learning process involves classification and the intelligible ordering of experience; but it also involves the ability to transcend conceptual categories. The transcendence of the normal conceptual categories draws attention to the riddle-subject and leads to fresh perception of its properties. Riddling, therefore, is an encapsulation of the learning process. We may be sure that popular, oral riddles were in circulation in Aldhelm's England, as they are in circulation everywhere in the world. Aldhelm evidently recognized that the riddle was a form of expression well suited to evoke fresh perception and appreciation of the properties of objects of the external world.

When riddles are written down they retain their basic form — that of a paradoxical/metaphorical contrast between opposing elements whose referent is to be guessed — but become capable of much greater verbal sophistication. Literary riddles have a lengthy tradition in western literature,[9] stretching back to the beginnings of Greek civilization.[10] Riddles (Greek *griphoi*) are attributed to Hesiod and Theognis, and by the fifth century B.C. the posing of riddles was a popular diversion at banquets (*symposia*), as we learn from Aristophanes and Aristotle.[11] Aristotle clearly recognized the metaphorical nature of the riddle, for he described it as follows: 'The very nature indeed of a riddle is this, to describe a fact in an impossible combination of words (which cannot be done with the real names for things, but can be with their metaphorical substitutes)'.[12] Large collections of Greek riddles are found in Athenaeus[13] and in the Palatine Anthology.[14] In Latin literature, by contrast, riddles are rare. Aulus Gellius records a riddle by Varro and several are cited by Petronius; a few more are preserved in the so-called 'African Anthology'.[15] For the Latin Middle Ages, however, and for the later history of the literary riddle, the most important figure is Symphosius, a Late Latin poet (fourth century? fifth century?) about whom nothing is known except that he composed the collection of one hundred three-line riddles that has come down to us.[16]

In the preface to his collection, Symphosius describes his riddles as *nugae*, 'literary trifles'; they were, he alleges, tossed off extemporaneously at a banquet — one is reminded of the practice of reciting riddles at Greek *symposia* — during the Saturnalia, after he had eaten and drunk a good deal ('post epulas laetas, post dulcia pocula mensae,/ deliras inter vetulas puerosque loquaces'). After the feasting had finished, recitations took place; and since Symphosius had brought nothing to recite, and did not wish to appear sane amid such insanity, he made up his riddles on the spot. His preface ends with a request to the reader for forgiveness, since his muse was far from sober ('da veniam, lector, quod non sapit ebria Musa'). Whether they were composed extemporaneously or

not, Symphosius's riddles are most noteworthy for their extreme
verbal dexterity: they consist mainly in simple paradoxes and
repetitions. Here is one example, the Key (no. iv):

> Virtutes magnas de viribus adfero parvis.
> pando domos clausas, iterum sed claudo patentes.
> servo domum domino sed rursus servor ab ipso.[17]

At their best Symphosius's riddles are engaging; but they are never
profound.[18]

Aldhelm clearly modelled his collection of one hundred
Enigmata on that of Symphosius. In his *Epistola ad Acircium* he
refers specifically to 'the poet Symphosius, endowed with
knowledge of metrical skill',[19] who composed *enigmata* in
'wanton language' (*ludibundis apicibus*). Aldhelm's castigation of
Symphosius's levity is valid, for there is a world of difference in
tone and intention between Symphosius's extempore *nugae* and
Aldhelm's *Enigmata*. As Aldhelm tells us (with characteristic
modesty!) in the metrical prologue to his collection, his theme will
be even mightier than those of Moses and David (prol. 29:
incipiam potiora): his theme will be the entirety of creation, visible
and invisible, and his intention will be 'to reveal the hidden
mysteries of things' (prol. 7–8: *pandere rerum enigmata
clandistina*). Aldhelm will have been familiar with the biblical
usages of the word *enigma*, for example with the injunction in
Proverbs that the wise man will only become wiser if he
scrutinizes the *enigmata* of wise men (Prv.I.6), and especially with
St Paul's statement that we now see God 'through a glass darkly' (I
Cor.XIII.12: *per speculum in enigmate*), whereas we shall then see
Him face to face. He will also have been familiar with Donatus's
definition of the *enigma*: 'a dark utterance (made clear) through a
hidden likeness of things'.[20] With these passages in mind we can
see that Aldhelm intended his *Enigmata* as glimpses — through a
glass darkly, as it were — into the hidden meanings of things. For
this reason we should best render the term *enigmata* as 'mysteries'
rather than 'riddles' (a term which perhaps implies the levity which
Aldhelm deplored in Symphosius). Aldhelm took the form and
structure of the *enigma* from Symphosius,[21] but by a bold stroke
he transformed it into a poetic genre which was to engage the
interest of medieval readers for several centuries.

Aldhelm's *Enigmata* explore hidden and subtle relationships
between objects of the visible world. Sometimes the relationship is
immediately clear from Aldhelm's juxtaposition of two *enigmata*:
thus Raven (lxiii), the first animal dispatched from the Ark,

alongside Dove (lxiv); or Apple-tree (lxxvi), the source of man's downfall, alongside Fig-tree (lxxvii), which supplied the covering for his shame; or Sling (lxxiv) alongside Hornet (lxxv). More often, however, the relationship between *enigmata* involves one of the four cosmic elements (earth, air, fire, water). Thus the aquatic Salamander (xv), which can also inhabit fire, is paired with the Squid (xvi), which though aquatic also inhabits the air. The aquatic Crab (xxxvii) walks on the sea-shore but also climbs the heavens (in a manner of speaking), whereas the Pond-skater (xxxviii) walks on both water and earth. The feathers in the Pillow (xli) can swell up to the clouds, whereas the feathered Ostrich (xlii) is earth-bound. As these subjects of Aldhelm's *enigmata* move from one element to the other, so there are other subjects which continually undergo elemental change. Salt (xix), for example, was once (sea-) water, undergoes fire and becomes earth. Fire (xlix) dissolves all things; the Diamond (ix), however, is not dissolved by fire but by goat's blood. And so on. In the *Enigmata* we see a universe in constant flux, made up of warring elements. The cosmic struggle is typified in the Cauldron (xlix), where all four elements are present and at war with each other:

I hang . . . neither touching the sky nor the vast earth, heated by the fire and seething with water. Thus I endure these two oppositions with their various dangers. . .

However, these warring elements are normally held in check by a bond of peace, as we see in the Double Cooking-Pot (liv):

Look: I carry fire *and* water in the inwards of my stomach; yet the surging waters do not overcome the fire, nor are the waters of the stream evaporated by the dark flames; rather, there are bonds of peace between the fire and water.

Nothing in the universe remains without the moderation of Natura (iv).[22]

Aldhelm's universe is in a continual process of gestation, birth and growth. Birth in the *Enigmata* is a dynamic process in which the whole of creation — animate and inanimate — participates. Nearly one third of the *Enigmata* contain an explicit reference to birth (the recurring verbs are *genero*, *gigno* and *nascor*).[23] Some *enigmata* are concerned solely with birth. Thus the Fountain (lxxiii) gives birth to thousands though it is itself devoid of life. The *enigma* of the Weasel (lxxxii) is occupied entirely with the unusual manner in which this animal becomes pregnant and gives birth. Aldhelm's concern with birth and the process of birth helps to explain the recurrence of one of the most striking images to be found in the *Enigmata*: that of *viscera*, 'inwards', or better, perhaps, 'womb'. In twenty of the *Enigmata* reference is made explicitly to the object's *viscera*.[24] Thus, for example, the Bookcase (lxxxix) bears divine words within its *viscera* which come to birth and life in the reader's mind. The Wine Cask (lxxviii) bears unfermented must in its *viscera* which eventually come to birth as wine. The *viscera* of the Silkworm (xii) produce silk; the *viscera* of the Organ (xiii) give birth to melodies; the *viscera* of the Candle (lii) give birth to light; the *viscera* of the Flour-sieve (lxvii) give birth to flour; and so on.

The universe depicted in Aldhelm's *Enigmata* is charaterized by subtle correspondences and relationships, and is in the continual process of gestation and growth. In one sense, everything in the universe would seem to share — to some degree at least — in these vital processes. Yet the profound difference between animate and inanimate nature is never lost sight of. The Bellows (xi) have breathing apparatus and breathe, yet they are not alive. A vital spirit passes through the *viscera* of the Trumpet (lxviii), but it is not alive. Distinctions such as these lead the reader to contemplate anew the inexpressible difference between God's creation and man's, and nowhere is this difference more acutely stressed than in Aldhelm's *enigma* on the greatest of man's creations, the Colossus of Rhodes (lxxii):

> The maker of my body fashioned all my limbs for me; nevertheless, I do not derive the normal funtions accruing to limbs from them: I cannot walk with my feet nor see with my eyes, even though there are wide-open windows beneath my forehead. No breath comes from panting inwards (*viscera*), nor do I strive to cast arrows with both arms. Alas, my creator made this gigantic frame in vain, since I am inwardly devoid of all feeling in my limbs.

In his *Epistola ad Acircium* Aldhelm had described his collection of *Enigmata* by saying that, 'having obtained materials concerning the diverse qualities of things both heavenly and terrestrial, [he] excerpted them in a cursory and summary fashion, considering now the great, now the meagre nature of creatures'.[25] This, for once, is a modest understatement of what Aldhelm attempted and achieved in his *Enigmata*. Rather than write a didactic treatise on cosmology (in the manner, say, of Isidore's *De Natura Rerum*), Aldhelm had the brilliant idea of casting his cosmology in the form of *enigmata* so that the reader would be led to consider the fabric of nature strand by strand (as it were) and so gain a fresh perception of the 'hidden mysteries of things'. The brilliance of his innovation was immediately recognized by his contemporaries, and the form of his work was avidly imitated.

Aldhelm had his imitators almost as soon as his *Enigmata* were published. His younger contemporary Tatwine, probably the scholar of that name who became archbishop of Canterbury in 731 and died in 734,[26] composed a collection of forty *enigmata*,[27] in which the influence and inspiration of Aldhelm is everywhere discernible. Alhdelm had prefaced his colletion of *Enigmata* with an acrostic prologue; Tatwine surpassed Aldhelm by linking the first and last letters of each of his forty *enigmata* in a vast acrostic and telestich which, spelled out, make up the following distich (note that each line has precisely forty letters):

> Sub deno quater haec diuerse enigmata torquens
> Stamine metrorum exstructor conserta retexit.

Tatwine's *enigmata* are indeed woven together by this complex acrostic scheme; but, as in the case of Aldhelm's *Enigmata*, they are also linked by various cosmological threads. Tatwine's principal concern appears to be with man's knowledge of God and the interpretation of His universe. Thus the first of Tatwine's *enigmata* is Philosophia (a term which apparently embraces all the disciplines of the trivium and quadrivium: 'septena alarum me circumstantia cingit'); the third concerns the four levels of scriptural interpretation (historical, spiritual, moral and allegorical); another concerns the five senses (xxvi), and various *enigmata* are concerned with writing and the transmission of knowledge (iv, v, vi and x). In his pursuit of human knowledge, Tatwine considers on the one hand the place of evil in the scheme of things (xxi–xxiii), and, on the other, the role of the virtues (ii and xxiv). The context in which contemplation of such themes is possible is clearly an ecclesiastical one, and a number of Tatwine's *enigmata* describe items of everyday monastic life: bell (vii), altar (viii), cross (ix), lectern (x) and paten (xii). It will be seen from these few examples that Tatwine responded sensitively to the challenge posed by the cosmological scheme of Aldhelm's *Enigmata*, and that his own *Enigmata* are of sufficient interest to bear comparison with those of his great predecessor.

For reasons unknown to us, Tatwine concluded his collection of *enigmata* at forty. A subsequent poet, one 'Eusebius',[28] probably a Southumbrian by training,[29] took the step of extending Tatwine's collection from forty to one hundred, the number canonized by Symphosius and Aldhelm. In the earlier part of his collection at least, 'Eusebius' attempted to follow the lead of Aldhelm and Tatwine, and to couch his *enigmata* in a theological framework. The unfolding of this theological scheme is seen in the sequence of the first few *enigmata*: God (i), Angel (ii), Devil (iii), Man (iv), Heaven (v), Earth (vi), and so on. Unfortunately, however, 'Eusebius' was unable to maintain this grand scheme, and for the final twenty or so *enigmata* was obliged to draw his subjects from a 'scientific' source (Isidore's *Etymologiae* certainly and a Latin *Physiologus* probably), so that his collection ends with a parade of wonderful beasts: Dragon (xlii), Tiger (xliii), Panther (xliv), Chameleon (xlv), Leopard (xlvi), Serpent (xlvii), Lizard (l), Scorpion (li), Chimera (lii), Hippopotamus (liii), and so on.

Aldhelm's *Enigmata* served as the inspiration for a literary experiment, quite different from that essayed by Tatwine and 'Eusebius', by the English scholar Wynfrith, who was later to win fame and martyrdom as the German apostle Boniface (*ob.* 754). Boniface was evidently struck by the moral implications of Aldhelm's *Enigmata*, for he composed a series of twenty *enigmata*, each in acrostic form, of which ten were devoted to the virtues and ten to the vices.[30] Each of Boniface's *enigmata* is devoted to a specific virtue or vice, with the acrostic spelling out the name of the subject: hence VERITAS AIT, FIDES CATHOLICA, SPES FATVR, and so on. However, in casting his *enigmata* in a straightforward dogmatic, hortatory form, Boniface lost the potential for imaginative exploration of the external world which characterizes the *Enigmata* of Aldhelm.

It was not only Anglo-Latin enigmatists who drew inspiration from Aldhelm, but vernacular poets as well. The so-called 'Leiden Riddle', probably a Northumbrian production of the eighth century, is nothing more than a translation of Aldhelm's *Enigma* xxxiii ('Lorica').[31] The large collection of Old English Riddles preserved in the tenth-century 'Exeter Book'[32] includes two which are simply translations of Aldhelmian *Enigmata*: Riddle 36 (= Aldhelm, *Enigm.* xxxiii) and Riddle 41 (= Aldhelm *Enigm.* c). But Aldhelmian diction and subject-matter are influential throughout the collection of Exeter Book Riddles, and it would appear that the compiler of this collection was attempting to emulate Aldhelm's collection by amassing nearly one hundred riddles.[33] Old English scholars have also seen the influence of Aldhelm's *Enigmata* on other Old English poetry.[34]

The poetry of these various Anglo-Latin and Old English poets testifies clearly to the influence of Aldhelm's *Enigmata* in Anglo-Saxon England. But his *Enigmata* were soon known farther afield.

The compiler of the so-called pseudo-Bede *Collectanea*, a miscellaneous collection of scholarly puzzles, made probably in the eighth century, possibly in Ireland or Wales, included several of Aldhelm's *Enigmata*.[35] On the Continent, the author of a collection of twelve *enigmata*, usually called the 'Lorsch Riddles' because they are preserved uniquely in a manuscript from Lorsch (now Vatican, Biblioteca Apostolica Vaticana, Pal. lat. 1753),[36] evidently drew inspiration from Aldhelm's *Enigmata*.[37]

That Aldhelm's *Enigmata* were soon being studied enthusiastically on the Continent — no doubt as a result of the Bonifatian mission — is proved by the large number of surviving manuscripts written in continental centres in the eighth and ninth centuries.[38] In fact the *Enigmata* were soon incorporated in the school curriculum[39] and were studied alongside the great Christian-Latin poets such as Juvencus, Caelius Sedulius and Arator. During the ninth century these Christian-Latin poets were provided with detailed commentaries by Carolingian scholars such as Remigius of Auxerre,[40] and it is interesting to see that the *Enigmata* too were provided with scholarly commentary. Some notion of this commentary, and hence of how Aldhelm's *Enigmata* were studied in early medieval schools, may be gleaned from the unprinted marginal glosses which accompany Aldhelm's *Enigmata* in a tenth-century manuscript of English (and possibly Canterbury) origin, now London, British Library, Royal 12. C. XXIII (the *Enigmata* occupy ff. 83r–103v of the manuscript).[41] Thus Aldhelm's *Enigma* no. i (*Terra*, 'Earth') is provided with the following gloss:

> Terra dicta a superiori parte qua teritur. Humus ab inferiori uel humidus. Terra uero sub mari. Tellus autem quia fructus eius tollimus. Hec et Ops dicta eo quod fert opem fructibus eadem et aruus ab querendo et colendo uocatur. Proprie autem terra ad distinctionem harene. Arida nuncupatur sicut scriptura ait, 'Porro uocauit deus aridam terram' (f. 84r).

This gloss is copied directly from Isidore, *Etymologiae* XIV.i.1–2. It does not, perhaps, elucidate Aldhelm's *enigma* very helpfully, but it indicates that the glossator had recourse to a standard medieval reference-work in commenting on Aldhelm. The *Etymologiae* were laid frequently under contribution by the Royal glossator,[42] but other sources were also used, such as Gregory the Great's *Moralia in Iob*[43] and some version of the *Scholia Bernensia* on Vergil.[44] We have no means of knowing whether these explanatory glosses were first applied to Aldhelm in England, or whether they were transmitted with the text from a continental exemplar. Whatever the case, there is abundant evidence that the *Enigmata* were carefully studied in tenth-century England.[45] Of all Aldhelm's works, then, the *Enigmata* proved the most popular from the time they were published until the eleventh century and beyond, both in England and on the Continent. The reasons for their popularity are apparent, and they will repay careful study even today.

ENIGMATA

Preface[1]

[p. 97] (Eternal) Judge, You Who with heavenly authority rule perpetually the sceptres (of power) and the resplendent royal court of heaven, controlling it with eternal laws — for in punishment You tortured the disgusting limbs of Behemoth when the ghastly (creature) once fell headlong from the lofty citadel (of heaven) — (You), protector, grant now to me, who am composing bright songs in verse, Your aid, that I may be able, (though) unskilled, to reveal by Your decree the hidden mysteries of things through my verse. Thus, God, do You freely bestow Your gifts on unworthy (recipients) [9]. *[p. 98]* I do not declaim my verses in the direction of the Castalian nymphs, nor has any swarm (of bees) spread nectar in my mouth; by the same token I do not traverse the summits of Apollo, nor do I prostrate myself on Parnassus, nor am I entranced by any poetic vision.[2] For God shall be able to augment the poetic undertaking for me, freely breathing His holy gifts into my obtuse mind: if He should touch my mind, my heart shall at once requite (the gift) with praise [16]. For biblical verses[3] make it clear that the prophet Moses long ago had chanted the glorious praises of an ancient victory far and wide among peoples everywhere [cf. Ex.XV.1–18], where the bright sun, on raising its head from the ocean's flood, shines forth. And the Psalmist, singing aloud the verses of his songs, announced a Child born through divine procreation which had risen in the skies before the Morning Star had poured its radiant light on the world when the ages were newly formed [Ps.CIX.3] [24]. But if these (present) *Enigmata* in verse, after all blemishes and awkwardness have been completely expunged, are to come off well at an hexametrical pace, and if no delusion seduces my mental efforts with empty

deception, I shall begin (to sing of) even mightier (themes), if God — [p. 99] Who once strengthened His warrior Job — shall refresh the parched inwards of His servant with a draught of everlasting dew. For You (God) once led streams of water from dry rocks, when the throng (of Israelites), having crossed the Red Sea, entered the desert: David sang of this in a psalm [Ps.LXXVII. 13–15]. You, Father, Who protect all ages from the citadel of heaven, deign now to forgive the unspeakable faults of my sins [36].

I. *Earth*

I am called the nurse of all things in my sphere, which the universe sustains — and deservedly, since wicked offspring never rend their (own) mother's breasts in such a way. In summer I am verdant with offspring; in winter-time I languish [4].

II. *Wind*

No-one can see me nor grasp me in his hands; I quickly spread the shrill whistle of my voice through the world. [p. 100] With my terrible-sounding strength I am able to shatter oaks. I touch the lofty skies and pass through (earthly) fields [4].

III. *Cloud*

In flight I vary my hue, leaving heaven and earth behind: there is no place on earth for me, none in the region of the skies. No other (creature) fears an exile of such cruelty; but I make the world grow green with my moist (rain)drops [4].

IV. *Nature*

Believe me, nothing exists without my controlling force, and yet no eye shall see my face and visage. Who doesn't know that the convex summits of heaven, the bright (course) of the sun, the fluctuations of the moon — all move at my command [4]?

V. *Rainbow*

In the writings of the ancients[4] I am conceived as the child of Thaumas, but I myself shall set out the first beginnings of my descent: I was born bright-red from the sun through the parturition of a watery cloud. I illuminate the skies at every turn, (but) I do not ascend in the wind [4].

VI. *Moon*

[p. 101] I now participate in the common fate of the sea, unrolling monthly patterns with alternating cycles: (for just) as the brilliance of my luminous shape decreases, so does the swelling sea lose the upsurge of its waters [4].

VII. *Fortune*[5]

It is well known that an eloquent poet once sang: 'where God and where hard Fortune calls, let us follow!' [Vergil, *Aen.* XII.677]. The ancients were accustomed — wrongly! — to call me mistress, as being the one who ruled the sceptres of the world — until (the advent of) Christ's grace which shall rule forever [4].

VIII. *Pleiades*[6]

The stupid ancients said that we were the offspring of Atlas. Our company is seven-fold, but one of us is scarcely to be seen. *[p. 102]* We walk at the summit of the sky and beneath the depths of the earth as well. We are visible in blackest darkness, but are hidden by daylight. We took our former name from that of spring [5].

IX. *Diamond*[7]

See, I do not fear the cutting force of hard iron, nor am I burned in a furnace of flames: but the hard force of my insuperable strength is softened by the blood of a goat. Thus blood overcomes that which causes fear in an iron mass [4].

X. *Dog*[8]

The mighty force of things long ago created me in such a way that I chase the fierce enemies of my master; bearing arms (as it were) in my mouth I accomplish deeds of war, and yet I'm quick to avoid a beating by fleeing from a child [4].

XI. *Bellows*[9]

Together with my twin brother I am fed by alternating blasts. There is no life in me, even though I have breathing apparatus. *[p. 103]* My craft supplies ornamentation for jewelled metals: no thanks are given to me, but another accepts the praise [4].

72

XII. *Silkworm*[10]

When the time of the year for weaving (silk) thread returns, my pale inwards swell with silken fibres; I quickly climb up to the leafy tops of broom so that, after making the little (silk) balls, I may rest in the peace allotted to me by fate [4].

XIII. *Organ*[11]

Although trumpeters may blow battle-trumpets made of hollow brass, and lutes may twang and horns resound with a great racket, yet my inwards belch out a hundred melodies: in my presence the music of stringed instruments is immediately dumbfounded [4].

XIV. *Peacock*[12]

I am outstandingly beautiful, acknowledged as a wonder throughout the world, (even though) I am created from bones and sinews and red blood. /p. 104/ As long as I live, the sheen of burnished gold does not glow more brightly (than I do); and when I die, my flesh never decays [4].

XV. *Salamander*[13]

Although I live in the midst of fires, I do not feel the flames, but rather I will treat the damages (inflicted by) the fire completely as a joke. I do not burn when the fire is crackling and embers are glowing, but rather the flames of the torrid furnace grow cooler [4].

XVI. *Squid*[14]

The spectacle offered by my life is a pleasing sight: in company with schools of scaly fish I explore the waters of the sea, and with flocks of feathery birds I likewise climb through the air; nevertheless, I cannot live by breathing air [4].

XVII. *Bivalve Mollusc*[15]

/p. 105/ I am born in the blue waters of the sea from twin shells, producing tawny fleeces from my spiky body. Notice that I provide the wool of cloaks as well as food from my flesh: thus in two ways I pay my debt to fate [4].

XVIII. *Ant-lion*[16]

For a long time I have borne a name of two components, inasmuch as I'm called a 'lion' and an 'ant' in Greek, giving rise to metaphorical meanings in my two names, since I am unable to fend off the beaks of birds with my own beak. Let a wise man investigate why I have this two-fold name [5]!

XIX. Salt[17]

Once upon a time I was sea-water, teeming with scaly fish, but, subject to a new decree of fate, this existence ceased, /p. 106/ when in the midst of blazing fires I undergo a searing ordeal: for (now) my face shines bright white like ash and snow [4].

XX. Bee[18]

Formed in wondrous ways and engendered without seed, I load my sweet inwards with booty from flowers. Through my craft the food of kings grows golden with honey. I always brandish the sharpened arrow-points of fierce warfare and (yet), lacking hands, I surpass the metal-work of smiths [5].

XXI. File

Gleaming with a furrowed body and steely brightness I am made for grinding down shapeless metal with my teeth. Being accustomed to polish the mass and substance of gold, I smooth down its surface while remaining the very coarsest of substances; lacking any voice myself I screech stridently with a piercing shriek [5].

XXII. Nightingale[19]

My glorious voice warbles with various melodies: I shall never sing my songs with a harsh-sounding beak. /p. 107/ For all that I am dusky in colour, yet I am not to be scorned for my singing; thus I do not cease singing in the face of a frightening future fate: for winter puts me to flight, but I shall return as soon as summer comes [5].

XXIII. Pair of Scales[20]

Nature once created us as twin sisters, whom the observance of just laws perenially controls: we are accustomed to scorn individuals and to maintain justice. Happy would be that age for mortals on earth if they would maintain the norm of justice in the manner of us sisters [5]!

74

XXIV. *Dragon-stone*[21]

The head of a terrifying dragon is said to have given birth to me. I enrich the brilliance of gemstones with my crimson hue. But no strength of rigid hardness will be given to me if the scaly dragon should die before I have been snatched bright-red from the very crown of its head [5].

XXV. *Magnet*[22]

/p. 108/ Nature's force, or rather the creator of heaven, gave to me that which is lacking in all the miracles of the ancient world: for I am able to suspend cold masses of steel in the air. Thus, conquering by means of this particular strength, I surpass other metallic natures. (However), in the presence of Cyprian adamant, I am immediately deprived of my potency [5].

XXVI. *Cock*[23]

Noisy in the darkness, it was my custom to have announced the shining rays of majestic light and the brilliance of the sun; I am feathered and I bear the name of a well-known people. Wearing weapons on my feet I engage in the hazards of war, sporting a jagged crest on the top of my head [5].

XXVII. *Whetstone*

I come forth cold from the frozen inwards of the earth. I shall polish the hardness of iron with my rectangular face; and I never fear the hazards of old age, /p. 109/ as long as Vulcan[24] [i.e. fire] shall not snatch away the number of my years with his fire: my rigid shape immediately grows soft in black flames [5].

XXVIII. *Minotaur*[25]

I am two-shaped, being different with respect to my face and my limbs: I am armed with horns, but my other limbs constitute a terrifying man. I am known by report through the fields of Cnossos, having been born a bastard of an unknown father in Crete. My name is taken from that of man and beast together [5].

XXIX. *Water*

Who would not be astonished at the spectacle of my nature? With my strength I support (the weight of) a thousand trees, but a slender point[26] is soon able to shatter these mighty efforts! The birds of the sky and the fish swimming in the sea once drew from me the beginnings of their life [5]. It is well known that a third part of the world is under my control.

XXX. *Alphabet*

/p. 110/ We were born seventeen voiceless sisters; we say that the six other bastards are not to be counted in our number.[27] We are born of iron — and we die once again by iron — or of the feather of a bird flying swiftly in the sky. Three brothers begot us of an unknown mother [5]. Whoever in his eagerness wishes earnestly to hear our instruction, we quickly produce for him silent words.

XXXI. *Stork*[28]

I have a gleaming white appearance and also one that grows darkly black, as I am made of the various hues of the feather. I lack a warbling voice, for I produce a rattling sound with my beak. Although in my ferocity I tear scaly snakes to pieces, /p. 111/ my body does not swell up with the deadly venom [5]: I am even in the habit of feeding my tender chicks and offspring with the poisonous flesh and foul blood of serpents.

XXXII. *Writing-tablets*[29]

My origin was from (the wax of) honey-bees, but my other outer part grew in the woods. Stiff leather provided me with my shoes. Now the iron point cuts into my comely face with its wandering movements, and carves furrows in the manner of a plough [5]; but the holy seed for the crop is brought from heaven, and it produces abundant sheaves from its thousand-fold harvest. Alas, this holy harvest is destroyed by fierce weapons!

XXXIII. *Breast-plate*[30]

The dewy earth produced me from its frozen inwards. I am not made from the bristling fleece of (sheep's) wool; no yarn is drawn (tight on a loom), no humming threads leap about (the spindle); nor do Chinese silk-worms weave me from their yellow floss; I am not gathered from spinning wheels, nor am I beaten by the stiff carding comb [5]: /p. 112/ and yet, nevertheless, note that I am described as 'clothing' in common parlance. I have no fear of arrows drawn from long quivers.

XXXIV. Locust[31]

Although to the farmers I may not be a welcome visitor — I cull the fruit of (their) fields from the green vegetation of the countryside, gnawing in throngs the bark of tree trunks — (yet) once upon a time I was renowned for devastating the kingdoms of the Nile when they and all their foul population experienced the ten plagues [Ex.X.14]. My heart is beneath my knees, for it stands enclosed in its case; in the manner of a venomous toad my chest is placed under my knees.

XXXV. 'Night-raven' (Screech-owl)[32]

My nature appropriately reproduces my name in two aspects, for the 'shadows' have part of me, and the 'birds' the other part. Only rarely does anyone see me in the clear light, particularly since at night-time I frequent hiding-places beneath the stars. It is my custom to chatter in mid-air in a harsh voice [5]. I am recorded in Romulean [i.e. Latin] books, although my name is Greek, while I inhabit nocturnal shadows through my name.

XXXVI. Midge[33]

/p. 113/ I am slight in body, (and) armed with sharp stings. I rise in throngs, flying aloft on my wings, taking bloody prey with my gory sword, sparing no four-footed beast; rather, I thrust forth my darts, goading the bristling flesh of flocks with wounds [5]. Once I was notorious for plaguing the Egyptian countryside [Ex.VIII. 16–17]; and boring through into the muscle, I am nourished with the blood of bulls.

XXXVII. Crab[34]

The ancient Latins called me 'nepa'; I walk along the wet shores of the foaming sea and, proceeding backwards, I traverse the ocean with inverted steps. And yet the ethereal heaven is adorned by me when I climb up in the sky, ruddy with my twelve stars [5]. The oyster, terrified by the hard stones (which I cast), fears me.

XXXVIII. Pond-skater[35]

/p. 114/ I walk on the waters borne up by my four feet, yet I do not fear that I shall drown in the watery main. Rather, I tread on foot equally on land and sea. Nature does not allow me to swim in the fast-moving beck nor to cross turbulent streams by bridge or by boat [5]; instead, I walk with dry feet over still waters.

XXXIX. Lion[36]

I, a rough-haired beast of the woods, destroy boars armed with tusks and antlered stags, although they bellow aloud; remorseless, I crush the arms of bears. With my gory maw, I do not fear the teeth and jaws of wolves, being frightening (myself and) sustained by my royal authority [5]. For I sleep with my eyes wide open, never closing them.

XL. Pepper[37]

I am black on the outside, covered with wrinkled rind, yet inside I have a glistening core. /p. 115/ I season the delicacies of the kitchen: the feasts of kings and extravagant dishes and likewise sauce and stews. But you will find me to be of no value at all [5] unless my inwards are crushed for their shining contents.

XLI. Pillow[38]

I would rather that you do not suspend your trust, even though what I say might be thought worthless; rather, open your believing mind to my words. I am able to swell up loftily to the clouds on high if, with all my body removed, my 'head' is taken from me; however, if I am borne down with the weight of someone's head pressing deeper into me [5], I will always appear to be diminished in size.

XLII. Ostrich[39]

The massive limbs on my bulky body sprout feathers. I am similar in colouring to the hawk, but dissimilar with respect to flying, since I do not traverse the upper air on my slender wings; instead, I walk on foot through dusty fields, offering the smooth shells of my eggs (to men) for their cups [5]. My homeland is said to be Phoenician Africa.

XLIII. Leech[40]

/p. 116/ Pale yellow in hue, I haunt the foul waters of swamps, for fortune has made for me a 'bloody' name, since I am nourished by thirsty mouthfuls of red blood. I am devoid of bones, arms and feet, but I bite dying bodies with three-forked wounds [5] and thus I provide a remedy from my health-bringing lips.

78

XLIV. *Fire*

My father and mother begot me of frozen hardness [*scil.* flintstone] while my youth soon grew strong in dry tinder. With my own strength I can surpass their lot, since nothing except water can conquer my nature. When I loose the bonds of my nature, I utterly destroy forests and cliffs and metals such as tin and iron [5]. When life is in me I am the likeness of a bright star; afterwards, however, overcome by fate, I am blacker than pitch.

XLV. *Spindle*[41]

[p. 117] I was born in the forest, green on a leafy bough, but fortune changed my condition in due course, since I move my rounded shape twirling through the smooth-spun thread; from this is made the royal covering of a robe. No hero (anywhere) is girded by a belt as long as mine [*scil.* the distaff]. They say that the Parcae decree the fates of men through me — yet severe cold would destroy men if I did not withstand it.

XLVI. *Nettle*[42]

I torment my tormentors, but I willingly would torment no-one, nor do I wish to harm anyone, unless he were first to incur the guilt and seek to pluck my green stalk. The limbs of the man who harms me immediately become hot and swell up: thus I avenge the injury and inflict punishment with my sharp stings [5].

XLVII. *Swallow*[43]

I spend several months wasting away without food, but sleep and slumber helps pass these lengthy fasts. *[p. 118]* When the pale fields burst out in brilliant luxuriance, my red throat immediately gabbles chattering songs. After producing my tender brood and the offspring of my kin is grown [5], I flee of my own accord and seek shady retreats. But if someone should harm the eyes of my chicks, I as physician supply a well-known poultice as remedy, (by) seeking a flower of the field whose name is the same as my own.

XLVIII. *Movement of the Heavens*

The kindly Creator of nature formed me thus: I am round, and traverse all the universe in vast orbits, bearing the expanse of the earth with all its weight on my bosom; so too I embrace the surging masses of the ocean and the sea. For there is nothing in the nature of things that would be as swift [5] — nothing which walks on foot or flies through the air or, as a denizen of the sea, speeds with fins through the blue-green depths, nor the wheel which a watermill drives in its circular course — none could run as fast as I, if the seven planets did not retard my course.[44]

XLIX. *Cauldron*[45]

[p. 119] I hang, ugly, round, large, made of beaten metals, neither touching the sky nor the vast earth, heated by the fire and seething with water. Thus I endure these two oppositions with their various dangers, as long as I put up with the liquid of the water and the fierce flames [5].

L. *Milfoil (Yarrow)*[46]

In the language of the Greeks and likewise in Latin I am called 'thousand-leaf', and am born from the green field; therefore I shall have my hundred-fold name ten times over, since no other plant, among all the countless furrows of the earth's expanse, blooms so abundantly on its tender stalk [5].

LI. *'Heliotrope'*[47]

I am born from the fertile field, flourishing of my own accord; the shining crown grows golden with yellow bloom. *[p. 120]* With the sun in the west I close up, and open again at sunrise: whence the learned Greeks devised my name [4].

LII. *Candle*[48]

I was formed from two-fold material by open hands. My insides glow brightly; my entrails, plundered from flax or indeed from the slender rush, glisten; but the outer parts of my body are golden yellow, (the produce of) flowers [i.e. bees' wax], and, belching fire, they pour out flame and sparks [5]; and moist tear-drops drip continuously from my brows. Nevertheless, I thus dispel the horrid shadows of night. My scorched inwards soon leave remnants of ash.

LIII. *Arcturus*[49]

At the summit of the universe I stand, hemmed in by starry throngs. I bear the name 'esseda' ['war-chariot'] in common parlance. /p. 121/ Revolving continually in a circle I never incline downwards, as do the other stars of the heavens (which) hasten to the sea. I am enriched by this endowment [5], since I am nearest to the pole, which stands out above the Rhipaean mountains of Scythia. I equal in number the Pleiades at the summit of the sky, the lower part of which is said to sink down in the Stygian or Lethean swamp among the black shades of hell.

LIV. Double Cooking-Pot[50]

Who could believe this exhibition of mighty events and who could control the states of things behaving contrary to their normal condition? Look: I carry fire *and* water in the inwards of my stomach; yet the surging waters do not overcome the fire, nor are the waters of the stream evaporated by the dark flames [5]; rather, there are bonds of peace between the fire and water. A hammer and anvil created me in the first instance.

LV. Ciborium (Chrismal)[51]

/p. 122/ I am venerated as a holy house, filled with a divine gift. But no-one unlocks my portals nor throws open my doors unless the roof is removed from my four chambers. And although there are gleaming jewels on the outside of my body and a golden boss glistens with its burnished metalwork [5], yet my teeming inwards are more richly endowed within, where the beauteous splendour of Christ shimmers: thus does the brilliant glory of these holy things bloom! In this church the (vaults of the) roof do not spring from beams or columns.

LVI. Beaver[52]

I am a guest dwelling on the edge of steep (river-)banks. I am not lazy, but am a warrior with teeth for weapons; what is more, I sustain my life through hard work, felling mighty trees with the curved hatchets (of my teeth) [4]. I frequently dive, moistening my head in the stream, down to the watery depths where the wet fish swims. Healing wounds to the vitals and limbs diseased with pestilence, I annul the deadly disease and plague. I am nourished by chewing the rind (of trees) and their bitter bark.

LVII. Eagle[53]

/p. 123/ Although deceitful poets might sing in their verses (that I am) the weapon-bearer of unlucky Jove and the abductor of

81

Ganymede, I was not that bird by whom the Trojan youth [i.e. Ganymede] was carried off; rather, I chase fleeing swans high in the air and drive screeching cranes (before me) beneath the summit of the heavens [5]. When weary old age destroys my body with senility, my limbs are moistened by being dipped in watery streams; thereafter I am renewed by the brilliant light of Phoebus [i.e. the sun].

LVIII. *Evening Star*

My name clings to me from the earliest time of night. I seize the western realms at the world's axis. When Titan [i.e. the sun] dips his life-giving body in the ocean and the sky, sinking downwards, is absorbed in the grey waves, then I follow concealing my light in the glass-green plains (of the sea) [5], and consider myself fortunate not to be snatched suddenly from the skies so that my light may drive away the dark shadows of night.

LIX. *Quill Pen*[54]

/p. 124/ The bright pelican, which swallows the waters of the sea in its gaping throat, once begot me (such that I was) white. I move through whitened fields in a straight line and leave dark-coloured traces on the glistening path, darkening the shining fields with my blackened meanderings [5]. It is not sufficient to open up a single pathway through these fields — rather, the trail proceeds in a thousand directions and takes those who do not stray from it to the summits of heaven.

LX. *Unicorn*[55]

In no way do I fear the attacks of cruel Mars, even though the hunter with his vainly baying hound should be babbling, a bowman shooting iron-tipped arrows; rather, sustained by my immense strength, I behave as an aggressive warrior (and) bring down mighty elephants [5]. /p. 125/ Alas, cruel Fortune, which thus tricked me by craft, since I slaughter mighty beasts but am overcome by a harmless virgin! For, laying bare her breast, the beautiful young woman straightway captures me and, having thus fulfilled her wish, she leads me back to a lofty city. The Greek language gave me my name because of my horn [10]; the Latins call me likewise in their language.

LXI. *Dagger*[56]

I was formed originally from the earth's bosom by means of skill; the remainder of my constitution came from fierce bulls, or rather it was manufactured from stinking goats [*scil.* to provide a horn handle]. Through me the eyes of many are closed in death — I who, while being naked myself, strive to protect the life of my master [5]. My house is constructed of leather cut to size as well as of shaved-down laths which they cut from a tree.

LXII. *Bubble*

I am born from raindrops falling from a wet sky and grow to size in a waterfall in the river; but no hand can touch me while I am swimming in the watery stream or else my inwards will burst at once with the touch /p. 126/ and my fragile breath will evaporate into thin air [5]. Before such time, I lead my cohorts in throngs through the waters, since my many companions share the same origin.

LXIII. *Raven*[57]

When savage floods were destroying the human race and new-made oceans were punishing all mortals — with very few exceptions, (namely those) who carried the seeds of the world — I first of all living things flaunted the bonds of the law [Gen. VIII.6–7] by refusing to bow my neck to the commandment of the patriarch [5]. Whence, I suspect, the poet [i.e. Caelius Sedulius] said long ago: '(The sin) which it [i.e. the raven] committed on the waters it washed away in the wilderness'. For I shall never stuff my young with feasts of food unless first I see their feathers grow black in the flesh. Let one letter be removed: henceforth I shall remain without offspring [10].

LXIV. *Dove*[58]

When God had punished (man's) unspeakable sins with the Flood and at the same time had washed away the contagion of evil with those waters, I carried out the first words of the command (issued by) the patriarch [Gen. VIII.11], indicating with the (olive-) leaf that well-being had returned to earth. Accordingly I always have a gentle heart [5] and I shall remain a blessed bird free of black gall.

LXV. Cat[59]

[p. 127] I am a sufficiently reliable guardian, watching over the house vigilantly. In darkest night I traverse black shadows, not losing the sight of my eyes (even) in pitch-black caves. I silently arrange snares to serve as deadly stumbling-blocks for the unseen thieves who ravage the stores of grain [5]. A roving huntress, I seek out the haunts of wild animals, but I will not chase the fleeing throngs in the company of dogs who, barking after me, provoke savage battles. A race hateful to me has given me my name.

LXVI. Millstones[60]

We are sisters, equal in our common lot, who through our labour provide food for everyone else. The work is the same for both of us, but our status is distinct: for the one runs around, something which the other never does. Nor are we goaded by the bitter stings of envy [5]: what either one eats, what it chews over open-mouthed, it humbly returns all crushed to pieces, without any (attempt at) wicked deceit.

LXVII. Flour-sieve[61]

Although dry myself, I pour out from my innumerable windows a frosty and gleaming snow, casting it down from my dark inwards. [p. 128] And yet everyone loves it, even though it is cold, thicker than cloud and mist, and is scattered throughout the hall. Without it, mortals proceed towards the separation of death [5] — thus do the vital spirits perish, when life comes to an end — but enriched by it, they scorn the portals of Dis [i.e. the underworld]. This snow never melts (when placed) on burning coals, but rather — marvellous to relate — it grows hard in the fire.

LXVIII. Trumpet

I who am hollow shall stir the hearts of warriors with my blast, urging the cohorts to battle with my shrill notes. Accordingly, I issue resoundingly in so great an uproar because no inwards dull the sound within me; rather, the blasts of wind have dominion throughout my body [5]. No chirping cricket can ever surpass me, nor can the lively nightingale, singing at the same time in the broom — the bird which the Greeks in their own language call 'acalanthis'.

LXIX. *Yew-tree*[62]

By having ever-green foliage on my leafy body I am at no time deprived of a thick covering, even though Circius [i.e. the west-north-west wind] and Boreas [i.e. the north wind] and the blasts of Caurus [i.e. the north-west wind] strive with their terrible force to strip off my exterior. */p. 129/* The fates of things[63] have made of me a bearer of pestilence [5], for when the poisonous branch spreads from my trunk, and ravenous gluttons consume it with gaping mouths, I straightway strike down dead the many corpses of those consuming me.

LXX. *Loaf of Bread*[64]

I arise from the earth, shield-shaped with a gleaming body of rich snow, growing hard in the heat of Vulcan [i.e. the oven] — and yet more valuable by far than other shields of battle; nor is there any iron boss in the middle of my shield-shape. Without me, what use is a shield (in the hands) of grim warriors [5]? Limbs and vital spirits would scarcely be freed from the pathway of death if I did not oppose Hades with powerful determination.

LXXI. *Fish*[65]

The kindly Creator deprived me at once of feet and hands when He first created the mighty world. I am not sustained in flight by the swift wing of a bird; nor does breath in alternating inhalations animate my body. Although while in the skies I gaze on heaven's vaulted summits [5], yet I do not scorn the waters of the surging sea.

LXXII. *Colossus*[66]

/p. 130/ The maker of my body fashioned all my limbs for me; nevertheless, I do not derive the normal functions accruing to limbs from them: I cannot walk on my feet nor see with my eyes, even though there are wide-open windows beneath my forehead. No breath comes from panting inwards [5], nor do I strive to cast arrows with both arms. Alas, my creator made this gigantic frame in vain, since I am inwardly devoid of all feeling in my limbs.

LXXIII. *Fountain*

I creep stealthily and speedily through empty hollows of the earth, winding my twisted route along the curves of its arteries.

Although I am devoid of life and utterly lacking in sensation, what number could embrace or what calculation encompass the many thousands of living creatures which I engender through birth [5]? Neither the stars of the glowing firmament in the sky nor the sands of the billowing sea can equal them.

LXXIV. Sling[67]

[p. 131] The gleaming crop of flax, blooming in the field's expanse, and the ox-hide provided me with the elements of my constitution. I consist of two bands of twisted cord; with a stone (launched) from these I felled a mighty tyrant [I Reg.XVII.40–50] when once the hosts of the Gentiles were bent on furious war [5]. I prefer to decide a battle with a smooth stone rather than by fighting with hard spears with their iron tips. Three fingers launch my entire body aloft: I whirl about the head and (then) am hurled into thin air.

LXXV. Hornet[68]

Now I soar through clear air on two wings, a detestable creature, and I produce the buzzing sound of my rough voice; and in a hollow stump I congregate in dense swarms, amassing sweet food for our own throngs — and yet these comestibles are rebarbative to human taste [5]. But if some cruel (enemy), breaking the bonds of peace, should seek to defile our home beneath its oaken roof, straightway I call out our allied forces to battle, and as they buzz in throngs and drive in their stings, the (enemy) troops withdraw, terrified by our savage darts [10]. [p. 132] Thus, guiltless, they cast their many spears — which are tinged with foul poison — at a guilty enemy.

LXXVI. Apple-tree[69]

The beginning of the new-born world was happy at first, until (man) was destroyed by the cunning of the devil. The cause of the original sin came then from me, who was dispensing sweet apples to the new inhabitants (of Paradise). I am a witness that salvation returned once more to the world [5], when the Judge of the World was hanged from a spreading tree and this glorious Son of the Thundering God washed away our sins.

LXXVII. Fig-tree[70]

Who in the world sooner provided the covering of a garment, or who more mercifully covered wretched (mankind) in need? I do not speak empty words nor fashion fictions: first of all on earth, as report has it, I produced from my own body a garment in the form of long leaves [5]. The fig bends me down while it provides food in clusters, which the diligent farmer eats during the winter months.

LXXVIII. *Wine-cask*[71]

/p. 133/ Look, I dole out cups of wine, making many men drunk — (cups of wine) which the vintner pressed from golden-yellow grapes and the vine produced from the green sprout of the grape, filling the wine-merchant's stall with nectar from the vine. Thus my inwards swell to the full with must [5], yet inebriation does not trouble my swollen body, even though someone might draw off this nectar in a hundred jars. I am a product of the earth, growing in deep woodlands; the country farmer splits my substance with wedges, toppling lofty pines and oaks with his axe [10].

LXXIX. *Sun and Moon*

The foul offspring of Saturn, namely Jupiter — whom the songs of poets picture as mighty — did not produce us, nor was Latona our mother on Delos; I am not called Cynthia and my brother is not Apollo. Rather, the ruler of high Olympus, Who now resides in His heavenly citadel on high, produced us [6]. /p. 134/ We divide up the four-part world with a mutual law: we rule the nocturnal hours and the limits of days. If we as brother and sister did not rule the unstable universe by law, mighty Chaos — alas! — would cover all in darkness [10] and the infernal realms of black Erebus would then hold sway.

LXXX. *Glass Goblet*[72]

From fissures in rocks I flowed forth in a slow stream while flames cracked open the hard inwards of stone and the heat of the furnace held sway, once the reins had been released. Now my receptive shape gleams forth, very similar to ice. To be sure, many people wish to grasp my neck with their right hands [5] and to seize my delightfully smooth body with their fingers. But I change their minds as I give kisses to their lips, applying these sweet kisses to their tightly-pressed mouths: and (thus) I strike down the tottering advances of their feet with disaster.

LXXXI. *Lucifer (the Morning Star)*[73]

I always precede the clear light of day with my brightness: I am the standard-bearer for Phoebus [i.e. the sun], who brilliantly illumines the globe. /p. 135/ I proceed through the sky, making my way along an oblique path. I best love the eastern regions, since my brilliance moves thence to the land of the Indians, who first see the light [5]. How happy I once was when God's law was being obeyed! Alas, I subsequently fell, proud in my impudent arrogance; accordingly, punishment overthrew the deadly enemy. Six companions, therefore, climb the heavens with me: the learned reader will be able to disclose (their names) through books [10].

LXXXII. *Weasel*[74]

A motley-coloured quadruped, I dwell in curving caves, engaging in battles with the deadly race of dragons. I do not become pregnant with beloved children, nor does my womb, made fertile by a male, produce offspring in the way other mothers receive the sperm of the embryo [5]. Instead, my inwards become pregnant with child from my ear. If, however, my offspring suffers the separation of death, I am said to have a skilfully-contrived new remedy.

LXXXIII. *Steer*

/p. 136/ Easing my parched mouth with foaming jaws, I thirstily drank up liquid from four fountains. While alive I break up the fertile sods of earth with its deep roots through the efforts of my mighty strength. But when the breath leaves my cold limbs [5], I am able to bind men with fearsome fetters.

LXXXIV. *Sow Pregnant with Five Piglets*[75]

Now I have twelve eyes in a single body; and six heads; but they are controlled by my other limbs. I walk sustained by twenty-four feet, but there are ninety-six (toe-)nails on my body; in number I am thus comparable to the (ninety-six) combined metrical feet[76] [5]. The poplar and the yew-tree and willow-trees with their green leaves are hateful to me; but I love the crooked beech-tree with its nuts and the acorn-bearing oaks with their flowering crowns; so too the shady holm-oak is not despised.

LXXXV. *Man Blind from Birth*

/p. 137/ I shall now say to you in words what you will scarcely be able to believe, even though it's true and not trifles to trick the mind. For once upon a time I gave a welcome gift to my son, a gift which no-one could ever have given to me, since God from on high had deprived me of the bright bounty [5] in which all other men's hearts rejoice.

LXXXVI. Ram[77]

I am armed, bristling with wrinkled horns; by mouthfuls I crop the grass growing in the meadows. And yet as I set forth I am surrounded by starry throngs which ascend the lofty summits of the heavens in droves. With the exertion of my head I shatter fortified cities [5], destroying town-walls with their lofty citadels. I clothe mortals with woven threads of garments. If the fifteenth letter (of the alphabet) stands in front, I am part of a house.

LXXXVII. Shield[78]

From the trunk of the willow-tree and from the shaved hide of an ox I am constituted, ready to undergo the bloody encounters of battle. /p. 138/ I shall always protect the body of my bearer with my own body, so that Orcus [scil. the underworld] will not snatch away his life. What (other) warrior sustains such great misfortunes or so many deadly wounds in battle [6]?

LXXXVIII. Serpent[79]

More cunning than all other creatures that breathe the air of the atmosphere [cf. Gen.III.1], I scattered the seeds of death far and wide through the world, whence a terrible crop grew up with its deadly harvest, which the Fornicator [scil. the devil] reaps for wicked purposes with his evil scythe. I greatly fear encounters with the antlered stag [5]. In old age I shall be deprived of my aged skin and once again I shall carry on, sustained with new-found youth.

LXXXIX. Book-cupboard[80]

Now my inwards are filled with holy words, and all my entrails support sacred books. And yet I am unable to learn anything from them. Unfortunately, I am deprived by fate of such a gift, since the deadly Parcae [i.e. the Fates] take away the illumination (which) books (provide) [5].

XC. *Woman Giving Birth to Twins*

[p. 139] I have six eyes, and I take things in from as many ears; but I have sixty toes and fingers on my body. Look, when forty of these have been torn from my flesh, I see that only twenty will remain [4].

XCI. *Palm*[81]

The omnipotent Creator, who fashioned all things by His command, granted to me that I have the name 'victorious' in this world. For the glory of kings flourishes in my name; and for martyrs as well, as they win the battles of this world they acquire the exalted rewards of celestial life [5]. The throng of warriors is covered with leafy crowns, and the soldier, the victor in the struggle, (is covered) with a green branch. At the apex of my crown sprouts a thick bush, from which the coverings of various textiles are woven. So too I provide sustenance with the honied nourishment of food [10], distributing foodstuffs for the people with my nectar.

XCII. *Lofty Lighthouse*[82]

[p. 140] On lofty cliffs, where the sea pounds the rocks and surging salt-waves swell the flood, construction-work raised me aloft with mighty structure so that, (acting) as a guide, I might point out the shipping-lanes to (passing) ships. I do not ply with oar the bounding main [5] nor cleave the sea in a bending course with keels; and yet, giving signals from my lofty height, I lead wandering ships, driven by mighty waves, safely to shore: the fireman kindles firebrands in my lofty towers as wintry clouds conceal the twinkling stars [10].

XCIII. *Spark*

What thing on earth is possessed of such mighty force, or boldly strives to exert a similar strength? At first my beginnings in life are insignificant; but, although meagre, I am accustomed to overthrow the mighty in death: the inwards of my own womb carry this death [5]. For, savage and greedy and hungry and fierce, *[p. 141]* I strew dense woodland forests and thickets and massive pine-clad mountain slopes beneath the skies. And yet I am smaller than a gnat with my slender body, when my cold mother [*scil.* flintstone?] brought me forth from her hardened womb [10], (so) producing first of all the offspring of her race.

90

XCIV. Wallwort[83]

The elder, as it grows green in the woods with its rotten smell, has leaves similar to mine; for I grow in the fields as a shoot, bearing black clusters of berries on my brow. Physicians, scouring the countryside, are said frequently to have sought me,[84] growing (wild) on the landscape, when the irritation of disease has crept into diseased skin [5]. I am able to bring relief, so that the poison of leprosy, horrendous in its devastation, does not spread, when it is attacking the inwards with its pestilence: thus I restore the stinking guts of men with my buds.

XCV. Scylla[85]

/p. 142/ Look, the Fates gave me the name of dogs — thus does the language of the Greeks render it in words — ever since the incantations of dread Circe, who stained the waters of the flowing fountain with her words, deceived me. Weaving words, the cruel witch deprived me of thighs together with shins, and calves together with knees [5]. Terrified mariners relate that, as they impel their ships with oars and cleave the sea, sweeping along the mighty waves while the tempest rages, where the broad blade of the oar runs through the water [10], they hear from afar the howling offspring that barks about my loins. Thus the daughter of Titan [scil. Circe] once tricked me, so that I should live as an exile — deservedly — in the salt waves.

XCVI. Elephant[86]

A grim creature, I have learned to regard the roar of battle without fear: the iron-clad battle-lines and the throngs of densely-packed soldiers, the wretches whom the empty desire for fighting impels, as they seek to stain the holy laws of the realm with their weapons, and the battle-trumpet sucks in the air with windy blasts /p. 143/ and the strident battle-horns resound with blazing rattle [5]. Although the Creator made me ugly at birth when, issuing from the womb, I took on the gifts of life, nevertheless the glory of my beauty follows upon my death, as the death-bringing terminus creeps into my open entrails [10]: fine sheets of gold, precious with their burnished metal — even though they be adorned with the sparkle of jewels (and the) flourish of ornamentation — are never able to surpass me [scil. as ivory]. Nature denied me the possibility of kneeling down when tired, or of giving my eyelids over to sleep on bended knee [15]: what is more, I am compelled to spend my life standing up.

XCVII. *Night*

Flowering earth bore me, black, from her body; and I produce nothing fecund from my sterile womb, even though the poets, telling in their verse of the Eumenides, claim that I gave birth to the race of Tartarus.[87] No substance of certain birth pertains to me [5]; but I embrace the four-square world in my darkness. The Titanian torch of Phoebus [i.e. the sun], who is a friend to all as it proceeds through the world, is inimical to me. /p. 144/ Grim thieves, whom I strive to protect in my dark bosom [10], are always accustomed to love me. Vergil sang this of my dear sister [i.e. Rumour]: 'She walks along the ground and hides her head in the clouds, this mighty and unspeakable monster, on whose body there are so many feathers, so many watchful eyes — marvellous to tell! — so many tongues, so many mouths and so many ears [15]. By night she flies in the shadows, midway between heaven and earth'.[88]

XCVIII. *Woody Nightshade*[89]

A purple flower, I grow in the fields with shaggy foliage. I am very similar to an oyster: thus with reddened dye of scarlet a purplish blood oozes by drops from my branches. I do not wish to snatch away the spoils of life from him who eats me, nor do my gentle poisons deprive him utterly of reason [5]. Nevertheless a certain touch of insanity torments him as, mad with dizziness, he whirls his limbs in a circle.

IC. *Camel*[90]

/p. 145/ Once I was a consul, when the Roman horse-soldier controlled the sceptres of power with his dominion. Now my body supports the frightful burden of a hump, and a load of killing weight presses on its large shape. I terrify swift herds of horn-footed horses [5] who flee at once in fright with four-footed motion as they spy the mighty limbs of my ferocious body.

C. *Creation*

The Creator, Who supports the world on eternal columns, the Ruler of (all) kingdoms, restraining lightning-bolts with (His) law while the suspended summits of the wide skies revolve, made me in all my variety when He first created the world.

I am vigilant at the watch; for it shall never be my pleasure to sleep; and yet my eyes are closed suddenly in sleep. For as God governs the universe with His own edict, so do I encompass all things beneath the pole of heaven. Nothing is more retiring than I, since a (mere) ghost terrifies me; /p. 146/ again, I am bolder than a bristly boar [10]. No-one, seeking the banners of victory, can conquer me — except God Himself, Who rules on high in His ethereal citadel. I am more fragrant than perfumed incense, exuding the scent of ambrosia, and I can surpass the lilies, growing in the earth in combination with ruby-red rose-bushes, through the full sweetness of the redolent nard; and then again I stink with the putrid stench of reeking filth. I rightly rule all things which lie beneath the sky and are subject to its sway, as the omnipotent Father ordained. I contain the most gross and the most delicate forms of things [20]. See, I am higher than the sky and can examine God's secrets; and nevertheless, being more lowly than the earth, I gaze into foul hell. Being older than the world I existed from time immemorial; yet look: this year I shall be born from my mother's womb. I am more beautiful than golden bosses on a shining brooch, more ugly than buckthorn, more vile than worthless seaweed. I am wider than the broad limits of earth and yet I can be enclosed in the middle of someone's fist. I am colder than winter and glistening hoar-frost, /p. 147/ although I burn hot in the searing flames of Vulcan [30]. I am sweeter on the palate than a taste of smooth nectar; yet again, I am more bitter than the grey wormwood in the field. I ravenously gulp down meals after the manner of gluttonous Cyclopes, although I can equally well live content without food. I am swifter than eagles, faster than the wings of Zephyrus, fleeter than a hawk; and yet the nasty earthworm and the slug and the slow swamp-turtle and the black beetle, offspring of stinking dung, all outpace me in a race more quickly than the telling. I am heavier than lead, I tend to the weight of rocks [40]; I am lighter than a feather, to which (even) a pond-skater yields. I am harder than flint, which pours dense flames from its entrails, or iron; but I am softer than cooked offal. I have no curly locks on the top of my head which adorn my forehead with fringe or my temples with ringlets, even though a crimped hair-do flows from my crown more kempt than that produced by curling-irons. I grow fatter by far than the grease of sows, as they stuff[91] their bodies with beech-mast /p. 148/ and swineherds are gladdened by the fattened flesh [50]; but grim starvation shall torment me, wasted with hunger, as I, pallid, am perpetually deprived of rich feasts. I am clear, I confess, brighter than Titan's orb; whiter than the snows, when the clouds let fleeces fall; and darker by far than the black shadows of the dungeon and the gloomy shades which Hell encloses. I am made smooth and round like the orb of the stars, or the globe of a ball or a crystal sphere; and, on the other hand, I am extended like Chinese spun-silk, stretched out to make smooth thread or the fibres of a garment [60]. See, I reach much farther, marvellous to relate, than the six[92] zones by which the wide world is measured. Nothing exists in the world beneath me nor above me, except the Creator of all things, controlling the world with His Word. (I am) larger than the black whale in the (sea's) grey waves, and smaller than the thin worm which bores through corpses, or the tiny atom which shimmers in the rays of the sun.[93] I march on a hundred feet through the grassy fields; I never ever walk on earth as a pedestrian. Thus my wisdom excels that of wise men [70]; /p. 149/ yet the precious letter in books did not instruct me, nor was I ever able to recognize what made up a syllable. I am dryer than the burning heat of the summer sun; yet again, dripping with dew I am moister than the water of a fountain. I am saltier by far than the waters of the swelling sea, but I trickle fresher than the icy water of streams. Adorned with the manifold beauty of all the colours with which the structure of the present universe is painted, I am now of ghastly hue, deprived of all colour.

Pay heed, you who believe the words of my utterance [80]! A learned teacher will scarcely be able to expound them orally; and yet the doubting reader ought not to think them trifles! I ask puffed-up wise men to tell what my name is.

THE CARMEN DE VIRGINITATE

TRANSLATED BY JAMES L. ROSIER

Introduction to the
CARMEN DE VIRGINITATE

Aldhelm's prose treatise *De Virginitate* was dedicated to Abbess Hildelith and a sorority of nuns at Barking Abbey. Towards the end of that lengthy work, Aldhelm expressed a promise to his dedicatees that, given life and health, he would

> try with artistry to adorn the renown of this same chastity, with Christ's co-operation, in the heroic measures of hexameter verse, and, as if the rhetorical foundation-stones were now laid and the walls of prose were built, so . . . build a sturdy roof with trochaic slates and dactylic tiles of metre.[1]

Some time later — we do not know how much later — Aldhelm completed the promised hexameter version, the *Carmen de Virginitate*. Although the poem bears no specific dedication, Aldhelm does advert to his earlier promise (line 22: 'Et dudum prompsit voto spondente libellus'); we may assume, but without the assurance of proof, that the *Carmen de Virginitate* too was sent to the nuns of Barking.[2]

In composing a verse counterpart to an earlier prose work, Aldhelm was following a literary tradition which had its roots in the schools of antiquity, namely that of *conversio* or paraphrase.[3] As a scholastic exercise ancient grammarians had required their pupils sometimes to turn prose passages into verse, sometimes verse into prose. As early as the third century B.C. works of Plato and Xenophon were turned into hexameters by one Soterichus, and Cicero refers to a prose paraphrase of the verse of Ennius. This double exercise eventually led to what medieval authors referred to as the *geminus stylus* or 'twin style',[4] that is, the composition of a 'twinned' work consisting both of a prose and a verse part. In fact Bede, in referring to Aldhelm's *De Virginitate*, describes it as an *opus geminatum*:

> He [Aldhelm] also wrote a most excellent book on virginity both in hexameter verse and in prose, producing a twofold work (*geminato opere*).[5]

The immediate model for Aldhelm's work, as Bede goes on to note, was Caelius Sedulius, a Roman poet of the fifth century,[6] whose *Carmen Paschale* (a verse account of Christ's life and miracles as related in the New Testament, suitably amplified by figural and allegorical allusions to Old Testament events) was later to be completed with a treatise on the same subject in prose, the *Opus Paschale*.[7] The *Carmen Paschale* was one of the most widely studied poems of the Latin Middle Ages, and was certainly well known to Aldhelm, who frequently quoted from it and who used it as a quarry for examples in his metrical treatise *De Metris*; the prose *Opus Paschale* was much less well known (it survives in a mere handful of manuscripts), and there is no certain evidence that it was known to Aldhelm. Nevertheless, Aldhelm certainly knew of the existence of Sedulius's *opus geminatum*, and this knowledge served as the inspiration for the poetic *conversio* of his earlier prose treatise.

The *Carmen de Virginitate* follows the structure of the prose work in broad outline, but with some important alterations. In lieu of the opening chapter of the prose work, in which Aldhelm in a brief autobiographical passage explains the genesis of the work and his relationship to its dedicatees, there is an acrostic *praefatio*, consisting of a simple invocatory prayer to God the Father. The lengthy introductory section of the prose work, consisting of chapters III–XIX and treating in theoretical terms the three grades of virginity (that is, *virginitas, castitas* and *iugalitas*) with frequent recourse to patristic authorities and to many extended similes, is drastically condensed in the *Carmen* so that the same matter is treated in only 247 lines (with the three-fold distinction occupying a mere twenty-three lines, 84–107). There is also a perceptible shift in emphasis: *virginitas* in the poetic account becomes a much more aggressive virtue, vigorously 'trampling' down foul vice, where the verb most frequently used is *calco* (99: *calcans ludibria falsa*; 117: *fetida calcantes spurcae contagia carnis*; 136: *calcat licitae commercia vitae*; 155: *haec calcat pedibus spurcae consortia vitae*; and so on). The sense of aggression associated with virginity is matched by the vocabulary of filth and foulness associated with the flesh. This heightened poetic vocabulary prepares the reader for the violent conflict between the virtues and vices which concludes the poem.

Following the brief introduction are the catalogues of male and female virgins (occupying lines 248–2445). The order and the exemplary virgins are largely the same in both works, but with some significant differences. Aldhelm omitted from the *Carmen* the accounts of Didymus/Thomas, Felix, Malchus, and Christina and Dorothea (both associated with Scholastica in the prose work); on the other hand, he added accounts of Jerome and of Gervasius and Protasius. More interesting is the fact that on a number of occasions Aldhelm amplified the account of a particular virgin from the prose work by adding new material. Such amplification occurs in his verse accounts of Jeremiah, Daniel, Clement, Silvester, Benedict, Julian and Constantina.[8] In some cases Aldhelm drew information freshly from his original source; in others he combined the information contained in the prose account with material drawn from an entirely different source. For example, Enoch is linked with Elijah in *CdV* 273–7, probably because Aldhelm had the apocryphal *Book of Enoch* before him; or the account of Clement (drawn originally from the *Liber Pontificalis*) is amplified by recourse to the pseudo-Clementine *Recognitiones*. In any case, these alterations and additions indicate that the *Carmen de Virginitate* is far from being a slavish versification of the earlier prose work.

At the end of the catalogues of virgins in the prose *De Virginitate* Aldhelm included (for no very obvious reason) accounts of Joseph, David, Samson, Abel and Melchisedech, followed these accounts with a diatribe against ostentatious dress (based on Cyprian's *De Habitu Virginum*), inserted an account of Judith, and then concluded with a peroration addressed to his audience, the nuns of Barking. The final section of the *Carmen de Virginitate* is entirely different from this: Aldhelm rejects all the concluding matter found in the prose work and adds in its stead a lengthy account of an allegorical confrontation between the Vices and Virtues (2446–760). Aldhelm presents each of the Eight Principal Vices in the following order: (1) *Ingluvies ventris* ('Gluttony'); (2) *Fornicatio* ('Debauchery'); (3) *Philargyria* ('Avarice'); (4) *Ira* ('Anger'); (5) *Tristitia* ('Despair'); (6) *Accidia* ('Sloth'); (7) *Cenodoxia* ('Vainglory'); and (8) *Superbia* ('Pride'). With some — but not all — of these Vices he pairs the corresponding Virtue: thus *Ira* with *Patientia*, or *Accidia* with *Constantia mentis*; but all Vices are opposed and 'trampled down' by Virginity (2468–71: 'Virginitas igitur, quae calcat crimina stupri. . . Contra bellantes studeat certare catervas/ Octenosque duces, quibus haerent agmina saeva') — the heightened poetic language of violence here recalling that of the introduction. The sequence of the Eight Vices and much of the terminology used to describe them is taken directly by Aldhelm from the fifth of Cassian's *Collationes* ('Collatio abbatis Sarapionis de octo vitiis principalibus'). But an allegorical confrontation of Vices and Virtues could not fail to recall Prudentius's *Psychomachia*, a poem which was undoubtedly studied in Anglo-Saxon England.[9] In Prudentius's poem, for example, one of the most memorable of the individual combats is that between Ira and Patientia: Ira exhausts herself by casting futile weapons at the imperturbable Patientia and, in a final burst of rage, commits suicide by throwing herself on her own spear. Aldhelm too matches Ira with Patientia, and arms her with the same weapon (a spear: Latin *contus*) which she wielded in Prudentius. Aldhelm like Prudentius introduces various biblical parallels in his treatment of the various encounters (the comparisons with Judith, Judas and Achar are all found in Prudentius, for example). Furthermore, there are various verbal parallels between Aldhelm and Prudentius:

> Aldhelm, *CdV* 2865: Quem Deus a nostri detrudat *pectoris antro*
> Prudentius, *Psych.* 6: Mens armata queat nostri de *pectoris antro*;

and,

> Aldhelm, *CdV* 2882: Et regnatoris stipant *sublime tribunal*
> Prudentius, *Psych.* 736: conscendunt apicem; mox et *sublime tribunal*.

These parallels might suggest that Aldhelm was indeed familiar with Prudentius's poem. On the other hand, one is bound to wonder why, if Aldhelm knew it, he did not make more use of Prudentius's brilliant characterization of the various vices and virtues. The matter is uncertain at present, but the answer may eventually lie in a more thorough analysis of Aldhelm's treatment of his sources; and such an analysis is long overdue.

Aldhelm concludes the *Carmen de Virginitate* with the topos that was used to conclude so many medieval poems: the sailor has crossed the stormy sea and now heads for the safety of the harbour.[10] He adds a passionate plea (like that found at the end of his prose treatise) for gentle treatment at the hands of critics, and ends with a prayer that he deserve to join the virgin saints in heaven.

In spite of its immense prolixity, Aldhelm's *Carmen de*

Virginitate was widely read and studied as a curriculum text during the early Middle Ages, both in England and on the Continent, as may be seen from the number of surviving manuscripts.[11] In England, in the early period, Alcuin excerpted various verses from the *Carmen* for his work *De Laude Dei*, a lengthy anthology of readings from biblical, patristic and Christian Latin sources intended apparently for meditational purposes.[12] From the later Anglo-Saxon period numerous manuscripts survive, many of them accompanied by dense glossing.[13] Only with the twelfth century does Aldhelm's poem — the earliest and longest Latin poem composed by an Anglo-Saxon — pass into oblivion.

CARMEN DE VIRGINITATE

PRAEFATIO

[p. 350] Let these metrical verses now celebrate chaste soldiers and let the Virgin[1] receive praise from the four corners of the earth! May the triune God in the citadel Who, in His might, created the world, may the Ruler of the world, ruling in His lofty seat, deign to grant me, unworthy as I am, peace in heaven with the blessed ones whom I praise here in these very verses. The Judge enthroned on high, Who preserves the celestial rule, *[p. 351]* allowed these to ascend through the cloudless threshold in the midst of the phalanx of saints, who with unceasing praise duly glorify the Thunderer ruling His kingdom [10]. All-possessing Lord, Creator and Maker of the world, grant to us in need sure assistance and do not allow us to be thrust back from heaven to our enemies, but rather, may (Your) right hand touch us poor men in protection, lest the deceitful Plunderer be able to shut the entrance of the heavens, or be able to deceive the blessed by a false show of harmful things; or lest the wily Thief thrust down into the dark pit those whom Christ, the Founder, the Shepherd watching over His fold, protects from high Olympus, lest the wrangling Robber ravaging the royal sheepfold be able to say 'puppup'[2] twice [20] — but may the Guardian protect all the fold even now. Noblest Mother, you who bear that mighty name by divine authority: deign to grant your aid through prayers. For you brought forth everlasting Light [i.e. Christ] from light, which the prophets by holy inspiration call Titan, whose splendour radiates from high heaven throughout the world and whose lightning likewise fills the heavens with shimmering: King of kings and Prince of peoples, so called from all time, Great from His Greatness, Ruler from His Universal Rule: neither the lands nor

102

the heavens can enclose Him [30], nor can the navigable sea with its foaming waters, nor the zones of the universe, which enclose the high heavens, surround Him. I, a poor man, shall proceed in these holy endeavours to set forth the lives of those distinguished men and women who by virtue of their chaste natures here on earth, aided by God, flourished in perennial bloom /p. 352/ — if, that is, a poor man may nevertheless set forth their great achievements worthily, when no one can expound all of them clearly in words:

SOTSAC ANIMRAC TNAMORP CNVN SENORIT ACIRTEM.[3]

· · · · · · ·

Almighty Progenitor, guiding the world by Your rule, Who are the Creator of the shining heights of the star-filled heaven, (Who) also formed the foundations of the earth by Your Word; You Who paint the pale greensward with purple blossom, and restrain the azure surface of the wave-wandering sea so that the shores of the lands are not submerged by water, but rather that obstacles of rocks may break the swollen waves; Who water the crops of the ploughed fields with a cool spring and swell the husks of corn by rain from cloud-bursts, Who remove the hiding places of the earth by a two-fold radiance [10] — /p. 353/ namely, Titan [i.e. the sun] that adorns the day and Cynthia [i.e. the moon] (that adorns) the night; Who ornament the expanses of ocean with plump fish, forming scaly squadrons in the greyish waters; Who similarly fill the clear air with swift-flying flocks of birds which, chirping with their beaks, pipe chattering songs and proclaim the Creator with their diverse voices: kind and merciful God, grant aid to me that by my verse I may be able to sing of the renowned work of saints of earlier days, as previously I praised chaste (virgins) in prose. Thus let these heroic [i.e. hexametrical] songs amass their praises [20], as I recall the previous sequence of my (prose) book to have done, and as my little book formerly set forth, so keeping a promise.[4]

I do not seek verses and poetic measures from the rustic Muses, nor do I seek metrical songs from the Castalian nymphs who, they say, guard the lofty summit of Helicon; nor do I ask that Phoebus, whom his mother Latona bore on Delos, grant me a tongue, expressive in utterance; never do I deign to speak by means of unutterable verses, as the clear-sounding poet [i.e. Vergil] is once said to have proclaimed [29]:

Open Helicon now, goddesses, and direct my song! [*Aen.* VII.641].

/p. 354/ Rather, I shall strive with prayers to move the Thunderer,

103

Who grants us the divine declaration of the gentle Word. I seek the word from the Word: the psalmist sang this Word engendered in the heart of the Father, that which is His only Offspring, the Word by which the Almighty Father created all things throughout the world. Thus may the propitious spirit of the Father and the Son mercifully grant aid to a weak servant. For in the Godhead there lies a single essence; in the Godhead there also exists a three-fold mode of being. The substance of God is therefore to be believed in a triple name [40] — but let His power be spoken of in a single name! For faith induces us to believe in three persons, but the nature of God, the noble Creator of heaven, guides in rule all generations as one.

Behold, let these promised songs be composed in new verse![5] Let the fluent page issue praise of virgins, and let the clauses and caesuras of the verse proceed with three types of foot: [p. 355] let the dactyl run its course except at the end of verses, let the syllable of the spondee avoid the fifth foot; thus let the final syllable of a trochee conclude the verse [50] which, always last, rejoices to be placed at the end. Thus may these metrical hexameters proceed with three (kinds of) feet!

I do not, of course, think anything difficult for You Who relax the laws of nature with frequent changes. For the monuments of ancient books give us modern men the example of the little ass speaking with human voice, which previously used to bray with its raucous throat, when a seer about to curse the people wished to proceed and to strike down the guiltless (ass) with the weapons of words [cf. Num.XXII.28–30]. Therefore I openly say that You are able to confer on me more poetic power [60], Who deign to shape (in me) a form of earth and inspire this insensible breast with vital breath,[6] Who provide minds with abilities and lips with speech, so that no one gives utterance to the lyre and composes songs with the strings of the cithara to Christ in vain. Indeed, if anyone rejects the songs of the lyre's strings and desires something better than to strike with a plectrum on the chords with which the holy psalmist [i.e. David] once accompanied his psalms, [p. 356] and so eagerly desires to nourish his mind with a great melody and refuses to be content with refined song [70], let that man, listening attentively to the greatest musical instruments with a thousand blasts, delight his hearing with their windy bellows, even though other songs glitter with gilded surfaces!

Who would be able worthily to know the mysteries of things or the concealed matters of God by the power of knowledge, if the hot coal or the burning pebble, taken up by the tongs of the altar, did not cleanse his impure lips? — the coal with which the Seraphim once purified the lips of the prophet [cf. Is.VI.6], so that straightway, glowing deservedly with heavenly inspiration, the excellent doctor released the locks of the Word [80], and with the white heat of scripture he consumed the offences of the people, so that by his doctrine he could convert many to Christ, transferring earth-dwelling ranks to the celestial kingdom.

There is said to be a three-fold diversity in the human race which now lives throughout the three corners of the world and strives on earth to obtain the kingdom of the Thunderer. Accordingly, matrimonial life receives some who, in the permitted law of wedlock, live their life virtuously, /p. 357/ and by all the endeavours of their minds strive to preserve God's teachings while remaining under the law of marriage [90]. There follows another grade and a second order of the chaste, who having once been married reject the union and sever the restraining bonds of indulgence allowed to them, abandoning the lurid associations of impure flesh so that they may preserve a lasting age when they rend the chains of marriage previously enjoined. A third life glows in the lamp of virgins whose distinction surpasses the customs mentioned above.

Virginity, treading upon the false frivolity of worldly indulgence, appears at the highest station of the virtues [100], since it is the most chaste sister of the angelic life: in her the false wantonness of this world does not hold sway, but rather her spirit struggles to curb rebellious flesh so that it can constrain hideous sins, and thus, gaining victory, destroys the enormous act of sin, which is normally accustomed to overcome even iron-clad minds, even though they appear to be as strong as whetstone.

To these categories, therefore, the Ruler of Olympus opens the gates of the celestial courts and the thresholds of life — those which we have already said were three in number [110]. Upon these also from fecund seed He bestows fruits, which the Glory of the eternal kingdom [i.e. Christ] has foretold (would) increase throughout the squalid plots of ploughed ground [Matth.XIII.8]. /p. 358/ By right of their merits, He promised fruitful bundles by the hundred-fold to the blessed virgins, who disdain in their hearts the false ostentations of the world, trampling on the fetid contagion of impure flesh. So too Christ, the glory of heaven, drew out sixty-fold fruit from the earth of the fields; the chaste reap these bundles as their own [120] who now break the yoked union of marriage, and by devout mind remove particular temptations, spurning the permissible joys of worldly pomp.

Finally, he who joins the nuptial bonds will receive thirty-fold bundles from the field as he reaps; he does not wholly tread under the (sexual) engagements of wedded life, but rather desires willingly to produce a progeny of offspring in the world and to beget a generation of kindred. Therefore let all, whom concern for modesty excites and whose hearts are pricked by love of purity [130], undertake a contract of spirit and pure flesh, just as the holy sentence [*scil.* of St Paul: cf. II Cor.V.1–6] teaches a two-fold life! For the blessed soul is preferred to the action of the body. Therefore a monarchy of the mind will rule continually so that deceits of the flesh do not taunt the soul; and a hand-maiden should not overcome her mistress by stupid behaviour, nor should a maid-servant ever rule with haughty contempt!

Now, therefore, let these songs gather rare flowers from which virgin crowns may be made! /p. 359/ What in our struggle (of life) pleases the citizens of heaven more [140] than love of purity reigning in a pure breast? For celebrations of chastity nourish the heavenly hosts. Although generations of offspring grow for it on earth, yet in heaven it (still) scales the summits of the virtues.

Virginity, which preserves chaste flesh without fault, defeats all other celebrations of virtue in glory. The bountiful spirit of the high-throned God claims a temple for itself if the pure will is thus aroused in the heart, as the blessed speech of apostolic words announces: 'Know you, that your loins are the temples of God [150]. The spirit of the Thunderer now rightly dwells in you' [I Cor.III.16]. It is unnatural to stain or pollute (this temple) by sin. Resplendent Virginity gleams like the jewel of a crown which encircles the head of the eternal King in a wreath. With her feet Virginity treads upon the association with impure life, completely eradicating the joys of wanton flesh. From the bosom of the earth, base gravel produces the substance of tawny gold and burnished metal, with which the contrivance of the present world is adorned. In this way chaste purity, the similitude of yellow gold [160], is born from the unclean flesh of earthly parents. Just as the rose excels all tinges of purple dye and scarlet colours at the same time with its ruddiness; /p. 360/ as pale gravel produces purple gems which are covered by clods of dusty earth; as the golden blossom spills out from the bark of the cornel cherry-tree in springtime, when the earth brings forth sprouts; just as the sweet date is pushed out at the top of the leafy palm and fruits burst out of dry branches; even as a gleaming pearl is nourished in the lowly sea-oyster [170] and excels its mother in its own glory; and as the base gravel beneath the green turf of a despised field forms golden filaments of yellow metal, so — in order that I might sum up six comparisons in two lines — does sacred Virginity, so beloved by the citizens of heaven, take the beginnings of its life from impure flesh.

Just as the glory of wine is to be found in fruitful fields, when the tendrils of the vine produce huge grapes and the vintager strips the leafy rows of vines with a reaping-hook; just as the stars yield to the extraordinary light of the sun [180] when Titan on his oblique course illuminates the earth, outshining all the stars of the upper skies — so likewise renowned Virginity, which adorns the saints, excels in providing all the rewards of saints. Chastity is also called the queen of virtues, so long as it is joined in chaste will to the companies of angels. This virtue, I say, rendered powerful by divine favour, surpasses gold amulets set with fiery jewels. /p. 361/ Virginity is as resplendent as the ruddy purple of kings, by which rulers in togas enjoy their privileges [190]. Purity of mind ruling in a chaste body is a virgin flower which knows not the ravages of old age, nor does it fall to the earth as plants droop their leaves. See how the lilies bloom in the fertile furrows, and how the rose with its blood-red petals thrives among the thorn bushes, from which he is adorned who is victorious by chance in the wrestling match and as victor in the circus-contest receives garlands. No differently will chastity, when rebellious flesh has been completely subjugated and the wicked laid low in defeat, wear beautiful crowns from the ruling Christ [200].

Although chastity is embellished by the praise of poetry and the life of the pure increases (in renown) through eternity, nevertheless the eternal gift of Christ is not withheld from those who maintain the sanctioned marriage of lawfully wedded life. Therefore the despised little piece of silver,[7] which a unit [i.e. an ounce] equal to twelve parts counterbalances (on the scales), is not neglected, even though a broach with its golden bosses stands out more, or burnished plates are surely more golden; the lantern will not become worthless for you, virgin, whether it is made from scraped leather and willow-wood [210] or with a thin covering of parchment, /p. 362/ even though the bronze oil-lantern perchance excels it, or the oil-lamp illuminating dark hiding places with its light. The pale light of the moon is not rejected at night when cerulean darkness blackens the world with gloomy shadows, even though Titan more radiantly pours out glimmers of light when the rain-clouds disperse and the parched upper sky is hot. Nor likewise do we disregard the deep water of a well which a pump lifts from a cistern, even though the excellent streams of a spring [220], which cold gravel bears with icy water, surpass it. The dark-winged diver, filling the maw of its stomach with scaly fish, is not utterly rejected; nor does the talkative black jackdaw, which tries to plunder the husks of corn and the crops of the delightful meadowland, snatching bundles of crops from the harvest, seem worthless, even though in contrast the multi-coloured feathers of the peacock glow with yellow hue and its shapely circles gleam redder than the reddish purple-fish — the peacock, whose handsome form and golden beauty far surpasses all the efforts of skilled workmen [230]. Thus its (the peacock's) flesh, wonderful to say, cannot decay, as the teachings of ancient man [e.g. Augustine, *De Civ. Dei* XXI.4] inform us: it is a sign and symbol of beloved Virginity, which by devout disposition is accustomed to tread down the wicked filth of the world, scorning the putrefaction of its flesh. *[p. 363]* Pomegranates with their round seeds surrounded by a covering are not spurned, even though the sweet fruit of the palm-tree excels them, reproducing the sweet tastes of nectar and honey. In the same way, I say, let chastity by its fame be venerated forever [240], so that this written page will not wish to snatch in its deceitful jaw(s) those chosen (people) who join the covenant of matrimony and live justly by the right of chaste marriage, especially since the letter of the ancient law tells how our ancestors led an excellent life, and by holy inspiration proclaimed the future gifts of God, when the Saviour Christ blessed the world.

. . . .

The prophet ELIJAH, whom the four books of Kings record as trusting in the distinction[8] of virtue, was a holy virgin, known by his fame throughout time [250]. Accordingly he performed many miracles on earth and declared by his words the secret prophecies of God, which the sequence of the book makes known in clear language. Once, supported by the thunderbolt of heaven, he ordered the two leaders of fifty men to undergo the flames of pyres and be burned, *[p. 364]* and he likewise thrust the hundred men obeying the commands of the tyrant to their death. He also was compelled to close up the starry sky in (its) four quarters for forty-two months, so that the dry heavens would not let rain fall from any clouds [260], so that water would be denied to the dying plants and the parched meadow would receive no nourishment of water [III Reg.XVII.1–15]. And then with his command he broke open the obstacle of the clouds, so that rain-showers might flow abundantly from a darkened sky and the earth swell again with fertile seed, producing from verdant fields abundant food for the multitude. The eternal Judge ordered this same prophet to ascend and enter the golden heights of heaven in a two-horsed chariot. He was fortunate, who never knew the separation of death, as the multitude of his ancestors throughout the world had endured [270], and as the throng of future descendants will endure; but rather this hero remains to this day in the vales of Paradise, just as Enoch, whom the divine power of heaven snatched up lest he endure the terrible damnation of a wicked world, dwells in Elysium in the same high abode: accordingly, the two of them carry the banners of the Thunderer into the bloody struggles of war against the Antichrist.[9] All the bodies will rise from their dark graves, /p. 365/ and the tombs throughout the field, having been closed, will open up by themselves when the trumpet blasts and the clear call of the horn resounds [280] with God's advent, Who metes out rewards to all — either divine rewards to the excellent or obviously cruel ones to the sinful.

Likewise the prophet ELISHA, glowing in virginal bloom, adorned the ages with renowned miracles. The golden heifer showed him to be a prophet, (since he was) born amidst its bellowing, because he destroyed the shrines of pagan gods. By a two-fold endowment he will be enriched by the Holy Spirit, which bestows the splendid duties of heavenly affairs, increasing individual gifts in holy minds. He aroused the corpse constricted with horrible death [290], even though it had already been put to sleep by death's lot [IV Reg.IV.34]. But the stupid children who, roaring in a loud clamour, sought to revile and mangle the holy seer, he gave over to the jaws of she-bears to be eaten up in retaliation for calling the prophet a bald-head in the manner of jesters [IV Reg.II.23–4]. In such a way does God avenge His saints with a dreadful wrath and duly punish sinners with a cruel lash.

Noble JEREMIAH was blessed with the two-fold gift; although of the innumerable gifts of virtue which the grace of Christ confers [300], he had as many as the richest hero, /p. 366/ nevertheless, as I have said, his two greatest gifts are clear [scil. purity and prophecy]. This man, preserving his entire life under the laws of purity, possessed a holy celibacy adorned with the flower of pure chastity, and presages sent from on high filled the rich prophet of God so that he could perceive things enclosed in darkness and could unlock the innermost secrets of heaven in understanding. God sanctified this pure man in his mother's womb even before he had known the light of this present life [Ier.I.5], so that he might be a seer, eloquently expressing oracles: concerning him the word of the heavenly Father says [310] that before he came forth out of the womb of his mother, this virgin would be sanctified by an extraordinary gift. Meanwhile[10] the prophet is straightway sent forth to prophesy, in order that he might destroy the kingdom of the devil and likewise the rule of the Tyrant in the world, relying on the strength of the Thunderer; that he might plant and build the Kingdom of Heaven, restoring the rule of heaven when the deceit of the evil one is destroyed [Ier.I.10]. He contemplates the twin branches of the growing twig, which signify perchance the form of the two peoples [319]; likewise in turn he discerns as many [i.e. two] baskets [Ier.XXIV.1]: but nevertheless a comparable interpretation portends twin peoples through the Old Testament.

Monuments of ancient writings clearly attest that the holy DANIEL always flourished as a virgin, /p. 367/ he who set for us a pattern of blessed celibacy and offered a mirror of life to his disciples. He therefore made known the prophetic times of Christ more certainly than all the ancient prophets in their prophetic announcements; explaining the numbers of years in right order he announced the birth of our King in this world [330], writing that beyond the passage of four hundred years there would be eighteen *lustra* [i.e. 90 years] of time until Christ would come forth as Ruler of the world. Truthfully again in his speech he treated of the future: that four rulers of the kingdoms will arise [Dan.II.31–45] — just as the cruel tyrant [i.e. Nebuchadnezzar], while in bed, had previously seen prophesies of a high statue made of (four) various metals. Subsequently, while sustained in his rule, he saw a sturdy tree with leafy branches growing in the earth, whose lofty crest touched the clouds [340], while beneath, throngs of birds and every kind of wild beast pluck the sweet nourishment of food from the branches [Dan.IV.7–14]; but Daniel, in his prophetic heart, knew straightway that by the high tree a tyrant was rightly signified, whose rule the power of heaven would destroy, while seven times would pass over and torment the proud king [Dan.IV.22], so that deservedly he would flee to roam in the bushy woodlands and, as long as he perceived the scourge of the raging Thunderer, squalid and shaggy he would seek the myrtle-groves inhabited by wolves — the tyrant, demented, having become a companion of four-footed beasts [350]. /p. 368/ In addition[11] Daniel destroyed the temple of the heinous Bel while the priests of wickedness suffered the separation of death; in the same way he punished with a bloody death the priests who were tricking the people under the deception of their pagan shrine [Dan.XIV.1–21]. At another time, subduing a dragon through his virtue, he threw a dark morsel into its dreadful jaws; and when the savage beast swallowed the pitch-black lump, the guts of the slaughtered monster immediately ruptured [Dan.XIV.26]. God always saved Daniel from (the king's) violent wrath, even though he might in his experience tolerate the tortures of evil men [360]. In the end, trusting in celestial armament, Daniel did not fear the savage jaws of beasts or the attack of lions, even though the excellent prophet was shut up by his cruel torturers and thrust into a dark pit. Thus Virginity always preserves a chaste friend, scorning foul dangers with their thousands of perils.

In a similar way the three boys [i.e. SHADRACH, MESHACH and ABEDNEGO], redolent of the flowers of chastity, had once preserved the rights of decency in spurning the golden image of the stolid tyrant [i.e. Nebuchadnezzar] who, by a threatening command, ordered all the multitudes [370] to venerate a deaf and dumb image of metal [Dan.III.1–11]. A trumpet with hoarse-sounding blasts resounded from on high; the reed-pipe reverberating with the cithara reached the skies; the sambuca responded to the frequent blasts of the trumpet so that, genuflecting with bended knee, the people throughout the fields would pray to the king's golden idols. /p. 369/ But the Hebrew youths, scorning this wickedness, refused to bow their heads to the heinous image. The evil king therefore threatened the chaste youths with the heat of the furnace, in order that the fire might induce worship [380], while hostile bonds would bind their holy arms [Dan.III.21]. Fire immediately consumed the cruel bonds, but could not burn the blessed limbs of those saintly boys. It is wondrous to speak of: that the flame of the furnace should harass the boys in the dreadful prison with harmless firebrands; but Chastity rejected the torments of the furnace while the hearts of these youths burned with glowing faith. For a blessed angel descended from the fiery stars to quench the burning fire with icy winds and to extinguish the red-hot lumps of coal with heavenly showers [390].

But why does my poem proclaim only ancient fathers whom the clear records of ancient books celebrate, when the new dispensation, by which the merciful Saviour blessed the whole world, surpasses the old law?

First of all, the prophet JOHN (the Baptist), filled with divine inspiration, gave a sufficient example for virgins. While still enclosed in his mother's womb he sensed the Lord, while Mary on this earth was bearing a heavenly pledge [Luc.I.41]. He dwelled in the forests, eating the wild food of honey [399] and the bodies of locusts for sustenance [Matth.III.4]; /p. 370/ other dishes of nectared array he disdained. Blessed Gabriel foretold his birth to his father [i.e. Zechariah] when, at the right hand of the altar, he (Gabriel) spoke prophecies to the priest (Zechariah) as he dutifully took the thurible in its golden shrine [Luc.I.8–20]. And when perchance this blessed precursor became a man and matured to prophetic age he, the bridegroom's attendant, foretold the coming of Christ in the world, converting great multitudes by his holy preaching. Indeed the pure Baptist immersed the salvation-bringing Thunderer in the stream, drenching Him with water [410]; thereupon this liquid straightway acquired the blessed gifts of salvation which are now sprinkled abundantly throughout the four corners of the earth, as people everywhere accept the gifts of baptism. Thus the blessed celibate, John the Baptist, shone forth, and is known forever as the messenger and precursor of the Lord. Although his mother lacked a fertile body and in her sterile womb was barren, he was born late in (his parents') life from the venerable stock of his father. No one, except the Physician of the world, the begotten Son of God, was born greater from the womb of a woman [420]. And thus, John, being pure, cleansed the other One, pure without stain, and in the river he bathed Christ (Who) consecrated the azure waters of the wavy sea and provided the gifts of birth with clear waters, as the old return again to the beginnings of life.

Then as Christ was leaving the blue surface of water and with devout steps walked on the banks of the river, the confines of lofty heaven opened /p. 371/ and the skies thundered, as the Ruler of Olympus, addressing His Son, spoke with words which flew through the air [430]: 'Behold, this is my beloved Son Who it is my wish should rule throughout the whole world' [Matth.III.17]. Coming in the form of a swift dove, the propitious spirit of heaven descended to Christ [Luc.III.22]. This bird, therefore, is blessed by the Holy Ghost, since it alone is lacking the bitterness of cruel poison with which the brawling crowd of other chafing birds is vexed: this radiant, prophetic bird bears a gentle heart. Now this prophet (John) underwent much torment for the sake of Christ: he endured the filth of prison and gloomy dungeons without light [440] because he condemned the marriage of the cruel king [i.e. Herod], who had broken the laws of consanguineity by defiling the bed of his own brother without the sanctity of lawful wedlock. Not fearing the hideous torments of an unspeakable death, John restrained the tyrant with his voice. Immediately platters were reddened with flowing blood and the

112

prophet's head, cut off, was carried to a banquet of people — the head which the ferocious queen [i.e. Herodias] had cunningly demanded through her daughter, who had been performing a dramatic entertainment with a maidenly dance [Marc.VI.21–8]. Now this horrible wound, with its bloody purplish gash [450], signified Christ as the Healer of the world: while suspended on the spreading branch of a cross He Who was innocent had to endure the violence of criminals.[12] /p. 372/ Nevertheless, generations experienced the salvation they desired, when God as Christ descended to the wandering shades of the underworld to break open the iron entrance of its bolted door. He shook the bronze bolts of the abominable gates, just as the prophetic Psalmist had previously proclaimed in song [Ps.CVI.16], saying that the Thunderer was to suffer at the end of the world.

Now I shall strive in my verse to proclaim the blessed JOHN (the Evangelist) [460], who was the most pleasing of those who slept upon the breast of merciful Christ [Ioh.XIII.23]. This learned man drank in rivers of inspiration from the sacred breast; he thirsted, and filled his stomach with eternal waters, and he preserved a beautiful state of chaste life, shrinking utterly from any association with false flesh. With reports of his virtues spreading afar, therefore, the seeds of his fame increased throughout the world. Accordingly, this discourse has not revealed individual particulars, but rather it tells of generalities, albeit in rough verse. From death he raises corpses put to sleep [470], which the fetters of chill death had bound tightly; touching the eyes of the blind he gave sight; /p. 373/ he commanded the crippled to go forth on firm foot; (through him) the deaf heard sonorous harmony with their ears and the mute unloosened their lips in speech; he permitted the maimed to live with healed hands. Although he swallowed lethal draughts down his throat, he did not feel the dark harm of black poisons.

We also read of one commonly called SAUL in ancient times: he suppressed the doctrines of Christ at the command of leaders [480]; he tortured the gentle limbs of blessed men because he wished the secret recesses of the ancient law to hold sway, and to prefer the rites of the ancient fathers to Christ. But a change was brought about: with a new name, blessed PAUL merited the renown of apostolic fame. This holy distinction caused him to flourish in chaste modesty, even though earlier he condemned to dark prison the bodies of many men who were preserving the covenant of Christ. But lofty God, who turns the hearts of criminals, rescued an excellent lamb from the savage jaws of wolves [490]; He Who very often changed gloomy dark-coloured ravens into doves white without grey bile — this very God, granting such wonderful gifts of divine value, mercifully lightens the punishments of criminals. And so it was he (Paul) whom the Father twice summoned from His high citadel; /p. 374/ and Paul, surrounded by darkness and devoid of bright light, fell with prostrate knee on his face. Although he experienced the loss of eyesight in blindness, yet he saw the sun shining from heaven, which always illuminated his heart with its kindly light [500]. This was the man who was the pre-eminent doctor and teacher of the world, who converted barbarian multitudes with his sacred teaching.

LUKE is presented in the likeness of a four-footed calf; he wrote lucid doctrines in the sacred book, setting forth the seventy-seven names of fathers from which Almighty Christ in the glory of royalty was descended and assumed birth in our own flesh [cf. Luc.III.23–38]. The sacred garlands of a virginal crown adorned (Luke); when he had lived seventy-four years and narrated the lineage of the Lord from its first origin [510], when obstructive chaos and the listless confusion of matter filled the awesome world with terrifying lurking places, with the key of heaven Luke unlocked the ancestral treasury, which reached back to the time when the all-powerful Founder of the four-cornered world formed the fecund world beneath the heavenly clouds. In days of yore this physician healed the wounds of the flesh, caring for the festering ulcers of internal organs with heat-treatment. By means of his doctrinal writing this disciple of Paul cured even more fully /p. 375/ the offences of souls and the behaviour of wickedness [520], which cause wounds of the mind. After his death he ornamented the seat of the Augustans with his sacred bones, where the absolute rule of the world after the power of Rome reigns beneath the summit of heaven.[13]

In ancient times Rome brought forth a clement priest to whom, by his just merit, clemency gives its name [CLEMENT]. Since he preserved himself pure for the gift of chastity, God freely enriched him with heavenly grace. Peter, who presides over the height of the apostolic seat, bore this offspring from the seed of the heavenly Word, and granted the holy beginnings of baptizing [530]. By his faithful steps this devote disciple equals the blessed doctor, who continually teaches doctrines and often makes clear the divine teachings of God. By chance, therefore, Clement happened to behold his aged parents and his own brothers, whom Peter, the famous fisherman of Christ in this world, had caught up with angelic nets from the sea of the world, and drew them to the stars of heaven to be blessed with him.[14]

At the same time when a renowned ruler shone forth on the earth, to whom the world gave the name Constantine [540], SILVESTER, a bishop, lived in the city of Rome: /p. 376/ this holy man directed the summits of the apostolic seat [i.e. he was pope]. As priest he displayed many signs of virtue which, being written down in records, are now read throughout the world. By his virtue he once fettered a scaly dragon, binding it in strong chains with iron links; previously the dragon, breathing from its lair with deadly breath, had plagued the populace of the Roman realm — and justly so, because they disdained to accept the one Christ, thinking that veneration of a horrifying serpent was preferable [550]. But when Silvester had bound the beast with a tight collar, choking off the deadly dragon's diseased breath, joy immediately arose among the happy subjects: 'The beast which so often raged furiously has been defeated!' Accordingly, the refulgent grace of baptism immediately illuminated the Roman citadels from heaven, like the sun.

Silvester also cured the sallow limbs of Constantine, removing repulsive sores covered with leprous scales, when he bathed the ruler in the waters of Christ. For this reason Rome destroyed the shrines of the (pagan) sanctuary [560], rejecting the ancient worshipping places of evil gods, and eagerly sought after the more powerful heights of the new [i.e. Christian] temple which, marked with the Saviour's blood, shone forth; and they thereby propagated the perpetual triumphs of (the Christian) God throughout the ages. Thus Silvester fully adorned the world with his conduct when he instructed the king of Rome with the teachings of Christ.

This same teacher waged a conflict with and fought against twelve masters of artifice /p. 377/ who with deceitful voice were denying the proofs of the pure one [i.e. Silvester],[15] when they spurned the gifts of the welcoming Mediator [570] Who opens the shining threshold of perpetual life. Relying on celestial weapons, therefore, Silvester obtained his wish and immediately gained victory in the struggle; and, as if struggling against mighty dogs gnashing their teeth which in vain fill the lofty air with howling, this soldier let fly the iron-tipped arrows of Scripture on a true course, until, in confusion, all his opponents turned their backs at once, all except Zambrius,[16] who relying on necromancy deceived the unwitting populace with wicked trickery. When the seductive magician whispered without voice to a bull [580], the quadruped fell to the ground giving up the ghost, and a vast cry of the multitude struck the upper sky of clouds. But Silvester adored his Lord and was undaunted, so that the people, whom Christ rendered immune by the purple of His precious blood once the evil one's deception had been removed, were not at all duped by the abominable fantasies of crafty Zambrius. Silvester straightway roused the bull's body, prostrate in death and, releasing and throwing off the chains and bonds of the spell, he made the gentle bull return to the herd. Then far and wide the people proclaimed the Thunderer with their voices [590]; praising the Lord they began to render thanks. This man was, as it is said, a companion of Chastity until that time when he ended his holy life.

[p. 378] At one time King Constantine searches certain presages and dreams of future events. For when he stretched his royal limbs on a cushion of feathers, he saw by chance and discerned in his vision the figure of a wrinkled woman misshapen, with an aged appearance, who stooped and walked troubled with trembling limbs; what is more, the cruel fate of death had already touched her [600]. The illustrious priest Silvester ordered the king to revive the decrepit limbs of the little old woman so that she would once again enjoy life. Then, through the prayers of the king, a beautiful young girl arose, the same whom the stern countenance of old age had previously disfigured and, although she formerly lay still as a corpse in the death of decay, nevertheless, she immediately becomes a girl lovely in appearance. When he beholds her, the rejoicing king crowns her with a wreath, binding her temples with a garland of glittering gold, and he adorns her with the covering of a robe as well as with gowns [610]. Like a queen she wears a ruby-coloured necklace around her neck — such was the excellent appearance of this beautiful virgin. Then Helen, in conversation, teaching the king what was to happen, explaining the future omens of the dream, said thus to the Augustan king: 'She will always be yours and will escape the finality of death, [p. 379] except for the time when the last ages shall burn in dire flames.'

The emperor lay awake in his high bed, frightened, pale, and gripped by fear of the dream. He gathered together in a group sophists eloquent in their skill, who cast about philosophical speculations with windy words [620]. In order that they might disclose secret destinies for him, he asked what future mysteries were signified in his dream. As it happened, however, they produced nothing by their vapid haranguing, but rather fashioned many trivialities with their false words. Then the emperor, fasting, chastised his temperate body and for seven days declined rich foods, begging that the prophecy be revealed by the Lord Christ.

Night fell and covered the world with its dark veil and embraced the earth with its black wings. Then when sleep took hold of the royal limbs in the bed [630], Silvester spoke to the emperor, revealing the mysteries of these things: 'The woman, whom you thought was old in grim appearance, who disgusted you so much by her decrepit senility, is the city which men commonly call by the name of Byzantium: henceforth let it be called Constantinople for all time. Indeed, in your name it will perform triumphs throughout all ages. In this city the once lofty heights of walls have grown old and now, fallen from their eminence, they lie strewn on the ground. The walls decay and battlements totter — decay shatters these things and infirm old age destroys them [640]. But I will order you to keep my commands: /p. 380/ transported on the back of a hoofed animal through forlorn countryside, remember to carve a furrow with the tip of a standard. Thus riding through the land you shall push the flag-staff in your right hand, digging four furrows in a continuous line [i.e. the four sides of a rectangular plot], on which, having erected lofty towers of a fortress, you shall renew the walls of the building with red brick. In it your offspring will reign and that of your grand-children — as the numerous offspring of your fathers have reigned — their offspring and the fathers of their fathers will be gathered in it' [650].

Now there was a priest of Italy, AMBROSE, famous through praise. Fulfilling the precepts of merciful Christ, he preserved the pledge of the spirit and of a chaste body; he bore a name taken from the nectar of 'ambrosia'. Once when he was a tender young boy in the cradle, he was found worthy to offer a great spectacle of future happenings. For by chance a swarm of bees in great number covered the child's face — wonderful to speak of! — and even though they crowded around his lips in a frightful swarm, still the body of the infant was aware of no peril [660]. Thus in rapid succession they filled the mouth of the boy lying there; and, in due course, they were eager to return again [i.e. whence they came] in swarms. After this, seeking in columns the heavenly clouds, they strove to depart straightway from human sight. His father, (also called) Ambrose,[17] was amazed at seeing this marvel, from which his child was assigned such a renowned name. /p. 381/ Indeed, this swarm of bees, with which the lips of the saint overflowed, portends the sweet words of nectared honeycombs, from which the hearts of people became abundantly sweetened. This venerable teacher composed a lucid little work [i.e. the *Hexameron*] [670], unfolding with devout reckoning how from the first beginnings the wisdom of the supreme Father had made this present world through six periods of days, disposing the ages with an eternal command. These things, I say, the holy man taught numerous times in his discourse, leading many souls into the heavenly realm.

Let my babbling writing now set forth praise of MARTIN, whom at its four corners the whole world celebrates. The Almighty Father blessed him with heavenly praise (one) night when he was not yet cleansed in baptism nor anointed by the sacred chrism of balsam [680], since he, being devoted to Christ, brought alms to the infirm and clothes to the needy when he was yet a catechumen. /p. 382/ Who, indeed, dependent on eloquent speech, would be eager to delineate all the signs of his virtue in records, so great were the gifts which God bestowed upon this devoted follower? Often he improved country-folk with health-giving doctrine, so that they might be more willing to eradicate their abominable rites and believe in Christ, the Creator and Ruler. For he destroyed the unholy holies of the pagans [690], rightly casting down the sanctuaries of guilty despots, and straightway, having broken up the deceit of the ancient shrine, this venerable priest built a temple to the high-throned God. So that error in worship would not deceive the people, he also destroyed a notorious pine tree with green-sprouting trunk to which the senseless chiefs were wont to offer incense — what a crime this was! — burning the entrails of sheep in the beginnings of spring. On three occasions he made dead corpses rise from death, disrupting the hideous infernal regions of burning death, and also, granting the bounties of life to the diseased [700], he bathed the ghastly limbs of disabled men. Although Martin was never known to have experienced the wounds of a sword nor as a martyr to have shed red blood nor even to have been burned with hideous fire-brands, nevertheless his confession (of Christ) merited the illustrious palm-branch, since his spirit was prepared to endure the dangers of death. This bishop continually remained an unfailing virgin, until he, a soldier (of Christ), departed to the heavenly court, /p. 383/ borne aloft by angelic hosts to the vault of heaven.

In ancient times Greece produced venerable fathers [710], from whose number stands out the most celebrated and blessed GREGORY (of Nazianzus), known by his fame above the skies, whom God taught to preserve his pure modesty, joining together the bonds of body and a chaste mind. For at a certain time, perceiving through a dream, he saw two maidens glowing in virginal bloom. Seeing them, he shrank back with harsh gaze, since he did not undertake to witness the female face. But they both addressed this holy man with pleasing voices: 'Young man, do not harshly spurn us devoted maidens [720] nor, indignant, despise the faces of us sisters, since we are joined to you in the perpetual love of a brother! For you have offered to us a pure sanctuary in your heart, where we both will always be joyful. Brother, you shall never be deprived of our friendship. One of us is called Virginity, of fruitful flower; the other, being sagacious, bears the name Wisdom; and we were sent here from angelic regions so that the fellowship of our life might remain with you' [730].

BASIL, at one time the greatest author of learned works, in his divine doctrine founded an excellent law [i.e. Basil's *Rule*] from which proceeds the norm of a balanced life, /p. 384/ which releases nothing to bend under perverse weight but balances the elect by the scale of just weight, returning in alternating turns messages to holy men, in such a way that the true harmony of brothers may be adorned, and the pledges of a just mind may perpetually shine forth. He also composed a book in fluent language revealing the first seeds of created things [Basil's *Homiliae* on the Hexameron], how the eternal Ruler formed the ages [740] and established the four-cornered world by His command, dividing the matter of the world in right order, while He created the golden stars of the arched heaven. From here the beginning of the infant world arose for us, so that the highest Prince [i.e. Christ] might forge the mechanism of things. This man (Basil) revealed that he had retained his virginal modesty, affirming thus in perfect speech: 'I have never in rashness known the female body, nor shamefully touched the limbs of women at all; yet I will not be called an innocent virgin by that name' [750].[18]

The Egyptian land produced illustrious fathers, purchasing the shining gifts of perpetual life, from whose number there prevailed by blessed lot the owner of the famous name of ANTHONY, /p. 385/ who diligently sought the highest kingdoms of the heavenly regions. This first inhabitant taught holy worshippers that they might seek uncultivated fields in woodland pastures, in which to pluck fruits of the contemplative life and become perpetually subservient to the Lord on high. This man, I say, warned those meriting the Kingdom of Heaven [760] to spurn pleasures and forsake the riches of the world, to follow the steep way and beware the sloping, since the two paths [i.e. of virtue and of sin] of life stretch in different directions: as one traverses the ethereal fields through the heights of heaven, so the other traverses the vast, endless underworld. Those who wish to know of his glorious life — by what signs this merciful man shone forth in the world, in what manner he cured foul injuries of the body, healing hideous ulcers by means of curative care, how as a physician, thwarting the plagues of the people [770], he restored the diseased inwards once the organs had been cured — let him[19] not be slow to look at the narration of the little book in which his abundant virtues are written [i.e. Athanasius's *Vita S. Antonii*].

No differently was PAUL (the Hermit) known by his miracles above the skies and in all the realms, where the lights of Phoebus shine in desert places. /p. 386/ No more distinguished, blessed soldier than he strives towards an eternal dwelling place. A faithless relation chose to deceive this innocent man by a treacherous deed, severing the bonds of peace. Fleeing, therefore, Paul sought refuge beneath a cliff [780] until the torments of savage persecution should decrease and the world would again be joyful in a peaceful time. The date of the palm-tree nourished him in a narrow den, and he wore leaves rather than the warm cover of a robe. He took away the fire of thirst with deep waters of a spring, which as soon as the gravel of the earth brought it forth shining, the waters again poured away into a sloping hollow. A winged bird fed him in the cave, beneath the high leaves of the palm, with the delightful nourishment of grain. The lions, having put away their ferocity [790], and wolves, having been ordered to tame their fierce jaws, were submissive to him. Depending on the favour of heaven, he lived happily on earth one hundred and thirteen years. Then at last, rightly attended by heavenly multitudes, /p. 387/ he went celibate to the fellowship of the eternal kingdom, to receive new joys as a victor on high.

Similarly, sustained by the extraordinary beauty of his virtues, a blessed man called by the famous name HILARION accomplished many astonishing miracles in the desert; the present world celebrates him with abundant fame [800], since he strove eagerly to fulfil the rule of his teacher and to imitate the values of his father. He bridled his wanton body with a strict rule, removing the torrid burning of his lascivious flesh. He repulsed the very beginnings of titillating lust, treading severely upon the first playfulness of youth. He became illustrious in Egypt, as I will briefly show in my poem. For he burned up with flames an enormous serpent, which for a long time had been swallowing up miserable countrymen in its venomous throat, when a pyre flaming with a huge pile of kindling-wood [810] burned the serpent with its flames as it crawled onto the coals. At length, when turbid seas with mountainous waves were for a long while spewing out seething floods from the watery main, and the swelling flood did not recognize the ancient coastline but, crested by the mountains of waves, the deep sea with its foamy flood scorned its proper coastline — /p. 388/ then all the people gathering together in a closely-pressed crowd placed the blessed old man before (to stand in the face of) the swelling flood and, trembling, they reverently beseeched their faithful protector to bring help to the miserable citizens by his own will [820]. Drawing in the sand, he furrowed the sign of the cross thrice: the dreadful motion of the salt waters grew to a peak rising straight up to the stars of the sky. Then he checked the raging billows of the cruel sea. Thus the soldier of Christ bridled the surface of the sea, so that deservedly the fame of this saint will never diminish.

So also there is said to have lived in Egypt (a man called) JOHN, an inhabitant of the desert who led a life without reproach; he bound up his own course of life with tight bonds, overcoming the carnal prison-house of a lustful mind [830] and sustaining the two-fold burden with just moderation, since the divine sentence taught a two-fold life which a leader ought to discern with balanced judgment and recognize as controlling the impulse of the flesh.[20] A renowned grace filled this new prophet so that he was able to unlock the sealed hiding places of things, opening secret mysteries with the key of virginity. For on one occasion a woman perceived through a dream how he was blessed with a rich gift of virtues; in other words, she received a desired remedy from the flesh [840], /p. 389/ even though previously, groaning, she bore a complaint in her heart.

At the time when Rome was flourishing, holding command of the world and directing the sceptre of authority throughout the world — at these same times fortunate BENEDICT rose to fame;[21] merciful God, the Creator, granted him to Italy so that he, as leader, would bring the wandering people of the Lord by direct course to the path of the eternal kingdom, a people which, at first, having been alienated by wrong turns, Error had thrust into the dark underworld of infernal burning. Often he destroyed the temples of former tyrants [850], who had denied the Lord of Light with dim hearts; he immediately fixed the conquering sign of salvation in those same places. Thus the soldier of Christ triumphed over the defeated enemy, restoring the basilica for the Lord and rebuilding the church. What measure or number or list of calculations can explain the abounding virtues of this man — virtues which exceed measure and counting — because of the (very) mass of his deeds? For he restored light to dead corpses which fortune, through the force of icy death, had destroyed. He

121

furnished the deaf with hearing and the lame with walking [860]; /p. 390/ he roused the sick, invigorating them with strength of limbs. Putting to flight the weapons of the evil spirit and shattering his arrows, he cured wounded hearts once the enemies had been destroyed. Once he renewed a vessel broken in a shatter of fragments, as a nurse poured out rivers of tears; (on another occasion) he had smashed a poisonous goblet, which held a potion of death, with his right hand extended in the sign of salvation. He also ordered the steel weapon of the Goth, which had fallen into deep water, to return again to the arms from which it came. He was the first to set forth in the struggle of our life [870] the way in which the monasteries might hold to a desired rule, and the way in which a holy man might hasten, ascending by the right path, to the lofty heights of the heavens. Pope Gregory once described his renowned life, revealing it in documents [i.e. in Gregory's *Dialogi*] from the beginning to the time when this blessed man departed to the heavenly citadel. In the number of his pupils we are gathered together rejoicing, whom fertile Britain bears in its bosom as citizens; it is from him that the grace of baptism flowed to us, and from him a venerable throng of teachers hastened (to us) [880].

/p. 391/ What shall I recount of two twin brothers[22] who, by a brotherly vow yielded their souls to the stars and their bodies to the earth? They were reddened with gore, having been made martyrs, venerating Christ who suffered by (His) purple blood. As the psalmist sang [Ps.CXV.13], they both yielded their place to the Lord: proceeding on the path of Christ they receive the saving cup amid draughts of death. At this time blessed Ambrose, being shown the way by St Paul, found them sleeping buried in the flesh, hidden in a rocky tomb cut four-square (in the stone) [890]. Holy Virginity adorned them with its heavenly flower which is always dear to angelic hosts. One was called GERVASIUS, the other PROTASIUS, names chosen according to the wishes of their parents.

Once there was a bishop by chance called NARCISSUS, redolent of the merits of his virtues, as bright as his name. Flourishing with a two-fold gift, he held at the same time the summit of the episcopacy together with the glory of his virginity. /p. 392/ For that reason he became famous throughout the world by a celebrated reputation [900], as the doctrine of his speech was supported by the merits of his life. He caused the water of a font to grow thick with oil and changed liquid streams into thick drops. At length, when the proper time for the Paschal Feast renewed throughout the world the annual devotions of the Christians, who

122

are accustomed to celebrate this triumph of Christ more fully than they celebrate other solemn feasts of the year, at that time the oil had run out in the empty lantern of glass, and the lamp, smoking, grew powerless with dark shadows since the hanging lantern burned without light. Trusting in the Lord, Narcissus soon ordered the holy priests to draw a portion of spring water [911] and to fill the empty glass with the clear liquid. Thereupon the water is poured through all the lamps: thus exorcizing them he blessed the lamps filled with water, and then the glowing liquid fed the devouring flames; the reed in the centre of the light shone brightly, and far more so than would the fuel of thick (olive-)oil and certainly more so than with the glowing fat of a sow in a glass. The multitude of the people, seeing these miraculous things, soon gave repeated praise and thanks in common to God [920]. /p. 393/ Yet the Adversary, who strives to destroy the human race with deceptions, did not allow his (Narcissus's) favourable reputation to flourish. A wicked council was gathered together with three witnesses who concocted with false accusation a horrible crime, so that with the teeth of a serpent they might assail the bishop's reputation and insult this saint with venomous fraud. From this number, one man first came forward, and although he had sworn an oath he falsified it with deceitful fraud: 'May I thus burn up entirely with dark fires and with flames fed by tinder if I fashion trifles in my speech' [930]. Another followed to bring his false complaint. He began to speak to the throng in an insolent voice: 'Thus may my body not be destroyed with jaundice, because my sworn statement offers truthful words.' Then the third man brought forth an accusation from his breast and unwisely he strove to bind together with lying words the links of his oath in intricate elaborations: 'May cataracts thus not darken my sight with gloomy shadows nor inwardly fill my half-blinded eyes, unless I, a truthful witness, speak false utterances' [940]. Accordingly, the holy man wished to endure exile; and, fleeing, he shunned the unjust stain of malice. Thus this father is said to have lived far off in the woods, plucking bundles of contemplation under a mountain, since in solitude he wished to become intimate with the only Christ, despising the hazardous joys of a false world.

Whereupon, vengeance soon punished the above-mentioned witnesses who concocted worthless lies with false oaths and desired to discredit the innocent saint. But see, that wicked witness [i.e. the first of the three] burns in scorching fire [950], /p. 394/ he who first hurled (verbal) weapons from his wicked lips in order that his malignant words might darken the life of the bishop; his lofty roof, having been scorched, resounded with the crackle of its burning ashes and the heat scorched throngs of his neighbours. So too did severe punishment torture the second man by afflicting his sallow limbs with jaundice until, decaying, he gave up the breath in his breast. The third man was deprived of the double windows below his forehead when his clear eyes were closed by dark shadows. Trembling, he had witnessed the torments of his predecessors [960], (seen) how the high-throned God had afflicted these deceitful men for their cunning — He exposed the shady scene of their terrible wickedness. Their fruitless scheme was uncovered by their blind frauds and the guilty man shed such a river of tears and flooded his face with the salty fountains of his eyes, that the pupils of his eyes were deprived of light. In such a way the triune vengeance of the Thunderer punished these criminals until their demise, when harsh Death raged upon them. So the eternal Judge, while He punishes the wickedness of these criminals, publishes bountiful praise of the chaste priest [970].

Meanwhile the Egyptian land was no less amazed by the reputations of its fathers renowned under the heights of heaven. From among these in times past arose blessed ATHANASIUS, whose tutor was the most holy Alexander. It was Alexander[23] who defeated wretched Arius, who was promulgating a savage schism; [p. 395] (Arius died) as he disgracefully expelled the foul contents of his stomach from the ruptured rectum of his posterior and filled up the hollow cavity of the latrine throughout its (inner) recesses. After the sacrifice of mass had been completed and the offering of the holy meal had been celebrated, blessed Alexander [980] saw to his astonishment a group of children on the shores of the sea, imitating in play the mystical gifts of God. Indeed, at a distance he saw that Athanasius on that occasion thus was anointing the children, wetting them in the waters of baptism, as if he were a bishop consecrated according to sacred law. Such signs portended that he was to be a holy man, which the favourable chance of things declares clearly. The serious decrees (of an episcopal synod) confirmed what had been done as a game, when holy Alexander ended his life in death [i.e. Athanasius was made bishop in succession to Alexander].

After this, Athanasius, flourishing in adulthood, succeeded him [990]; as pastor of the flock he kept watch over the sheepfold against the injury of beasts and the jaws of wolves, creatures which are accustomed to frequent cattle-pens and sheepfolds. This bishop, by uprooting the teachings of the stupid, endured perverse schismatics and a thousand dangers. These same schismatics,

124

telling lies in a thick flock, attempted to dishonour him, contriving false empty stories, as when they showed an arm ripped from a body to the king [Constantius], and carried the mutilated arm in a coffin as a spectacle for the people. The fools said this had been done by magical artifices [1000], /p. 396/ basely saying that he, Athanasius, had mutilated the body of Arsenius, who had once been a reader on the pathway of books. Thereupon the Emperor Constantius ordered that this kindly prophet be summoned immediately from his far-off place. But it turned out differently from what the cockeyed plan envisaged, when the above-mentioned reader laid bare the dark deception. When the wicked fraud had been discovered, the holy bishop said: 'Lo, behold the reader's right hand in good health, and, all of you, observe the vigorous left hand.' Then the new triumph is noised abroad in praise of the innocent man [1010] when they realized that the blessed priest was without blame. The foe was stupified when the pretence of deception was revealed. Oh how many idle men did ashen whiteness cover over as confusion filled their red faces! Thus with God's aid do guilty inventions fail. But, (even though) ground down on the rack, the viper [i.e. Satan] raised up its head and once again belched forth black venom from its mouth. For they tried to trick the saint by yet another deception. Indeed, a wanton woman instructed in vile tricks attempted to accuse the saint with a charge of debauchery [1020]. But more quickly than can be said, a priest [i.e. Timothy] dulled the sting of the words with a shield, overcoming the adulteress with his effort — (Timothy) whom the ignominious hand of the deceitful (woman) was clasping. But nevertheless, the bishop, relying on the protection of Christ, now evaded the envious deceits of those perverse men. Going down into the deep recess of a cistern — /p. 397/ which, being empty of water, provided the covering of a roof (for him) — he hid himself inside for a period of six years. They say he concealed himself there as many years passed, with the result that he nowhere saw Phoebus (the sun) shining with light [1030]. But in fact he never ceased in his mind's eye from gazing on the light of justice of the seven-fold heavens, which sacred writing in excellent books describes [i.e. Rufinus's additions to Eusebius's *Historia Ecclesiastica*].

Let my loquacious document make known the glory of BABILAS, setting forth the many praises of the distinguished bishop, who had been instructed by the written teachings of the Book to build a defence for the flock and an enclosure for the sheep against the open jaws and bites of ferocious wolves. When the emperor [i.e. Numerianus] who ruled the extensive empire of Rome — indeed the three-cornered earth as far as its known limits [1040] — wished to cross the threshold of the sacred church — and not with hesitating steps — under the malicious stimulus of the Evil One, the holy bishop, reproaching the proud emperor with his voice, censured him showing no respect for his royal diadem. Defending by his words the entrance of the sacred sanctuary, he bravely warned the one stained with bloody gore not to touch the apse of the church with his black hands. Whereupon the bishop is led to the imperial court so that in an exchange of words he might speak with the perverse emperor. The intemperate ruler began to compel by means of punishments [1050] the venerable worshipper of Christ, bound by tight knots, so that as a suppliant he would pray to the images of ancient gods, /p. 398/ pouring libations and offering burnt-offerings to the statues in the temple. But the blessed priest rejected this as though it were filthy poison and did not bow his neck to the allurements of that shrine. Then the emperor ordered that three youths, bound by the link of brotherhood, who had earlier been instructed by the bishop in the doctrines of Scripture, be tortured with limber whips, to the extent that their hearts might be swayed by inflicted lashings, (hearts) which had previously refused to obey the wicked emperor [1060]. But even so, the bodies of these youths did not yield to punishment — rather, their hearts overcame the dreadful rods, even though the beating brought forth bloody streams and bloody weals grew moist all over the tender flesh. At last, having patiently suffered capital punishment, the bishop sought the blue heavens, triumphing in victory over death. And the beardless boys, that is, young men, when their teacher had ascended on high, were crowned with garlands of red roses and likewise rejoicing entered the lofty summit of heaven, joined to the angelic multitudes [1070].

Who is able to speak, in speech urbanely polished, glowing praises of saints, renowned beneath the heaven's summit where Titan pours down his golden rays on the world, as he illuminates the wide earth on his return course? Nevertheless, may this verbose page now begin to celebrate and announce in rough verse the outstanding men whom the motherly womb brought forth into the world as twins doubly named, /p. 399/ one called COSMAS, the other, DAMIAN. Education provided these two with a cure for this world [i.e. they studied medicine] [1080], and divine favour freely assisted them, so that they were able to drive out malignant corruptions from internal organs and apply a saving cure for diseased persons, expelling by their skills terrible destruction from the body. The mute and maimed, the halt and those found deaf, the one-eyed and squinting who had the use of distorted light [i.e. vision], the stammering and stuttering, who, in speaking, corrupt words by their twisted expression — indeed, whatever disease men bore — they restored with the gifts of Christ from heaven, and so dispelled the torment of foul flesh by means of their medicine [1090]. And yet, rich with the extraordinary gift of virtue, they did not carry pouches stuffed full of deceitful gold, but rather despised purses of money as though such were black venom, giving all their efforts without reward as heavenly alms. Meanwhile, a savage emperor, who then held rule of the world, was punishing martyrs with his cruel edicts. He immersed the two aforementioned brothers, who relied on the power of the Thunderer, in the sea with its whirlpool of swirling water. But the cold waters grew mild with a clear, calm motion, and more quickly than can be said the waters carried the saints to shore [1100]. Thus the power of the sea, restrained by holy strength, subdued the turgid surface of the wavy waters, while the right hand of the Father made a harbour visible in the waves. Whereupon, seeing the standards of (the brothers') victory, the ungodly emperor attempted other tortures of Gorgon-like venom. For the fierce ruler ignited the cruel sustenance of flames and stuffed a furnace full of brushwood tinder; into this blaze he ordered the holy men to be thrust /p. 400/ so that the conflagration would consume, in a fire of live coals, the guiltless limbs — which the sea, swirling for a long time in a whirlpool could not submerge in the murky waves of its waters [1111]. Likewise the flash of fire grew cold in the tinder of the furnace so that the soldier(s) of Christ, heedless of the storm of fire, gave great thanks for their unharmed lives, just as a salamander often exults over the flames of a hearth even though it is by chance gathered up into a wood pile for a fire.[24] Then they were forced to climb onto the broad wood of a cross and suffer the arrows thick from quivers. At once the eternal Father, Who rightly exalts holy men, shattered the dreadful darts of the guilty torturers [1120]. Thereafter they assumed the bloody wreath of martyrdom, passing on to the arched summits of the lofty heaven.

I do not hesitate to record the brilliant renown of CHRYSANTHUS, whom the world deservedly celebrates with much-mentioned praise. First, at an early age, his father handed the budding youth over to the teachers of rhetoric, so that the young boy of ability might learn the knowledge of books, which the wisdom of the world cherishes with dull comprehension. This boy was, so it is said, endowed with a clever mind, glowing in ability and prudent in heart [1130]. Following this training, when as a distinguished reader he absorbed with his ears the sacred books written in the language of heaven, he immediately rejected the teachings of ancient cults, /p. 401/ and trampled upon the false trivialities of old laws, and more quickly than can be told, by obtaining the fundamentals of faith he washed away the disgrace of sin with the waters of baptism. Soon he began of his own will to preach Christ publicly to the pagans, spurning as he did so the torments of arrogant threats. Then his father, putting aside the laws of nature, thrust his son into the dark recesses of a confined prison [1140], because he greatly feared the decisions of the wicked treasury. Trembling, he feared above all a cruel, capital punishment. But when the mind of the young man willingly endured torments, the father soon arranged a contrivance according to a different scheme, and subjected his son to the hazardous delights of worldly display, presenting him with a silken covering in the form of a purple robe, which a dying silk-worm had produced from its fruitful womb, and thus he adorned his eminent son, who glittered in the precious robe. Then by the father's order girls, who were adorned in varied garments and lovely in appearance, brought bountiful banquets and an extravagance of food [1151], in order that the brave soldier might be softened by such displays, to which the iron hearts of men often yield. Nevertheless, this young soldier, armed with the protective shield of Christ, scorned the dangerous kisses of maiden-lips and did not allow the sharp sting of debauchery to penetrate his heart, but rather shook off the arrows launched in deceit. The 'honey-sweet lips' did not, as the poet sang in the betrothal song, 'cling to his rosy lips' [Claudian, *Epith. Laurentii*, 80], /p. 402/ but rather Christ's sweet lips lingered upon his [1160].

As a final attempt there came a mature vestal maiden, Daria, her beautiful face blushing, whom a golden necklace adorned with greenish jewels. She tries to entangle the young man in a bond of love to the point that he would turn his mind to the union of a wedding chamber. This well-adorned young lady relied on eloquent words. Accomplished teachers were, in a word, astonished at the ability of the girl, which was supported by a knowledge of books. Indeed, she was sure in writing and quick in reading. But the event of dark fortune turned out otherwise [1170]: while the holy youth opposed the contrary turnings of fate, Daria, who for a long time had observed the divine authority of Vesta, came to believe in the high-throned God Who holds the rule of heaven; the maiden was converted by the eloquent words

128

of Chrysanthus. They then arranged by pledge a union feigning wedlock, and they both live harmoniously together in chaste behaviour, in order that deep within their hearts they might avoid the impure blemish and black stain of mortal love once they had expelled it from their hearts. After this Daria was anointed with the sacred waters of baptism so that it might strip the ancient garbs from her mind [1180] and she could assume a new covering from the clear water. Thereupon the maiden rejected the lessons of ancient books and followed the doctrines of the four-fold Gospels. Who would be able to count the mighty multitudes of people whom Chrysanthus and Daria led to believe in Christ through their example?

/p. 403/ Whereupon Chrysanthus, about to be tortured, with seventy men in a tight-packed troop guarding him, was consigned to bitter punishment unless he would offer incense at the shrine of Hercules. When the champion refused, trusting in the divine power of the Lord, a cruel soldier began to torment him [1190] and bound him with wet, rough knots of thong in readiness to undergo the scorching heat of the flaming sun. Quicker than a moment the thongs were loosed from his arms when Almighty God released the evil ropes. But fetters of stocks once again confined his calves and bound his swollen limbs to rigid posts: immediately, the Ruler of Olympus clove the stocks, even though the fools (still) bound him in their blind stupidities. Then a cruel attendant ordered that he be sprinkled with urine — a liquid which, as they say, will dispel dark phantasms — soaking his holy limbs with a putrid stench [1200], since the attendant thought the Lord's servant to be dependent on necromancy; but the stench exuded sweet ambrosia of nectar. The torturer then ordered that a heifer be flayed of its hide and that the limbs of the martyr be bound with the raw skin, ready to endure the sun burning with light. But flaming Titan [i.e. the sun] restrained his torrid heat so that the limbs of the innocent man suffered no burning at all. /p. 404/ Then renewed confinements enclosed the holy man, for now fetters of tight chains bound his arms [1210] and tied his neck to his two ankles — but suddenly the holy Judge broke loose the closely-bound knots and straightway ripped apart the chains of steel. Then a luckless soldier, who took pleasure in red blood, would have carved up the saint with a knotted scourge. But — a wonder to speak of! — the blessed martyr did not feel the severe lashes of the cudgels with their sharp blows; indeed, the pliant switches grew gentle as a feather to the saint, or as green papyrus which becomes soft in the river. Moved by these miracles,

Claudius (the tribune, in command of the soldiers) willingly believed [1220]: converting his seventy men with clear doctrine he had them immersed and purified in the water of baptism. Thus the now-fortunate soldier led them, sprinkled with reddish-purple blood, to heavenly Olympus — even those men who, being buried together and shut in a cave, would see the radiant gifts of perpetual life.

When these had deservedly gone to the lofty summit of the heavens, Daria suffered torment together with steadfast Chrysanthus. But he who was unwearied, bound by the force of iron (chains), was thrust into the dark recesses of prison [1230] to suffer where stinking excrement flowed through the fetid crypts; yet the stench gave way to nectar as shadows to light. Meanwhile Daria was handed over to corrupt harlots, and she who was without perverse sin was made to enter a lewd brothel; but a roaring lion was sent from the narrow grates of a cage /p. 405/ to keep safe the virginal limbs of the girl. If anyone should desire to dishonour her holy chastity by violating her pure body with illicit actions, as once the infamous Oza touched the ark [II Reg.VI.6], immediately the lewd man, his face confused, would die by fierce jaws [1240] and, gnawed by the lion's teeth, he would feel an avenging punishment in meeting (such a) savage death.

At last Chrysanthus and Daria assumed red crowns in death, following the decree of the emperor who held the rule of Rome, and they who were tormented in life by bloody punishment rest buried together in a crypt in the sand. When the earth spontaneously splits open and mankind emerges from dark tombs, we believe that He Who releases the world from bondage will awaken to (everlasting) peace from the depths of the grave those who are rightly gathered in blessed throngs [1250].

When this time had passed, the savage tempest, bloodying the holy Church of Christ with pagan weapons, gathered together a thousand hazards of death for holy martyrs, torturing these innocent men who were without guilt of crime, such that a soldier of Christ, at the point of a drawn sword, would even deny (Christ) when he suffered the brutal lashes of his evil torturers. Among these a certain martyr by the name of JULIAN underwent horrible trials (filled) with bloody punishments. /p. 406/ When he had grown to a proper age his father sent him to school so that he might learn the dialectical doctrines of things from manuals [1260] and at the same time the rhetorical arts of books. Even though the handsome lad was still growing in tender years, this student, a scholar by instinct, copied the clear contents of ancient volumes.

130

When his aged father saw that his son had grown up, he tried to persuade him — since he was descended from famous ancestry — to assume the responsibilities of marriage, in order that there would be an offspring of grandchildren to succeed him for posterity, if only he would choose to marry a rich wife. The son demanded that an interval of seven days pass [1270], so that during this time he might beseech the Thunderer with his voice, eagerly seeking a divine sign to his entreaties, so that he would more certainly know the divine will of almighty Christ. As the time passed the venerable young man was resting on a couch, having given his limbs to sleep, when he duly saw a supernatural vision. The blessed man absorbed with his ears these celestial words: 'Straightway make haste to rise from your couch, soldier! Do not fear, young man, that a young woman [i.e. Basilissa] be allotted to you with dowry and do not cross the agreeable decisions of your parents by your stubbornness; but remember to preserve as a holy companion [1280] /p. 407/ the maiden who is joined to you with pure body! For she will remain an unwearied companion of purity. By your words many thousands of people everywhere will serve me and have faith in the rule of heaven.'

So the young man carried out the orders of his father and, agreeing to a feigned marriage for his mother's sake, he received the girl adorned with jewels and gold. The high-throned Ruler of the four-cornered earth protected the chaste husband and the virgin betrothed to him [1290], so that they together would never blacken their own limbs with sin; with sanctified loins they restrained the excesses of flesh, especially since Christ, touching their pious hearts, exhorted them in their sleep to preserve chaste purity. For in their bedroom they saw the text of the Book, written in golden language and inspired by the King of Olympus, in which it was commanded that holy virginity be preserved. Thereafter they who sustained the rule of righteousness according to the prescribed course founded monasteries for the followers of Christ. They also established lowly cells for (female) celibates [1300]. Even though these celibates were kept separated by the lower order of their sex, yet they were not made separate by the lower rank of their virtues. Indeed, in these monasteries ten thousand holy monks flourished: here both day and night they continually served with incessant songs and frequent chanting of psalms, besieging the court of heaven with unbroken strength while they seek the entrance of starry Olympus with their prayers.

/p. 408/ Meanwhile black poisons belched out from the maw of the ancient Dragon which tortured the holy multitudes of Christ.

The soldier of Christ was then bound by tight shackles [1310] and undeservedly suffered beatings by a knotty club; the lashes resounded with noise from the bloody scourge until his purple blood dripped in streams. Thus the servant followed His Lord with devout mind, going by a narrow course to the heavenly citadels, even as before the Master went by a narrow path, removing the sins of the world with His purple blood when He dutifully deigned to ascend the extended wood of the cross. At that time the martyr's torturer suffered the loss of an eye and became one-eyed, being struck by the lashes and a blow of the switch intended for the martyr [1320]; he, however, restored light to the one-eyed man, even though the priests of the temple, who permitted (this) mockery, were not able to restore the light which had been torn out by the switch.

Moreover, in overthrowing ancient structures Julian had destroyed to its very foundation the lofty temple so solidly constructed, together with the fifty[25] metal images which stood there. Not even wound-inflicting Mars,[26] who spreads the seeds of war, inflaming loathsome hearts with Gorgonian venom, was able to aid the statues of the temple with his shields; nor were Venus or her most foul offspring [i.e. Cupid] of any avail [1330]; /p. 409/ the golden statues of Minerva, the goddess whom dullards have said is powerful by her cleverness, were flattened on the ground; nor was Bacchus — for whom the branches of the vine ripen, as the fictions of old books falsely relate — able to sustain by his will the tottering columns of the temple. But the temple's marble statues tottered with crumbling surfaces, and the building, its stones broken to pieces, fell headlong to the ground. Neptune, by reputation the alleged ruler of the seas who holds command of the sea with its swelling waves, was not at that time able to sustain the false effigies of ancient gods, which they sculpted in clear marble [1340] or which golden plates with burnished garlands adorn. Splendid Hercules is said to have been victor over the Centaur, and to have checked the flaming blasts of the predator Cacus when he belched forth fumes from his smoky mouth as Hercules's hand squeezed him in his cave — but his club did not rebound with firm strength in the temple, where the suppliant servant of Christ poured out his prayers. Limping Vulcan, whom they imagined to be powerful with fire, regulating torrid lightning-bolts with fiery reins [1350], perished completely, undone by the blaze of fire.

In such a way the shattered contrivance collapsed in a heap of fallen images, as true history relates in the ancient Book of Kings [I Reg.II.12–36]. /p. 410/ For when the priest saw that the two

132

offspring had transgressed, and that the father's severity had not restrained, nor had his increasingly violent vengeance punished, the guilty children, the vengeance of the Thunderer accordingly burned fiercely, such that, after the ravages of dreadful carnage, the ark of the Lord would be taken through Azotos, and He would cast down the high image [I Reg. V. 1]. Then Dagon fell on his face with his knees broken [1360] — and his abominable head had parted company with his deadly limbs, the head which the citizens could see on the threshold torn from his shoulders, while saffron-coloured Dawn shone from her golden chariot, and the golden sunshine grew yellow throughout the four-cornered earth and poured forth rosy beams on the open fields — and Dagon's broken spine was all that was left of his body [I Reg. V. 3–5]: it was in no other wise that the Ruler of Olympus raged against the pagan gods, whose shattered power fell to the ground, so that no one was free of the terrible danger, as the sequence of this writing reveals in its present manner [1370].

Thus also Phoebus took flight, his divine power rent asunder . . .[27] Jupiter, who was the fierce son of unfortunate Saturn and whom songs of poets glorify as mighty, seized the power of his father by driving him out, a eunuch, against nature, as the ancient works record; the miserable exile, castrated, hid in Latium, avoiding the danger of his harsh son. Neither was Pluto of any avail, he who guides the infernal region with his loathsome sceptre and reigns in the dark court of that infernal place; /p. 411/ he it was who carried the daughter of Ceres to the black shades [1380]; but the queen Proserpina was unwilling to follow her mother, as it is said with deceitful words in old books. Nor was Pan — whom the people of Arcadia worship by offering entrails, when many internal organs roast in the flames on spits — able to bring aid to the crumbled foundations of the temple.

The high edifice tumbled when its roof, broken, cracked open: adhesive cement could not bind firmly the ramparts of the walls nor is the hard rock joined together through the bonding of mortar. And so when the power of the ancient gods was exhausted and the huge structure of the majestic temple had crumbled [1390], the avenging severity of the Thunderer scattered it in ashes, just as the martyr [i.e. Julian], suppliant in prayers, had beseeched with his voice that the pagans might through these outstanding miracles believe in the high-throned God Who reigns in glorious heaven. Then the sole offspring of a prefect believed of his own will when, embracing the divine utterances of the martyr, the blessed young man opened his devout heart to the fruit-bearing words. But at once they were thrust into the dark recesses of prison, where the decaying corpses of the condemned seethed foully within with black worms [1400]; but even so the nostrils of the innocent men were filled with the fragrance of nectar, breathing indeed the heavenly scent of ambrosia; /p. 412/ nor did a shaft of light, shut out from the prison, cease, but clear brightness drove away dark shadows: thus does God triumph through holy virtue in His saints. A warder, seeing such miraculous things, believed in the high-seated King, Saviour of the world; and, receiving baptism, he was accompanied by a crowd of soldiers who previously had kept watch over the dark prison.

Meanwhile Julian ordered a corpse, punished by death [1410], which before had been wrapped up tightly in bandages, to rise (up) from the dark recesses (of death), its soul returning. The dead man awoke, disrupting gloomy Tartarus. The crowd, shouting out questions and causing a great disturbance, urged the young man to tell in truthful words how he could enter the dark portals and the gloomy recesses of the infernal world as a dead man and how he, having been brought back to life again, could see the shining sun. Quickly the dead man, rising, revealed the statutes of death; alive once more, he proclaimed angelic assistance to the multitude [1420].

Yet again, with the deceit of the Serpent prompting, the holy martyrs were thrust into vats filled with kindling wood in which a black mass of burning pitch glowed. The fire belches sulphurous flames and consumes the nourishment of brushwood from the district, until the flames would (seem to) burst into the high boundaries of the atmosphere. But nevertheless Christ's assistance protects the guiltless men. Then a rope soaked in oil bound their fingers and a devouring fire soon consumed the rope in fierce flames, although it did not burn the arms of the saints in its firebrand [1430].

/p. 413/ And yet again the Serpent, wound in malignant coils, raised his cerulean neck with its noxious venom. The martyrs were now bound by rope and thrown into an arena so that lions might gnaw the saints' limbs with their jaws, and the torturers' bloody punishment would force innocent arms to endure the crunching bites of bears. But it turned out differently, for the palm of victory was given to the saints: the beasts, showing obedience, licked the feet of the holy ones with their tongues as they completely forgot their recent prey. Thus, through God's transformation, the hearts of beasts become gentle [1440], even though the hearts of stupid men grow senseless, as once the poet [i.e. Caelius Sedulius] spoke in verses: 'And ferocious lions learned to protect their prey' [*Carm.Pasch.* I.203].

After this the martyrs purchased the bloody crown and ascended to the clear heights of starry heaven. Following the entombment of cold death there came to their tomb ten lepers with rough-skinned bodies who, having been immersed in the sacred water of baptism, straightway received in their hearts a cure of spirit and of flesh.

In ancient times there was a certain renowned servant [1450] who duly attended upon lofty Christ; the famous land of the Nile brought him forth in the world to seek the holy rewards of chaste men. According to many reports the Egyptian(s) called him AMOS. This devout man performed many signs of virtue. He was an inhabitant of Nitria with its leafy brambles, attending to the uncultivated lands of that waste country. /p. 414/ This place was given the name Nitria from the mineral natron:[28] at times it is believed that the world produces names by way of chance — if it is right to believe in such things [1460], if indeed there is any such thing as chance or fate or collocation of stars, if the Parcae sparing none[29] guide the threads of mortals' lives and threaten men by turning the spindle which moves the mill(wheel) in a smooth turning; but I believe instead that Nitria thus purged the errors of the guilty, as bodies are cleansed of evil filth by means of natron and so cleansed they sparkle.

At one time Amos came upon the swelling Nile, which irrigates the fertile Egyptian kingdom with its waters. But wishing to cross over, he lacked the necessary boat [1470]. A sense of shame of appearance prevented him from uncovering his body, lest by his nude flesh he dishonour the proprieties of modesty. Then, quicker than words, like a winged bird he was borne by divine agency to the other side, across the waters foaming at the shore, just as long ago at a time of importance a steward [i.e. Habakkuk] /p. 415/ traversed the Chaldean kingdom in the grasp of an angel so that cakes of grain might nourish the servant [i.e. Daniel] of the Lord [Dan.XIV.32–8].

Now consider a certain boy who had been mangled by the teeth of a wild dog and who had suffered wounds inflicted by the rabid jaws, was deprived of his rational mind, and went mad [1480]. Iron chains bound him in tight bonds because, out of his mind as he was, he would rush about frantically in erratic steps. Accordingly the parents of the boy lamented his fate and, weeping, they sought out a remedy from the venerable saint, that he might cure their poor son's misfortune and grievous disability. Amos is said to have given them advice with these words: 'Return to the widow at once the bullock taken deceitfully, and your beloved son (will) accompany you safe and sound'. They were astonished that he knew their hidden theft, which previously they believed had been done in secret places [1490]. When they returned what had been stolen in this ill-omened robbery, the happy father rejoiced in the deliverance of his son. Thus it was brought about as the truthful man had promised by his words.

At another time he demanded that a large jar be brought, which two men undertook to do; but one of the men broke his oath. Therefore Amos destroyed the humped camel, constricted by cold death, on which the man had failed to bring the vessel. But the other truthful man who, being generous, fulfilled his promised vow, enjoyed the use of an unharmed donkey. Blessed Anthony (the Egyptian hermit) once saw this excellent soldier [i.e. Amos] [1500], when he had left behind the fetters of flesh, borne by a multitude of angels, entering the beautiful threshold of perpetual life.

/p. 416/ In ancient times there was also holy APOLLONIUS: the land of the Nile gave birth to this man, made famous by his miracles. He was honoured by praise in the four corners of the world, offering a just example [scil. as abbot and rector] to five hundred brothers. In the time of adolescence he sought out the desert, for at the age of fifteen he fled from mortals[30] of his own will. He lived and passed through forty years [1510], praying nearly a hundred times (each night) in his nocturnal retreat, and he did so about as many times each day, so that bowing down with bended knee, face to the ground and relying on the mercy of the Thunderer, he entreated the Father. His woven robes were flaxen coverings which would never suffer old age while he lived. Thus he stood out, glowing with celebrated fame. But far off, where there stood a temple dedicated according to ancient custom, a pagan cult of the people persisted; thence priests, carrying images [1520] according to an oft-repeated rite of the Bacchantes, wandered about in long circuitous routes. When Apollonius by chance saw that the demented multitude was carrying a wicked statue from the temple in their peregrinations, then with his knees firmly fixed he called upon the Thunderer with his voice, and straightway he made the bacchanalian throng stand in a column, so that not a single one could proceed anywhere on his feet, but all alike stood as rigid as bronze statues suffering the torrid torch of the blazing sun, as Titan [i.e. the sun] scorched them the more with the heat of the summer season. As they realized whence their suffering came [1530], they pledged their hearts, believing in the holy man's words of doctrine, and receiving the mystical gifts of heavenly baptism — if only the priest would break off the hostile bonds by his prayers, /p. 417/ so that the path through the fields would lie open to their hastening steps and they would be able to go away on their usual path. He removed the delay by pouring out prayers upward, urging lofty Olympus in frequent succession. Thus the powerful Creator loosened the locked bonds to such a degree that the multitude, having got their wish, would depart purged of their sins by the holy water of baptism [1540], (while) at the same time shattering the broken idols and breaking them in pieces.

Once a violent dispute broke the honourable peace between those believers who profess Christ in their hearts and those disbelievers who refute Christ with deception: for Bellona, the fierce goddess of war, infected hearts with her poison and, bearing bloody weapons, she disrupted the treaty of peace. With troops pressed close together, the armies advance. Dreadful Mars exults in the bloody contest: the harsh horn sounded and the war-trumpet resounded its fanfares, while phalanxes incited war with booming voices [1550]. Then the aforementioned priest came swiftly forward; he desired to settle the savage struggle of war, endeavouring to extinguish the kindled flame of deception and to pacify the senseless tumult of horrendous slaughter. But a certain rabble-rouser raged in wicked intent; he who was the savage head, leader and standard-bearer of war /p. 418/ stood forth, saying that he would never prefer a pledge of peace until he should bring about loathsome death by violence. Then the holy man spoke, boldly disclosing future destinies: 'So may the bloody fortune of death befall you [1560], just as you wish by your words, and you will come to a bitter end! You alone, dying, will witness harsh death, while the others, rejoicing, observe a life of salvation. And after your death the earth will not offer you a grave, but savage beasts will rend you with rabid jaws and the beaks of birds will likewise mutilate your mangled body!' Thus it was as the truthful priest said in his speech: after his [*scil.* the rabble-rouser's] death had occurred, the corpse was covered with gravel; when morning light again broke through the twilight they saw that the body had been dug out from its burial place by beasts [1570] and that the beaks of birds had ripped apart the evil limbs. Then everywhere the people believed that Apollonius was a prophet, since the swift outcome of things revealed the picture (he had drawn in his words). All those who had offered incense at the shrines eagerly forsook the ghastly images of the ancient cult and pursued the pure gifts of cleansing baptism.

This renowned father, while celebrating the Paschal Feast, ordered the squadrons of people of the desert everywhere to join together and the faithful group to assemble in companies. After this, when the harmonies of the mass were ended [1580], and they all would seek the humble courses of a customary meal, they were fed with the dry nourishment of meal and grain, which in the springtime the garden produces from its lap as the earth swells up with grass. Then the holy man addressed the companies with this voice: 'If we truly bear believing hearts, brothers, /p. 419/ let us now besiege with prayers the Lord Who rules in the heavenly citadel and Who holds power as He governs the sceptres of the world, and let us seek worthy consolation so that the Judge may provide sustenance to us poor men [1590]; on this feast day the reins of severity shall be relaxed!' And thus, they beheld at the entrance of a cave splendid feasts and plentiful services of food, of which it is wonderful to tell. Food-bearers stood there, whom no man had seen before even though he had wandered through the fields of Egypt. They saw pomegranates full of seeds and pips, grapes and figs and many loaves arrayed in order. Even the fruit of the high palm-tree was seen there, and the sticky honey enclosed in hives by the structure of wax, and yellow nectar distilled from the liquid of the honey-comb [1600], and there too in abundance the biestings, brilliantly milk-white. When these things had been produced, the bearers disappeared, and the people began to render thanks to bountiful Christ, Who filled their dishes with rich feasts. Until the day of Pentecost — as they call it — Almighty God, Who knows all secrets, fed His own foster-children with such delights.

At length famine punished the multitude of Egypt with disaster. Observe: they came in throngs, tightly packed in groups, so that all of them in their misery might together in the same manner seek nourishment of food [1610]. /p. 420/ Then the priest measured out three baskets filled with bread which previously he had blessed in prayer with his holy hand. Thereupon he fed them all for four months, in such a way that he absolutely never denied bits of grain, nor did the basket run out, its supply of bread exhausted. He also once increased the essence of the fatty olive, as once the prophet Elijah is read to have increased the thick liquid of the cruse (of oil), making it abundant by his words [III Reg.XVII.13–14].

Now, I will relate the virtues of a glorious saint [i.e. JEROME],[31] the very thought of whom has struck the inwards of my heart [1620]; his fame increases throughout the four-cornered earth and his wisdom shines throughout the farthest boundaries. He was a virgin guardian and interpreter of chastity, who translated the Hebrew prophecies into Roman words, for he revealed the depth of the New and Old Testaments, disclosing the two books of the foreign Septuagint, which his version now sets out on holy pages. Moreover, he composed tractates rightly to be marvelled at; he unravelled the secret words of the prophets in a certain commentary, /p. 421/ revealing the mysteries of things [1630]. As a renowned teacher he continues to live throughout the ages by his writings, which are now duly copied throughout the four-cornered world. Indeed, he is celebrated by a throng of readers all over the world. He was the son of a father called Eusebius, as he himself [i.e. Jerome] revealed when he listed the works of the ancient fathers [i.e. Jerome's *De Viris Illustribus*], produced after the time when our Saviour assumed the cradle of our flesh on earth and cleansed the sins of the world, when He mounted the gallows of the cross with His holy body and, having suffered wounds, purged with His red blood the human race polluted by the trickery of the Evil One [1640]. Whoever attempts to examine the words of the two laws with so much zeal or so skilfully as this teacher studied the sacred books, as the psalmist sings, both day and night? But a vicious rival [i.e. Rufinus], tainted because of this by the plague of envy, savaged the saint with horrible jaws: thus glory is snatched by the black jaws of jealousy and the praise of holy men is damaged by the deceit of the wicked. For dogs crowd closely in on the boar with their baying, surrounding him on all sides in a tight circle [1650]. /p. 422/ But he disperses these hostile hounds with his teeth and, gaining his desire, he shall reign in the meadows of heaven.

. . . .

Now the praise of blessed men has been recorded, to whom fair virginity, dear to the inhabitants of Paradise, granted that the vast world may celebrate their praises until the world is dissolved in final flames, when hills will melt like wax and woodlands droop away — indeed, when the cycle of Olympus comes to an end after the world dissolves, the garlands of these saints (will) radiate more brightly before the Throne. The time is now at hand to make known holy women in these verses [1660], how Chastity gave to virgins who had attained the height of virtue the right to wear refulgent crowns, they who scorn in their hearts wicked delights of the world, who leave behind the foul joys of sinful displays so that they might follow with devout mind the Lord of Light, when the virgin(al) throng in close companies surrounds the Lamb in the ethereal height of the heavens, and the white flock shall rejoice with its holy Shepherd in that fertile land where fields bloom with purple flowers, where the savage wolf does not gnash his teeth with fearful jaws [1670], where pastures know not the ravages of a cruel thief, but where the perpetual harmony of peace reigns continually.

Therefore I now honour MARY in this chaste report. /p. 423/ In my verses I endeavour to praise this illustrious maiden, whose renown the whole world rightly celebrates, who was the famous seed of the race of Israel, a virgin abundant with child, betrothed to a suitor. But Almighty God — the Creator of the four-cornered earth, from Whom proceeded the plan of this world, to Whom all secrets are exposed before His high summit [1680], and Who illuminates all hidden things with His light — seeing the undefiled heart of the chaste virgin, preferred that this virgin should give birth to the divine offspring — Who, by His coming, should take away the foul guilt of the world — when He gave (her as) a temple for Christ and (as) a sanctuary of chastity. Soon she bore the true Light from the light of the Father, so that Christ might free the world from gloomy darkness, where mankind had grown senseless in the black world, until the time when the rays of the gleaming Sun shone forth, about which the prophets had already sung their words [1690].

This Virgin,[32] I tell you, pregnant with heavenly offspring, produced from her womb the King Who redeems all ages, Who alone rightly controls the government of the world — just as this young maiden had previously learned from an angelic announcement, when the high-throned Father sent Gabriel (down) from the stars. It was she whom the excellent prophet [i.e. Solomon], who once ruled as a wealthy man over the fields of Jerusalem, revealed in his song: /p. 424/ '(My sister, my spouse) is a garden closed up, verdant on the flowering summit [scil. of Libanus], a fountain sealed up, welling from the heavenly pool [cf. Cant. IV.2], a quivering dove' [Cant. II.14, V.2 and VI.8]. To her the prescient [1700] angel began to speak: 'Behold, you shall beget an immortal offspring and you, a mother about to give birth, shall bring forth an infant; let this Son of the high-throned (God) be called blessed for all eternity! The Holy Spirit shall come unto you from heaven; behold, its might provides a (shady) bower for your heart; the heavenly power of the Father, holy maiden, shall protect you.'

When this had been said the mother's womb swelled with the child Who, when He had been born, delivered the world from its lamentable defect (of sin) and, when He had been crucified, wiped away its foul wickedness.

Now to continue. What page of these metres can worthily fashion in its verse an enduring praise of CECILIA [1721]? She turned her betrothed to the teaching of Christ, scorning sweet sports of carnal excess, since she loved instead the sweet kisses of Christ, embracing His fair neck with her lovely arms. Even though musical instruments vibrate with many harmonies and songs resound with melody sacred to the Muses, even so the deceitful pomp of the impious — which fixes snares for saints so that a soldier of Christ may not attain the joys of Paradise [1720] — did not move the depth of her soul. Meanwhile, as they went to an inner chamber as the law of marriage permitted, she addressed (her husband), saying thus: 'See, an angel came from the celestial stars. /p. 425/ This protector strengthens me by a heavenly pledge, so that I cannot love anything at all of the flesh; for He preserves my body continually for all eternity so that no-one inflamed by foul passion can defile my limbs with shameful sin. Quickly in punishment my Protector will avenge with angelic weapons those who attempt to seize me with polluted hands' [1730]. Thus the devout woman converted her betrothed to God, as well as her (future) brother-in-law, releasing them from an ancient error and so, believing at last, they might obtain the gifts of the baptismal font; suffering tortures of the flesh, they both were made martyrs and became fellow-inhabitants in the highest regions.

The land of Sicily — which the blue waters of the sea surround and which the fury (of the sea) forever beats with salty waves — produced AGATHA, a maiden fitting for the service of Christ, whom the inhabitants of Sicily celebrate with famous praise, (for) she willingly devoted herself to divine worship [1740]. At the time of her adolescence she blossomed forth in Christ, despising in her heart the vain riches of the world and, as a dedicated young lady, she followed Christ the Lord, at once leaving behind all the adornments of secular life. Who indeed can express in words the harsh punishments, and who can speak of the dark calamities of torture which this little virgin endured on her body while on earth? She suffered the terrible pains of a wound-inflicting sword, which mutilated her body with its bloody edge: her fair bosom was deprived of its virgin breasts [1750] /p. 426/ and dark-red blood flowed in drops from her flesh. Torturers also burned the maiden with flame, roasting her chaste limbs in black fires — but swifter than words the flame lost its own power, burning the limbs of the girl with now-harmless fire. There was not a single persecution of her body, but rather a triple torment racked her limbs: the burning pyre, the fragments of red tile, and the cruel cutting of the unbending sword bloodied her limbs, which were without any guilt of foul sin [1760]. Then the Almighty Father, the Sustainer of the devout girl, cast down His eyes on earth from celestial regions, rejoicing to behold the triumph of the maiden's character. At once the merciful Protector of the needy gave help to the girl so that she might become stronger than those who were viciously torturing her. After this she purchased the garland of a martyr, and rising above flesh she assumed the perpetual wreaths of the Kingdom.

Finally, after her death she was not lacking in miracles, although her bones rested in the tomb of a sepulchre and her holy spirit rejoiced in the starry heaven [1770]. For at one time Mt Etna, boiling over with fire, thrust out burning sulphur in flame-belching streams: then, leaving behind the scorched summit, the masses of stone and the liquefied bowels of the mountain rushed headlong. Then a Sicilian priest, seeing the flashes of flame, placed the holy tomb containing her body in the path of the fire — /p. 427/ and quicker than words the threats of the furnace died down. Because of this the land of Sicily rejoices for all eternity.

When the stupid leaders, who ruled the kingdoms of the world, undeservedly put to death martyrs after their bodies had been mistreated [1780] — or rather, they honoured the saints by shedding their blood — there was a certain young virgin among those who were to suffer, LUCIA, who unremittingly loved the Lord Christ. As she was born from good descent of an illustrious family, several young men wished to accept her in marriage, but since she was consecrated to God she rejected any marriage-contract because of her chaste behaviour and in order to gain the Kingdom of Heaven. She advised her mother, who was exhausted by a weakness of the blood, to touch the tomb in which the body of the gentle virgin Agatha was confined and rested in peaceful death [1790], just as once another woman, troubled by an issue of blood, unobserved touched Christ; that woman was healed and made whole by the hem of His robe, the Lord bestowing health upon her [Matth.IX.20]. Lucia's mother, therefore, believed, and through the holy power of the tomb was made able to close up her open veins so that the blood-stream in her veins never again flowed (so) freely and, quicker than can be said, the effusions of her blood dried up. Thereupon the daughter began to explain in

142

words to her mother that she wished to serve Christ continually as a virgin and, as a virgin, she desired to reject the (proposed) marriage of her suitor [1800], relinquishing the golden amulet ostentatiously adorned with jewels, that she might rather give the adornments given to her by suitors to strangers, /p. 428/ bestowing alms upon the poor and gifts on the needy, and might thereby build up treasures in the citadel of heaven. At once the daughter by her words won over her mother as a friend; she opened her heart to her daughter's chaste words so that together, as wealthy persons, they might offer their patrimony to Christ.

When this fact was made known and was spread in conversation among the people, and their ears were worn out by such holy reports, the black heart of the suitor, infected with poison [1810], raged with Gorgon-like evil because the maiden had been snatched from him, the maiden whom the Saviour joined to Himself as a mature spouse, betrothing this maiden promised with a dowry of (martyr's) blood. The frantic hearts of the enraged people became inflamed and the consul Paschasius [i.e. the suitor][33] was vexed by terrible anger and this cruel tyrant berated her with words, attempting to take from Christ a beautiful bride. But she did not yield to the harsh goading of words: nor could she be persuaded by the flattering deceitfulness of pimps, even though she was dragged by rope to a dark brothel [1820] and at the same time (a herd of) cattle pressed forward[34] the gentle girl (bound) in cords; and although torturers roasted the tender maiden with a fire in which black streams of pitch and of fatty oil crackled in a horrifying inferno of fire, as the townspeople continued to increase the fuel for the flames, all in order that the blessed girl might feel the horror more. But quickly the scheme of tormenting punishments failed: the live coals roasted her limbs with harmless embers, since God was protecting her and driving away the flames of the pyre. /p. 429/ Then, however, the prosecutor [i.e. Paschasius], who was troubled by a terrible disorder of the mind [1830], could not bear the shame which had been done to him by the maiden, and he violated her fair inwards with a rigid sword, and dark red blood immediately flowed from her flesh. Nevertheless, this brutal tyrant did not exult in her death nor did he, victorious, have cause to rejoice for the death of the virgin of Christ, since the Sicilians squeezed his neck with tight shackles and quite rightly bound his arms with knotted chains. Thus the guilty consul came to the Roman city so that a severe sentence could punish a monstrous crime as the blood of the innocent, by causing the blood of the guilty to be shed [1840], worthily punished him for such undertakings.

Thus also in this song I shall sing about chaste JUSTINA, who attained the golden Kingdom by her virgin purity. Despising the florid traffic of worldly life, she rejected the earthly bonds of a matrimonial union. A noble suitor, inflamed with base love, did not cease putting together snares of words — in vain! — in order that this dowried virgin might be his for eternity, and from whom there might come the posterity of descendants. But since this man, wicked in his mind, desired such a vile act [1850], and yet was unable to persuade the innocent girl with his deceits and thereby inflame her senses with blind passion, he endeavoured to stain this excellent creature by means of magic potions. At that time there lived one Cyprian, famous for his cunning trickery and learned in the terrible skill of evil magic. He promised to bring aid to anyone who sought it, devising many corruptions and subversions of the devout mind to such an extent that he might carry on his struggle with the fearful weapons of the devil. /p. 430/ The venomous magician continually sent these devices to the holy maiden in order to beat upon her heart with enticements of debauchery [1860]. Yet when the virgin of God spurned all trifles of the flesh, thus destroying the lurid weapons of her black-hearted ravishers, Cyprian came to believe in high-throned Christ, Saviour of the world; and now faithful in his whole mind he was converted to the Lord: so at last the magician repented and gave up his foul idols, having discovered what dangers the virgin could endure, she who never could be overcome by a thousand devices of evil, but shunned the evil sin of unchastity.

After this, when Claudius (Caesar) ruled the world by his command, the evil man [i.e. Claudius] compelled the saints with his cruel edicts [1870] — what a crime! — so that they might deny Christ with the voice of the damned. But because they were unwilling to comply with the tyrant's decrees, oh how severely they suffered the cruel torments of death! Even so, Justina was not afraid to submit her neck to the sword or to pour forth streams of blood from her veins. Thus the blessed maiden was adorned by a two-fold triumph: not only was the venerable martyr reddened with wreaths of roses, but the fair woman blossomed with the garlands of a virgin. Together with her, Cyprian, the champion of God bleeding with his spilled blood [1880], merited the standards of bloody martyrdom. And so these saints, together, ascended to the stars of heaven, even as together they had endured the most terrible torments of death.

/p. 431/ Now what can an unlearned boor by the verses of these metres ever worthily tell of EUGENIA, born of a distinguished family, a ruby-red jewel glittering with virgin crown, whose praises the wide world celebrates everywhere under the pole of heaven, and whose glory the court of heaven intones with harmony? When she had not yet undergone the sacred birth of baptism, she venerated Christ with such a wondrous love [1890] that although a woman, she cut off her hair, despising her dark locks, (and) she took up the standard of Christ; and, by disguising her sex, her male tonsure could by this new plan hide the female concealed underneath. Whereupon the heroic maiden, rejoicing and taking up the cross of the Lord with a devout mind, left her carriage empty to proceed with the servants whom she had deceived by her clever device, in order that she, a wise virgin, might hasten on foot through by-ways to the thresholds of the saints and, seeking out the bishop, might receive the bounty of baptism [1900]. Soon, however, the carriage was returned to the home which she had left; as soon as her parents realized that the carriage was returning rejected, their drooping hearts grew rigid with oppressive care. Then, also moved by this chance of fortune, a large group of those near at hand uttered a lament from their breasts and poured forth a salt-river of grief from their eyes: /p. 432/ they drenched their sad faces with flowing showers (of tears). At that time the lovely young woman was attended by two eunuchs so that suspicion could produce no accusation.

God, the divine helper of those in need, protected the defence-less, innocent girl [1910] with the shield of His right hand, as the renowned prophet sang long ago [cf. Ps.XVII.36]. For the tongue (of an accuser) was lying with venomous words, attempting to condemn the girl with charges of debauchery. But the Almighty Father, Who knows all secrets, wished to reveal the triumphs of the chaste virgin by defeating the author of the accusation in the presence of the people. For, just as the matron [i.e. Melanthia], driven by the goads of the Evil One, sought to dishonour the illustrious servant of Christ by wanton words, disregarding the laws of nature [1920], just so this unfortunate woman [i.e. Melanthia], when a crowd of people had gathered, endured[35] the great mockery of laughing words, and her distraught countenance rightly punished the offence, so that men would never say, 'Where is their God?' [Ps.XIX.10].

A certain young virgin of Christ, whom her aged parents called AGNES, flourished in the world. /p. 433/ This outstanding girl had been glowing with the virtue of purity — her thirteenth year on earth had just passed by — when, growing in young age, she despised in her heart the foul filth of the world [1930]. But a suitor, the son of a prefect, who was famous in his royal office and a Roman citizen, sought through earnest prayers to take noble Agnes in marriage. He offers a golden amulet with ruby gems, also promising many talents of silver; in this way he undertook to seduce the chaste girl with the glue of gifts, as a bird-catcher snares a bird in intricate traps. But quickly the young virgin realized the deadly risk if she should listen too frequently to his foul words or if she, as a virgin, should be set upon by his shameful kisses [1940]: fearing this mousetrap, she spurned the wanton man with her words. For she vowed that, preserving her body at all times in a virginal contract, she would be a spouse of Christ, Who duly pledged her with a dowry of faith and Whose ring consecrated the maiden's body. Therefore, suffering many dangers, the innocent virgin endured dark prisons (while) on earth. But seeing the hardships of the struggling maiden, the Judge dispersed the terrifying shadows of the prison and poured forth a clear Light of light from heaven [1950] so that the girl's eyes might not suffer the gloom of darkness. Then the chaste girl was driven into a murky brothel of harlots /p. 434/ so that she might be stained by the sin of impurity and her holy life be marked by shameful talk, which seeks to dishonour the names of Christ's servants, just as baying hounds usually tear with their teeth. Then the suitor, accompanied by a large crowd, came to her brandishing garrulous darts from his chattering lips; because of her chaste vows she had disdained marriage with him — but God, Who justly brings victory to the innocent [1960], punished his guilt with the sword of heaven's anger. Thus, quicker than words, he who wished to defile the saintly one with foul gestures gave up his life and arrived in the infernal regions of horrid Dis. Straightway, however, Agnes broke the chains of death by her prayers, thus restoring with reddish hue his limbs which were stiff from punishment in the coldness of death. This was done so that there would be celebrations of praise for Christ where before there had been abuses by foul words [1969]. And the tomb of the sepulchre, the grave wherein the limbs of the maiden rested, cured Constantina so that the daughter of the ruling king [i.e. Constantine] could render mighty thanks for her restored life to the eternal King of Kings, Who reigns in heaven.

In ancient time there lived a girl dedicated to God; /p. 435/ her aged parents called her THECLA. She was converted by the holy teaching of Paul and followed Christ, renouncing the contracts of marriage. The love of virginity which glowed in her heart rejected the sweet unions of worldly life [1980]; in this pursuit the favour of heaven strengthened her mind, which the things of the world could not soften at all, so that she was harder than iron when it came to bloody torturers. Both her mother and father, having contracted a betrothal, busily arranged to give her in marriage for the purpose of bearing offspring for the family; but the girl's mind, glowing with virgin flames, could not be cooled in the bath of worldly water, even when her parents descended upon her with a storm of words, just as the heavens pour down showers of rain. And so the fire and scorching flame were kindled [1990]: Vulcan raged on all sides with black firebrands, so that the holy virgin could suffer the pyre's torments, which would consume her blessed flesh unmarred by corrupting guilt. Evil men sought to mutilate her female frame on the rack so that, limb by limb, her bloody bones would be emptied of marrow, if that were possible. But God from His eternal citadel protected the virgin so that she, having her prayers answered, would escape the flames of the fire. Then the virgin was thrust towards the jaws of lions to be torn asunder, so that they would gnaw her feminine limbs with ferocious bites [2000]. But the beast(s) did not dare to mangle her holy body, since God was protecting her devout limbs, although they would never spare her tender flesh of their own accord. Thus the Creator bestows the golden rewards of the heavenly kingdom upon the elect when they struggle in the arena of this world. This maiden adorned the last hours of her life: /p. 436/ bathing her holy body in red blood, as a martyr she ascended to the threshold of eternal heaven.

Now let these metrical songs undertake to venerate blessed EULALIA, made known previously by praises in (my) prose [2010]! She loved nothing mortal with empty love, nor did she seek to prefer anything of this world to the Thunderer. Rather, she despised all wealthy displays alike so that, having utterly rejected all delights of treasure as a likeness of squalid filth, she might be free to follow Christ. Hence she renounced the luxuries of the nuptial bed and the tempting joys of conjugal life, as well as the fortunes of transitory glories, (and she did this) so that the heavenly lover of chaste virtue, the Almighty Judge, might offer the gifts of life — He Who is accustomed to arm the chaste with continual victories [2020] and to open the gate of heaven to His soldiers when these saints win the battles of this deceitful world and bear their battle-standards in garlanded companies.

At the time of the Goths there lived a certain young girl who, because of her learning, took the name SCHOLASTICA. God abundantly enriched her with heavenly gifts, and she gained golden rewards by her vow of virginity. The outstanding report of her blessed life characteristically makes known, wherever the wide world extends, that this virgin, by her earnest entreaties, undertook to urge her brother [i.e. St Benedict], who was bound to her by a brotherly bond [2030], (to remain with her) /p. 437/ that they might at night take sweet meals of the Scripture and feasts of the Holy Word, these things from which the hearts of people are thoroughly satiated and the souls of holy men are nourished. But her faithful brother was not persuaded by any of her entreaties; moreover, by his reply he showed scorn of his holy sister. Thereupon the girl besieged merciful Christ in her heart that He might deign to heal the wound of her sorrow. At once the whole heaven grew dark with a cloudy storm [2040] and the summits of the sky (were shrouded) in the darkened heavens. Huge thunder, mixed with flashing fires, resounded, and the trembling earth shook with the mighty roar; thick-laden clouds rained down with heavy drops and the air drenched the earth with dark rainfall; the valleys were filled and vast floods flowed over the land. Then he remained unwillingly, who previously of his own will had refused what his anxious sister in lamenting had sought. Thus, God hears those who pray with a devout mind, even though they might not derive words of solace from anyone [2050].[36]

A very beautiful and noble virgin, CONSTANTINA,[37] lived in Rome, offering examples of the new life to all those who wish to live chastely, renouncing the foul contaminations of their previous life. /p. 438/ This blessed virgin, I say, relying on her heavenly Patron, despised the world flourishing with false adornments, as the dried-up refuse of chaff is cast aside and rejected. And that you may be the more astonished, hear the reputation of her parents!

For her father, majestically guiding the rule of the kingdoms, held the command of the world when Christ reigned [i.e. Constantine was the first Christian emperor] [2060], and he was given the name Constantine for all eternity. As the praises of his life travelled far and wide, he loved his blessed daughter with a wonderful tenderness. This eminent father pledged this maiden (in marriage) with a dowry, since she had now grown to adolescence in virgin(al) years. She was promised to an excellent suitor, a man more distinguished than any others except the kings who rightly rule the world, and to this end a pledge of dowry had been contracted. But God, resolving to keep the girl chaste, pricked the mind of the suitor, a provincial governor, with sharp stings [2070], so that he rejected completely the world's rich splendour, and, thus liberated, would choose to serve the High King rather than live a rich man in the world's rich delights. A miraculous beginning of salvation thus came about for him.

For at a certain time the Scythian army, a multitude armed with terrible weapons, advanced in close formation and devastated helpless Thrace with its innumerable troops. But the emperor's future son-in-law was defended only by a small military force. /p. 439/ Soon, shut up within the walls, he mounted the fortifications, having no trust in weapons as the savage tumult was approaching [2080]: so that there was a violent spectre of horrible death and his desperate soldiers were listless in the city. Then, with the promptings of Paul and John, the consul hastily swore an oath and pledged vows to heaven that he would serve the Saviour for the rest of his life and that, as a good Christian, he would abandon the ancient temples, if only the generous mercy of Christ would relieve immediately the imminent massacre of the people and the gruesome dangers of war, restoring peace by breaking up the tempest of violence. When these words were issued by the mediating voice of him making the vows [2090], the praetor immediately recognized the consolation of Christ, as the heavenly citizens straightway protected the city, and the enemy battalions everywhere turned their struggling backs in rampant flight. Peace encompassed the people with its wreaths of salvation. When the leader whose prayers had been answered finally came to the city, having received an ornamented standard of triumph and bearing back to the Romans this celebrated trophy from the enemy, he, now a hero, set free ten times five hundred slaves, that is five thousand enslaved servants, and made all of them Roman citizens [2100]. Nor did he ask Constantine to render to him the bride which had been promised, but of his own will he completely rejected the celebrated marriage. Thus he spurned the fetters of wealth and threw off the reins of the world, /p. 440/ so that as a poor soldier he could follow Christ in need, fulfilling now by his deeds the words of the Scripture which say: 'Make vows to God, rendering the pledges which are owed' [Ps.LXXV.12].

In this manner Almighty God protected (Constantina, His) loving servant, who had besieged the kingdom of the Thunderer with constant prayers, so that the Creator, a lover of chastity, might protect her who had abandoned the evil deceptions of foul luxury [2110]. She converted great multitudes to Christ by her teaching and also, shining with renowned fame, by her example. Indeed, the two sisters Attica and Artemia, who were born of the blood of the praetor, the suitor whom ancient times called Gallicanus, gave manifest witness to this fact. Constantina

149

advised his [Gallicanus's] daughters just mentioned to preserve their virginity by chaste behaviour, and they likewise merited the garlanded trophy of virtue as they left the world when their time of life had been completed and blessedly hastened on high to the stars of heaven [2120].

Meanwhile, there flourished in no lesser degree in Rome a young soldier of Christ, EUSTOCHIUM, the daughter of venerable Paula. She served the rights of chastity according to angelic laws and the refulgent sign of pure youth adorned her, even though the fortune of the world bound her sister Blesella to a union of the marriage-couch and the nuptial torches, to endure the seductive bonds of a luxurious marriage. Nevertheless, the bride greatly lamented the loss of her virginity when her husband had concluded his earthly time, just as a matron is accustomed to lament the loss of her husband [2130] when, in grief, she bewails his death by sobbing. /p. 441/ Yet these lamentations — which the fortunes of the world cause and deadly disease provokes with its cruel termination — Eustochium, a virgin, did not feel with bitter tears, for she despised the honied contagion of worldly pleasure. She spurned kisses on her cheeks as the bite of an asp, but rather pressed the sweet kisses of Christ to her lips and gave in return pure kisses to her supreme Spouse, as once the ruler [i.e. Solomon] who held control of the kingdom of Jerusalem sang in a famous poem [i.e. the Song of Songs] [2140], representing the part of Christ in the drama of betrothal. Thus, I say, having obtained her wish, the maiden lived out her life in such a way that her fame will be duly celebrated for the rest of time. The holy translator Jerome wrote many works for her; he it was who interpreted the words of the New and Old Testaments, converting Hebrew prophecies into the Roman language and Greek words into the Latin tongue. This same translator, rich in his knowledge of obscure books, brought to the Latin world (many) foreign volumes, so revealing their contents; he (thus) brought to light the Greek treasury of books [2150] which a foreign shadow had obscured, unlocking the phrases of words with the keys of Latin. Moreover, for the servant of Christ [i.e. Eustochium] this same teacher wrote a book adorned in polished language /p. 442/ which describes the kind of garland by which fair chastity is adorned, preserving pure limbs without blemish of wanton lasciviousness, and in which the praises of chaste life are represented [i.e. Jerome's *Epistola* XXII]. This most excellent daughter of Paula lived a virgin in such a way until her time of life reached its conclusion; then, quickly, her spirit entered the golden kingdoms of heaven [2160], as her soul returned to the celestial multitude.

Here also let the blessed honour of the holy virgin DEMETRIAS be spread throughout the world by the praise of these verses. Although great multitudes in dense numbers celebrate this maiden, born of prosperous parentage in Europe, yet her praises also astonish the Carthaginian kingdom, which marvels at the outstanding fame of this virgin among the people. For just as a lamp is not hidden in the shadows of a bushel but rather, glowing, is placed on the highest summit to shine forth brightly to all [2169], illuminating all with its light [Matth.V.15], so this virgin consecrated to God lived in chastity on earth, sustained by her divine Patron. This glorious maiden was born of a noble stock of parents and received by birth a splendid heritage, but in God's presence she stood more nobly-born by far, gleaming with the merits of virtue as a jewel in a crown. Beautiful with respect to her hair, pleasing with her curls, fair of face, this virtuous virgin of God (nevertheless) wore a frown on her brow. Throngs of wealthy suitors eagerly desired to receive this radiant girl in marriage [2180], /p. 443/ since, being lucky, she possessed a large inheritance of rich treasures, and of pure gold metal with shining jewels; and the virgin was resplendent in an ornamented gown. But the still unmarried maiden wished to abandon all this inherited ostentation and instead of it to cling to the kisses of the divine Spouse, offering sweet kisses, cheek to cheek. And recently I read a book [i.e. Pelagius, *Epistola ad Demetriadem*] written in an elegant style, which tells about the extraordinary life of this virgin in prose, a writing which the girl's holy mother requested through earnest entreaties, when her holy letter urged a teacher across the sea [2190] that he duly write down the holy (Christian) doctrine for her daughter so that she might store up a treasure in the incense-box of her heart, preserving her virgin chastity without any stain of disgrace.

At a time when the persecutions of a cruel tyrant forced persevering champions of Christ to suffer bloody tortures, three renowned sisters [i.e. CHIONIA, IRENE and AGAPE] received splendid crowns, weaving them with purple garlands, while pure-white chastity and blood-red martyrdom obtained two-fold gifts for these virgins of Christ, whose names I recorded in prose some time ago [2200]. The impious emperor, who ruled the kingdoms of the world, desired that these servants of Christ should marry, promising the holy maidens many gifts if they would all give consent to suitors, receiving the fine dowry of these noble men. /p. 444/ If, however, they were not willing to enter into the marriage agreement, he would order the devout maidens to suffer tortures and to endure filthy prisons in tightly-bound chains, where they would receive no nourishment other than that of scanty crusts of bread.

But blessed Anastasia, offering sustenance to the wretched [2210], did not cease to feed the innocent servants of Christ. She provided the donation of her money and the patrimony of her wealth to martyrs who endured the perils of death. For this reason the world publishes her fame and a perpetual issue of praise goes forth forever. She rejected the despicable patrimony of her suitor and, despising the condition of marriage, she followed the Lord. And for this the woman suffered bloody punishments, which books now set out in order, and her blessed martyrdom is read on inscribed leaves (of parchment) [2220] when the time returns annually for celebrating her feast.[38]

At length brutal executioners led the aforementioned like-minded sisters from the dark prison. The cruel governor, Dulcitius, seeing them together, so beautiful in appearance, burned with an impure flame and was seized with lustful motives and dark passion. This deceitful man promised numerous gifts to the maidens if they would only fulfil his vile intention. But the shield of purity protected Christ's servants and they rejected in their hearts the evil arrows of debauchery [2230].

But when nocturnal rest possesses weary limbs, after the sisters had sung sweet songs to Christ /p. 445/ and called upon the gates of heaven with psalms, the savage governor, inflamed with foul love, with gross footsteps boldly dared to break into their cell. God, however, was keeping watch, and the evil creature was blinded in his heart, as foolishly he bestowed kisses on black cooking-pots. This mindless governor, blackened and sooty from pots and frying-pans, thus sported throughout the night, while God kept watch and protected the sisters [2240]. At length the miserable man left the cell and went out. Because of his foul appearance his comrades could not recognize him and they withdrew far off, shrieking in consternation; thinking he was a ghost, they abandoned the frightful spectre. The wicked official had impaired his own vision: the adulterer alone did not perceive (through) the fog of deception that which others, who were not viciously deceived, were able to discern. He grew angry, and in a complaint he sought the permission of the emperor to punish the crimes of the allegedly guilty sisters by whip-lashes. At his appearance, however, the leaders who had gathered in a dense throng [2250] struck him with blows and the pliant switch of the scourge, so that the bewitched spectre of the corrupt man would flee far off.

He was conducted to his own chamber by his attendant slaves and soon the house resounded with the outcries of his dependants when they beheld their master sooted over with black. In vain he asserted that the blessed maidens, helped by the power of magicians, had produced this terrible wound. He then commanded that the saintly ones be stripped of their robes that he might feast upon their nude bodies with impure glances, /p. 446/ which previously the phantom appearance had deceived in the darkness [2260]. But God on high, who rightly gives victory to saints, defended His helpless servants with His strong right hand so that no one was able to remove the robes from their bodies. At last the hateful leader Sisinnius came, (proclaiming) that if the sisters were unwilling to burn incense or to perform heathen rites at the temple, he would kill them together by means of a cruel death. But no one, by means of terrifying threats, was able to dissuade the resolute holy minds from the worship of Christ, even though the savage (torturer) applied a hundred stripes [2270]. Then he ordered two of the sisters to be burnt in a crackling fire; and praying, rather than suffering defeat, they were borne in angelic arms to the stars of heaven. And the third followed to behold the heavenly multitude, going by a different path to the rewards of life; the wounded virgin, having suffered arrows taken from long quivers, succumbed to her many wounds as purple blood flowed from tender flesh.

Furthermore, tradition proclaims twin sisters who had been born and raised in Rome [2280]: one was called blessed RUFINA, the other, younger in respect of age, was called SECUNDA. Their father, Asterius, and mother, Aurelia, consulted them about a fine dowry offered by noble suitors. However, these illustrious maidens rejected their betrothal rights and spurned all the patrimony of the deceitful world, /p. 447/ in order that they might be joined perpetually in marriage to the Spouse who reigns in heaven, where fair youth blooms and old age, furrowed with wrinkles, never approaches [2289]. But the girls' intended spouses, who before had borne pure faith in their hearts, now rejected the path of Christ and pursued by-ways of errors on a rough and rugged track. Therefore the maidens, spurning their suitors' rights, left the lofty citadels of the Roman city so that the accusing words of the guilty suitors might not prove disturbing to their peaceful minds. Together, in a litter, they sought a country estate known to them which they happily managed in a remote part of Etruria. But

153

again, their suitors betrayed them; soldiers were sent and both girls were quickly returned to the city [2300] (of Rome) to endure the gloomy squalor of prison.

Then one sister, Rufina, refused to obey impious commands that she offer homage (forbidden to her as a Christian) at the shrines. For this the maiden was carved up with limber whips so that her sister Secunda, looking on, would soften in resolve when she beheld her sister's holy limbs suffer dreadful lashings. But it turned out differently than the cruel executioner expected, since the virgin did not speak with faltering words. Without flinching, Secunda spoke firmly: 'Inflict all bloody tortures on us at the same time [2310] — fires and swords and blood-drawing switches; ropes and clubs and rocks in hard hailstorms drawing blue-black weals with rivers of blood — but I shall carry away as great a prize when the executioner is defeated: however many kinds of torture you harshly inflict, /p. 448/ however many dangers of violent death you cause, that many crowns shall we have in the heavenly region!'

Now the sisters were shut up in a prison devoid of the brightness of (a lantern's) light, there to suffer torment in reeking excrement — but the brilliance of light shining from the axis of the skies [2320] drove away the dark shadows of the shadowy prison and the stench of the dung emitted an odour like incense. After this, however, they thrust the two girls, sustained by the divine will, into scalding baths heated with a burning firebrand; yet the power of heaven quickly extinguished with moisture the flames crackling with tinder in the baths, and the shield of purity protected virgin limbs so that the coal hurt no-one with its harmless embers — the torch, tinder and live coal lost all vigour, and the firebrand burning in vain quieted and grew cool [2330]. The vicious torturer then ordered that the holy servants be bound by the neck with weights of rock, so that the channel of the Tiber could submerge in its shining waters those whom the kindled firebrands previously had not dared to burn — but the surface of the waves bore aloft Christ's servants; the cold waters became still with glassy billows, while the virgins' bodies floated like the planking of a ship, and they returned again to the shore, their life intact. Then by the cruel order of this unrelenting commander the limbs of the saints were reddened with purple blood [2340] and both, purchasing bloody garlands of martyrs, /p. 449/ justly obtained virgin triumphs. Leaving behind the earth they eagerly attained to the kingdoms of heaven. Even though the earth covers their bones and the tomb of a sepulchre encloses these limbs, which suffered death for Christ, until the blazing coal shall consume the earth, nevertheless their spirits ascended to the abodes of heaven, bearing without confusion triumphal banners in a dense multitude, as they surround the seat of judgement in throngs.

At the time when Decius ruled the three-cornered earth [2350], bringing about perils of death for the soldiers of Christ, there arose in Rome a story of two sisters which reached all ears with excellent reports. The executioner was unable to overcome them with tortures, even though he punished the innocent girls with bloody death, in the hope that they might turn their minds from the Author of life. One was called blessed ANATOLIA, the other bore the true name of VICTORIA. Noble-born suitors wished to marry these maidens for the sake of offspring [2360], but their minds, burning with virgin flames, consumed the flax of luxury with a fire-torch of purity, and so in their hearts they rejected the transitory filth of the world. They scatter their wealth and, giving away their patrimony, they tread down golden bawbles with their purple jewels; soon, they had given all their adornments to the miserable poor, saving nothing for themselves, in return for a heavenly gift. A winged messenger, dazzling in appearance and glowing with snow-white brilliance, descended from high heaven, bearing the staff of a sceptre in his holy right hand [2370]. He addressed the girls in this way: /p. 450/ 'Drive away paleness far from your face and let not fear shake the inwards in your fearful breast, for a nuptial couch is prepared for you in the seat of Paradise, in which the company of the eternal Spouse is never lacking and where there is long-lasting bliss, if virginity, an unweared companion, should protect you!'

Just as the angel had given the precepts of holy purity, so both maidens preserved the partnership of a chaste life until life's departure, when death bays on the threshold [2380], robbing fading hearts of vital breath. When these events had taken place [scil. the dispersal of the dowries], the suitors' savage hearts, polluted with the deadly poison of jealousy, snarled when they realized that their intended spouses had given away their extensive wealth. Meanwhile, the virgin Victoria, leaving Rome as an exile, was taken to a place of exile, the city of *Tribula* [i.e. Monteleone in the Sabine hills]. There a death-dealing dragon belched its breath from its stomach, polluting the clear air with lethal poisons, to such an extent that the citizens, frenzied in a great tumult, now preferred to abandon the city polluted with its breath [2390]; they detested the lair where the horrible monster lurked. Victoria promised these miserable people, if they would open faithful hearts to the Lord Christ and abandon the foul idols of their

155

pestilent cult, that quicker than words she would drive away from the people the serpent with its deadly breath, which tortured the crowds with bloody destruction — provided, that is, they would choose to believe in Christ. When the multitudes promised this with a unanimous voice, the virgin straightway drove away the scaly serpent and ordered it to crawl far off in empty wastelands [2400]. Overcome by the weight of her words, the serpent with its scaly skin /p. 451/ immediately abandoned its dark habitation.[39] Thus the blessed maiden, relying on the triumph of heaven, expelled the huge serpent by her holy power, so that it would never again break into its cave; rather, as an exile it withdrew far away into uncultivated fields — just as she had ordered the dragon to leave with her terrifying command, giving victory to the citizens when the serpent had been expelled. Then the blessed servant of Christ asked the citizens that in the hollow, from which the evil beast had fled, they deign to build a shelter for her [2411]. Soon thereafter, just as the venerable suppliant virgin of God had requested, they sent sixty maidens to join her who would praise the Thunderer with their voices in frequent prayers, singing the holy songs of the odes of David [i.e. the psalms]. In due course, her suitor Eugenius, supported by the priest of the temple, ordered her to offer incense and sacrifice to Diana; but the holy girl refused to fulfil this wicked command. Accordingly her cruel tormentor exercised a sharply-pointed sword, pouring out her flowing blood [2420] and consecrating her virgin limbs with red blood. Straightway the murderer realized the peril of his victory when his right arm, drying up and withering, grew numb; moreover, experiencing leprosy on his blistered body and swelling up with worms, he breathed out into the air his last breath.

So also blessed Anatolia shone forth with great miracles, having endured exile at the hands of a savage tyrant. Behold, by driving off demons she revived the panting breast of a consul's son, who had been bound by tight bonds /p. 452/ and experienced loss of feeling and a wandering mind [2430]. While this report was still fresh, the country people brought those afflicted with various ailments and gathered them in a multitude around the saint, and the virgin gave them the cure they desired. By breaking the bonds of a serpent she likewise immediately saved a snake-charmer who had aroused the savage snake with his incantation so that the fierce beast would bite the saint's limbs with open jaw and ferocious teeth, and which had previously gathered the motionless enchanter into its coils. But witnessing his own salvation by such power, he hastened to believe in Christ [2440]. Moreover, he increased his deserts with the purple of his blood, and was ready to receive his rewards among the blessed companies of heaven. Afterwards, the fair martyr followed (him) with two crowns: chastity fashioned for her its white shining crown and martyrdom its red crown; her virtue being thus rewarded.

. . . .

Now that holy praises of the blessed, whose fame blazes under the summits of heaven, have been set forth, it remains for this poem to present the battles ensuing from the Vices, /p. 453/ which will deny the realm of heaven to the Virtues and the virgins of Christ [2450], and will close the flowering threshold of the brilliant gate, unless, driven far off by God's power, they collapse and flee into dark shadows, while Christ presses hard upon them.

Behold, the troops gather in companies for battle — the companions of Justice and the holy battle-line of the Virtues; opposite them stands the malignant camp of Vices who cast dense showers of darts of evil (deeds), just as the rival throng of two hosts bearing standards prepares to fight, while the trumpet sounds its fanfare and the horns of the legions rouse War with their song [2460]. Opposite these Vices, I say, stand more Virtues in dense formation — they bear the war-standard, the helmets with breastplates as well as the shield of battle and the sword of the Word (for) killing the manifestations of sin [cf. Eph.VI.17] — as they take themselves into position for the battle for the world. When they had taken position by joining shields, the Virtues beat back the cruel thrust of the wicked spears. Therefore may Virginity, which tramples the sins of debauchery, (and) whom the evil scar of vice never disfigures, be eager to contend against the battle-troops [2470], and may the virgin with armed force strive to defeat those eight leaders to whom the savage battle-lines adhere.

It profits not only to overthrow the practitioners of debauchery and to torment their flesh with fierce lashings /p. 454/ unless the other transgressions of the seven Vices are cast to dire death with attacking weapons: just as the Lord's people left behind the Egyptian rule, walking through the wet sea with dry feet, and completed a period of forty years — that is to say, a long revolution of eight *lustra* [2480] — until they gained the kingdom of the Promised Land.

But the Egyptian people, submerged under the Red Sea which destroyed their dense throngs in its abounding waves, can rightly signify Gluttony of the belly. Therefore may the virgin, subduing the wicked army, defeat this foul plague in the first combat. A dissolute array follows Gluttony, excess of food, drunkenness and intoxication of the soul, which always nourishes Gluttony with sumptuous feasts. But Gluttony which devours courses of sweet food [2490] and longs to fill the innermost recesses of its belly, and is eager to stuff the stomach with rich delicacies — this seductive (enemy) is destroyed by the powerful weapon of fasting. For the first man, whom the King of Olympus formed — and had moulded with holy hands this new inhabitant of the earth, filling his breast with the heavenly breath of life — a long time ago fell prostrate to gluttonous seduction /p. 455/ when he, a glutton, plucked the forbidden apple from the tree; from him a pestilent seed grew up in the world, whence sprang a harvest thick with foul grain [2500].

Drunkenness usually weakens the soul of men: for the begetter and ruler of the world after the Flood [i.e. Noah] — when the waters punished the human race with their billows — planted a vine with leafy shoot in the ditches, and drinking the nectar he shamefully exposed his private parts, so that his son [i.e. Ham] laughed stupidly with an impudent voice; his brothers, the third and the first [i.e. Sem and Japheth], wished to hide this shameful deed of their father, covering him under the clothing of a robe. If Bacchus was able to force the venerable prophet to curse his son and his whole race of descendants [2510], saying, 'May the servant Canaan be cursed forever' [Gen.IX.25], then may the virgin fear cups of new wine all the more, lest she might lose the triumph of the heavenly crown, since a drunkard knows not how to pursue the narrow path of life.

Did not Lot also, who lived generously among wicked men and as a host offered the shaded comfort of a couch and gave abundantly the comfort of food to all [Gen.XIX.2], when dark thunderbolts with sulphuric flashes set afire the fornicators and sodomites [Gen.XIX.24], softened by baseness, who were committing vile deeds of Sodom in a heinous fashion [2520] — did not he, the father, drunk, know his grown daughters in debauchery [Gen.XIX.33–4]? Unknowingly he wandered into their chambers; yet he would never have done this deed, unspeakable in its perversity — unless drunk with wine, he would not have known the rights of their beds.

/p. 456/ Why do I recall Nabal, drunk with the nectar of new wine, who an exile in his inebriation, laughing with a raucous voice, reproached his race and the name of his grandfather [I Reg.XXV.10]? And had the wise matron, his wife [i.e. Abigail], not known — by her ever-watchful sense — that damnation would

158

come to her wicked husband: alas, how many and how violent would have been the slaughters [2530] which Nabal, sluggish in his chamber, would have endured from the spurned king [i.e. David], so that the wall would have known not one defiling urinator before dawn sprinkled her rosy light on the fields!

For this reason may the virgin strive to overcome this beast, lest the devouring monster destroy the gates of Heaven so that the soul is not able to ascend to the realm of Paradise! Indeed, the Virtues continually wage harsh wars against Gluttony which overcomes iron-clad hearts; Integrity, however, opposes it with strength of fasting, so that the fortress of the spirit may not be overwhelmed by feasting [2540]. Thus the virtuous virgin scorns honey-sweet draughts of nectar and flees from sumptuous banquets for the sake of Christ, in order that blessed Virginity may be able to serve the Thunderer.

Thereafter, the seductive wars bring forth a second encounter, (that) of Debauchery against those who chastely serve exalted Christ. Truly, chaste virginity tramples with her feet upon the house of prostitutes in the likeness of stinking filth. From this monster are born the foulest words as well as lewd jesting, sports with ridiculous gestures, trifling and false affection, and excess of (sexual) desire [2550]. Oh how many and what kinds of men, celebrated with praise, has this fierce Enemy thrust under gloomy Tartarus, thereby taking away the virginal triumph through crafty deception!

/p. 457/ The appearance of beauty was not able to force the excellent Joseph thus to lose his crown of virtue; he rejected the mistress who set snares of sexual allurement for him, and fleeing from disgrace he left behind the covering of his cloak [Gen. XXXIX.7–8]. For that reason the blessed man earned the Egyptian rule; the whole world proclaims him renowned!

What shall I say of Judith, born of noble stock [2560], who with her pure body scorned the king's brothel and despised with her heart the loathsome disgrace of sin? When her fellow citizens had endured dangers of death, the chaste girl carried the blood-spattered trophy in a sack, while she devoutly preserved undefiled her womanly honour [Idt.XIII.10]. Thus pure chastity rejects in blessed triumph the vice of wicked flesh with its defiled filth, repulsing rivalling conflicts with virtuous arrows, lest the lurid poison of the brothel creep into the delicate fibres of the body and scorch the marrow with fire [2570].

Next, a third Vice, Avarice, foments a battle, a Vice which is, perhaps, best explained as 'greed'. A dense army surrounds this leader of combat; she does not walk as a lone pedestrian through public roads, bearing bloody spears and other weapons smeared with poison. Resplendent with false witnesses, she gathers into battle-formation her evil accomplices, that is, a thousand lies, frauds and thieves, worthless characters with deceitful actions, passions for ugly gain, empty oaths /p. 458/ and profits stained with the violence of robberies [2580]. As the Psalmist says, bewailing the sins of the accused who are always willing to be slaves to Avarice for money, 'He stores up treasures and knows not to whom it goes' [Ps.XXXVIII.7]; the learned Paul, in an apostolic utterance, taught the same, maintaining that this was the cause of all evil [I Tim.VI.10].

Therefore may Virginity try to destroy this fault — since Judas, the greedy purse-bearer, committed a monstrous crime against the Lord of Light with a dark trick: with ravenous hands he secretly took and carried off the purse entrusted to him and thus in his greed he stealthily confiscated the alms of the needy poor [cf. Io.XII.6; XIII.29] [2590]. Therefore revenge punished this guilty man with miserable death, and afflicted the thief with a cruel beating; he who, insanely blinded by a reward of silver, sold the King of Heaven, Who redeemed the world with His blood.

Hear also of the greedy king of the Hebrew nation, Ahab [III Reg.XXI.1–29], by whom the blooming vineyard belonging to Naboth was taken by fraud, when Ahab's cruel wife [i.e. Jezabel] forged a heinous document (in Ahab's name). The Avenger, looking down from the high heavens, punished this crime brought about by their fraudulent sin. For dogs licked up the flowing blood of the tyrant [2600], where Naboth, the innocent leader who had harmed no-one with weapons, lay buried under a shower of rocks. The savage dogs, however, fiercely tore Jezabel to pieces with their teeth and crushed her limbs, drenched with purple gore, into the ground — Jezabel, who had written the letter to the town and had cruelly punished the righteous followers of the Lord [IV Reg.IX.10].

Thus also when the walls of the city were shattered the leader (Achar) lost his life because of his greed for gold [Ios.VII.18–25]; /p. 459/ such also was the death of his miserable followers, whom a shower of stones crushed to death [2610], at the same time as the Lord's people surrounded the seven pinnacles of the wall in a dense throng armed with gleaming weapons. The sound of the war-trumpet and the clang of rattles struck terrible fear in the hearts of men. Soon the heights of the shattered city, which had stood with its seven citadels for a long time, were overthrown and

160

fell [Ios.VI.5]. And so, greedy for gain, heaping up gold trinkets, the wretched man continually stuffs his sack with gold coins; and just as the fires of a kindled hearth crackle [2620] more and more with flames the more nourishment that is given to the fires, the more they desire to be fed with more wood, yet Achar's burning madness is denied fulfilment. Thus the greedy man and the fire of hell may be compared by this three-fold example of events [i.e. of Judas, Ahab, and Achar].

Now a fourth company is gathered by fierce Anger who, always raging, lusts for the perils of war and arouses by means of her contentiousness the hearts of brothers to conflict, as she breaks treaties joined for righteous peace. From her are born massacres with vile butchery, clamorous voices and gnashing indignation [2630]. Yet temperate Patience carries a small shield in opposition and, prepared to fracture the skull of rampaging Anger made bloody by the sword, she silences the loud cry lest the greatest of furies be able to conquer minds — even though this fury, stained with Gorgon blood, /p. 460/ hisses and gnashes, biting with her poisoned snakes, as this daughter of black Night raises her head from the infernal regions and so rising out of murky Styx into the world Allecto incites stupid minds to sin. She is accustomed to bring to the battle iron spears [2640] which would inflict grievous wounds on holy souls, were it not that the Lord protects our defenceless breasts.

In a fifth column, the advancing attacks of Despair break down the defences and battlements of the virtues and harass the soldiers of God with savage weapons; this obstinate desperation of the faint-hearted mind overwhelms the unwary with a veil of bitter rancour. But with his shield the soldier of Christ quickly checks the spears of Despair, and likewise every other kind of blade which is wont to prick the mind; lest perchance they weaken [2650], the joys of a troubled heart and a spirit which tempers the heart with joyful movement heals this disease so that hardness and rancour do not corrode the innermost part of the mind, whereby the soldier of Christ would be unable to live in peace. Thus, let dark Despair rather be destroyed at once, lest the (upright) stature of the swaying soul should fall headlong into ruin if it lacks the strong foundation in our own Christ, Who by His grace always generously protects those in fear and trembling and permits no-one to fall from this mortal wound — /p. 461/ unless the sick and despairing man should reject this Physician [2660]! That name (*Tristitia*) is believed to divide itself into two parts, and its conditions are thought to be distinguished by a two-fold path, one of salvation leading to the threshold of Light, the other, fatal, one, descending into the dark underworld [II Cor.VII.10] — from which may God in heaven deign to save us!

Next sluggish Sloth leads the sixth assault: she nourishes leisure and idle sleep as well as the distressing emptiness of careless words and fickle attitudes of mind and actions of the body. Likewise Restlessness is surrounded by a huge force [2670]. Ever-watchful Perseverance of the mind, which seeks to defend its life with the shield of Christ, tramples upon this menace; when the enemy is driven away, it gains untroubled peace. For this vagrant spirit desires that a man's mind seek leisure and that sleepiness seize upon his dulled senses, so that attentive reading may not harass his troubled heart nor the eyes of the wakeful follow the path of the Scriptures.

A seventh army follows, dense in arms, a menace which the ancient Greeks called *Cenodoxia*, which is translated into Latin by the name *Vana gloria*, 'Vainglory' [2680]. As the Promoter of Evil was urging terrible sin, Vainglory enticed the first man by deception, *[p. 462]* when words such as these broke from her black heart: 'On whatever day you are willing to pluck the fruit, the eyes of your face will be opened at once and divine honours will follow you' [Gen.III.5]. Oh what devious nonsense the lying Criminal promised in order to blacken the gifts granted by the new life! Would it not have been enough that the world with its four corners, which the turning of the sky encircles with long revolutions [2690], duly serve human use for ever, even if the distinction of heaven were not to enhance earth's children? Alas, what a sin, alas! From this source evil arose for wretched mortals: the first man, relying especially on Vainglory, had no fear and was engulfed by empty hope.

From this tinder other disastrous vices follow: first of all, a precipitate dispute of a death-bringing word: then heresy spreads and boasting grows; from this also proceeds fierce striving for novelty. But the soldier, protected by the unbroken shield of Christ [2700], fends off the horrible point of this wounding spear.

Ferocious Pride amasses an eighth army, *[p. 463]* which brandishes weapons of sin at the warriors of Christ. With pompous deceit she aims to gather a band of followers, and strides ahead always accompanied by vile Disdain; and while in deceit she moves her feet through the sins of the world, her crested head shakes under dark clouds. For she generally strives to overwhelm the righteous with her own spears and she commits murders with the weapons of others.

162

From that root is born a black and leafy bush [2710] and a shady grove arises from the ominous seed: at first there is contempt of (one's) elders who teach (the) precepts, while pride of mind swells in a conceited breast; then the menace of envious hatred arises, which with swelling arrogance is wont to despise those who are equals and, by rejecting its attendants, to reign proud. For such death-bringing power thrives through envy, as when the deceitful Robber and lover of black death enticed the author of the human race with vain trickery, so that the throng of his descendants would not ascend to the high citadels of heaven [2720]. Thus, corrupted by the immense putrefaction of malice, one brother broke off the splendid covenant with his brother, who had been the first to burn the fatty inwards of a lamb, while God despised the votive offerings of cruel Cain [Gen.IV.3–16]. Thence an evil harvest of rough brambles grew up thickly, when the recreant sprinkled the fields with purple blood. Thence the mutterings of proud voices are born, /p. 464/ as well as the sin of the heart which refuses to obey commands, and also the savage slander of the tongue which lacerates men.

The other seven armies, which I enumerated previously [2730], originate among mortal men of earthly stock; that Monster, however, of which my page is now speaking, took his beginnings on the high summits of heaven, when the angelic leader and the first shining light of heaven eagerly desired to promote his own greatness from the north and in his wickedness vowed to be like the Lord. Then bedecked with the lovely shape of nine gem-stones he began, in vain, to swell up against the Creator, as he pondered a horrendous crime in his dark breast, namely that in his boldness he might be equal to the Lord with his own powers [2740]. Accordingly, accompanied by his followers, Lucifer deserted the ethereal region and filled the black Underworld. This Beast overpowered many proud inhabitants of heaven, who before in their brilliance glowed with angelic light and by their blessed lot flourished in high abodes: but while a third part of the(se) stars fell headlong, twice as many radiant stars remained above. And indeed, if this Serpent, belching deadly poison from his jaws, was able to prostrate the companies of heaven, then let the terrestrial cultivator of the field of this world [2750] be far more concerned to destroy the arrogant Serpent here on earth.

A humble man who does not know how to swell with arrogance of mind is able to overcome such monsters /p. 465/ and (hence) treads upon the offences of their proud habits. In vain does chastity obtain the distinction of renown if a gnawing worm

163

burrows into the integument of the heart; if empty pride fills the centre of the mind, it is in vain that virtue find praise in the words of men: the humble virgin is able to climb to the lofty heights if he or she follows Christ, Who offers a model to His children [2760] and has atoned for the sins of the world by shedding His blood.

. . . .

But the mass of this subject weighs me down like a heavy burden, so that this record cannot contain all virgins' crowns; more remains to be done by others who prefer to learn about an untreated subject and who do not want the whetstone of their talent to grow dull: they do not corrupt the keenness of their hearts with scabrous rust nor do they permit leisure to weaken their minds. Rather they turn over sacred books in their mind, frequently searching into those previously-written books of the laws [2770] which in their sweetness surpass the delightful taste of honey and of yellow honey-combs of which the poet [i.e. Caelius Sedulius] sings in his verse [cf. *Carm.Pasch.*, praef. 13–14]. Thus the skilled reader and expert lover of the Book strives to pluck the chosen fruits of Scripture, as from the meadow a cow munches the wild grass, which she chews over and over again when she reclines during the night. But the pig, accustomed to the muddy filth of its wallow, */p. 466/* cannot redigest its food in its fat gullet — the bloated porker which sleeps lying on the strewn straw, stables, and bundles of fern [cf. Lev.XI.7] [2780].

The day itself I say, even though hot July or even August might prolong daylight on earth, will run out before I could relate all of the glory which proclaims the praise of chaste virgins, and these babbling pages are perhaps not able perfectly to convey in their hoarse-sounding verse their mighty chastity, even though my lips greatly praise them in thousands of words, as organs bellow with droning blasts and musical lyres sing out with brief humming. My small vineyard offered to me golden grapes [2790], although the young shoot grew in a slender field; whence, plucking the grapes of chastity from the vine, I all too quickly pressed out the little must in my verses. But I do not think the wines will grow sour with age or that the teeth of those who drink them will perchance grind on the sediment, unless a deceitful wine-merchant pour in some watered-down trickery — (the kind of merchant) who now and again deceives those who are buying — as he aims to ruin the juice of the grape in the vats with water, asserting that it was thus that the bunches grew on the vine, from which the grapes were trodden by feet in the press [2800].

Now time forces me, (who am) composing these rustic songs to glorious saints, to conclude my running verses, as the end of the poem draws nigh (as it were) to the harbour; as a sailor crosses the foamy waves of the ocean, /p. 467/ having measured out the great sea in his tiny boat, wearied by the water he reaches the longed-for shore, taking down the swelling sails from the wind-beaten masts and at the same time loosening the sailyard from that part of the rigging. Now may the metrical anchor hold fast the sea-wandering boat, so that the wave-tossed sailor [2810] moving at last towards repose in the harbour may enjoy his desired lot!

Therefore I, a poor suppliant, beseech these patron saints who shape their own eternity by acts of virtue, and, miserable man, will in my prayers ask the Lord's servants, who merit the Kingdom of Christ by their chastity and ascend to the radiant heights of starry heaven, that they with a loud voice may call upon the Lord, Who willingly shows mercy to His unworthy servants and loosens the chains of sins from penitent sinners, so that, before the day which closes the light of life [2820] — and before that same day which opens up the threshold of death — all the acts of my offences may be cleansed and eternal Christ, the Glory of Heaven, may abolish whatever evil my wanton youth committed: mercifully granting indulgence may He remit my wicked sins of deed or of word as well as those of thought alone! /p. 468/ Thus may the highest power of the saints — those whom I described in my poem on virginity so that the crowns for the chaste would not lie hidden throughout the world [2830], crowns such as they had merited by their own flesh — deign to bring to me, now miserable, faithful assistance in turn.

And you [*scil.* the nuns of Barking?], whom the head-band adorns with its virgin wreaths, defend this work against querulous rogues, by shutting the lips of those who utter blame, even though I do not at all fear the words of readers who are scoundrels, who prefer to mangle the pages of singing poets, as in the light they seek out dark shadows of the word and look for rough, winding pathways in the level countryside, if the letter should hesitate or the syllable falter, or if gender, number and case should deviate from the rule [2840], if the triple person and the double figure should remain and if the tenses of the verb run five-fold according to prescription — and yet they do not correct the style of the faltering poet. Thus they always wish to tear apart the writings of authors, as the shaggy goat with his tooth gnaws at clusters of grapes, depriving the vines, with their leafy tendrils, of flowers — the goat which once carried the guilt of the people into the desert [i.e. the scapegoat: cf. Lev.XVI.16–28], /p. 469/ an act which the holy decrees of the Old Testament made binding. Let the fearful writer be afraid of such weapons, who although he is ready to wage war never trusts in his own arms [2850], nor learns how to protect his head with a helmet of verses nor knows how to defend his back with a breast-plate of prose. May a sword arm his right hand as a shield arms his left, and may his legs not be without greaves nor his thighs without iron: a writer should not fear the follies of the tongue that tries to frighten! For it is a ghost which terrifies the fearful in the darkness of night, a ghost which is wont to babble in the murky darkness. So too the crested appearances of spectres fade when the bold soldier, who presumes to take confidence in his boxing-gloves, dares to have faith and does not shrink from a ghost or spectre [2860].

. . . .

Since I have clearly discussed saints of both sexes, who ascend to the high regions of the heavenly heights, and by the elegant key of words have also exposed the eight-fold total of dark sins — may God drive it out from the hollow of our heart and banish it far from the light into murky places of concealment! — now, at the end, I beseech those reading my prose and verse to peruse this work thoroughly with kindly mind while, with their eyes open, they survey the text which is by chance two-fold in two distinct books [i.e. in prose and in verse] [2870], so that they may loosen the bonds of sin from me with their prayers, /p. 470/ and pay the price of the book with frequent supplication — so that He who preserves the heavenly kingdom by His rule, having no beginning or end and being timeless, to Whom the world's long existence gave and took away nothing, that He the Judge may have pity on me now and forever.

There will the saints rejoice throughout the heights of heaven, and in hosts will praise the Thunderer with their voices — first of all the Patriarchs, who gave birth to the flowering of a holy race, and to the progeny and new stock of their descendants [2880]: altogether they will advance in a dense crowd in throngs to crowd about the lofty judgement seat of the Ruler; there also rejoices the throng of the ancient Prophets, who once proclaimed the birth of our Christ, when He the Redeemer would renew the fallen ages and in His mercy cleanse the records of ancient sins; there everlasting life blooms for the martyrs, who with cruel wounds sought blessed rewards, purchasing with purple blood the Kingdom of Heaven which lay open to them; there holy throngs

166

of confessors will rejoice [2890], and although they did not shed their blood, /p. 471/ nevertheless their confession merited outstanding glory; there the glory of the Kingdom is granted to virgins, who abandoned the foul joys of earthly flesh, as they sing with ten times ten thousand songs and chant together four times eleven songs to Christ [cf. Apc.XIV.1], all following the Lamb Who once atoned for the vile transgressions of a sinful world with His red blood. With these saints who dwell in heaven, who enjoy blessed fortune and bear, crowned, the standard of victory [2900], and who in hosts surround the heavenly judgement-seat in thronged thousands above the stars, may I, least and last, trusting in the divine gift, deserve to be led to rest while Christ reigns throughout the heavens!

THE CARMEN RHYTHMICUM

TRANSLATED BY MICHAEL LAPIDGE

Introduction to the CARMEN RHYTHMICUM

In addition to his more ambitious essays in Latin quantitative verse, Aldhelm also composed a brief but fascinating poem in continuous octosyllables, a rhythmic verse-form on which he left the imprint of his originality and of which he was possibly the inventor. The poem bears no title in the unique manuscript which preserves it, and it may conveniently be referred to simply as Aldhelm's *Carmen Rhythmicum*,[1] following Ehwald's editorial designation. The poem is an autobiographical narrative, and concerns a mighty storm which occurred somewhere in southwest England, and its devastating effects on a local church — presumably a church located somewhere in Aldhelm's own diocese of Sherborne.

The poem is preserved uniquely in Vienna, Österreichische Nationalbibliothek 751 (Mainz, s. ix^{med}), a manuscript which was apparently copied from materials assembled by Lul, archbishop of Mainz (754–86), the successor of St Boniface and a former *alumnus* of Malmesbury.[2] Lul at one point had written from the Continent to an (otherwise unknown) English colleague named Dealwine, asking for 'some works of Aldhelm, either in prose or metre or rhythmical verse'.[3] There is reason to suspect that the rhythmical verse preserved in Vienna 751 is a copy of materials sent by Dealwine in answer to Lul's request. Now the (unique) copy of the *Carmen Rhythmicum* in the Vienna manuscript bears the following subscription: *Finit carmen Aldhelmi* (with Aldhelm's name copied out in full). Given the source of the materials which lay behind the Vienna manuscript, the evidence of this subscription and its explicit attribution of the poem to Aldhelm, must be taken on the highest authority.

Nevertheless, the manuscript's attribution of the poem to Aldhelm has been doubted — wrongly, in my view — by many

171

scholars, Ehwald among them,[4] and it is worthwhile briefly to examine the causes of doubt.[5] The first suspicion of doubt was sown by the fact that the *Carmen Rhythmicum* is prefaced in the Vienna manuscript by the rubric *Incipit carmen al̄*. This rubric, according to earlier commentators, means 'Here begins a poem of Aldhelm' (expanding the abbreviation *al̄* as *Aldhelmi*). This would not have caused a problem in itself, were it not for the fact that the same manuscript contains four further poems in continuous octosyllables, three of them[6] bearing the same rubric *Incipit carmen al̄*. Since these four poems are manifestly not by Aldhelm (one of them is addressed *to* him), the scribe's alleged attribution to Aldhelm is apparently in error; therefore, so the argument runs, the subscription *finit carmen Aldhelmi* is not to be trusted either. But this doubt is founded on misunderstanding and ignorance. In fact the abbreviation *al̄* in the rubrics has nothing to do with Aldhelm and is a *nota communis* or Latin manuscript abbreviation meaning simply *aliud* or *aliter*;[7] that is, *incipit carmen al̄* means nothing more than 'here begins another poem'.[8] Rubrics of the form *incipit carmen al̄* are frequently found in early medieval manuscripts of poetic anthologies and are used to mark the ending of one poem and the beginning of another: see, for example, the famous Codex Salmasianus (now Paris, BN lat. 10318 [Middle Italy, s. viii/ix]) of the so-called 'Latin Anthology'.[9] In other words, the existence of the rubric *Incipit carmen al̄* in Vienna 751 offers no grounds for doubt about the authenticity of the subscription also found there, *finit carmen Aldhelmi*. A second cause of doubt is equally without foundation. It was formerly thought that the wordplay on *casses* and *obses* in the first two lines of the *Carmen Rhythmicum* was a disguised reference to Aldhelm himself (with *casses* corresponding to the second theme of Aldhelm's name: OE *-helm*); and since the poem was therefore thought to be addressed to Aldhelm, it could not very well be *by* him. However, as Bradley[10] long ago pointed out, *casses* + *obses* corresponds to OE *helm* + *gisl*, not to *eald* + *helm*; and the OE name *Helmgils* formed from these themes (with customary metathesis in the second) is well attested in an early source.[11] In other words, the poem was not addressed *to* Aldhelm, but to someone named Helmgils. There is no obstacle, therefore, to accepting the authority of the manuscript subscription (*finit carmen Aldhelmi*): namely, that the first of the octosyllabic poems in the Vienna manuscript is by Aldhelm himself.

It is difficult to learn anything of the circumstances in which Aldhelm's *Carmen Rhythmicum* was composed. It is addressed to one Helmgils; but although this name is attested in an early Northumbrian source,[12] we know of no Southumbrian Helmgils who might have been Aldhelm's addressee.[13] Nor is it possible to date Aldhelm's poem. He mentions that he had formerly (*pridem*) promised to send a poem to Helmgils; but such a statement is too vague to allow any interpretation. Nor is it possible to identify the church where the storm occurred. Aldhelm's indications of geography are vague in the extreme. He reports that the storm occurred once when he had set out (*profectus fueram*) to travel 'as far as Devon' (*usque ... Domnoniam*) 'by way of' or 'through' Cornwall (*per ... Cornubiam*). If one set out from (say) Malmesbury, one would normally travel *through* Devon to get to Cornwall, not vice versa. Aldhelm's words would best make sense if, after a stay in Cornwall, he set out to travel from Cornwall back eastwards to Devon (and eventually to Malmesbury or Sherborne). In this case the church might have been located in Devon. But this interpretation is still problematical, for we do not know the precise geographical extent of Devon in the late seventh century; presumably *Domnonia* did not then extend further eastwards than the River Parrett.[14] We may deduce from Aldhelm's poem that the church in question was adjacent to the sea (lines 103–14) since the storm is shown pounding the promontories; and perhaps that it was near a river estuary, since rivers are seen overflowing with the violent rainfall (lines 49–50). Our knowledge of the sites of minster churches on the Devon coast (near river estuaries) is not full for this early period, but minsters at Whitchurch (on the Char) or Exminster (on the Exe) are perhaps in question. On the other hand, if — as the poem may suggest[15] — the church in question was a monastery, perhaps only Exeter itself would satisfy these various criteria. But Aldhelm's description of the church and its site is too vague to permit even a conjectural identification. We can only surmise that the church was in the diocese of western Wessex of which Aldhelm was bishop late in life (706–709/10), and that he may have been visiting it on pastoral business.

Somewhat more can be learned about the verse-form of Aldhelm's *Carmen Rhythmicum*: continuous octosyllables. The origin of this verse-form lay in the quantitative iambic dimeter hymns of late antiquity, particularly those of St Ambrose (*ob.* 397). Ambrosian hymns consisted of eight stanzas of four lines each (the stanzas were clearly designed to be sung alternately by choirs); within each line the second and fourth feet were regularly iambs (˘ -), although the first and third could also be spondees

(- -) or even anapests (⌣ ⌣ -) instead of iambs.[16] There were frequent elisions and no hiatus. Consider, for example, the following Ambrosian stanza:

> Dĕūs | crĕā+tŏr ōm+nĭum
> pŏlī+quĕ rēc+tŏr vēs+tĭēns
> dĭēm | dĕcō+rŏ lū+mĭne
> nōctĕm | sŏpō+rĭs grā+tĭā.

From the fourth century A.D. onwards, awareness of the quantity of Latin vowels decreased, with a correspondingly increased awareness of the rhythmic stress of words. Within the basic framework of the eight-syllable line of the iambic dimeter, therefore, we find stanzaic hymns where quantity has been abandoned and where the concern is with the natural stress of words — and sometimes, even, with mere syllable-counting. The Irish, in particular, seem to have been sublimely unaware of Latin quantity. There are several surviving Hiberno-Latin hymns of seventh-century date which preserve the framework of the eight-syllable line,[17] but in other respects are utterly unlike the iambic dimeter hymns of late antiquity. For example, the Hiberno-Latin poem *Altus Prosator*,[18] which consists of twelve-line stanzas (each line being of eight syllables) arranged in alphabetical sequence. Here is the beginning of the Y-stanza:

> Ymnorum cantionibus
> Sedulo tinnientibus
> Tripudiis sanctis milibus
> Angelorum vernantibus
> Quattuorque plenissimis
> Animalibus oculis . . .

The words have apparently been forced into a rhythmical strait-jacket. Throughout the poem there are no elisions but frequent hiatus. Lines consisting of only two words are frequent — a device found rarely (if at all) in Late Latin hymns. The poet is apparently concerned principally with the stress on the antepenultimate syllable (or proparoxytone, abbreviated *pp*)[19] of each line. He is concerned too that each line end in a word of no fewer than three syllables (*milibus, oculis* here) and most often a line consists in two quadrisyllabic words. Beyond these concerns, the poet is only interested in obtaining a syllable-count of eight syllables per line, with the result that there is no regular rhythm to speak of in the first five syllables in any line. For him, the principal stress — indeed the only important stress — in each line falls on the antepenultimate syllable: *cantiónibus, tinniéntibus, mílibus, vernántibus, pleníssimis, óculis,* and so on. Note also that each pair of lines is linked by either bisyllabic or monosyllabic rhyme (again, rhyme is a feature never found in Late Latin hymns). The rhythmic structure of *Altus Prosator* may be designated (in the terminology of Norberg) as 8*pp* + 8*pp*.

Aldhelm's continuous octosyllables owe a good deal to this Hiberno-Latin verse form.[20] Like it, Aldhelm's octosyllables rhyme in couplets (with either monosyllabic or bisyllabic rhyme) and have a stress-pattern of 8*pp* + 8*pp*. Aldhelm too seems to be concerned principally with syllable-counting and with the stress-pattern of the final word, which for him — as for the poet of *Altus Prosator* — consists of no fewer than three syllables. However, there are important features in Aldhelm's octosyllables which distinguish them from those of his predecessors. Aldhelm was apparently the first poet to abandon completely the stanzaic structure of the Late Latin and Hiberno-Latin hymns, and to use octosyllables for purposes of extended narrative: his *Carmen Rhythmicum* is two hundred lines long (for that reason I refer to the verse-form as practised by Aldhelm as *continuous* octosyllables).[21] Another feature of Aldhelm's octosyllables is the frequent alliteration which, as in his prose, is prominent if not absolutely regular:

> Neque *c*aelorum *c*úlmina
> Carent *n*octurna *n*ébula
> Quorum *p*ulchra *p*laníties
> Perlucebat ut glácies
> Donec *n*imbo ac *n*úbibus
> *T*orve *t*eguntur *t*rúcibus.

This aspect of Aldhelm's octosyllabic verse has been associated with the alliterative patterns of Germanic verse, but without definite results.[22] In any case, Aldhelm forged a versatile and resonant vehicle for the purposes of narrative, and his achievement had important consequences for later Anglo-Latin poetry.

In respect of his rhythmical verse, as of so many of his other literary achievements, Aldhelm's innovation soon found a host of imitators. A student of Aldhelm named Æthilwald wrote to the master enclosing three poems, of which the first was said to be in hexameters (now apparently lost) and the other two in octosyllables:

> . . . the third, wrought not according to the measure of feet, but written swiftly and with ploughing pen, with eight syllables

arranged in any one verse . . . I have dedicated and dispatched to you, O wisest father; the middle (poem), regarding the pilgrimage of transmarine journeys, likewise composed of quite similar lines of verses and syllables, I sent without delay to my and your colleague Wihtfrith.[23]

As mentioned above, the Vienna manuscript preserves five poems in continuous octosyllables of which the first is Aldhelm's *Carmen Rhythmicum*. Of the remaining four,[24] one (Ehwald's no. II) is manifestly the poem addressed by Æthilwald to Wihtfrith, for it describes a journey to Rome undertaken by three men, of whom one died in Rome while the two others returned to England bearing many gifts; another (Ehwald's no. IV) is addressed to Aldhelm, and is apparently the poem referred to by Æthilwald in his letter. Of the remaining two poems, one (Ehwald's no. V) is a verse epistle by Æthilwald addressed to one *Hova* (= Ofa or Offa, otherwise unknown), and it is a reasonable assumption that the final poem (Ehwald's no. III), a brief prayer to God, is by Æthilwald as well. These poems all show close adherence to the principles of rhythmical composition worked out by Aldhelm — syllable-counting with regular stress on the antepenultimate syllable, rhyme and frequent alliteration — and indicate that continuous octosyllables were an extremely flexible instrument for epistolary exchanges. They were used as such not only by Aldhelm's immediate circle of students, but also by numerous Anglo-Latin authors of the late seventh and early eighth centuries.[25] While still in England the scholar Wynfrith (later to be known as Boniface) addressed a letter of moral exhortation to one of his students named Nithheard, and concluded it with twenty-eight octosyllables of valediction.[26] Others in the circle of Boniface's correspondents, notably Berhtgyth and Lul, similarly used octosyllables for epistolary purposes.[27] In the later Anglo-Saxon period, octosyllables were used for narrative purposes by the hagiographer Lantfred, writing at Winchester *c.* 975, and other octosyllabic poems survive to indicate that that verse-form was a useful medium.[28] Once again it was Aldhelm who began a literary tradition which was still flourishing in England at the time of the Norman Conquest.

CARMEN RHYTHMICUM

[p. 524] Gentle reader, catholic *Helm-* [i.e. 'helmet'] and heroic *-gisl* [i.e. 'hostage']:[1] driven on by your prayers earnestly entreating (me), I the poet have composed this poem and have thereby fulfilled the undertaking I contracted long ago [7].

When I had set out for nasty Devon and was proceeding through Cornwall — which is devoid of any flowering vegetation or grasses in any abundance — the mighty elements and the chaotic masses (of the universe) were driven to collision under the fiery dome of the vaulted sky [16]: *[p. 525]* while the structure of the universe trembles[2] under the power of the winds, suddenly, during the night a wintry gale arises whose force shatters the earth and whose might overwhelms it, since, once the compact (which holds the winds in check) has been broken, the winds may rage unchecked in the upper atmosphere, and, with their bonds shattered,[3] they howl furiously throughout the world [26]. Then, once they have seized power and their bondage has been cast off, their impulsive blasts muster in battle-array — the winds whose twelve names are found in learned books.[4] Their leader, violently sweeping along the foam and surging wildly with its impetus, came from that compass-point where the burning lanterns of Titan [i.e. the sun] set [38]; and since those winds were not raging (as it were) at some undistinguished victory, the earth shuddered in disorder, and the (mighty) oaks uprooted (by the wind) crashed down with their crowns and their roots both shattered. Nor did the raindrops sprinkle down gently, but rather they threateningly drenched the entire expanse of the universe with their saturating downpour [48]. And when the rivers were nearly filled to overflowing with this violent rainfall, the storm attacked the earth with polished hailstones which poured down in masses from the black clouds above. Nor were the summits of heaven free from these clouds of

177

night: their bright sheen glistened as usual like ice — until they were grimly obscured by the darkness and the savage clouds. In fact, with the normal order of things upturned, the brightness of the sister of Phoebus [i.e. the moon] and the gleaming stars grew dark in the storm; nor did Lucifer [i.e. the morning star], the fiery herald of day, glisten and arise as a golden star as it customarily does; rather, it was blackened by the gloom as if by the darkest soot [70]. /p. 526/ The exquisite turnings of the Plough[5] are not clearly visible from the northern region of the North(-star), carefully keeping its course; and likewise the beautiful constellation of the Pleiades, offspring of Atlantis,[6] with its seven gleaming lights lies hidden: these stars climb through the heavens from the sun's (first) rising. Then the gleaming scale of Libra, with its finely-poised balance, grows slack; the circle of the Zodiac — which, I have learned, was called Mazaroth in ancient times[7] — with all its throng of twelve stars glistening in the heavens, is darkened [88]. Nor did the reddish star of Sirius gleam as it usually did, for the pitch-black mantles of cloud obscure the heavens. Nevertheless, lightning-bolts flash everywhere across the summit of the skies when the drooping fastnesses belch forth yellowish flames; their fiery nature derives from the clashing clouds. Similarly the waves of the sea crash in upon the gravelly beach, where the violence and aggression of the winds make their assault. On the surface[8] of the sea the salty waves were white-capped, since the surging whirlpool was seething with wintry floods; and the ocean with its mighty strength and savage flood-tides[9] was pounding the promontories with victory near at hand [110]: in such a way the sea swelled with the savage blasts of wind, driven by its force up against the rocky shores.

What shall I say of the mighty works of Almighty God, Whose number no-one can reckon on a counting-board?[10] Indeed, many (such works) are now apparent in the manifest miracle (which I am about to relate) — /p. 527/ Christ's undoubted mercy is revealed through these recent events [122]!

When the fourth cockcrow — as if it were the fourth vigil of the night — had roused the slumbering masses with its clarion calls, then standing in two responding ranks we were celebrating matins and the psalmody of the Divine Office:[11] suddenly with a blast of wind the pillars (of the church) trembled in their foundations; then the entire wooden structure[12] with its mighty beams shuddered and tottered, shaken in every corner of the church [136]. Amidst these mighty gales and tempests of terror our hearts trembled when our eyes beheld such horrendous events: the vault of the roof was creaking with terrifying moans and groans. At this point the congregation, fleeing across the shattered vestibule, finally seeks the door of the church in flight with disaster striking: danger is averted (only) through the Virgin's intervention! Some (of the congregation), in order to avoid the disaster, fled in two[13] bounds to the steep and slippery banks of the nearby hillside, for they feared greatly that the church would be levelled by the uproar [156].

However, when the black clouds and shadows (of night) had passed and the veil (of darkness) had been sundered by the brightness of the sunrise, and the impenetrable darkness had been cleft as if it were the likeness of death, then, seeing the fragments of the church's roof scattered everywhere, I say: look, the terrifying display of last night is now visible [166]; here the roof-beams of the church, where the most glorious (and) sweet delights (of prayer) were customarily taken, have crashed to their foundations. /p. 528/ See, here, the foliage of the leafy broom, basking in the sun, has been blasted from the walls by the wind's battering-ram. Alas, the roof's protective covering is lying all over the street [176]. Here, look, the roof-thatches have collapsed, leaving no defence (against the weather). These are the wanton sport of the cruel wind's blasts!

Furthermore, if the holy feast-day of St Paul [i.e. 29 June] had not been offering protection to the terrified souls of the fearful (congregation), we might perhaps have been struck with lightning once the roof was shattered — just as the evangelical words of the Threefold Thunderer state that the ruins of the tower [*scil.* in Siloe] fell mercilessly on some eighteen people with immense slaughter [Luc.XIII.4] [192].

Therefore let us all, snatched from danger, give thanks with gratitude to Christ Who reigns forever! Glory be to the unbegotten God and to the begotten Son together with the Holy Ghost ruling all ages beyond [200]! FINIT CARMEN ALDHELMI.

APPENDIX
ALDHELM'S PROSE WRITINGS ON METRICS

TRANSLATED BY NEIL WRIGHT

INTRODUCTION TO
ALDHELM'S PROSE WRITINGS ON METRICS

Aldhelm was the first Englishman to write a treatise on quantitative Latin verse, the *Epistula ad Acircium* (see pp. 10–11 above). The study of Latin metrics was probably introduced in England by Archbishop Theodore and Abbot Hadrian at Canterbury.[1] Aldhelm, himself a pupil of Theodore and Hadrian, describes his studies there in a letter; he tells us that metrics was a subject, 'whose obscurity the careful reader finds more intractable as the number of authorities grows less'.[2] Indeed the difficulties which Theodore and Hadrian faced in teaching metrics to English students must have been enormous. Composition in Latin verse demanded the grasp of a system of prosody alien to the English language and the combination of words of the correct scansion into various metrical schemes — the most important being the hexameter — which were quite unrelated to the patterns of stress and alliteration characteristic of Old English poetry. In spite of these difficulties, Aldhelm mastered metrics sufficiently well to become a prolific, if mechanical, composer of hexameters (see pp. 19–24 above). For this reason his *Epistula ad Acircium* is of great interest; it allows us to establish the sources on which Aldhelm drew when studying metrics and, more importantly, the extent to which he modified these sources to meet the needs of English pupils.

The *Epistula ad Acircium*, compiled between 685 and 705 and dedicated to Aldfrith, king of Northumbria, is in fact a composite work, divided into an introduction and three main sections. The introduction (cc. I–IV) consists of a dedication to King Aldfrith and a lengthy exposition of the allegorical significance of the number seven, ostensibly intended to strengthen the special relationship enjoyed by Aldhelm and the king. There follows a brief introduction to the subject-matter of the *Enigmata* (cc. V–VII; see p. 63 above). These do not, however, follow immediately. Instead, cc. VIII–X, known somewhat misleadingly as *De Metris*, are devoted to the structure of the hexameter, the metre employed in the *Enigmata*. The *Enigmata* themselves constitute cc. XI–CXI (translated by Michael Lapidge, pp. 70–94 above). The final section[3] of the letter (cc. CXII–CLII) consists of *De Pedum Regulis*, which deals with the various feet employed in metrical poetry. The work is concluded by an epilogue addressed to King Aldfrith (c. CLIII). In effect, the *Enigmata* are somewhat awkwardly positioned between two quite separate tracts on different aspects of metrics.

In the first chapter of *De Metris* (c. VIII), Aldhelm stresses the importance of the laws of prosody and announces his intention to provide examples of the metrical feet. In fact, this promise is only fulfilled in *De Pedum Regulis*, and even there Aldhelm does not explain the basic rules of Latin quantity; apparently he expected his audience to be already familiar with these rules.

Before discussing the contents of *De Metris* proper, it is necessary to explain some basic features of the Latin hexameter.[4] The hexameter line consists of six feet, the first four of which may be dactyls (a foot of one long and two shorts: $-\smile\smile$) or their metrical equivalents, spondees (a foot of two longs: $--$); the fifth foot is regularly a dactyl, while the sixth consists of a spondee or less commonly a trochee (a foot of one long and one short syllable: $-\smile$). Thus the first line of the *Aeneid* is scanned:

$$- \smile \smile \mid - \quad \smile \smile \mid \parallel \; - \mid \parallel \quad - \mid - \smile \smile \mid - \; -$$
arma virumque cano ‖ Troiae ‖ qui primus ab oris.   [*Aeneid* I.1]

The internal division of the line is also important. When a word terminates within a foot, the resulting division is called a caesura. Division after the first long of a dactyl or a spondee is termed a strong caesura (represented as $- \parallel \smile \smile$ or $- \parallel -$); division after the first short of a dactyl is termed a weak or trochaic caesura ($- \smile \mid \smile$). Within the hexameter line, the main caesurae occur in the third and fourth feet (they are also known as the penthemimeral and hephthemimeral caesurae respectively). The majority of hexameters have strong caesurae in the third and fourth feet (as in *Aeneid* I.1, quoted above), or in the third foot (usually supported by another strong caesura in the second), as in the following line:

$$- \smile \quad \smile \mid - \quad - \mid \parallel \; - \mid - - \mid - \smile \smile \mid - \; -$$
prima quod ad Troiam ‖ pro caris gesserat Argis.   [*Aeneid* I.24]

One pattern without a third strong caesura is also common. This

consists of strong caesurae in the second and fourth feet and a
trochaic caesura in the third:

‾ ˘ ˘�─ ‖ ‾ �─ ˘ ⏐ ˘⏐‾ ‖ ‾ ⏐ ‾ ˘ ˘ ⏐ ‾ ‾
quidve dolens ‖ regina ⏐ deum ‖ tot volvere casus.   [*Aeneid* I.9]

Other combinations of caesurae are far less usual.[5]

The first main section of *De Metris* (c. IX), however, does not
proceed directly to basic hexameter-structure, but deals with the
related question of elision. Elision occurs when a word ending
with a vowel or vowel + *m* is followed by a word beginning with a
vowel or *h*. Under these circumstances, the final vowel or vowel +
m has no metrical value and is elided, as in the following line,
which contains two elisions:

‾ ˘ ˘ ⏐ ‾   ‾ ⏐ ‾ ‾ ⏐‾‾ ⏐ ‾ ˘ ˘ ⏐‾ ‾
litora, mult(um) ill(e) et terra iactatus et alto.   [*Aeneid* I.3]

Originally the elided vowel was probably pronounced with
reduced emphasis, but in the Late Latin classroom (and
presumably in England) it was entirely suppressed. Such elision
had no counterpart in Old English and must have proved a major
stumbling-block for English students. Aldhelm therefore explains
the device at length and gives copious examples drawn from
Christian and Classical poets. Elision in general he terms a
metaplasm, subdivided into synaloepha (elision of a final vowel)
and ecthlipsis (elision of a final vowel + *m*); this terminology is
drawn from Late Latin grammatical theory. Aldhelm's discussion
of elision, however, marks an improvement on that found in Late
Latin grammars. There, elision was classified as only one of several
metaplasms, or metrical licences, which, combined with the fact
that the metaplasms were usually discussed separately from metrics
itself, tended to disguise the true role of elision in hexameter
poetry.[6] By giving elision such prominence at the beginning of his
treatise, Aldhelm stresses its importance, at least in scansion.[7]

The next chapter (c. X) deals with the hexameter itself. Cast in
question-and-answer form, it is largely borrowed from Audax's
Excerpta, a grammatical compilation of uncertain, though
probably late, date.[8] The chapter falls into two main sections, the
first on combinations of dactyls and spondees in the line, and the
second on caesurae.

Unfortunately Aldhelm's discussion of hexameter-structure
retains all of the irrelevancies and confusions found in the
Excerpta. His initial remarks contain only two useful statements:
that the line consists of six dactyls or spondees 'arrranged mutually
or placed alternately' and that the fifth foot is regularly a dactyl
(see pp. 195–202 below). The body of the chapter is devoted to the

schemata or combinations of dactyl and spondee possible in the line. There are thirty-two such combinations (since the sixth foot, always disyllabic, is treated as a spondee on all occasions). These can most conveniently be set out in tabular form:[9]

Line	Schemata
Without dactyls	SSSSS.
With 1 dactyl	DSSSS; SDSSS; SSDSS; SSSDS; SSSSD.
With 2 dactyls	DDSSS; DSDSS; DSSDS; DSSSD; SDDSS; SDSDS; SDSSD; SSDDS; SSDSD; SSSDD.
With 3 dactyls	DDDSS; DDSDS; DDSSD; DSDDS; DSDSD; DSSDD; SDDDS; SDSDD; SDDSD; SSDDD.
With 4 dactyls	DDDDS; DDDSD; DDSDD; DSDDD; SDDDD.
With 5 dactyls	DDDDD.

According to whether they belong to the groups permitting one, five, or ten combinations, lines are classified as *monoschemi*, *pentaschemi*, or *decaschemi*.

The value of the *schemata* is purely theoretical, yet they clearly exercised on Aldhelm all the fascination of a new toy. First, following Audax closely, he notes that, depending on its scansion, a hexameter may have between twelve syllables (for a hypothetical line of six spondees) and seventeen syllables (for a line with five dactyls); lines which apparently exceed this upper limit do not in fact do so since they always contain elision. Aldhelm then laboriously illustrates each of the *schemata* by composing entirely

186

artificial hexameters on the theme: 'Christ on the cross saved the world'. Although he also quotes a few additional lines of Christian and Classical poetry, Aldhelm is entirely concerned with theory rather than practice.[10] Indeed, his catalogue of the *schemata* is concluded by a completely erroneous discussion of the possibility of a dactyl in the sixth foot, which could only mislead the pupil (see further p. 266, n. 27 below).

This tension between theory and practice is also implicit in Aldhelm's examination of the *schemata* used by Vergil.[11] Although he gives full examples, Aldhelm's observations amount to no more than the fact that Vergil employed all those combinations which do not have a fifth-foot spondee (i.e. all the patterns regularly used by any hexameter poet!) and that Vergil used only one type of line with a spondaic fifth foot (which is false: see p. 267, n. 30 below). In this way Aldhelm completely fails to examine the hexameter rhythms preferred by Vergil.[12] This disappointing section of *De Metris* concludes with definitions of the metrical terms 'catalectic' and 'hypercatalectic', neither of which have any real relevance to hexameter-structure.[13]

The second part of *De Metris* is primarily concerned with caesurae, to which Aldhelm adopts two differing theoretical approaches. The first, entirely derived from Audax, depends on the relationship of word-ending and foot-division throughout the line. Aldhelm distinguishes three main types: *districtus*, in which no word-ending coincides with a foot-division; *divisus*, in which all word-endings coincide with a foot-division (a purely artificial type never in practice encountered in hexameter verse); and *mixtus* which combines the two former (as in the majority of hexameter lines). Clearly, this approach is too abstruse to allow the beginner to understand the role of the main caesurae in the hexameter. Aldhelm's second discussion is more helpful. He gives examples of the strong caesurae of the third and fourth feet (penthemimeral and hephthemimeral) and of the third and fourth trochaic caesurae, although in the case of the two latter his definitions are incorrect (see p. 210 below); moreover he neglects to explain how these various caesurae were normally combined in the hexameter line. To make matters worse, Aldhelm also includes a section on the *pathe* or *passiones* of the hexameter line. In fact, these licences are never found in Latin verse, but occur very occasionally in the Homeric hexameter, when a short is substituted for a long at various points in the line. Aldhelm's attempt to provide an example from Vergil's *Aeneid* only involves him in further error (see p. 209 below). On the whole, the second section of *De Metris* is of only limited value for the student.

De Pedum Regulis is a more original composition, although it too is marred by Aldhelm's pedantry. The first chapter (c. CXII), for instance, deals with the internal division (i.e. caesurae) of the twenty-eight individual feet found in metrical poetry; this was unnecessarily complicated for the English student, who was unlikely to be concerned with much more than the division of dactyls and spondees by the main caesurae of the hexameter and elegiac couplet. The bulk of *De Pedum Regulis*, however, consists of twenty-eight chapters (cc. CXIII–CXL), each devoted to one of the principal feet and giving copious lists of words which exemplify its scansion. This structure is quite different from that found in Late Latin technical treatises, where the feet are normally named, defined, and illustrated by one word only in a brief chapter.[14] While the urge to supply full lists of examples can be paralleled in the Latin grammars compiled by Anglo-Saxon scholars, Aldhelm clearly has a further purpose. As we have already seen, the major problem for the English student of metrics was the system of prosody. Aldhelm's word-lists, which often contain strings of rhyming words, provide a useful aide-mémoire to their quantities. In effect, Aldhelm converted the conventional dry catalogue of metrical feet into a rudimentary *gradus*, or metrical dictionary, of real practical value. After these extensive lists, *De Pedum Regulis* is completed by two further chapters (cc. CLI–CLII), one dealing with the rules of accentuation which are closely related to quantity, and the other on the *synzugiae*, or combined feet of five or six syllables.

As a metrical treatise, then, the *Epistula ad Acircium* is of uneven quality. *De Metris* is, with the exception of the section on elision, characterised by Aldhelm's understandable, but excessive, respect for the authority of Late Latin metrical theory. He reproduces its mechanical approach along with much that is irrelevant and misleading, besides introducing additional confusions of his own making, instead of compiling a clear introduction to the hexameter, tailored to the requirements of English pupils. His concerns are theoretical, not practical; from Aldhelm the attentive student could learn how to scan a hexameter and to recognise elision and the principal caesurae, but to master composition, the characteristic rhythms and word-patterns of the hexameter, and the combination of lines, he would have to turn to the hexameter poets themselves and to his own ear. Conversely, *De Pedum Regulis* is more successful. While it purports to be a discussion of the feet, it is in fact the first metrical *gradus* composed for non-Latin speakers.

For all its limitations, the *Epistula ad Acircium* reflects the kind of instruction in metrics which Aldhelm had received at Canterbury. In the letter which describes his studies at that centre (see p. 183 above), he gives the following details of the subject:[15]

> how, that is, the hidden components of the metrical art itself are formed from letters, words, feet, poetic figures, verses, accents, and *tempora*; the seven divisions of the discipline of the *pathe* (that is, the varieties of the *acephalos, lagaros, procilios* and the rest); which verses are counted as *monoschemi*, which *pentaschemi*, and which *decaschemi* by the fixed measurement of their feet; and how catalectic, brachycatalectic, and hypercatalectic lines are recognised by skilled argument.

In this catalogue, 'letters, words, feet, poetic figures, verses, accents, and *tempora*' largely represent the main divisions of prosody as expounded in Late Latin manuals;[16] it was on this framework that Aldhelm drew when composing *De Pedum Regulis*. Similarly, the *pathe, schemata*, and catalexis are all important elements in *De Metris*, principally drawn, as we have seen, from Audax. However, some of Aldhelm's terminology cannot be precisely paralleled in the Late Latin metrical treatises. This has led some scholars to suggest that Aldhelm drew directly on Greek sources, but this is hardly credible since his knowledge of Greek was probably no more than could be gleaned from glossaries.[17] It is far more likely that Aldhelm reproduced these terms because they had regularly been employed in the classroom by Hadrian and Theodore, the latter himself a Greek from Tarsus.[18] The *Epistula ad Acircium*, then, allows us to form a picture of the ways in which metrics was first taught to English students at Canterbury.

In spite of their obvious importance, the sections of the *Epistula ad Acircium* concerned with metrics have never been translated, although Michael Herren has published an English version of the introductory discussion of the number seven (cc. I–IV) and the epilogue (c. CXLIII).[19] In this Appendix I have translated *De Metris* in its entirety (pp. 77–96 of Ehwald's text). The body of *De Pedum Regulis*, however, consists of lengthy lists of Latin words exemplifying the scansion of particular feet. As these lists are readily accessible in Ehwald's edition, there seemed little point in reproducing them in English; accordingly, I have translated only the introductory chapter on the internal division of the feet

189

(c. CXII) and the final chapters on accentuation and the *synzugiae* (cc. CXLI–CXLII), in addition to one chapter (c. CXII: *On the Pyrrhic*) to serve as an example of those dealing with the feet themselves. No apology is made for the literal rendition of Aldhelm's extravagant prose style, which in the exchanges between master and pupil sometimes borders on the comic; but I have at all times striven to avoid ambiguity.

DE METRIS

VIII. *On the Rules of the Twenty-eight Feet*

[p. 77] In order that the theory behind these things[1] should be more clearly apparent, I have added the twenty-eight regular metrical feet from which stem not only all eight principal types (of metre) but also the kinds which, growing from the same bough, are woven with the hundred-fold leaves of metre.[2] For each foot I have heaped up as great a number of examples *[p. 78]* gathered from the various parts of speech, as I believe suits the requirements of the present small work in giving a tolerably clear introduction. Since my most famous predecessors are known to have written with examples drawn uniformly from nouns, I will follow closely in their footsteps and explain a richer set of examples. The wood of the whole of Latin is very dense with bushy groves of syllables where, as the venerable tradition of the ancients declares, many small branches of rules have sprouted from each of the roots of words. Hence this discipline is not easily grasped by beginners, especially if they lack training in the art of metre and do not know how and by what method to recognise long and short syllables and also common syllables — termed *dichronae* by the Greeks — which may be either.

IX. *On Metaplasm, Synaloepha, Ecthlipsis and the Scansion of Verses*

The whole theory of metre can be seen in this three-fold definition of syllables rather than in the spring or mount of the Muses, of which Persius Flaccus says,[3]

nec fonte labra prolui caballino
nec in bicipite somniasse Parnasso
memini me.   [*Satirae, prol.* 1–3]

By it we may correctly determine which lines are *monoscemi*,
which *pentascemi*, which *decascemi* with, unless they end with a
trochee, twenty-four *tempora*.[4] The whole versification of the
heroic hexameter or the scansion of the caesurae rests principally
on this triple rule of discernment. However in lyric and satiric
poets, because of the demands of metre, there are frequently
interspersed the coming-together, as it were, of synaloephae and
additions removed by elision. *[p. 79]* These are chiefly caused by
vowels or syllables ending with the semi-vowel *m*. Junius Juvenal
in the Fifth Book of his *Satires* elided both these at one time in the
course of one line,[5]

- - | - - ⌣ ⌣|- - |- - | - ⌣ ⌣ |- -
oment(a)? ut video nullum discrimen habendum (e)st.
                                                          [*Satirae* XIII.118]

This scans: ōmĕn spondee, ṭaŭtvĭdĕ dactyl by synaloepha, ōnŭl
spondee, lŭmdĭs spondee, crĭmēnhă dactyl, bēndŭmēst spondee by
synaloepha.[6] Again the same satirist in the Fourth Book writes,

- - | - ⌣ ⌣ |- - |- -|- ⌣ ⌣ ⌣ |-
bellor(um) exuviae, truncis affixa tropeis.   [*Satirae* X.133]

This scans: bēllō. rŭmēxŭvĭ by synaloepha. āetrŭn. cĭsāf. fĭxātrō.
pĕis. In this way Annaeus Lucanus, the poet of Cordoba, in his
Eighth Book elided twice in one line,

- ⌣ ⌣| - -|- ⌣ ⌣ |- ⌣ ⌣ |- ⌣ ⌣ |- -
quar(e) agit(e) Eoum comites properemus in orbem!
                                          [*De Bello Civili* VIII.289]

Again in the *Tenth Book* he says,

- - | - - |- ⌣ ⌣ |- ⌣⌣ |- ⌣ ⌣ ⌣|- -
hinc terg(o) insultant pedites; via nulla saluti;
                                          [*De Bello Civili* X.538]

and elsewhere,

- - |- ⌣ ⌣ |- - |- ⌣ ⌣ |- ⌣ ⌣ |- ⌣
extremoqu(e) epulas mensasque petemus ab orbe!
                                          [*De Bello Civili* IX.430]

Hence Paulus the Quaestor elided the letter *m* thus,[7]

- ⌣ ⌣| - - |- ⌣ ⌣|- ⌣ ⌣ |- ⌣ ⌣|- -
Tartare(am) in sedem sequitur nova nupta maritum.

Thus also Prosper, the poet and orator, is known to have elided
the same letter twice in the book he entitled *Epigrammata*, saying

```
 -   -  |  -   -  |-   -  |-   -  |- ᴗᴗ |  -   -
```
non coept(um) aut auctum, non hic mutabile quicquam (e)st,

[*Epigrammata* III.5]

and again later,

```
 -  -  |  -   -  ᴗ +   -   |-   -  |  -  ᴗ  ᴗ |-  -
```
caelest(em) ad patriam tendens cognosce vocantem!

[*Epigrammata* XXXI.1]

The same synaloepha can be found in the verses of the Sybilline poetess, who says,[8]

```
 -   -|   -   - |-   ᴗ  +   -  |-   ᴗ  ᴗ |-   -
```
tunc ill(e), aeterni species pulcherrima regni.

The grammarian Phocas provides an example of synaloepha in his first line,

```
 -   ᴗᴗ|   -  -|-       -  |-  ᴗᴗ |  -  ᴗ  ᴗ +  -
```
ars mea multorum (e)s, quos saecula prisca tulerunt!

[Keil, *Grammatici Latini* V.410.1]

/p. 80/ Isidore elided vowels in this manner,[9]

```
 -  -|-     -  |-   ᴗᴗ +  -  |  -ᴗᴗ|-  ᴗ
```
argutusqu(e) inter latices et musica flabra,

[*Anthologia Latina*, no. 483, line 2]

and Vergil in his Eleventh Book,

```
 -  ᴗᴗ |   -  ᴗ ᴗ|-  -  |-   -    -  |-  ᴗ  ᴗ|-  -
```
Ocean(um) interea surgens Aurora reliquit.   [*Aeneid* XI.1]

In *Aeneid* Book VII he also includes both synaloepha and ecthlipsis in one line:

```
 -   ᴗ  ᴗ|   -   - +  - |-       -  |-  ᴗ  ᴗ|-  -
```
nunc repet(o): Anchises fator(um) arcana reliquit.   [*Aeneid* VII.123]

This scans: *nŭnc rēpĕ. tŏānchī. sēsfă. tŏrūmār. cănārĕ. lĭquīt.* The ambiguity of scansion often confuses these two metaplasms. They are distinguished by the following difference of definition; if [in the line quoted above] the first vowel is elided, this will be synaloepha, if the second, it will be ecthlipsis,[10] as may be read with care in the final line of the *Book of Kings* [i.e. Cyprianus Gallus's metrical version of the Heptateuch]:[11]

```
 -  ᴗ +  -|-   -  |-     -  |-  ᴗ  ᴗ|-  -
```
purpureis maior Persar(um) in sede tyrannis.

Vergil's book entitled *Pedagogus* begins,[12]

carmina si fuerint te iudice digna favore,
  reddetur titulus purpureusque nitor;
si minus, aestivas poteris convolvere sardas
  aut piper aut calvas hinc operire nuces.

```
```

In it he too elided a syllable,

```
 -      ⌣ ⌣  |  -  -|   - | -   ⌣  ⌣
dur(um) iter et vitae magnus labor.
```

Arator the subdeacon elides the final syllable of a genitive in his first line,

```
 -   ⌣ ⌣ |-  - |   -|-    -  |   ⌣⌣ | -   -
moenibus undosis bellor(um) incendia cernens,
```

[*Epistula ad Vigilium*, 1]

and below in an elegaic line he added,

```
 -        ⌣  ⌣|  ⌣ ⌣ |-  -  ⌣ ⌣|-  ⌣  +
inqu(e) humeris ferimur te revelante piis.
```

[*Epistula ad Vigilium*, 6]

Andreas the orator writes,

```
 -⌣⌣  |        ⌣  ⌣|-   -  ⌣⌣ |   ⌣  ⌣ |-
filius ips(e) hominis, qui deus est hominis.
```

[*Anthologia Latina*, no. 494c, line 10]

/p. 81/ I have tried to investigate and explain these two types of metaplasm from the total number of fourteen [metaplasms][13] because they are often enough found contained in the whole body of poetry-books and, unless they are first recognised by wise understanding, they are accustomed to create various obstacles of difficulties and problems of errors for those, travellers as it were, who scan them. Therefore I have gathered in throngs various metrical lines illustrating the metaplasm of synaloepha. Once they have been examined, no confusion of removed elision or hidden pit of slurred synaloepha can thereafter darken the light of the scanner or blunt the gaze of the reader.

X. *On the Exchange of Alternate Question and Answer Signified by Two Different Letters.*

In order, therefore, that the three-fold rules of the heroic hexameter can be more firmly understood,[14] I shall attempt briefly and in summary to set them out as the revered authority of the ancients is shown to have handed them down. I think that I will be able to reveal them more simply and clearly if for a short while my treatise is varied by the alternate exchange of question and answer. This was demonstrably the practice of blessed Augustine in the texts of many books — the *Soliloquies*, *On Free Will*, the book he entitled *On the Teacher* and the six books *On Music* — and of

194

Isidore in the two volumes entitled *Sinonima* or *Polionima* (this type of composition was, I think, borrowed from the eleventh class of common nouns).[15] In the same way Junillius, dedicating to Primasius, bishop of the Apostolic See, the *Regular Institutes* which he had learned from Paul the Persian, a man well instructed in the schools of the Syrians, writes 'lest there should be any confusion caused, as it often is, by negligence of antiquities, I have assigned the Greek letter M to the teacher, Δ to the pupils so that all error can be completely removed by these foreign characters, *[p. 82]* which are not used in Latin writing'.[16] Indeed the mind's intellect is better and more wisely sharpened by this method as though on a whet-stone. Thus, omitting the remaining types of metre, which are divided into a hundred various kinds,[17] let me elucidate, by setting out alternately and in turn the aforementioned characters of letters, the rules of the dactylic hexameter, which are most important, because it holds the citadel and crown of all the others.

Δ How many types of line are there in the dactylic metre? M Five. Δ What is dactylic metre? M That which consists of dactyls and spondees. Δ Surely the last foot of the line is often a trochee? M Several scholars endowed with skill in the metrical art have concluded that this foot should be excluded from the line, since any syllable at the end of the line is *adiaforos* — that is, it is ambivalent and it makes no difference whether it is long or short. For this reason some consider that the line which admits a trochee is incorrect. Theory demands that in a full line there be twenty-four *tempora*. If a trochee is allowed, the number of *tempora* is reduced to twenty-three; such a line is termed *colobos*.[18] Δ You said before that there were five types of line in the dactylic hexameter, tell me them by name. M Hexameter, pentameter, tetrameter, trimeter, dimeter.[19] Δ Which is more correct: hexameter or hexametrus? M Either, as in the case of Evander and Evandrus, the first of which derives from Greek, the second from Latin. Δ Into how many feet, then, is the hexameter or hexametrus divided? M Six, dactyls and spondees arranged mutually or placed alternately. Δ How many types of hexameter line are there? M Three. Δ Which? M Dactylic hexameter, heroic hexameter, iambic hexameter, which is also called a senarius (consisting of six single feet) and a trimeter (consisting of double feet).[20]

Δ Well then, if a hexameter line consists of six spondees, can it be called dactylic? M The line is called a *spondiazon* but the metre is dactylic. For this combination only occurs in the dactylic metre. Δ Which are dactylic hexameter lines? *[p. 83]* M Those consisting of six dactylic feet and concerning anything other than war and the deeds of heroes, as, for example, the *Bucolics*, the *Georgics* and suchlike. △ Which are heroic hexameters? M Those dealing with wars and the actions of heroes, such as the *Iliad* of Homer, the *Aeneid* of Vergil and the books of Lucan versifying the struggles of Caesar and Pompey.

△ What is the fifth foot? M A dactyl. △ Why is the fifth suitable for a dactyl? M Because the dactyl always has a special place in the fifth foot of the line, though it is placed variously in the other feet, and a line which has a fifth spondee is too rough. It is called a *spondiazon*; for example,

$$- \ -\!\mid \!\smile \ \smile\!\mid \ - \ -\!\mid \ - \!\mid \ - \!\mid \ - \ -$$

aut leves ocreas lento ducunt argento. [*Aeneid* VII.634]

For this reason one ought not to place a dactyl at the end of the line nor a spondee in the fifth foot. Hence the spondee is called the final foot by some because it makes the sixth foot its own.

△ What is the limit to syllables in the dactylic or heroic hexameter line? M Every dactylic or heroic hexameter has from twelve to seventeen syllables, since the shortest line has no less than twelve. △ But then, surely we often find lines of eighteen, nineteen and twenty syllables, for example,

$$- \ \smile \ \smile\!\mid \smile \ \smile\!\mid \ \smile \ \smile\!\mid \ \ - \!\mid \smile \ \ \smile\!\mid \ - \ -$$

sed revocare gradum superasqu(e) evader(e) ad auras,

[*Aeneid* VI.128]

or

$$- \ \smile \ \smile\!\mid \ - \!\mid \ - \ \ \smile \ \dashv \ \ - \ \smile \ \smile\!\mid -\smile \ \smile\!\mid \ - \ -$$

laurus erat tect(i) in medi(o), in penetralibus altis,

[*Aeneid* VII.59]

or

$$- \ \smile \ \smile\!\mid \ - \ \smile \ \dashv \ \ \smile \ \dashv \ \ - \!\mid - \ \ \smile \ \smile\!\mid \ - \ -$$

aut oner(a) accipiunt venient(um) et agmine facto,

[*Aeneid* I.434 and *Georgics* IV.167]

or

$$- \ \smile \ \smile\!\mid \ - \ \ \smile\dashv \ \ \smile \ \ \smile \ \dashv \ \ \smile \ \smile\!\mid - \ \smile \ \dashv \ -$$

cara mih(i) ant(e) alias nequ(e) enim novus iste Dianae.

[*Aeneid* XI.537]

M Indeed there are many of eighteen syllables, but those of nineteen are found rarely and those of twenty scarcely, if ever. But it must be noted that in metrical theory those syllables are never counted which, as I said before, form the metaplasm of synaloepha. In this way all lines which seem to exceed the aforementioned number of syllables *[p. 84]* are reduced, when the

196

elisions are discounted, to seventeen, sixteen or even fifteen syllables, as in the case of your examples above. Therefore you should know that no dactylic hexameter line can be found which is seen to exceed seventeen syllables and thus all range from that number down to twelve. △ Please explain this more lucidly and untangle it more clearly. M The dactylic hexameter line, if it consists only of spondees, will have twelve syllables, if it has one dactyl, thirteen, if two, fourteen, if three, fifteen, if four, sixteen, if five, seventeen. Each time a dactyl is added, there is an extra syllable.

△ Through how many forms can the dactylic hexameter line be seen to vary? M According to metrical theory it has thirty-two *schemata*. △ Explain the forms of these *schemata* more clearly in order. M In a line of twelve syllables there is one form, which, as I said before, is called *monoscemus*. This invariably contains only spondees and is termed a *spondiazon*, for example,

$$- \ - |- \ - |- \ - |- - | - \ - \ | \ \vdash \ -$$
hi producuntur legati Minturnenses.

This type of versification is so harsh and dour that Albinus in his book on metrics forbids[21]

spondeo totum concludere versum.

Rather the line is better decorated by the addition of a dactyl in the fifth foot. △ In a line of thirteen syllables how many *schemata* are there? M Five without a shadow of doubt. △ How? In what way? M Since in it a single dactyl is admitted amongst the spondees and is placed freely in any of the five feet.

△ The minds of those who ponder in pursuit of the twice sixteen ambiguities of the dactylic metre are more easily persuaded by numbers of examples, produced to illuminate the dark lair of foolish ignorance, than by the unsupported rambling of wandering words. M The hexameter line of thirteen syllables with one dactyl and four spondees takes, as I have said, five forms. The dactyl is placed in the first foot thus,

$$- \ \ \smile \smile | - \ - |- \ \ - | - \ \ \ - |- \ -|- -$$
in cruce confixus mundum Christus salvavit,

in the second thus,

$$- \ - | - \smile\smile \ |- \ -| - \ - |- \ -| \ - \ -$$
Christus filius aeterni salvavit mundum,

in the third thus,

$$- \ -| \ - \ -| - \ \ \ \smile \smile| - \ - \ | \ - \ \ -| \ - \ -$$
Christus per lignum crucis aufert mundi noxam,

[p. 85] in the fourth thus,

```
‒  ‒ |‒  ‒ | ‒    ‒ |‒  ‿ ‿|‒  ‒ | ‒ ‒
```
scandens in ligno Christus dedit arram vitae,

in the fifth thus,

```
‒  ‒ |‒    ‒ |‒    ‒|‒   ‒ |‒ ‿ ‿|‒   ‒
```
suspendens mundi Christus peccamina dempsit.

△ How many *schemata* does the line of fourteen syllables have? M It is most certainly defined as having ten *schemata*. △ Go through these forms in order. M The dactyl is placed in the first and second feet, the first and third, the first and fourth, the first and fifth, or the second and third, second and fourth, second and fifth, or the third and fourth, third and fifth, or the fourth and fifth: a total of ten alternating forms of *schemata*. △ Demonstrate this with examples! M The Spaniard Juvencus in the first line of his prologue reveals knowledge of this matter:

```
‒  ‒ |‒ ‿ ‿|‒  ‒ |‒ ‒ |‒ ‿ ‿|‒ ‒
```
immortale nihil mundi compage tenetur.   [*Evangelia, praef.* 1]

This scans: $\bar{\imath}mm\bar{o}r.$ $t\bar{a}l\breve{e}n\breve{\imath}.$ $h\bar{\imath}lm\bar{u}n.$ $d\bar{\imath}c\bar{o}m.$ $p\bar{a}g\breve{e}t\breve{e}.$ $n\bar{e}t\bar{u}r.$; and below,

```
‒ ‿ ‿|‒    ‒ |‒  ‒ |‒   ‒ |‒ ‿ ‿|‒ ‒
```
accumulant quorum ‖ famam ‖ laudesque poetae.

[*Evangelia, praef.* 8]

Similarly Sedulius in his metrical preface of catalectic[22] hexameters and pentameters composed his first line as a *decascemus*,

```
‒    ‒ |‒  ‒ |‒   ‿ ‿|‒  ‒ |‒ ‿ ‿|‒ ‒
```
paschales ‖ quicumque dapes ‖ conviva requiris.

[*Carmen Paschale, praef.* 1]

Juvenal writes in the Fifth Book of *Satires*,

magna quidem sacris quae dat praecepta libellis.   [*Satirae* XIII.19]

This scans: $m\bar{a}gn\bar{a}qu\breve{\imath}.$ $d\bar{e}ms\bar{a}.$ $cr\bar{\imath}squ\bar{a}e.$ $d\bar{a}tpr\bar{a}e.$ $c\bar{e}pt\bar{a}l\breve{\imath}.$ $b\bar{e}ll\bar{\imath}s.$; and below,

```
‒  ‒ |‒  ‿ ‿|‒ ‒ |‒  ‒ |‒ ‿ ‿|‒ ‒
```
quae tam festa dies, ‖ ut cesset prodere furem,   [*Satirae* XIII.23]

Lucan writes in his Tenth Book,

```
‒ ‒ |‒  ‿ ‿|‒ ‒ |‒ ‒ |‒ ‿ ‿|‒ ‒
```
felix praedo iacet ‖ terrarum vindice fato.   [*De Bello Civili* x.21]

△ In these verses which you seem to have advanced as examples, in no way have all ten regular *schemata* been clearly illustrated, but only three forms with dactyls first and fifth, second and fifth, and third and fifth; the remaining seven *schemata* are missing, as yet

198

unexemplified. Therefore I think it would be useful if, going back over the same *schemata* in order, you now try to explain comprehensively, rather than with incomplete specificity, a matter which through a passive, generalising definition you have in no way expounded fully. M The heroic hexameter line of fourteen syllables has a dactyl in the first and second feet thus,

- ˅˅ |- ˅ ˅ |- - | - - |- - | - ˅
arbiter omnipotens mundi dempsit peccata;

[p. 86] in the first and third thus,

- ˅˅ |- - | - ˅˅ |- - | - - |- -
abstulit in ligno Deus omnem mundi labem;

in the first and fourth thus,

- ˅ ˅ | - - |- - |- ˅˅ |- - | - ˅
lurida quassavit diri Deus Orci sceptra;

in the first and fifth thus,

- ˅ ˅ |- - | - - |- - |- ˅˅ | - -
triverat in ligno pendens mundi mala Christus;

in the second and third,

- - | - ˅ ˅ | - ˅ ˅ |- - |- - | - ˅
Christus de cruce tetra tulit mundi peccata;

in the second and fourth,

- - | - ˅ ˅ | - - |- ˅˅ | - - | - ˅
Christus de cruce contrivit mala mundi cuncta;

in the second and fifth,

- - | - ˅ ˅ | - - |- - | - ˅ |- -
Christus de cruce salvavit iam saecla triumphans;

in the third and fourth,

- - | - - |- ˅ ˅ |- ˅ ˅ |- - |- -
Christus purgavit generis maculas humani;

in the third and fifth,

- - | - - |- ˅ ˅ | - - |- ˅ ˅ | - -
sacra salvavit genus humanum cruce Christus;

in the fourth and fifth,

- - | - - | - - | - ˅ ˅ | - ˅ ˅ |- -
Christus nos servet iam crimina cuncta relaxans.

△ How many *schemata* does the line of fifteen syllables contain? M According to the explanations of the ancient authorities it consists, like that above, of ten *schemata*. For just as in the line of fourteen syllables there are ten variants of dactyls, in this there are the same number of spondees. △ I wish to be shown examples of these matters with lines exhibiting this form. M Lucan explains this in his Eighth Book, saying,

- ⌣⌣ | - ⌣ ⌣ ⊦ ‖ - ⊦- - ⊦ ⌣ ⌣ ⊦ - -
ardua quippe fides ‖ robustos exigit annos;

[*De Bello Civili* VIII.282]

and also in the Fifth Book,

- ⌣ ⌣ ⊦ ⌣ ⌣⊦ ‖ - ⊦- -⊦⌣ ⌣ ⊦ - -
fertur ad aequoreas ‖ ac se proiecit in undas.

[*De Bello Civili* V.800]

This scans: *ferturad. aequore. asac. sepro. iecitin. undas.* Vergil in the *Georgics* writes,

- -⊦- ⌣ ⌣ ⊦ ‖ - ⊦- ⌣ ⌣ ⊦ ⌣ ⌣ ⊦ - -
Ascraeumque cano ‖ Romana per oppida carmen;

[*Georgics* II.176]

and Paul the Quaestor says,[23]

- ⌣⌣ ⊦ - ⊦- ‖ -⊦- ⌣ ⌣ ⊦ ⌣ ⌣ ⊦ -
arbiter aurarum ‖ qui fluctibus imperat atris.

Thus lines of this type are termed *decascemi*. △ I consider this kind of answer completely unsatisfactory, unless these specifically excerpted lines are increased to ten by a comprehensive list. M The hexameter line of fifteen /p. 87/ syllables with three dactyls has ten *schemata* in this way: dactyls in the first, second and third feet,

- ⌣ ⌣⊦ ⌣ ⌣⊦ ⌣ ⌣⊦ - ⊦- - ⊦- -
iam veneranda Dei suboles mundum salvavit;

in the first, second and fourth,

- ⌣ ⌣⊦ ⌣ ⌣⊦ -⊦ ⌣ ⌣ ⊦ - - ⊦- ⌣
iam memoranda Dei proles cruce salvat saecla;

in the first, second and fifth,

- ⌣ ⌣⊦ ⌣ ⌣⊦ -⊦ - ⊦ ⌣ ⌣ ⊦ - -
en veneranda Dei proles salvat cruce mundum;

in the first, third and fourth,

- ⌣ ⌣ ⊦ - - ⊦- ⌣ ⌣ ⊦ ⌣ ⌣⊦ - - ⊦ - -
in cruce suspensus sine crimine salvat mundum;

in the first, third and fifth,

- ⌣ ⌣ ⊦ - ⊦- ⌣ ⌣⊦ -⊦ ⌣ ⌣⊦-
omnibus in ligno tribuit sperare salutem;

in the first, fourth and fifth,

- ⌣ ⌣ ⊦ - -⊦ - ⊦- ⌣ ⌣⊦ - ⌣ ⌣ ⊦ -
in cruce confixus iam saecula prisca novavit;

200

in the second, third and fourth,

    ‒ ‒ |‒ ⌣ ⌣ |‒ ⌣ ‒|+ ⌣ ⌣|‒ ‒|‒ ‒
mundum iam veneranda Dei suboles salvavit;

in the second, third and fifth,

    ‒ ‒| ‒ ⌣⌣ |+ ⌣ ⌣ |‒   ‒| ‒ ⌣ ⌣|‒ ‒
Christo concelebretur honor, qui saecla beavit;

in the second, fourth and fifth,

    ‒ ‒| ‒ ⌣⌣ |+   ‒ |‒ ⌣⌣|‒ ⌣⌣ | ‒ ‒
Christo concelebret praeconia debita mundus;

in the third, fourth and fifth,

    ‒   ‒ | ‒ ‒| ‒ ⌣⌣ |‒ ⌣ ⌣ |‒ ⌣ ⌣ | ‒ ‒
emptus Christo concelebrans cane carmina mundus.

△ How many *schemata* does the line of sixteen syllables have?
M The same number as I have already demonstrated in the case of
the line of thirteen syllables: five. △ Give examples of these
schemata drawn from the books of the authors. M Lucan in his
Third Book writes,

    ‒ ‒|‒   ⌣ ⌣|‒|| ⌣ +|‒   ⌣ + ⌣ ⌣|‒ ‒
fractarum subita‖ratium periere ruina.   [*De Bello Civili* III.597]

This scans: *frāctă. rŭmsŭbĭ. tărātĭ. ŭmpĕrĭ. ĕrĕrŭ. īnă.* It should be
noted that metricians consider this and similar lines praiseworthy
because after division by scanning no part of speech is found intact
— as is often the case in the other types of *schemata*.[24] Paul the
Quaestor in the *Action of the Graces* says,[25]

    ‒ ⌣⌣ |‒   ⌣ ⌣ +|| ‒ | ‒ ⌣ ⌣ +| ⌣ ⌣ |‒ ‒
Oceanum rapidis ‖ linquens repetensque quadrigis.

Vergil writes in the *Bucolics*,

    ‒ ⌣⌣ |⌣⌣ ⌣+|| ⌣ ⌣ +| ‒|‒ ⌣ ⌣ +| ‒
pergite, Pierides! ‖ Chromis et Mnasullus in antro.

                                      [*Eclogues* VI.13]

/p. 88/ Persius Flaccus says in two consecutive verses:

    ‒ ⌣ ⌣ | ‒ ⌣ ⌣+|| ⌣ ⌣ +|‒ ‒|‒   ⌣⌣|‒ ‒
non equid(em) hoc studeo, ‖ populatis ut mihi nugis
    ‒ ⌣ ⌣|‒ ‒|‒|| ⌣⌣ ⌣|‒   ⌣ ⌣ |‒ ⌣⌣|‒ ‒
pagina turgescat‖dare pondus idonea fumo.   [*Satirae* V.19–20]

Just as in the line of thirteen syllables a dactyl can be found in five
positions, the line of sixteen can have a spondee in these same
places in turn. Such lines are called *pentascemi* because of these five
schemata. △ I think it would not be foolish to set out correctly
and in order the five forms of these *schemata*, which have been
illustrated above by lines from the poets. M The heroic line of

sixteen syllables with four dactyls has five forms thus: dactyls in the first, second, third and fourth feet,

— ˘ ˘ |— ˘ ˘|— ˘ ˘|— ˘ ˘ | — — | — —
iam veneranda Dei suboles cruce mundum salvat;

in the first, second, third and fifth,

— ˘ ˘ |— ˘ ˘ |— ˘ ˘|— — |— ˘ ˘ | — —
iam veneranda patris soboles salvat cruce mundum;

in the first, second, fourth and fifth,

— ˘ ˘ |— ˘ ˘|— — |— ˘ ˘|— ˘ ˘ |— —
en veneranda Dei proles cruce saecla coruscat;

in the first, third, fourth and fifth,

— ˘ ˘ |— — |— ˘ ˘|— ˘ ˘|— ˘ ˘|— —
iam pietas immensa Dei cruce cuncta beavit;

in the second, third, fourth and fifth,

— — |— ˘ ˘|— ˘ ˘|— ˘ ˘|— ˘ ˘|— —
mundum iam veneranda Dei soboles cruce salvat.

△ Well then, how many *schemata* do you think must be counted in the line of seventeen syllables? M I can tell you that, like that of twelve, it has one *schema*. △ How and in what way can it come about that the smallest and largest lines have the same fixed number of *schemata*, when they are so different in syllables? M Because the one has spondees in five feet, the other dactyls in the same feet — with the exception of the sixth foot, which must be disyllabic, so that the number of syllables does not increase further. △ I open my heart to believe the tenets of the teacher and the words of the master, but I wish to learn this more certainly from the venerable poems of the ancients. M Eusebius's *Chronicles* tell us that in the fear of imminent death Vergil composed a metrical epigram for the last rites of his funeral — this is called an epitaph — saying,

Mantua me genuit, Calabri rapuere, tenet nunc.
[Migne, *Patrologia Latina* XXVII.554]

[p. 89] This scans: mantŭă. mĕgĕnŭ. ītcălă. brĭrăpŭ. ĕrĕtĕ. nĕtnunc.
His rival Lucan imitated him with these words,[26]

— ˘ ˘ |— ˘ ˘|‖ ˘ ˘|— ˘ ˘ | — ˘˘|— —
Corduba me genuit, ‖ rapuit Nero, proelia dixi;

also in the Sixth Book,

— ˘ ˘ |— ˘ ˘|— ˘ ˘|— ˘ ˘|— ˘ ˘ |— —
undique praecipiti scopulis removentibus aequor.
[*De Bello Civili* VI.24]

This scans: *úndĭquĕ. prāecĭpĭ. tīscŏpŭ. līsrĕmŏ. vēntĭbŭs. āequŏr.*
Elsewhere the aforementioned bard of Mantua writes,

at tuba terribilem ‖ sonitum procul aere canoro.　　[*Aeneid* IX.503]

Amongst other things Sedulius says this in a *monoscemus* line,

laudat et egregiae ‖ tribuit sua vota rapinae.

[*Carmen Paschale* III.128]

Prosper in his *Epigrams* composed in the same way,

recta volens animus ‖ sapiens et amator honesti.

[*Epigrammata* LXVII.1]

△ Is a dactyl, then, never placed in the sixth foot? M According
to Vergil it can be, but not in a verse in which all the other feet are
dactylic, as in the *Georgics*,

aut spumas miscent ‖ argenti vivaque sulphura.　　[*Georgics* III.449]

Some people invert this and read,

[aut spumas miscent ‖ argent(i)] et sulphura viva.

Again in the Sixth Book of the *Aeneid* he writes,

bis patriae ‖ cecidere manus, ‖ quia protinus omnia.

[*Aeneid* VI.33]

Some exclude this line on the grounds of synaloepha, but they do
not realise that synaloepha is caused by the coming-together of
vowels, either alone, as Vergil does in Book Four,

quam t(u) urbem, soror, hanc cernes, quae surgere regna,

[*Aeneid* IV.47]

and Lucan in his Fifth Book,

saeva quies pelagi maestoqu(e) ignava profundo,

[*De Bello Civili* V.442]

or with a consonant intervening as,

longius et volvens fator(um) arcana movebo.　　[*Aeneid* I.262]

This cannot be admitted in the above mentioned case, because
omnia is a separate foot as, in the *Bucolics*,

omnia fert aetas,　　[*Eclogue* IX.51]

and

203

<pre>
-   ͝ ͝ | -   ͝ ͝ |-
</pre>
omnia vincit amor.   [*Eclogue* X.69]

Thus, unless it is rejected by present-day metricians, it is even possible for a line to consist of six dactyls, as in this verse,

<pre>
   - ͝ ͝ -|- ͝ ͝ |- ‖ ͝ ͝ |- ͝ ͝ | - ͝ ͝ | - ͝ ͝
</pre>
/p. 90/ interea tenero ‖ mihi bucula pascere gramine,

and elsewhere,

<pre>
- ͝ ͝ |- ͝ ͝ |-   ‖ ͝ ͝ |-   ͝ ͝ |- ͝ ͝ | - ͝ ͝
</pre>
at tuba terribilem ‖ sonitum procul excitat horrida.[27]

△ How have metricians named these verses which end with a dactyl? M Such verses are termed acatalectic by metricians as, for example,

<pre>
- ͝ ͝ | - ͝ ͝ | - ͝ -|- ‖ ͝ ͝ |- ͝ ͝ |- ͝ ͝
</pre>
sidera pallida defugiunt ‖ face territa luminis,

and the above two examples.[28]

△ Now that you have catalogued the thirty-two kinds of *schemata*, I beg you to set out in an orderly and clear list of examples how many kinds can be found in the poems of Vergil, Lucan, Persius Flaccus or Terentius Afer.[29] M Of the above thirty-two types I have been unable to find more than seventeen in the poetry of those authors, with the exception of Terence, who following Menander wrote comic volumes rather than heroic verse and gave their prologues to the stage in his defense (apologies as it were), when he was gnawed by the dog-like tooth of his rivals. △ I wish to know these seventeen types more clearly. M In the line of thirteen syllables Vergil used two *schemata*, those with dactylic second or fifth feet. A second foot dactyl is found in,[30]

<pre>
-   - |- ͝ -|- ‖ - | -   - |-   - | -   -
</pre>
aut leves ocreas ‖ lento ducunt argento,   [*Aeneid* VII.634]

and a fifth foot dactyl in,

<pre>
-    - |- - |- ‖ - | -   -| - ͝ ͝ | - -
</pre>
sed vos electi ‖ ferro qui scindere vallum,   [*Aeneid* IX.146]

and below,

<pre>
-    - |-   - | - ‖ - |- -| - ͝ ͝ |- -
</pre>
ductores Teucrum ‖ primi dilecta iuventus.   [*Aeneid* IX.226]

△ How many types did he use from the line of fourteen syllables? M Only four: either a dactyl is placed in the first and fifth foot as,

<pre>
- ͝ ͝ |-   - |- -|‖- |-   -|- ͝ ͝ | - -
</pre>
/p. 91/] filius huic contra ‖ torquet qui sidera mundi,

[*Aeneid* IX.93]

or in the second and fifth,

```
  -   -  |-  ∪  ∪|-    ‖  - |-   -  |  -  ∪  ∪  |-  -
```
et nox atra polum ‖ bigis subvecta tenebat,   [*Aeneid* V.721]

or in the third and fifth,

```
     -      - |-    -  |-  ‖  ∪  ∪  |-  -  |-  ∪  ∪ |-  -
```
urb(em) orant, taedet ‖ pelagi perferre laborem,   [*Aeneid* V.617]

or in the fourth and fifth,

```
  - -  |   - - |- |-  ‖  -  |-  ∪  ∪ |-  ∪  ∪ |-  -
```
stridens traiecto ‖ haesit tepefacta cerebro.   [*Aeneid* IX.419]

△ How many types did he employ from the line of fifteen
syllables? M Although the line is called *decascemus*, he took six
types from it: either a spondee is found in the first and second feet
as,

```
  -  -  |-  -  |-  ‖ ∪  ∪  |-   ∪  ∪ |  -  ∪  ∪ |-  -
```
scindit se nubes ‖ et in aethera purgat apertum,   [*Aeneid* I.587]

or in the first and third,

```
  -  -  |-  ∪  +   ‖- |-  ∪∪ |-  ∪  ∪|-  -
```
interclusit hiemps ‖ et terruit auster euntes,   [*Aeneid* II.111]

or in the first and fourth,

```
  -   - |-  ‖  ∪  ∪ |-   ∪ | ∪ |-  ‖  -  |- ∪  ∪ |- -
```
cum fletu ‖ precibusque tulit, ‖ per sidera testor,

                                                               [*Aeneid* III.599]

or in the second and third,

```
  -  ∪∪ |-  - |-  ‖  - |-  ∪  ∪ |- ∪  ∪ |-  -
```
adnuit et totum ‖ nutu tremefecit Olimpum,   [*Aeneid* IX.106]

or in the second and fourth,

```
  -   ∪  ∪|-  - | -  ‖  ∪  ∪ |-  -  |-  ∪  ∪ |-  -
```
iamque vale! torquet ‖ medios nox umida cursus,   [*Aeneid* V.738]

or in the third and fourth,

```
  -  ∪  +  ∪  ∪ |-‖ - |-  - |-  ∪  ∪ |-  -
```
Ascanius meriti ‖ tanti non immemor umquam.   [*Aeneid* IX.256]

△ How many types is he known to have taken from the line of
sixteen syllables? M Although the Greeks called this line
pentascemus, our poet employs four types: either a spondee is
found in the first foot as,

```
  -  - |-  ∪  ∪ |-   ∪  +  ‖ ∪  ∪ |-  ∪  ∪ |-  ∪
```
Cartago premat Ausoniam, ‖ nihil urbibus inde,   [*Aeneid* X.54]

and elsewhere in two consecutive verses,

```
  -  - | -  ∪  ∪ |-‖ ∪  ∪ |  -  ∪  ∪    |-  ∪  ∪ |- ∪
```
cernat semineci ‖ sibi me raper(e) arma cruenta
```
  -  - |-   ∪  ∪ |-   ‖  ∪  + ∪∪|-  ∪  ∪ |- -
```
victoremque ferunt ‖ morientia lumina Turni,   [*Aeneid* X.462–3]
```

205
```

or in the second,

$$- \; \smile \; \smile \; \vert \text{-} \; - \vert \; - \; \Vert \; \smile \; \vert \text{-} \; - \; \smile \; \smile \vert \text{-} \; \smile \; \smile \; \vert \text{-} \; -$$

dentibus infrendens ‖ gemitu graditurque per aequor,

[*Aeneid* III.664]

or in the third,

$$- \; \smile \; \smile \; \vert \text{-} \quad \smile \; \smile \; \vert \text{-} \; \Vert \; - \vert \text{-} \; - \; \smile \; \smile \vert \text{-} \quad \smile \; \smile \; \vert \text{-} \; \smile$$

Graiugenumque domos ‖ suspectaque linquimus arva,

[*Aeneid* III.550]

or in the fourth,

$$- \quad \smile \; \smile \vert \text{-} \; \smile \smile \vert \Vert \; \smile \; \smile \vert \quad - \; - \vert \text{-} \; \smile \; \smile \vert \text{-} \; -$$

hunc cape consiliis ‖ soci(um) et coniunge volentem,

[*Aeneid* V.712]

and again,

$$- \; \smile \; \smile \vert \Vert \; \smile \; \smile \vert \quad - \; \smile \vert \smile \; \vert \text{-} \; \Vert \; - \vert \text{-} \; \smile \; \smile \vert \text{-} \; -$$

Ascanius ‖ gale(am) ante pedes ‖ proiecit inanem.   [*Aeneid* V.673]

△ Finally how many types does he use from the line of seventeen syllables? M It rejoices in only one sort of *schema*, without which it is seen to completely lack other types of *schemata*. The line is called *monoscemus* in Greek, since all the feet except the last scan as dactyls,

$$- \quad \smile \; \smile \vert \text{-} \; \smile \; \smile \vert \text{-} \; \Vert \; \smile \; \smile \vert \text{-} \; \smile \; \smile \; \vert \text{-} \; \smile \; \smile \vert \text{-} \; -$$

nos procul inde fugam ‖ trepidi celebrare recepto;

[*Aeneid* III.666]

[p. 92] Similar is the first line of the Tenth book,

$$- \quad \smile \; \smile \vert \text{-} \; \smile \smile \vert \Vert \smile \; \smile \; \vert \text{-} \quad \smile \; \smile \vert \text{-} \quad \smile \; \smile \vert \text{-} \; -$$

panditur interea ‖ domus omnipotentis Olimpi,   [*Aeneid* X.1]

and in the Twelfth Book,

$$- \quad \smile \; \smile \vert \text{-} \; \smile \; \smile \vert \Vert \smile \; \smile \vert \text{-} \quad \smile \; \smile \vert \text{-} \; \smile \; \smile \vert \text{-} \; -$$

tum lapis ipse viri ‖ vacuum per inane volutus,   [*Aeneid* XII.906]

and in the *Georgics*,

$$- \; \smile \quad \smile \vert \text{-} \; \Vert \; \smile \; \smile \; \vert \text{-} \; \smile \vert \smile \vert \; - \; \Vert \; \smile \; \smile \; \vert \text{-} \quad \smile \; \smile \vert \; - \; -$$

ille volat ‖ simul arva fuga ‖ simul aequora verrens.

[*Georgics* III.201]

△ What is a catalectic heroic line? M Vergil provides an example saying,

$$- \quad \smile \; \smile \vert \text{-} \quad \smile \; \smile \vert \text{-} \; \smile \quad \smile \vert \text{-} \quad \smile \; \smile \vert \text{-} \; \smile \smile \vert \; - \; -$$

et tonicae manicas et habent redimicula mitrae;   [*Aeneid* IX.616]

This scans: *ettŏnĭ. caemănĭ. căsēthă. bentrēdĭ. mĭcŭlă. mītrae.*;
and in the Eleventh Book,

$$- \; \smile \; \smile \vert \text{-} \quad \smile \; \smile \vert \Vert \; - \vert \text{-} \quad - \vert \; - \; \smile \; \smile \vert \text{-} \; -$$

fecerat et tenui ‖ telas discreverat auro;   [*Aeneid* XI.75]

206

and in the *Book of Judges* [i.e. Cyprianus Gallus],

septuaginta prius ‖ truncarat corpora regum;

and Lucan in his Third Book,

primus Caesareis ‖ pelagi decus addidit armis.

[*De Bello Civili* III.762]

△ What is a hypercatalectic hexameter line? M When one syllable is added to the fixed number of the six feet. △ Quote a verse composed in this way! M,

alma Venus Paphon ingreditur, ‖ rosa luceat ex aditis

and elsewhere,

rumpere claustra manu ‖ socios gelidis dare de scopulis.

A hypercatalectic verse is also admitted in a dactylic pentameter; for example,

O Deus omnipotens ‖ largire viam precibus

and elsewhere,

pulchra puella comas ‖ ambit sibi palmitibus.[31]

△ How many types of caesura are there in the hexameter line? M Four. △ Tell me the names of these caesurae! M *Districtus, divisus, mixtus* and *priapeius*.[32] △ Which line is *districtus*? M That in which no part of speech, when scanned, coincides with a foot. △ I would learn better from examples than unsupported eloquence. M Arator provides an example,

mortalisque sibi studium proponat origo.

[*De Actibus Apostolorum* I.871]

[p. 93] This scans: *mortā. līsquĕsĭ. bĭstŭdĭ. ŭmprō. ponāto. rīgo.*: here no complete word is found in any foot. Elsewhere he writes,

largiri ‖ salvantis opem ‖ numerusque dierum.

[*De Actibus Apostolorum* I.883]

Prosper in his *Epigrams* says,

fallaces semper ‖ curis torquentur amaris;

[*Epigrammata* LXVIII.1]

207

and Vergil,

‒ ‒ | ‒ ‖ ‒ ⊦ ⌣|⌣ ⊦ ‖ ⌣ ‒ ⌣|‒ ⌣ ⌣|‒ ‒
infandum ‖ regina iubes ‖ renovare dolorem.   [*Aeneid* II.3]

The poet Symphosius produces a *districtus* line, saying,

‒ ⌣ ⌣ |‒ ⌣ ⌣ ⊦ ‖ ‒ | ‒ ‒ |‒ ⌣ ⌣ ⊦ ‒
dulcis odor nemoris, ‖ flamma fumoque fatigor.

                                        [*Aenigmata* XLVII.1]

△ Which line is *divisus*? M That in which the parts of speech
are divided in scansion — that is, it has as many parts of speech as
feet — for example,

‒ ⌣ ⌣| ‒‒ | ‒ ‒ | ‒ ‒ |‒ ⌣ ⌣|‒ ‒
dic mihi Clio quisnam primus fingere versus.

But a line of this kind, lacking a penthemimeral or hepthemimeral
caesura, is not freely admitted in the dactylic hexameter by
modern practice.[33]
  △ Which line is *mixtus*? M That which contains both, part
districtus, part *divisus*. △ I shall follow the theory more easily if
you provide examples. M Vergil in Book Four writes,

‒ ‒ ⊦ ⌣ ⌣ ⊦‖ ‒ | ‒ ‒ | ‒ ⌣⌣| ‒ ‒
at regina gravi ‖ iamdudum saucia cura   [*Aeneid* IV.1]

and next,

‒ ⌣ ⌣ ⊦ ‒ ⊦ ‖ ‒| ‒ ‒| ‒ ⌣ ⌣ ⊦ ⌣
vulnus alit venis ‖ et caeco carpitur igne.   [*Aeneid* IV.2]

The Sybilline prophetess says,[34]

‒ ⌣ ⌣ ⊦ ⌣ ⌣ ⊦ ‖ ‒ | ‒ ⌣ ⌣| ‒ ⌣⌣ |‒ ‒
denumerat tacitis ‖ tot crimina conscius ultor.

Elsewhere a poet says,[35]

‒ ⌣ ⌣ |‒ ⌣ ⌣ ⊦ ‖ ‒| ‒ ⌣ ⌣ | ‒ ⌣ ⌣ ⊦ ‒
Petrus apostolicae ‖ qui culmina praesidet arcis;

This scans: *Pĕtrūsă. pŏstŏlĭ. căequī.* — the *districtus*-section —
cŭlmĭnă. prăesīdĕt. ārcĭs. — the *divisus*-section.
  △ Which line has a priapeian caesura? M That which is found to
be written in the priapeian metre. △ What is the priapeian metre?
M When the first three feet of the hexameter line are bound
together but divided and separated from the following three. △ I
wish to be shown examples of this from real verses. M Vergil
provides one in the *Bucolics*,

‒ ⌣⌣ ⊦ ‒ ⊦⌣ ‖ ⌣ ⌣ ⊦ ‒ ⊦‒ ⌣ ⌣ ⊦ ‒
ut puero Phoebi ‖ chorus adsurrexerit omnis;   [*Eclogues* VI.66]

208

also a sybilline verse illustrates this,[36]

vivat ut aeterno ‖ bonus ac malus ardeat igne;

[p. 94] also Symphosius,

ore procax non sum, ‖ non sum temeraria lingua;

[*Aenigmata* XCVIII.2]

and Vergil,

aut Ararim Parthus‖bibat aut Germania Tigrim.　　[*Eclogues* I.62]

△ Why is it called the priapeian metre? M Because most poems of this kind are written in honour of Priapus; for which reason many consider this type of composition more suitable for bucolic poetry.
△ What is the pithian metre? M The same as the hexameter.
△ Why is it called pithian? M Some think it is because in this metre were first composed the oracles of Apollo, who is named Pithius after the python which he killed. When, it is said, he pursued that snake with arrows on Parnassus to avenge his mother, the inhabitants of Delphi praised him with eloquent rhetoric in this metre.
△ How many *pathos* do you maintain are included in the dactylic hexameter and what are they?[37] M *Pathos* are called *passiones* in Latin and are six in number: *acephalos, procephalos, lagaros, procilios, dolichuros* and *miuros* or *spicodis*. △ What is *acephalos*? M A line without a head, when the first syllable is lengthened against its nature. △ Give an example drawn from an authority. M The second line of Vergil's *Aeneid* is *acephalos*:[38]

Italiam fato profugus.　　　　　　　　[*Aeneid* I.2]

[p. 95] He permitted the *barbarism* of the substitution of a tribrach for a dactyl. Similarly the other *passiones* are found in the middle or at the end of the verse. △ Since it is tedious to examine and illustrate these *passiones* in order, let only the last be explained! What is the *miuros* or *spicodis*? M *Mys* in Latin means 'mouse' or 'shrew-mouse' and from this first element is derived *miuros*, 'mousey'. △ What is a *spicodis*? M In Greek *spix* signifies 'hornet': hence *spicodis*. Both *miuros* and *spicodis* can be seen to have one meaning, since the limbs of both animals end in a thin and graceful tail. So too does the line, which ends with a pyrrhic.
△ What is the penthemimeral caesura and what does it mean?

M Penthemimeris is *semiquinaria* in Latin. *Emis* means *semi* just as *emispherium* is translated by *semispera* in Latin — that is the half of the sky poised with equal balance above or below the earth. The penthemimeris occurs in the heroic line when, after the first two feet, there follows a syllable which ends a part of speech, as,

– – |– ˘ ˘ ⊦ ‖ ˘ ˘ ⊦ – |– ˘ ˘ |– –
truncum terra tegit, ‖ latitant in caespite limphae.

[Symphosius, *Aenigmata* LXXII.1]

Similarly Prosper writes in his *Epigrams* about prayer to the Lord,

– ˘ ˘ |– ˘ ˘ ⊦ ‖ – ⊦ – |– ˘ ˘ |– –
cum prece sanguineas ‖ fundebat corpore guttas.

[*Epigrammata* LXXI.3]

△ What is the hephthemimeral caesura? M In Latin it is called *semiseptenaria* and occurs when, after the first three feet, there follows a syllable which ends a part of speech, as,

˘ ˘ ˘ ⊦ – ⊦ ˘ ˘ ⊦ ‖
Musa mihi causas memora, ‖   [*Aeneid* I.8]

and elsewhere,

– – |– ˘ ⊦ – – | –
nec pepli radios poscunt. ‖   [Symphosius, *Aenigmata* XVII.2]

Phocas writes,

– – ⊦ ˘ ˘ ⊦ ‖ ˘ ˘ ⊦ ‖ ˘ ˘ |– ˘ ⊦ –
te longinqua petens ‖ comitem ‖ sibi ferre viator.

[Keil, *Grammatici Latini* V.410.7]

[p. 96] △ Which is the caesura *trititrochaicus* or the third trochee? M When the third foot ends with a dactyl,[39] as the poet [i.e. Symphosius] demonstrates, saying,

– ˘ ˘ |– ˘ ˘ ⊦ ‖ ˘ ˘ |– ˘ ˘ ˘ |– ˘ ˘ ⊦ –
hoc volo, ne breviter ‖ mihi sillaba prima legatur,

[*Aenigmata* LXXXIV.3]

and elsewhere,

– – |– ˘ ˘ |– ‖ ˘ ˘ ⊦ – |– ˘ ˘ ⊦ –
nec iam terra vocor, ‖ licet ex me terra paretur.

[*Aenigmata* XCI.3]

An epigram of Prosper also exemplifies the third trochee,

– ˘ ˘ | – – ⊦ ‖ ˘ ˘ |– – |– ˘ ˘ ⊦ –
at bona, quae vere ‖ bona sunt nec fine tenentur.

[*Epigramata* XCIV.5]

△ What is the definition of the caesura *tetartitrochaicus*, which some call the fourth bucolic. M When in the fourth foot a part of speech ends with a dactyl.[40] △ Please make this more apparent with a clear list of examples. M In the first *Eclogue* Vergil states,

          - ˘ ⊦ - ⊦ ‖- | - ˘˘|
nos patriae fines ‖ et dulcia linquimus arva;   [*Eclogue* I.3]

and below,

        - ˘ ˘ ⊦ - | - ‖˘ ˘ ⊦˘ ˘ |
saepe tener nostris ‖ ab ovilibus imbuit agnus.   [*Eclogue* V.8]

Paulinus [of Nola] in his first line begins,

        - ˘˘| - ˘ ˘ ⊦‖ ˘ ⊦ ˘ ˘ |
annua vota mihi ‖ remeant, simul annua linguae.   [*Carmina* XV.1]

It should be noted that the rules of bucolic poetry demand that the
fourth foot always ends with a dactyl; Vergil overcome by the
difficulty of the task neglected this rule.[41]

△ Now that you have explained the daunting difficulties of the
metrical art more clearly than day, the moment and your plan
demand that you reveal the problematical riddles, which you
promised, in verses of shining urbanity and then teach the orderly
theory of each of the feet, with the exception of the unnecessarily
complicated *synzugiae*. M I would already be doing so, were not
your exacting questions anticipating me and forcefully, as it were,
preventing me from hurrying on.

[NOTE: at this point in the *Epistula ad Acircium* Aldhelm inserts
his hundred *Enigmata*; the prose treatise *De Pedum Regulis*
follows the *Enigmata*].

DE PEDUM REGULIS

CXII. *A Second Tract of Alternate Questions and Answers on the Rules of the Feet.*

[p. 150] △ Now that you have laid out the proposed *enigmata* and discussed melodious metres, your promised method of progress demands that you reveal the many rules of the feet with examples drawn from the various parts of speech, and especially of those feet which the grammarians are known to have made their own. M The entire collection of all the feet consists of three times forty plus four, or one hundred and twenty-four, but of this confusing multitude only twenty-eight are used by the metricians skilled in the eloquence of poetry: those which in no way exceed four syllables. △ It would please me to hear this explained more clearly and openly. M There are four feet of two syllables, eight of three and sixteen of four. These feet are the special province of the grammarians and from them sprouts the discipline of the hundred-fold metres. △ How many are the feet of the rhetoricians, which belong to the rules of oratory and aid urbane prose writing? M Thrice thirty and thrice two, or ninety-six, which Greek learning terms *synzugiae*. Thirty-two feet consist of five syllables and sixty-four *synzugiae* are formed by various combinations. △ How many attributes do the feet have? M Seven: arsis and thesis, number of syllables, *tempus*, resolution, *figura* and metre. △ What is the difference between arsis and thesis? M Arsis means 'rising' and thesis 'falling'. Arsis falls on the first part of a noun or verb, thesis on the second. They say that this distinction was discovered to differentiate the *tempora* of the feet, e.g. *polus* in which *po* is the arsis and *lus* the thesis. This rule is naturally followed by *crocus, thronus, torus, aetas, aestas* and all the nouns and verbs *[p. 151]* whose form demands their inclusion below as examples of the pyrrhic and spondee.[42]

△ How many types of divisions are there within the feet, especially those which are known to concern the grammarians? M According to the tradition said to be passed down by the authority of our forebears this division is three-fold. The division of some feet is *aequa* [one to one], of some *dupla* [two to one] and of several *sescupla* [three to two].[43] Ancient knowledge has formalised their names as dactylic, iambic, paeonic respectively. △ I beg you to expound the rules of this three-fold division more clearly. M There are ten feet which are divided one to one and are weighed as it were by an equal balance of *tempora*, since their arsis and thesis are equally poised: the pyrrhic, spondee, dactyl, anapaest, proceleumatic, dispondee, diiambus, ditrochee, antispastus and coriambus. △ How many feet are divided by separation of two to one? M Six: iamb, trochee, molosus, tribrach, ionicus minor and maior; whose arsis or thesis rises or falls with an unequal balance of *tempora*. △ What is division of three to two, why is it so called and which feet are so divided? M It is called *sescupla* to represent half the two to one, since one part exceeds the other not by twice its size, but a half thereof, so that it exceeds the one to one — by the extent as it were of a small measure — by the addition of a *tempus*, although the two to one excels it by virtue of its double *tempus*. Seven feet divide three to two: the bacchius, palimbacchius, amphimacrus and the four paeons. △ How and by what method *[p. 152]* can one ascertain whether the arsis or thesis have more *tempora*? M All syllables of nouns, verbs or any other part of speech are counted from the end not the beginning. Thus the *tempora* of the arsis and thesis are indicated by the accent which may fall in three fixed positions: the final, the penultimate and the antepenultimate. If the antepenultimate has an acute accent (it never has a circumflex) the arsis has more *tempora*, but if the penultimate has an acute or a circumflex, then instead the thesis will have the larger number.

CXIII. *On the Pyrrhic.*

△ Now I breathlessly await to hear the list of examples of the pyrrhic foot, particularly those drawn from the major parts of speech, the regular nouns and verbs. M These are the nouns which are recognised to have sprouted from the manifold root of the five declensions: *deus, decus, pius, genus, pecus, bonus, modus, domus, lupus, lepus, latus, chorus, crocus, torus, thronus, dolus,*

nemus, novus, scelus, opus, locus, equus, cibus, reus, comes, Ceres,
seges, acus, manus, malus — if it means 'bad', is a pyrrhic of two
shorts, e.g.

    ‒ ˘ ˘|‒   ˘ ˘|
ille malus Calabris errans in saltibus anguis,   [*Georgics* III.425]

and in the *Eclogues,*

    ‒ | ‒ ˘ ˘ |
ut me malus abstulit error;   [*Eclogues* VIII.41]

but if it means the mast of a ship, to which the sails and ropes of
the yard-arms are attached, it is a regular trochee of a long and a
short, as in the Fifth Book of Vergil's *Aeneid,*

      ⊢   ‒|‒   ‒ |
quis innexa pedem malo pendebat ab alto;   [*Aeneid* V.511]

also if *malus* is the fruit-tree — also called *melarius* — it is
feminine and is again a trochee, as in the *Georgics,*

    ⊢   ‒|‒   ‒ |
et steriles platani malos gessere valentes —   [*Georgics* II.70]

apis, lapis, avis, canis, cinis, famis, sitis, chelis, clamis, cutis, polus,
globus, homo, leo, caro, Maro, ovis, scrobis. This foot can also be
found with the termination *r*, though not always in the same
declension: *pater, puer, piger, niger, siler, socer, gener, aper, caper,*
tener, miser, celer, iter, scaber, sacer, ruber, amor, glomer, iubar,
cruor, honor, sator, soror, labor — but if this is the deponent verb,
then the *la* is long, e.g.,

    ‒ ˘ ˘ |
labitur invalidae deformis gloria flammae —
                 [Sedulius, *Carmen Paschale* V.92]

iecur, ebur, ager, timor, liquor — if this is the noun of the third
declension, then it is a pyrrhic, as in Arator,

    ‒   ˘ ˘ | ‒ ‒
de rore dapes, de caute liquores
                 [*De Actibus Apostolorum* II.59]

and below,

    ⊢   ˘ ˘ | ‒   ˘ ˘ |
aereusque liquor solidis induruit escis,
                 [*De Actibus Apostolorum* II.62]

but if *liquor* is a verb of the third conjugation, or order, as the
grammarian Valerius pleased to call it, it is a trochee, as in Vergil's
Georgics,

        canis cum montibus umor

‒ ᵕ ᵕ |

liquitur et zephiro putris se glaeba resolvit —   [*Georgics* I.43–4]

rosa, faba, aqua, mora, rota, coma, via, toga, gula, scola, plaga: if
plaga designates a quarter of the sky, it is a pyrrhic, as is shown by
a hexameter of Ambrose, bishop of Milan,[44]

                ⊦ ᵕ ᵕ |

dumque colorati rutilat plaga caerula mundi,

and by Sedulius,

   ⊦ ᵕ ᵕ ⊦   ‒ |

quattuor inde plagas quadrati colligit orbis;

                     [*Carmen Paschale* V.190]

but if it is a revenging blow, it is a regular trochee, as the same
bard shows in the verse of the gospel poem,

        ⊦   ‒ ⊦   ᵕ ᵕ |

qui tegit et plagam trepidat nudare medenti.

                     [*Carmen Paschale* IV.78]

It should be noted that some monosyllabic nouns produce a
pyrrhic in the oblique cases — that is, genitive and ablative — *crux
crucis, nux nucis, grex gregis, lar laris, sal salis, mas maris, nix nivis,
nex necis, pix picis, prex precis, pes pedis, grus gruis, trabs trabis,
bos bovis, dux ducis, trux trucis.*

△ Now that you have completed this limited summary of
regular nouns which belong by right to the domain of this first
foot, add examples of verbs. M Verbs of both the first and third
short conjugation scan in the same way: *voco, veto, levo, seco,
neco, puto, cavo, lito, voro, nego, amo, frico, plico, dico — dicas,
dicat* with a short *i*, as in the poet,[45]

             ⊦ ᵕ ᵕ ⊦ ‒

virgo Maria tibi Sixtus nova templa dicavi.

/p. 154] This belongs to the first conjugation; but *dico dicis dicit*
third conjugation has a long *i*, as in

‒ ᵕ ᵕ |

dicitis agricolis nautisque venire fragosam —

              [Juvencus, *Evangelia* III.299]

*paro, aro, crepo, sono, tono, novo, cibo, cubo, ligo, mico, creo, meo,
beo, rigo, lito, labo, loco, rogo, iugo, fugo, lavo* — this differs from
labo 'to totter' in that the former is transitive, the latter intransitive
— *roto, pio, hio* — its frequentative, or iterative, is *hieto hietas hietat*
and its inchoative *hisco hiscis hiscit* — *volo* — both *volo volantis*
and *volo volentis* can be shown to exemplify the pyrrhic, e.g.

ᵕ ᵕ |-
volitans per aequora mundus,

[Sedulius, *Carmen Paschale* II.1139]

and

| - ᵕ ᵕ |- -
et plura volentem/ dicere deseruit —   [*Aeneid* II.790–1]

cano, cado, fremo, gemo, fero, gero, tero, sero, sino, ago, meto, peto, tego, colo, bibo, rego, lego, traho, scio, cio — hence *excire* — *vomo, pluo, spuo, emo, nuo, queo, eo, fluo, luo, ruo, struo, loquor, precor, sequor, queror, reor, fruor, moror.* Defective verbs also belong to this class: *libet, placet, piget, pudet, iuvat, decet, liquet, licet.* △ Then these verbs of the two conjugations will always be pyrrhic when they end in -*o*? M As long as the final syllable is shortened, they are without doubt pyrrhics, e.g.

‾ ᵕ
malo manere niger, minus ultima fata verebor,

[Symphosius, *Aenigmata* LVIII.3]

or

‾ ᵕ ᵕ
nec gero magna simul, sed congero multa vicissim,

[Symphosius, *Aenigmata* XXII.3]

and again,

|- ᵕᵕ |
nolo sepulcra pati, scio me submergere terrae;

[Symphosius, *Aenigmata* LIII.3]

but if that syllable is lengthened, then most certainly they become an iamb, as in Vergil:

‾ ‾ |-   ᵕ ᵕ |- ‾ |- ᵕ ᵕ |- ᵕ ᵕ| ‾ ‾
Ascraeumque cano Romana per oppida carmen.   [*Georgics* II.176]

This scans: *Ascrāe. ūmquĕcā. nōRŏ. mănăpĕr. ōppĭdă. cārmēn.*[46]
△ Can a pyrrhic or an iamb be placed in a hexameter line seeing that you have produced examples in hexameters? M If the verbs of these conjugations are adduced independent of other parts of speech and without metrical versification, then they will follow the rules of the pyrrhic of iamb: /p. 155/ but in a dactylic poem the theory of scansion and division by caesurae into *cola* and *commata* will force them to be separated and subordinated to the demands of the dactyls and spondees. This could be easily proved without frivolous trickery or deceit by a thousand lists of examples. △ With what accent or *prosodia* do we pronounce this complex

216

assembly of nouns and verbs which scan as pyrrhics? M In disyllables of two shorts the penultimate has an acute accent.

[NOTE: I omit from my translation a number of chapters, each devoted to one particular metrical foot, which consist almost entirely of lists of Latin words. The metrical feet in question are the spondee, iamb, trochee, tribrach, molosus, anapest, dactyl, amphibrach, amphimacrus (or cretic), bachius, palimbachius, proceleumaticus, dispondee, diiamb, ditrochee, antespastus, choriamb, major and minor ionic, first, second, third and fourth peon, first, second, third and fourth epitritus. These various chapters constitute pp. 155–99].

CXLI. On Accentuation.

[p. 199] An accent is a speech-sign showing the right path to the reader. There are ten accents: acúte, gràve, circumflêx, long, short, *dasia* , *psili, apostrofus', hyfen-, hypodiastoli,.* These are divided into four categories: *toni, tempora, respirationes* and *passiones.* A *tonus* either emphasises or diminishes the middle of a strongly voiced syllable ... There are three *toni*: acute, grave and circumflex. An acute *[p. 200]* is an oblique stroke ascending to the right, e.g. *páx, píx, núx.* A grave is a down-stroke to the right, e.g. *hòmo, bònus, pàrvus.* A circumflex is a combination of the acute and grave, e.g. *mêta, mûsa, côepi. Tempus* is a sign revealing hidden quantity. There are two *tempora*: long and short. A long denotes a long vowel, e.g.

arma virumque cano, Troiae qui primus ab oris;   [*Aeneid* I.1]

a short denotes a short vowel, e.g.[47]

ingentes actus carmina nostra canunt.

A *spiritus* is produced by the voice and is either hurried or soft. There are two *spiritus*: *dasia* and *psili. Dasia* denotes a syllable which is aspirated e.g. *homo habitans habens; psili* denotes a syllable produced at the tips of the lips, e.g. *orator adiit orare.* A *passio* is unpronounced and differentiates between joined, whole and divisible. There are three *passiones*: *apostrofus, hyfen* and *hypodiastoli. Apostrofus* signifies an omitted vowel or — in Greek but not in Latin — two vowels. A *hyfen* denotes a compound of two part or whole words, e.g. *lucifer unigenitus* and *primogenitus.*

A *hypodiastoli* divides adjacent letters to prevent ambiguity, e.g.

viridique in litore conspicitur, sus.   [*Aeneid* VIII.83]

Thus no-one makes the error of reading *ursus*.

According to the Greeks the acute may fall in three places, according to the Romans in two: the penultimate and the antepenultimate. Penultimate means having the accent one syllable from the end, e.g. *árma, órna, ónus*; antepenultimate means having the accent two syllables from the end, e.g. *Basílius, Gregórius, Bobátius*. The circumflex may fall in two places according to the Greeks, but according to the Romans in one. This accent falls one syllable before the end, e.g. *câelum, câeli, caelôrum. Tempŏra* are placed on vowels when they are long or short, e.g. *nĭhil, ămem, flamĭna, mĭnus*. A *spiritus* is placed on an initial, or more rarely a medial, vowel, e.g. *huius, traho, [p. 201] inveho*. An *apostrofus* is placed above, but is used in Greek not Latin. A *hyfen* is placed below to the right, e.g. *sub, urbanus*. A *hypodiastoli* is placed below in the opposite way to the *hyfen*, e.g. *Constantinopolis*.

CXLII. *On the Synzugiae*

Since I have now set out the regular metrical feet of the grammarians, which, as I have already stated, number twenty-eight, I think it would be best for my treatise, pressed as I am by the goad of speed, to try to pass over the many, various combinations of the *synzugiae*, which belong to the discipline of rhetoric. Their names are known to be *proxilius, diprolius, diopros, trampus, cribussus, namprossimalus, phymarus, atrorbus, rivatus, pranulus, linuatus, machaus, matrimus, phynulus* and *febrinus*.[48] These feet are the special property of the rhetors, which the metricians reject with complete disdain, since they exceed four syllables. The *proxilius* consists of three longs and three shorts and may be represented - - - ⌣ ⌣ ⌣. By contrast the *diprolius* has three shorts and may be represented ⌣ ⌣ ⌣ - - -. The *diopros* and the *trampus* differ by the alternate positioning of two syllables, respectively - - - ⌣ ⌣ ⌣ and ⌣ ⌣ ⌣ ⌣ - -. The remaining *synzugiae* vary by regular alternations similar to the above. The name *synzugia* means a composite figure and can in a genitive plural reach nine syllables and twenty-two letters, e.g.   *Constan-*

tinopolitanus if we say *pontifex Constantinopolitanus* and in the genitive *pontificum Constantinopolitanorum*.

[NOTE: the *Epistula ad Acircium* concludes with an *Allocutio excusativa* addressed to King Aldfrith, translated by Michael Herren in *Aldhelm: The Prose Works*, pp. 45–7].

NOTES

GENERAL INTRODUCTION (pp. 1–4)

[1] Bede, *Historia Ecclesiastica* V.18 (ed. B. Colgrave and R. A. B. Mynors [Oxford, 1969], p. 514): 'Scripsit et alia nonnulla, utpote uir undecumque doctissimus; nam et sermone nitidus, et scripturarum, ut dixi, tam liberalium quam ecclesiasticarum erat eruditione mirandus'.

[2] Ehwald (as cited in full in n. 20 below), p. 498; trans. M. Herren, in M. Lapidge and M. Herren, *Aldhelm: The Prose Works* (Ipswich, 1979) (hereafter cited as *Prose Works*), p. 167.

[3] Thus, for example, a letter by Lul to one Dealwine, dated 745 x 746, requests certain works of Aldhelm, either in prose or metre or rhythmic octosyllables, to serve as consolation in his (voluntary) exile: M. Tangl (ed.), *S. Bonifatii et Lullii Epistolae*, Monumenta Germaniae Historica, Epistolae Selectae I (Berlin, 1916), p. 144. Lul addresses Dealwine as *iam dudum magistro*; since we know Lul to have come from Malmesbury, there is some presumption that Dealwine was at Malmesbury as well, where manuscripts of Aldhelm's writings were no doubt readily at hand. No manuscripts from Malmesbury of this early period are known to survive; but note that the fragmentary Miskolc manuscript (Z. Mady, 'An VIIIth Century Aldhelm Fragment in Hungary', *Acta Antiqua Academiae Scientiarum Hungaricae* XIII [1965], pp. 441–53) was written in England and is of continental provenance.

[4] For example, the see of Würzburg was established by Boniface in 742 and its first bishop was the Englishman Burghard. In a booklist surviving from Würzburg and dating from c. 800, there is an item *liber althelmi* (see E. A. Lowe, 'An Eighth-Century List of Books in a Bodleian Manuscript from Würzburg and its probable Relation to the Laudian Acts', *Speculum* III [1928], pp. 3–15). It is worth noting that one of the earliest surviving manuscripts of the prose *De Virginitate*, now Würzburg, Universitätsbibliothek M. p. th. f. 21, was copied at Würzburg in the mid-ninth century from a manuscript in Anglo-Saxon minuscule script, now lost. Possibly the lost manuscript was identical with the item in the booklist; in any case it shows that manuscripts of Aldhelm were available at Würzburg soon after its foundation; and similar assumptions may be made with respect to Fulda and Mainz.

[5] See G. Glauche, *Schullektüre im Mittelalter: Entstehung und Wandlungen des Lektürekanons bis 1200 nach den Quellen dargestellt* (Munich, 1970), pp. 18, 24, 29–30, 33 and 93.

[6] See G. Becker, *Catalogi Bibliothecarum Antiqui* (Bonn, 1885), nos. 6 (Reichenau, 822), 11 (Saint-Riquier, 831) and 22 (St Gallen, s. ix); see also nos. 26, 28, 37, 38 and 59.

[7] *Alcuin: The Bishops, Kings, and Saints of York*, ed. P. Godman (Oxford, 1982); the reference to *Althelmus* is in line 1547. Aldhelm's influence on Alcuin is pervasive; for example, line 1449 of Alcuin's poem is simply Aldhelm, *CdV* 1625. Godman indexes Alcuin's debts to Aldhelm on pp. 143–4.

[8] Two manuscripts which were written on the continent in the late ninth century but which were in England by the tenth are London, British Library, Royal 15. A. XVI, and Oxford, Bodleian Library, Rawlinson C. 697.

[9] Some impression of the density of glossing which often accompanied manuscripts of Aldhelm may be gained by consulting the facsimile edition of Brussels, Bibliothèque Royale, lat. 1650, by G. van Langenhove, *Aldhelm's De Laudibus Virginitatis* (Bruges, 1941); a similar amount of glossing is found in Oxford, Bodleian Library, Digby 146 (Abingdon, s. x^{ex}). Old English glosses to Aldhelm have frequently been the subject of study (see the Bibliography, above, pp. 27–8); the Latin glosses have attracted less attention.

[10] See F. C. Robinson, 'Syntactical Glosses in Latin Manuscripts of Anglo-Saxon Provenance', *Speculum* XLVIII (1973), pp. 443–75, and M. Korhammer, 'Mittelalterliche Konstruktionshilfen und altenglische Wortstellung', *Scriptorium* XXXIV (1980), pp. 18–58, esp. 29 and 55–6.

[11] See M. Lapidge, 'The Hermeneutic Style in Tenth-century Anglo-Latin Literature', *Anglo-Saxon England* IV (1975), pp. 67–111, esp. 73–5.

[12] See above, pp. 44–5.

[13] See above, pp. 67–8.

[14] See the verbal parallels between Aldhelm and the Bonifatian correspondence noted in the edition of Tangl (cited above, n. 3) as well as those noted by Ehwald.

[15] Ed. W. Levison, Monumenta Germaniae Historica, Scriptores rerum Germanicarum (Hannover, 1905), pp. 1–57; see esp. pp. xiii–xiv, and the parallels cited in Levison's apparatus.

[16] Hygeburg, *Vita Germanuum Willibaldi et Wynnebaldi*, ed. O. Holder-Egger, Monumenta Germaniae Historica, Scriptores XV.1 (Hannover, 1887), pp. 80–117; see also E. Gottschaller, *Hugeburc von Heidenheim* (Munich, 1973), pp. 59, 81, etc.

[17] D. A. Bullough, 'The Educational Tradition in England from Alfred to Ælfric: Teaching *utriusque linguae*', *Settimane di studio del Centro italiano di studi sull'alto medioevo* XIX (1972), pp. 453–94, at 466–73.

[18] On Aldhelm's influence on Byrhtferth, see M. Lapidge, 'Byrhtferth of Ramsey and the Early Sections of the *Historia Regum* attributed to Symeon of Durham', *Anglo-Saxon England* X (1981), pp. 97–122, at 113.

[19] The waning of Aldhelm's influence is reflected in the dates of surviving manuscripts. As against the large number of manuscripts surviving from the tenth and eleventh centuries, Ehwald (pp. 541–2) lists only six of twelfth-century date; and at least one of these (London, British Library, Royal 6. B. VII) is more accurately to be dated to the second half of the eleventh century.

[20] R. Ehwald, *Aldhelmi Opera*, Monumenta Germaniae Historica, Auctores Antiquissimi XV (Berlin, 1919) (hereafter cited simply as Ehwald).

ALDHELM'S LIFE (pp. 5–9)

[1] Bede, *Historia Ecclesiastica* V.18 (ed. Colgrave and Mynors, p. 514).
[2] Faricius, *Vita S. Aldhelmi*, in J. A. Giles, *Vita Quorundum Anglo-Saxonum*, Publications of the Caxton Society (London, 1854), pp. 119–56.
[3] William of Malmesbury, *Gesta Pontificum*, ed. N. E. S. A. Hamilton, Rolls Series (London, 1870) (hereafter *GP*); the *uita* of Aldhelm constitutes Book V of that work (ed. Hamilton, pp. 330–443).
[4] There is a critical treatment of the sources for Aldhelm's life by myself and Michael Herren in *Prose Works*, pp. 5–10.
[5] Ehwald, p. 229 ('contribulibus necessitudinum nexibus conglutinatae'); *Prose Works*, p. 59.
[6] On the nature of Aldhelm's sponsorship of Aldfrith, see discussion by Herren, *Prose Works*, p. 32.
[7] *Prose Works*, pp. 52 and 56.
[8] On Aldhelm as a member of Ine's *witan*, see M. Lapidge, '*Beowulf*, Aldhelm, the *Liber Monstrorum* and Wessex', *Studi Medievali* 3rd ser. XXIII (1982), pp. 151–92, at 155.
[9] *GP*, p. 354.
[10] Faricius, ed. Giles, p. 122; *GP*, pp. 332–3. Note that the name *Kenten* looks suspiciously like that of Centwine, a well-attested early West Saxon king (cf. below, pp. 233, n. 10, and 234, n. 12).
[11] *GP*, p. 332: 'non minor decedens septuagenario'.
[12] *Ibid.*, p. 385: 'nam annos aetatis eius nulla scriptura misit in calculum; sed est coniectura non fallax grandaevum fuisse sanctum...'
[13] The conversion of Wessex is described by Bede, *Historia Ecclesiastica* III.7 (who gives no date, however); the date derives from the *Anglo-Saxon Chronicle*, s.a. 635 (the baptism of King Cynegils at Dorchester).
[14] Ehwald, p. 494; *Prose Works*, p. 164.
[15] See A. S. Cook, 'Hadrian of Africa, Italy and England', *Philological Quarterly* II (1923), pp. 241–58, and R. L. Poole, 'Monasterium Niridanum', *English Historical Review* XXXVI (1921), pp. 540–5.
[16] *GP*, pp. 333–4.
[17] See further *Prose Works*, p. 7, together with the *caveat* by D. Ó Cróinín, *Peritia* II (1983), pp. 242–4.
[18] Ehwald, p. 478; *Prose Works*, pp. 153–4.
[19] *Historia Ecclesiastica* IV.2 (ed. Colgrave and Mynors, pp. 333–5).
[20] There is no evidence that Aldhelm was ever associated with a monastery other than Malmesbury.

[21] William of Malmesbury, who did not know Aldhelm's Letter to Geraint, put the beginning of Aldhelm's abbacy in 675 (*GP*, p. 385); but on no known evidence. That William himself was not entirely confident of the date is shown by the fact that he tampered with it in his autograph copy of the *Gesta Pontificum* (Oxford, Magdalen College 172).

[22] On the institution of the *Eigenkirche*, see the older studies by U. Stutz, *Die Eigenkirche als Element des mittelalterlich-germanischen Kirchenrechtes* (Berlin, 1895), and H. Boehmer, 'Das Eigenkirchentum in England', in *Texte und Forschungen zur englischen Kulturgeschichte: Festgabe für Felix Liebermann* (Halle, 1921), pp. 301–35; on Aldhelm's familiarity with the institution, see Lapidge, '*Beowulf*, Aldhelm, the *Liber Monstrorum* and Wessex' (cited above, n. 8), pp. 156–7.

[23] There is of course Leuthere's foundation charter in favour of Malmesbury (Ehwald, pp. 507–9), but most authorities regard this as spurious (see P. H. Sawyer, *Anglo-Saxon Charters: An Annotated List and Bibliography* [London, 1968], no. 1245; see also A. S. Cook, 'A Putative Charter to Aldhelm', in *Studies in English Philology: A Miscellany in Honor of Frederick Klaeber*, ed. K. Malone and M. B. Ruud [Minneapolis, 1929], pp. 254–7). It would be safer to declare our ignorance of Malmesbury's foundation until all the relevant documents have been subjected to thorough scrutiny.

[24] William of Malmesbury is the source of our information on Aldhelm's church-building activities: *GP*, pp. 345 (Malmesbury), 346 (Bradford on Avon and the monastery next to the river Frome, perhaps at Frome itself), 363 (Wareham) and 374 (Bruton).

[25] On the difficulty of ascertaining the date, which is conventionally given as 705, see *Prose Works*, p. 10.

[26] *Historia Ecclesiastica* V.18 (ed. Colgrave and Mynors, p. 514).

[27] *GP*, p. 378.

[28] See H. M. and J. Taylor, *Anglo-Saxon Architecture*, 3 vols. (Cambridge, 1965–78), II, pp. 540–3, where it is suggested that the fabric is of tenth-century date, and hence much later than Aldhelm's time. If the remaining fabric is indeed part of the church seen by William, his attribution of the building to Aldhelm is untrustworthy. See also J. H. P. Gibb, 'The Anglo-Saxon Cathedral at Sherborne', *Archaeological Journal* CXXXII (1975), pp. 71–110.

[29] *GP*, p. 382.

[30] *Ibid.*, pp. 383–4.

[31] Faricius (ed. Giles, pp. 138–9) reports a story to the effect that Ecgwine, bishop of Worcester, learned of Aldhelm's death in a vision as he was preparing to go on a penitential journey to Rome. On his way to Rome, Ecgwine stopped at Malmesbury to render homage to Aldhelm; he was subsequently absolved in Rome — *sicut in eius Vitae legitur uolumine*. William of Malmesbury (*GP*, pp. 383–4) embellishes this story considerably: according to William, Aldhelm died at Doulting in Somerset. Ecgwine, learning of Aldhelm's death in a vision, hurried to Doulting and transported Aldhelm's remains back to Malmesbury. Stone

crosses were erected every seven miles along the route, and according to William, all of them were still to be seen. (G. F. Browne, *St Aldhelm* [London, 1903], pp. 148–80, devotes much effort to identifying the sites of these stone crosses.) The source of William's embellishment was Dominic of Evesham's *Vita S. Ecgwini* (*c.* 1100): see M. Lapidge, 'Dominic of Evesham, *Vita S. Ecgwini episcopi et confessoris*', *Analecta Bollandiana* XCVI (1978), pp. 65–104, at 72–3. Since Ecgwine's earlier hagiographer, Byrhtferth of Ramsey (*fl. c.* 1000), knew nothing of the story of Aldhelm's appearance in Ecgwine's vision, it is probable that the whole story was fabricated by Dominic; in other words, no reliance can be placed on it.

THE WRITINGS OF ALDHELM (pp. 10–18)

1 *Historia Ecclesiastica* IV.26(24) and V.15.
2 Ehwald, pp. 61–75; *Prose Works*, pp. 34–45.
3 Ehwald, pp. 75–96.
4 *Ibid.*, pp. 150–201.
5 *Ibid.*, pp. 201–4; *Prose Works*, pp. 45–7.
6 Ehwald, pp. 228–323; *Prose Works*, pp. 59–132.
7 Ehwald, p. 229; *Prose Works*, p. 59.
8 Ehwald, p. 494; *CdV* lines 2855, 2844, 2845 and 2843 respectively.
9 See the arguments of M. Herren, *Prose Works*, p. 144.
10 Ehwald, p. 229.
11 *Ibid.*, pp. 475–503; *Prose Works*, pp. 152–70.
12 J. A. Giles, *Sancti Aldhelmi Opera* (Oxford, 1844), pp. viii–ix. The first to recognize that Aldhelm could not be the author of the metrical Heptateuch was L. Müller ('Zu Ennius und den christlichen Dichtern', *Rheinisches Museum* XXI [1866], pp. 123–33, at 126), who observed that the Heptateuch was evidently the work of a native Latin speaker. Müller's suggestion was endorsed by Manitius ('Zu Aldhelm und Baeda', pp. 543–4); the attribution was finally rejected by R. Peiper (*Alcimi Aviti Opera*, Monumenta Germaniae Historica, Auctores Antiquissimi VI.2 [Berlin, 1883], pp. liii–lxiii).
13 P. Lehmann, 'Ein neuentdecktes Werk eines angelsächsischen Grammatikers vorkarolingischer Zeit', *Historische Vierteljahrschrift* XXVI (1931), pp. 738–56; see also his qualified retraction, 'Die Grammatik aus Aldhelms Kreise', *Historische Vierteljahrschrift* XXVII (1932), pp. 758–71.
14 See N. Fickermann, 'Die Widmungsbriefe des heiligen Bonifatius', *Neues Archiv* L (1935), pp. 210–21; it is now ed. G. J. Gebauer and B. Löfstedt, *Bonifatii (Vynfreth) Ars Grammatica*, Corpus Christianorum Series Latina CXXXIII B (Turnhout, 1980), pp. 9–12.
15 Ehwald, pp. 79 and 93 (*bis*). Note that the poem is not quoted by any other Anglo-Latin author (nor apparently by another medieval author) besides Aldhelm.

[16] W. Bulst, 'Eine anglo-lateinische Übersetzung aus dem Griechischen um 700', *Zeitschrift für deutsches Altertum* LXXV (1938), pp. 105–11; see also B. Bischoff, *Mittelalterliche Studien*, 3 vols. (Stuttgart, 1966–81), I, pp. 154–5.

[17] Cf. Ehwald, pp. 68 and 235.

[18] See D. Schaller and E. Könsgen, *Initia Carminum Latinorum saeculo undecimo Antiquiorum* (Göttingen, 1977), no. 8497.

[19] See *Prose Works*, pp. 8–9; and cf. the remarks of V. Law, 'The Study of Latin Grammar in Eighth-century Southumbria', *Anglo-Saxon England* XII (1983), pp. 43–71, at 50–2.

[20] Cf. line 30, 'Restituens *seu* digna bonis *seu* iusta *profanis*' with Aldhelm, *CdV* 282, '*Seu* pia perfectis *seu* certe saeva *profanis*'.

[21] *HE* V.8 (ed. Colgrave and Mynors, p. 474).

[22] Colgrave and Mynors, p. 475:
'Here lies a holy bishop's mortal frame;
In Grecian tongue is Theodore his name.
A great high priest was he, the church's head,
Who in sound doctrine his disciples fed'.

[23] *Ibid.*:
'September was the month, the nineteenth day,
When from the flesh his spirit took its way,
Climbing in bliss to share new life and love
With angel-citizens of heaven above'.

[24] See C. W. Jones, *Bedae Pseudepigrapha* (Ithaca, N.Y., 1939), pp. 69–70.

[25] Ehwald, p. 477; *Prose Works*, p. 153.

[26] Cf. the remarks of D. Ó Cróinín in *Peritia* I (1982), pp. 406–7.

[27] So it was understood by William of Malmesbury, *GP*, p. 344.

[28] *GP*, p. 336.

[29] *HE* IV.24(22) (ed. Colgrave and Mynors, pp. 414–20).

[30] Three of the charters in question are listed by P. H. Sawyer, *Anglo-Saxon Charters*, nos. 230, 1166 and 1245, and printed by W. de G. Birch, *Cartularium Saxonicum*, 3 vols. and index (London, 1885–99), nos. 50, 54 and 37 respectively. The two other documents printed by Ehwald are a confirmation of privileges by Pope Sergius I for Malmesbury (no. IV = Birch, no. 106) and a confirmation by King Ine concerning abbatial succession at Malmesbury (no. V).

[31] Ehwald, pp. 507–16; the first two of the charters printed by Ehwald are translated *Prose Works*, pp. 173–5.

[32] See the remarks of A. S. Cook, 'A Putative Charter to Aldhelm', in *Studies in English Philology*, pp. 245–7.

[33] See L. G. Whitbread, 'The *Liber Monstrorum* and *Beowulf*', *Mediaeval Studies* XXXVI (1974), pp. 434–71.

[34] In the *Liber de Natura Rerum* of the thirteenth-century Dominican scholar Thomas of Cantimpré (ed. H. Boese [Berlin, 1973]), some thirty citations are attributed to one 'Adelmus' (a common variant spelling of the name 'Aldhelmus'): of these citations, fourteen are from Aldhelm's *Enigmata*, the remaining sixteen from the *Liber Monstrorum*. The

225

implication must be that Thomas of Cantimpré was using a manuscript in which the *Liber Monstrorum* was attributed to Aldhelm. No surviving manuscript of the work bears such an attribution, however.

35 The best edition is that of F. Porsia, *Liber Monstrorum* (Bari, 1976); it is also ed. C. Bologna, *Liber Monstrorum de diversis generibus: Libro della mirabili difformità* (Milan, 1977) and M. Haupt, *Opuscula*, 2 vols. (Leipzig, 1876), II, pp. 218–52.

36 See M. Lapidge, '*Beowulf*, Aldhelm, the *Liber Monstrorum* and Wessex', *Studi Medievali* 3rd ser. XXIII (1982), pp. 151–92.

37 Thomas Wright (*Biographia Britannica Litteraria*, 2 vols. [London, 1842–6], I, p. 219) refers to a passage of Aimoin of Fleury as quoted in the *Floriacensis vetus bibliotheca* (Lyon, 1605) by the seventeeth-century historian Jean Dubois (Ioannes a Bosco). The text of Aimoin in question is his *Sermo de S. Benedicto*; Dubois's edition is reprinted in *Patrologia Latina* CXXXIX, cols. 851–70. Near the end of this work Aimoin writes: 'Nihilominus Adhelmus Anglus, primum abbas, post episcopus factus, in libro de laude sanctorum, a se edito, huius sancti patris (*scil.* Benedict) hoc modo meminit' (col. 866), and goes on to quote some seventy lines from the allegedly lost work *De Laude Sanctorum*. In fact the lines are simply the passages on St Benedict and his sister Scholastica from the *Carmen de Virginitate*, lines 842–80 and 2024–50.

38 Manitius ('Zu Aldhelm und Baeda', pp. 538 and 545), basing himself on Giles's edition of Aldhelm's writings, noted that in his *Epistola ad Acircium* Aldhelm apparently referred to a work of his own in six books entitled *De Nomine*: 'coniux, quod nomen in nominativo et vocativo cum additamento n litterae libro VI. de nomine recolo disseruisse' (Giles, p. 279). Manitius accordingly treated the work *De Nomine* as a lost grammatical treatise by Aldhelm. However, as Ehwald noted (p. 156), the manuscript used by Giles was defective in that the word *Priscianum* had fallen out after *nomen* (*Priscianum* occurs in all manuscripts collated by Ehwald). In other words, Aldhelm was simply recalling that Priscian had treated the word *coniux* in Book VI of his *Institutiones Grammaticae*.

ALDHELM AS LATIN POET (pp. 19–24)

1 Ehwald, p. 202; *Prose Works*, p. 45.

2 See the discussion of Neil Wright, above, pp. 183–90.

3 Thus the hymns in the famous Antiphonary of Bangor (*c.* 700) which are *certainly* of Irish composition are rhythmic, not quantitative. On Hiberno-Latin rhythmic verse, see W. Meyer, 'Die Verskunst der Iren in rythmischen lateinischen Gedichten', in his *Gesammelte Abhandlungen zur mittellateinische Rythmik*, 3 vols. (Berlin, 1905–36), III, pp. 303–28, and D. Schaller, 'Die Siebensilberstrophen "De mundi

transitu" — eine Dichtung Columbans?', in *Die Iren und Europa im früheren Mittelalter*, ed. H. Löwe, 2 vols. (Stuttgart, 1982), I, pp. 468–83. Much turns on whether the quantitative verses which pass under the name of Columbanus were in fact composed by the Columbanus who was trained at Bangor, founded the monasteries of Luxeuil and Bobbio, and died in 615. However, there are persuasive reasons for thinking that the quantitative poems in question were composed by an unknown Carolingian Columbanus who was active *c.* 800: see M. Lapidge, 'The Authorship of the Adonic Verses "Ad Fidolium" attributed to Columbanus', *Studi Medievali* 3rd ser. XVIII (1977), pp. 815–80. And if these reasons can be accepted, there is no further evidence that quantitative verse was composed in Ireland as early as the seventh century.

⁴ *HE* IV.2 (ed. Colgrave and Mynors, pp. 332–3).

⁵ Ehwald, p. 477; *Prose Works*, p. 152.

⁶ See the fuller discussion by M. Lapidge, 'Aldhelm's Latin Poetry and Old English Verse', *Comparative Literature* XXXI (1979), pp. 209–31. A thorough study by Neil Wright of Anglo-Latin metrical practice is in preparation.

⁷ For helpful introductions to the hexameter, see S. E. Winbolt, *Latin Hexameter Verse* (London, 1903), and G. C. Cooper, *An Introduction to the Latin Hexameter* (Melbourne, 1952).

⁸ It was a canon of style that the *ictus* or musical 'beat' (which in a hexameter fell on the first syllable of every foot) should coincide in the last two feet of the hexameter with the natural accent of the words. Obviously this coincidence could most easily be arranged by the employment of a trisyllabic word in which the natural accent fell on the first syllable (as in *culmina*) followed by a bisyllabic word in which the accent was inevitably on the first syllable (as in *caeli*), or by a bisyllabic word (*fonte*) followed by a trisyllabic word with the accent on the second syllable (as in *rigabis*). It was no doubt the simplicity of these two arrangements which commended their (repeated) use to Aldhelm.

⁹ Statistics for the classical poets are taken from G. E. Duckworth, *Vergil and Classical Hexameter Poetry: A Study in Metrical Variety* (Ann Arbor, Mich., 1969).

¹⁰ Cf. also *Enigm.* lxvii.8 (*haec nix*), *CdV* prol. 21 (*iam nunc*), *CdV* 556 (*ut sol*) and 1460 (*fas est*).

¹¹ See *Enigm.* praef. 26 (*rusticitate*) and xxx.2 (*annumerandas*).

¹² See Lapidge, 'Aldhelm's Latin Poetry and Old English Verse', pp. 223–31.

¹³ Cf. also C. W. Jones, 'Carolingian Aesthetics: Why Modular Verse?', *Viator* VI (1975), pp. 309–40.

INTRODUCTION TO THE CARMINA ECCLESIASTICA
(pp. 35–45)

[1] A more appropriate title might be *Tituli* or *Sylloge Titulorum* or the like.

[2] See M. Lapidge, 'Some Remnants of Bede's Lost *Liber Epigrammatum*', *English Historical Review* XC (1975), pp. 798–820; see esp. nos. 2, 6, 7, 8 and 10.

[3] *Ibid.*, pp. 805–6 (no. 10); see also L. Wallach, 'The Urbana Anglo-Saxon Sylloge' (cited below, n. 11), pp. 144–6, who prints the opening six lines of the poem from a fragmentary manuscript now in Urbana, Illinois; these six lines were not copied by the antiquary John Leland, and hence are not printed by Lapidge, 'Some Remnants'.

[4] Ed. E. Dümmler, Monumenta Germaniae Historica, Poetae Latini Aevi Carolini I (Berlin, 1881), pp. 304–44; see discussion by L. Wallach, *Alcuin and Charlemagne: Studies in Carolingian History and Literature* (Ithaca, N.Y., 1959), pp. 178–97.

[5] See Lapidge, 'Some Remnants', pp. 804–5, as well as L. Traube, 'Perrona Scottorum', *Sitzungsberichte der phil.-hist. Classe der königlich Akademie der Wissenschaften zu München 1900* (Munich, 1901), pp. 469–538, at 488–9; K. Meyer, 'Verses from a Chapel dedicated to St Patrick at Péronne', *Ériu* V (1911), pp. 110–11; and W. Levison, 'Zu den Versen des Abtes Cellanus von Péronne', *Zeitschrift für celtische Philologie* XX (1933–6), pp. 382–90.

[6] The principal scholarly collection of *tituli* is still *Inscriptiones Christianae Urbis Romae*, ed. G. B. de Rossi, 2 vols. (Rome, 1861–88), to be supplemented by *Inscriptiones Christianae Urbis Romae septimo saeculo Antiquiores, Nova Series*, ed. G. B. de Rossi, A. Silvagni and A. Ferrua, 5 vols. (Rome, 1922–71). See also H. Leclercq, 'Inscriptions (histoire des recueils d')', *Dictionnaire d'archéologie chrétienne et de liturgie*, 15 vols. in 30 (Paris, 1907–53), VII, cols. 850–1089, esp. 850–905 for the early medieval period.

[7] See *Epigrammata Damasiana*, ed. A. Ferrua (Rome, 1942), a superb edition of some 59 *tituli* of Damasus, some of which are preserved in manuscript but many of which are preserved as lapidary inscriptions (often fragmentary) in Roman churches. On the preservation of Damasus's *tituli* in medieval *syllogae*, see pp. 13–17.

[8] In his *Ep.* xxxii, Paulinus discusses at length the question of *tituli* and quotes a number of examples composed by himself for his church at Nola; see W. Hartel, *Sancti Pontii Meropii Paulini Nolani Epistulae*, Corpus Scriptorum Ecclesiasticorum Latinorum XXIX (Vienna, 1894), pp. 275–301, and discussion by J. Engemann, 'Zu den Apsis-Tituli des Paulinus von Nola', *Jahrbuch für Antike und Christentum* XVII (1974), pp. 21–46.

[9] See *Venanti Fortunati Opera Poetica*, ed. F. Leo, Monumenta Germaniae Historica, Auctores Antiquissimi IV.1 (Berlin, 1881), esp. I.ii–xiii, II.xi–xiii and III.vi–viii. Book IV consists entirely of epitaphs, many of which may have been inscribed on tombstones and elsewhere.

10 Most of these are printed by de Rossi, *Inscriptiones Christianae Urbis Romae*, vol. II, pt. i.

11 See L. Wallach, 'The Urbana Anglo-Saxon Sylloge of Latin Inscriptions', in *Poetry and Poetics from Ancient Greece to the Renaissance: Studies in Honor of James Hutton*, ed. G. M. Kirkwood, Cornell Studies in Classical Philology XXXVIII (Ithaca, N.Y., 1975), pp. 134–51; see also the corrections and qualifications suggested by D. Schaller, 'Bemerkungen zur Inschriften-Sylloge von Urbana', *Mittellateinisches Jahrbuch* XII (1977), pp. 9–21.

12 See P. Sims-Williams, 'Milred of Worcester's Collection of Latin Epigrams and its Continental Counterparts', *Anglo-Saxon England* X (1981), pp. 21–38, and 'William of Malmesbury and *La silloge epigrafica di Cambridge*', *Archivum Historiae Pontificae* XXI (1983), pp. 9–33.

13 Ehwald, p. 153.

14 De Rossi, *Inscriptiones Christianae Urbis Romae* II, p. 60.

15 See discussion by J. Higgitt, 'The Dedication Inscription at Jarrow and its Context', *The Antiquaries Journal* LIX (1979), pp. 343–74.

16 Ed. E. Okasha, *Hand-list of Anglo-Saxon Non-Runic Inscriptions* (Cambridge, 1971), p. 85 (no. 61); it is also printed by Higgitt, 'The Dedication Inscription', pp. 343–4.

17 J. Scott, *The Early History of Glastonbury: An Edition, Translation and Study of William of Malmesbury's "De Antiquitate Glastonie Ecclesie"* (Woodbridge, 1981), pp. 94–6; the poem is also cited and discussed by M. Lapidge in *Anglo-Saxon England* VIII (1979), pp. 290–1.

18 Some clear notion of the length of a poem which could be inscribed may be gained from Alcuin's epitaph for Pope Hadrian I (*ob.* 795), which consists of thirty-eight lines of verse (elegiac couplets) followed by a brief sentence in prose stating the day and year of Hadrian's death (the poem is ed. Dümmler, MGH, Poetae Latini Aevi Carolini I, pp. 113–14). This poem is inscribed in elegant square capitals on a block of limestone measuring approximately 7' 3" by 3' 10" and may still be seen in the entrance hall of St Peter's, Rome (there is an illustration in *Karl der Grosse: Werk und Wirkung*, ed. W. Braunfels [Aachen, 1965], pl. 7). By comparison, Ine's *titulus* is only twenty-six lines long, and could have been accommodated on a smaller piece of limestone (Scott [*The Early History of Glastonbury*, p. 199] thinks that the Ine *titulus* was not inscribed and was a confection by William of Malmesbury, but he is excessively sceptical in this respect).

19 Giles, *Vita Quorundum Anglo-Saxonum*, p. 128.

20 It is not clear, however, what particular *ecclesia* Faricius had in mind. No major church in Rome was dedicated to *both* SS. Peter and Paul. There were dedications to St Peter singly (S. Pietro in Vincoli; the Vatican itself), to St Paul singly (S. Paolo fuori le mura) and to SS. John and Paul jointly. There was a small monastery dedicated to SS. Peter and Paul associated with the titular church of S. Martino ai Monti (see R. Vielliard, *Recherches sur les origines de la Rome chrétienne* [Paris, 1959], p. 143), but Faricius is unlikely to have known of this.

229

[21] See W. Levison, *England and the Continent in the Eighth Century* (Oxford, 1946), pp. 259–60.

[22] *GP*, p. 345. One may doubt, however, that there was any church on the site of Malmesbury before Aldhelm became abbot (see above, p. 8).

[23] See below, p. 233, n. 3.

[24] See Lapidge, 'Some Remnants of Bede's Lost *Liber Epigrammatum*', p. 803.

[25] The poem is quoted by Ehwald, pp. 6–7.

[26] *GP*, p. 361.

[27] Levison, *England and the Continent*, pp. 263–4.

[28] *GP*, p. 374.

[29] It is not easy to decide whether *CE* II or *CdV* was the original home of these verses. However, the lines follow the prose *De Virginitate* so closely (including the quotation from the Song of Songs) that one can best assume that they were originally composed as part of *CdV*, and were not interpolated into that context from elsewhere. This would imply in turn that *CE* II was a later composition than *CdV* — if it was indeed Aldhelm himself (and not a later scribe) who interpolated the verses into *CE* II. See also below, p. 233, n. 8.

[30] Note that the second of these two hexameters is taken entire from *CE* III.40.

[31] M. Tangl (ed.), *S. Bonifatii et Lullii Epistolae*, Monumenta Germaniae Historica, Epistolae Selectae I (Berlin, 1916), p. 21 (no. 14).

[32] The reasons are mainly chronological: the Bugga addressed by Boniface died *c.* 760, and would thus have been too young to have built and consecrated a church before Aldhelm died in 709 or 710.

[33] See Sawyer, *Anglo-Saxon Charters*, nos. 1255 and 1429; the second of these two charters is thought by students of Anglo-Saxon diplomatic to be authentic.

[34] See Lapidge, 'Some Remnants of Bede's Lost *Liber Epigrammatum*', p. 815, and the references there cited.

[35] *Ibid.*

[36] *Ibid.*:

> Hic Christi vernae corpus sub marmore iacet:
> supremus mundi concludit terminus isthic
> quam famulam prisci vocant de nomine Buggae...
> Coentuuini haec etiam fuit en pia filia regis
> dapsilis et clemens, Christi pro nomine felix...
> ter denis egregium servansque ovile decenter
> quattuor et simul annos pia rite regebat.

[37] On the source of Faricius's information, see below, p. 233, n. 10.

[38] Giles, *Vita Quorundum Anglo-Saxonum*, p. 122.

[39] The *Breviarium Apostolorum* is listed by the Bollandists, *Bibliotheca Hagiographica Latina*, 2 vols. (Brussels, 1899–1901), no. 652, and is printed in various places, of which the most accessible is *Analecta Bollandiana* II (1883), pp. 9–10; see also B. de Gaiffier, 'Le *Breviarium Apostolorum* (*BHL* 652), tradition manuscrite et oeuvres apparentées',

Analecta Bollandiana LXXXI (1963), pp. 89–116. In one of his poems, that known as *De Virginitate*, Venantius Fortunatus gives a brief synopsis of the lives of the apostles (VIII.iii.137–50), but there is doubt about whether Aldhelm knew the poetry of Venantius (see the discussion by Lapidge in *Anglo-Saxon England* VIII (1979), pp. 288–9).

40 Cynewulf's 'Fates of the Apostles' is ed. K. R. Brooks, *Andreas and The Fates of the Apostles* (Oxford, 1961), pp. 56–60; see discussion of Cynewulf by K. Sisam, *Studies in the History of Old English Literature* (Oxford, 1953), pp. 1–28, and by D. G. Calder, *Cynewulf* (Boston, 1981), esp. pp. 27–41. On the sources of the poem, see J. E. Cross, 'Cynewulf's Traditions about the Apostles in *Fates of the Apostles*', *Anglo-Saxon England* VIII (1979), pp. 163–75.

41 See discussion by E. Bishop, *Liturgica Historica* (Oxford, 1918), pp. 139–40. Note that the sequence of saints in the litany in the Irish Stowe Missal (A.D. 792) (ed. G. F. Warner, Henry Bradshaw Society XXXII [London, 1915], p. 15) is very nearly that followed by Cynewulf; cf. W. Ginsberg, 'Cynewulf and his Sources: *The Fates of the Apostles*', *Neuphilologische Mitteilungen* LXXVIII (1977), pp. 108–14.

42 B. Botte and C. Mohrmann, *L'Ordinaire de la messe* (Paris, 1953), pp. 76–8. Note that there is no disparity between Gelasian and Gregorian sacramentaries in this respect.

43 The work is listed by E. Dekkers and A. Gaar, *Clavis Patrum Latinorum*, 2nd edn. (Steenbrugge, 1961), no. 1191; it is ed. Patrologia Latina LXXXIII, cols. 129–56.

44 See A. Vaccari, 'Una fonte del *De ortu et obitu*', in *Miscellanea Isidoriana* (Rome, 1936), pp. 165–75.

45 See B. Bischoff, 'Die europäische Verbreitung der Werke Isidors von Sevilla', in his *Mittelalterliche Studien*, I, pp. 171–94, at 180–1, 183 and 186. The work is elsewhere used by Aldhelm as a source for entries in his prose *De Virginitate* (e.g. those for John the Evangelist and Luke).

46 Note that the order of the apostles in Isidore is different from that followed by the Canon of the Mass and by Aldhelm.

47 Isidore (*De ortu et obitu*, c. lxix) records the following incidents in the life of St Paul: that he sowed the seed of God (*uerbi gratiam seminauit*), that he was called by God, that he ascended the third heaven, that he spent a night and a day in the depths of the sea, that he defeated the Pythonissa of Delphi and saved a girl, that he brought the adolescent boy Eutychus back to life, that he blinded a sorcerer Elymas, that he cured a lame man, that he overcame the bite of a viper and that he cured the father of Publius. Aldhelm (*CE* IV.ii) follows this sequence of miracles precisely, with the small exception that he reverses the order of the last two. Aldhelm does not include any miracles that are not mentioned by Isidore. It could not be a matter of chance that two commentators select the same Pauline miracles and present them in the same order.

48 Patrologia Latina LXXXIII, col. 151.

49 For example, those in London, British Library, Royal 2. A. XX (ed. A. B. Kuypers, *The Prayerbook of Aedeluald the Bishop, commonly*

called the Book of Cerne [Cambridge, 1902], p. 212) and in the Stowe Missal (ed. Warner [as cited above n. 41], p. 15).

[50] Ehwald (pp. 8 and 32) therefore errs in referring the poem to an actual church: 'In sancti Mathiae apostoli <ecclesia>'. He is followed by Levison (*England and the Continent*, p. 262) and by Lapidge and Herren (*Prose Works*, pp. 11–12, who compound the error by referring to Matthew rather than Matthias!).

[51] See Lapidge, 'Some Remnants of Bede's Lost *Liber Epigrammatum*', pp. 816–17.

[52] See Godman, *Alcuin: The Bishops, Kings, and Saints of York*, p. lxviii.

[53] *De Abbatibus*, ed. A. Campbell (Oxford, 1967), p. xlvi.

[54] Ed. K. Strecker, Monumenta Germaniae Historica, Poetae Latini Aevi Carolini IV.3 (Berlin, 1896), pp. 943–61; see Strecker's full apparatus of *fontes*. The poem is in effect a cento of verses from Aldhelm and other earlier poets.

[55] Three manuscripts are in question: Paris, Bibliothèque Nationale, lat. 8318, ff. 73–80 (s. x); St Gallen, Stiftsbibliothek 869 (s. ix^{ex}), and Vatican City, Biblioteca Apostolica Vaticana, Reg. lat. 251 (s. ix[1], not s. x, as stated by Ehwald).

[56] See Dümmler, MGH, Poetae Latini Aevi Carolini I, p. 164; Schaller, 'Bemerkungen zur Inschriften-Sylloge von Urbana', p. 14, and Sims-Williams, 'Milred of Worcester's Collection of Latin Epigrams', p. 35.

[57] The two *tituli* are listed by Schaller and Könsgen, *Initia Carminum Latinorum*, nos. 6598 and 6793; they are printed by Ehwald, pp. 6–7.

[58] Listed by Schaller and Könsgen, *Initia Carminum Latinorum*, no. 14738, and printed by Ehwald, p. 20. (It is also printed with the poems of Boniface in Corpus Christianorum Series Latina CXXXIII, p. 315.) The two manuscripts in question are: Cambridge, University Library, Gg. 5. 35 (St Augustine's, Canterbury, s. xi^{med}) and Vatican City, Biblioteca Apostolica Vaticana, Pal. lat. 591 (s. xv).

THE CARMINA ECCLESIASTICA (pp. 46–58)

[1] As mentioned above (p. 38), this poem is not preserved in any surviving manuscript, but was apparently included in Milred of Worcester's *sylloge* of epigrams, whence it was known to Faricius and William of Malmesbury, both of whom quote it *in extenso* (Giles, *Vita Quorundam Anglo-Saxonum*, pp. 128–9, and *GP*, pp. 345–6). Although there are minor variants between the two quoted versions (note especially: line 5 *uenerantur* Faricius, *celebrantur* William; line 7 *candida caelorum recludens* Faricius, *candida qui meritis recludis* William; etc.), it would seem that the disparities are to be attributed to the copying habits of the two authors, rather than to the supposition that they were copying from different manuscripts. William at least was a notoriously careless transcriber: see Lapidge, 'Some Remnants of

Bede's Lost *Liber Epigrammatum'*, pp. 813–14 and 820. A cento of lines excerpted from the poem is preserved in Berlin, Deutsche Staatsbibl., Phillipps 167 (*olim* Cheltenham 1825) (Saint-Aubin of Angers, s. ix), on which see above, p. 45.

² The church in question was probably Aldhelm's own church at Malmesbury, which was dedicated to SS. Peter and Paul; see above, p. 38.

³ This line ('Claviger aetherius portam qui pandis in aethra') is a conflation of two hexameters from Arator, *De actibus apostolorum* (I.899, 'Claviger aetherius', and I.1076, 'qui portam pandit in astris'). Note that Aldhelm's line is quoted in his *Epistola ad Geruntium* (= Letter IV; Ehwald, p. 485), which may indicate that *CE* I was composed earlier than the *Epistola ad Geruntium*, a work which can be dated fairly precisely to 672 or 673 (*Prose Works*, pp. 141–3). However, Aldhelm used the same line on other occasions: *CE* IV.i.2 (Ehwald, p. 19), *Epistola ad Acircium* (Ehwald, p. 68), and prose *De Virginitate*, c. LV (Ehwald, p. 314). The ubiquity of the line in Aldhelm's work renders useless its value as a dating criterion.

⁴ This poem is preserved in the three continental manuscripts listed above, p. 232, n. 55; some nine lines of it are also preserved in Berlin Phillipps 167 (see below, n. 8).

⁵ On the identification of this church dedicated to St Mary — probably a second church at Malmesbury — see above, p. 39.

⁶ Virtually the same line (*CE* II.6) occurs as *CdV* praef. 25.

⁷ These two lines have been recycled from *CE* I.8–9.

⁸ Lines 13–31 of this poem correspond verbatim to *CdV* 1691–1709. On the chronological implications of this interpolation, see above, p. 230, n. 29, where it is suggested that the original home of the verses was *CdV*, not *CE* II. It would be interesting to know whether the interpolation was done by Aldhelm himself: certainly he was not above recycling lines of his verse, as the two previous notes will demonstrate. It may be significant that Berlin Phillipps 167, which preserves only part of *CE* II (lines 1–2, 4–8, 10 and 12) and which was evidently copied from an Anglo-Saxon exemplar, preserves no trace of the interpolated lines 13–31.

⁹ The identity of this church depends in turn on the identity of Bugga; see above, p. 40 and below, n. 11.

¹⁰ Recall Faricius's statement that Aldhelm was of *regia stirpe* and was the son of one *Kenten*, apparently a misspelling of Centwine (Giles, *Vita Quorundam Anglo-Saxonum*, p. 122). Faricius's sources for this statement were some Anglo-Saxon documents which he could not understand — he was Italian — but which were explained to him by an English interpreter: 'antiquissimis Anglicanae linguae schedulis saepius ex interprete legendo audiuimus' (*ibid.*). If they had any genuine basis, these documents might indicate that Aldhelm was the son of King Centwine, and hence was the brother of the Bugga in question; but the matter is problematical, to say the least.

[11] The identity of Bugga is unknown (see above, p. 40). Her name is evidently a hypocoristic form of a name with the theme *-burg*, such as *Æthelburg* or *Cuthburg* or *Osburg* or the like. Recall that Aldhelm dedicated his prose *De Virginitate* to a sorority of nuns at Barking Abbey, among whom was one Osburg, who was said to be related to Aldhelm *contribulibus necessitudinum nexibus* — words which could conceivably describe a sister.

[12] Centwine was king of Wessex 676–85; see Bede, *Historia Ecclesiastica* IV.12 and *Anglo-Saxon Chronicle* s.aa. 676, 682 and 685. On Centwine, see C. Plummer (ed.), *Venerabilis Baedae Opera Historica*, 2 vols. (Oxford, 1896), II, p. 221, and H. M. Porter, 'Centwine', *Notes & Queries for Somerset and Dorset* XXIX (1968), pp. 40–2. It is worth asking at least if this Centwine was Aldhelm's father: see above, p. 233, n. 10.

[13] The word used by Aldhelm, translated here as 'government', is *imperium*. Bede, in describing West Saxon politics of this period, makes an apparent distinction between *regnum* ('acceperunt subreguli regnum gentis') and *imperium* ('Caedualla suscepit imperium') (*HE* IV.12), where it has been thought that Bede is drawing a distinction between control of a sub-kingdom and overlordship of more than one; cf. F. M. Stenton, *Anglo-Saxon England*, 3rd edn. (Oxford, 1971), p. 68, n. 3 ('Aldhelm's statement that Centwine *imperium Saxonum rite regebat* proves that he was overlord of the whole West Saxon kingdom') and the more recent discussion of the term *imperium* by P. Wormald, 'Bede, the *Bretwaldas* and the Origins of the *Gens Anglorum*', in *Ideal and Reality in Frankish and Anglo-Saxon Society*, ed. P. Wormald (Oxford, 1983), pp. 99–129, at 107–9. The point at issue is whether Aldhelm was aware of an implicit distinction between *regnum* and *imperium*. Since Aldhelm elsewhere apparently uses the words synonymously (cf. *Enigm.* ic. 2, 'Arbiter imperio dum regni sceptra regebat' and *CdV* 1588, 'Et regit imperium'), it is doubtful if his words here concerning Centwine's realm will bear the onus of interpretation placed on them by Stenton.

[14] On the estates granted by Centwine, see P. H. Sawyer, *Anglo-Saxon Charters*, nos. 237 and 1667–9; of these, the last three have not been preserved, and the first is thought dubious by many authorities. See also H. P. R. Finberg, *The Early Charters of Wessex* (Leicester, 1964), nos. 361–3. In effect, Aldhelm's statement cannot be endorsed by surviving charters; but there is nevertheless no reason to doubt it.

[15] The context suggests perhaps that these 'recently-established churches' were *Eigenkirchen*; on which see above, p. 223, n. 22. Note also Bede's vehement remarks on the subject of such private churches or monasteries in his letter to Ecgberht (Plummer, *Venerabilis Baedae Opera Historica*, I, pp. 414–16).

[16] Unfortunately, the identity of these three battles is unknown. Our sole source for the military undertakings of Centwine is a notice in the *Anglo-Saxon Chronicle*, s.a. 682: 'In this year Centwine put the Britons

to flight as far as the sea' (D. Whitelock *et al.*, *The Anglo-Saxon Chronicle* [London, 1961], p. 23).

17 Plummer (*Venerabilis Baedae Opera Historica* II, p. 221) suggested that Centwine may have entered a monastery 'possibly compelled to do so by Cædwalla'. However, early Anglo-Saxon kings frequently entered monasteries in their declining years: see C. Stancliffe, 'Kings who opted out', in *Ideal and Reality in Frankish and Anglo-Saxon Society*, ed. P. Wormald (Oxford, 1983), pp. 154–76, at 155.

18 Cædwalla's brief reign lasted three years, from 685, when, according to the *Anglo-Saxon Chronicle* (s.a. 685), he 'began to contend for the kingdom', until 688, when he abdicated, went to Rome, was baptized by the pope, and died. The principal sources for Cædwalla are the *Anglo-Saxon Chronicle*, s.aa. 685, 686, 687 and 688, and Bede, *HE* IV.15 and V.7; see also Plummer, *Venerabilis Baedae Opera Historica* II, pp. 278–80.

19 The phrase *clementia Romae* is apparently a periphrasis for 'the pope'. It is curious that Aldhelm does not name the pope in question. The pope in 688 was Sergius I (687–701), whom Aldhelm was alleged to have visited and who allegedly granted a papal privilege in favour of Malmesbury: see *GP*, pp. 365–70. Note that Bede (*HE* V.7) gives the pope's name as Sergius.

20 There are some striking verbal similarities between Bede's account of Cædwalla's baptism (*HE* V.7) and Aldhelm's:

Bede: et in *albis* adhuc positus, languore *correptus* … solutus a carne, et beatorum est *regno* sociatus in caelis.

Aldhelm: Post *albas* igitur morbo *correptus* egrescit

Alta supernorum conquirens *regna* polorum

However, it is difficult to know what construction (if any) to place on these similarities. The simplest hypothesis may be that Bede and Aldhelm shared a common written source, now lost.

21 Ine was king of the West Saxons from 688 until his abdication in 726. See Bede, *HE* V.7 and the *Anglo-Saxon Chronicle*, s.a. 688; see also E. A. Freeman, 'King Ine', *Proceedings of the Somersetshire Archaeological and Natural History Society* XVIII (1872), pp. 1–59 and XX (1874), pp. 1–57.

22 In spite of Aldhelm's claim that Bugga's church was *praecelsa mole*, it is apparent from surviving remains that Anglo-Saxon churches of this period were small and simple in structure (see H. M. and J. Taylor, *Anglo-Saxon Architecture*, 3 vols. [Cambridge, 1965–78], III, p. 967). Aldhelm is apparently describing a double-cell building of which the eastern chamber was apsed (line 41), perhaps similar to that which survives at Stoke d'Abernon, Surrey: see Taylor and Taylor, *ibid.*, II, pp. 573–5, and B. Cherry, 'Ecclesiastical Architecture', in *The Archaeology of Anglo-Saxon England*, ed. D. M. Wilson (London, 1976), pp. 151–200, esp. 160–1; on the apse, see also below, n. 39. The twelve altars (line 40) need not imply twelve porticus or structural adjuncts, nor indeed a basilican (that is, aisled) structure; the altars

could have been recessed in the walls of the church. Aldhelm also states that the church was 'rectangular' (*quadrato*): see below, n. 30.

23 Aldhelm is here referring to a perpetual liturgical calendar. Early English examples of this type of liturgical book include the Calendar of Willibrord (see H. A. Wilson [ed.], *The Calendar of St Willibrord*, Henry Bradshaw Society LV [London, 1918]) of the early eighth century, and the Walderdorf Calendar, a fragment in Anglo-Saxon half-uncial of the mid-eighth century (see P. P. Siffrin, 'Das Walderdorffer Kalendarfragment saec. viii und die Berliner Blätter eines Sakramentars aus Regensburg', *Ephemerides Liturgicae* XLVII [1933], pp. 201–24).

24 Aldhelm describes separate choirs of monks (line 50: *fratres*) and nuns (line 51: *turba sororum*), probably segregated on either side of the church (line 47: *classibus et geminis*): compare the description of the performance of the Divine Office in Aldhelm's *Carmen Rhythmicum*, line 127 ('tum binis stantes classibus', above, p. 178). The implication here is that Bugga's church is a double monastery of men and women. On this institution in early Anglo-Saxon England, see M. Bateson, 'Origin and Early History of Double Monasteries', *Transactions of the Royal Historical Society* XIII (1899), pp. 137–98; S. Hilpisch, *Die Doppelklöster: Entstehung und Organisation*, Beiträge zur Geschichte des alten Mönchtums und des Benediktinerordens XV (Munster, 1928); and J. Godfrey, 'The Place of the Double Monastery in the Anglo-Saxon Minster System', in *Famulus Christi: Essays in Commemoration of ... the Venerable Bede*, ed. G. Bonner (London, 1976), pp. 344–50.

25 Aldhelm is here describing the performance of the Divine Office, with psalms, hymns, (antiphons) and responsories (line 52). Unfortunately, virtually nothing is known of the form of the Office in England at this period. No early office books survive (see H. Gneuss, 'Liturgical Books in Anglo-Saxon England and their Old English Terminology', in *Learning and Literature in Anglo-Saxon England*, ed. M. Lapidge and H. Gneuss [Cambridge, 1985], pp. 91–141, at 110–21). It might be surmised that the hymns in use were those of the Old Hymnal; see H. Gneuss, *Hymnar und Hymnen im englischen Mittelalter* (Tübingen, 1968), pp. 208–9. It is symptomatic of our ignorance that a recent account of the liturgy and prayer of the early English church (H. Mayr-Harting, *The Coming of Christianity to Anglo-Saxon England* [London, 1972], pp. 168–90 and 272–5) does not even mention the Office. Whatever can be learned must be learned by analogy of continental and Roman practices; for this reason, the evidence of Aldhelm — however vaguely worded — is very valuable.

26 Because Aldhelm in the following line refers to the ten strings of the lyre, it is probable that by *psalterii* (line 54) he is referring to the psaltery rather than the psalter itself. The psaltery at this stage was delta-shaped, and strung with ten strings over a hollow wooden sounding-box, as we learn from Isidore: 'est autem similitudo citharae barbaricae in modum △ literae; sed psalterii et citharae haec differentia est, quod psalterium lignum illud concavum, unde sonus redditur,

superius habet et deorsum feriuntur chordae, et desuper sonant ...
Psalterium autem Hebraei decachordon usi sunt propter numerum
Decalogi legis' (*Etym.* III.xxi.7); see also the article 'Psaltery', *The New
Grove Dictionary of Music and Musicians* ed. S. Sadie, 20 vols.
(London, Washington and Hong Kong, 1980), XV, pp. 383–7. What is
unusual is Aldhelm's statement that the psaltery was used in Bugga's
church to accompany the psalmody. Although King David is often
pictured holding a psaltery in illuminated Anglo-Saxon psalters of this
period (see, for example, J. J. G. Alexander, *Insular Manuscripts 6th to
the 9th Century* [London, 1978], pls. 74 and 146), there is apparently
no evidence that psalmody in the Divine Office was accompanied by
musical instruments of any sort. Aldhelm's evidence on this point is
precious, therefore.

27 It is worth noting that in Bugga's double monastery nuns participated
in the Divine Office by reading the scriptural lessons. The part taken
by lectors in the performance of the Office may be seen from the clear
exposition in K. Young, *The Drama of the Medieval Church*, 2 vols.
(Oxford, 1933), I, pp. 44–75.

28 On feasts of the Virgin in early Anglo-Saxon England, see M. Clayton,
'Feasts of the Virgin in the Liturgy of the Anglo-Saxon Church',
Anglo-Saxon England XIII (1984), pp. 209–33. Aldhelm's reference is
problematic, for the reason that the Nativity of Mary was celebrated on
8 September. The feast of Mary celebrated on 15 August was the
Assumption. Aldhelm, however, specifically refers to the *nativitas* of
Mary ('Istam nempe diem ... Nativitate sua sacravit virgo Maria': lines
59–60). Clayton (*ibid.*, pp. 213–18) faces the difficulty by suggesting
that Aldhelm was referring only to the day on which Bugga's church
was consecrated (line 59: 'qua templi festa coruscant'), not to a
liturgical feast of Mary. This solution is not entirely satisfactory, but
the matter could only be finally resolved if we could recover a liturgical
calendar used at Bugga's church (cf. above, n. 23).

29 On the use of glass for windows in Anglo-Saxon churches at this
period, see the remarks of Bede, *Historia Abbatum*, c. 5 (ed. Plummer,
Venerabilis Baedae Opera Historica, I, p. 368), who records that
Benedict Biscop sent to Gaul for glaziers, which at that time were
unknown in England: 'misit legatarios Galliam, qui uitri factores,
artifices uidelicet Brittanniis eatenus incognitos, ad cancellandas
aecclesiae porticumque et caenaculorum eius fenestras adducerent'
(Bede is referring to a time in the 670s). Aldhelm himself shows some
familiarity with glass-making in *Enigm.* lxxx (above, p. 87).

30 Translating *quadrato* as 'rectangular'; on the structure of the church,
see above, n. 22.

31 Unfortunately, no altar-cloth survives from early Anglo-Saxon
England. That elaborate liturgical embroideries were used elsewhere in
England at this time is clear from an early eighth-century epigram that
was included in Milred of Worcester's *sylloge* of inscriptions (the
epigram is ed. M. Lapidge, 'Some Remnants of Bede's Lost *Liber*

Epigrammatum', pp. 812–13 [no. 20]), and some idea of their luxurious appearance may be gleaned from the surviving Maaseik embroideries: see M. Budny and D. Tweddle, 'The Maaseik Embroideries', *Anglo-Saxon England* XIII (1984), pp. 65–96. On written evidence for altarcloths, see J. Braun, *Der christliche Altar*, 2 vols. (Munich, 1924), II, pp. 21–7 (the passage in Aldhelm is discussed on p. 26).

32 On medieval chalices in general, see J. Braun, *Das christliche Altargerät in seinem Sein und in seiner Entwicklung* (Munich, 1932), pp. 17–196, esp. 30–8, and pls. 1–40, and H. Leclercq, in *Dictionnaire d'archéologie chrétienne et de liturgie* II, cols. 1595–1645, s.v. 'calice'. The chalice in Bugga's church was made of gold and covered with jewels. That Anglo-Saxon chalices were often very lavishly decorated is clear not only from contemporary written evidence (see C. R. Dodwell, *Anglo-Saxon Art: A New Perspective* [Manchester, 1982], pp. 203–7), but also from surviving specimens of chalices of Anglo-Saxon or Insular inspiration or workmanship, such as the Trewhiddle Chalice, the Ardagh Chalice, and the Tassilo Chalice; see illustrations in D. M. Wilson, *Anglo-Saxon Art* (London, 1984), pls. 3, 151 and 161 respectively (on the Tassilo Chalice, see also G. Haseloff, *Der Tassilokelch* [Munich, 1951]). For another (less lavish) example recovered from the River Thames, see D. M. Wilson, *Anglo-Saxon Ornamental Metalwork 700–1100 in the British Museum* (London, 1964), pp. 179–81 (no. 90) and pl. XXXIV.

33 No Anglo-Saxon patens appear to survive from this early period. For patens from elsewhere in medieval Europe, see Braun, *Das christliche Altargerät*, pp. 197–246, esp. 198–203, and pls. 41–7, and H. Leclercq, *Dictionnaire d'archéologie chrétienne et de liturgie* XIII, cols. 2392–414, s.v. 'Patène'.

34 The cross described here was not an altar-cross in the modern sense; modern altar-crosses did not exist before the eleventh century (see Braun, *Das christliche Altargerät*, pp. 467–8). In Anglo-Saxon times, the cross stood behind the altar. That these crosses, too, could be very lavishly decorated is clear from contemporary written evidence (see Dodwell, *Anglo-Saxon Art: A New Perspective*, pp. 210–13) and from surviving specimens such as the Brussels or Drahmal Cross and the Rupertus Cross (see illustrations in Wilson, *Anglo-Saxon Art*, pls. 240 and 158 respectively).

35 On medieval thuribles or censers, see Braun, *Das christliche Altargerät*, pp. 598–632, esp. 608–11, and pls. 126–37, and H. Leclercq, in *Dictionnaire d'archéologie chrétienne et de liturgie* V, cols. 21–33, esp. 25 (on this passage in Aldhelm), s.v. 'encensoir'. Thuribles too were lavishly decorated and elaborately wrought in the Anglo-Saxon period, as is clear from contemporary written evidence (see Dodwell, *Anglo-Saxon Art: A New Perspective*, p. 218) as well as from surviving specimens: see Wilson, *Anglo-Saxon Art*, pls. 209–10; see also three tenth-century examples listed in Wilson, *Anglo-Saxon Ornamental Metalwork*, pp. 122–4 (no. 9), 151–2 (no. 44) and 157–8 (no. 56), and pls. XII–XIV, XXIV and XXVI.

³⁶ Saba in Arabia was famous for its incense, as Aldhelm will have known from Pliny (*HN* XII.52), or perhaps simply from Vergil, *Aen.* I.416 and *Georg.* I.57.

³⁷ The word *iubentur* is curious here: does it imply that, in a double house such as Bugga's church, the priests say mass only at the abbess's request? Compare a passage in the contemporary *Vita S. Bertilae*, c. 6, where the abbess Bertila is said to have ordered (*iubebat*) priests to say mass (MGH, SRM VI, p. 105).

³⁸ The poems which make up *Carmina Ecclesiastica* IV and V were clearly conceived by Aldhelm as a set, a sort of verse 'Fates of the Apostles'; it is therefore perhaps unwise to seek to identify a particular church in which the altars were found. But recall that Bugga's church had precisely twelve altars (*CE* III.40; see above, p. 48).

³⁹ In the early Anglo-Saxon period, the preference for apsidal east ends on single- or double-cell buildings is found predominately in churches associated with a Kentish group; see the remarks of B. Cherry in *The Archaeology of Anglo-Saxon England*, ed. D. M. Wilson, pp. 173–4.

⁴⁰ As noted above (p. 43), Aldhelm's principal source for *CE* IV is Isidore, *De ortu et obitu patrum*. However, Aldhelm frequently amplifies Isidore's account of a particular apostle by adding details from various other sources. His account here is amplified by reference to Matth. IV.18–20 and Luc. V.1–11 (apparently it is Christ, not Peter, who is in the boat).

⁴¹ Aldhelm again amplifies Isidore by introducing details from Act. V.15 and IX.36–41.

⁴² Isidore (*De ortu et obitu*, c. lxviii: Patrologia Latina LXXXIII, col. 149) makes only cursory mention of Simon Magus's attempt to fly: 'Simonem etiam magicis artibus coelum conscendentem ad terram elisit'. Aldhelm introduces a number of details (the tower, the bone-shattering fall) probably drawn from the apocryphal *Actus Petri cum Simone*, cc. xxxi–xxxii (ed. R. A. Lipsius and M. Bonnet, *Acta apostolorum Apocrypha*, 2 vols. in 3 [Leipzig, 1891–1903], I, pp. 81–3).

⁴³ Here Aldhelm amplifies Isidore's account of Peter's death by drawing on Jerome, *De viris inlustribus*, c. i: 'A quo [*scil.* Nerone] et affixus cruci, martyrio coronatus est, capite ad terram verso, et in sublime pedibus elevatis, asserens se indignum qui sic crucifigeretur ut Dominus suus' (Patrologia Latina XXIII, col. 607).

⁴⁴ St Paul is also treated by Aldhelm in the prose *De Virginitate*, c. xxiv, and the *Carmen de Virginitate*, lines 479–502. Here Aldhelm follows precisely the sequence of events of Paul's life as recorded by Isidore, except that he reverses the order of the miracles of the serpent's bite and the father of Publius (see above, p. 231, n. 47).

⁴⁵ On the word *occa* ('ploughed field'), see R. I. Page, 'OE "fealh", "harrow",' *Notes & Queries* XXVI (1979), pp. 389–93.

⁴⁶ The ultimate source here is II Cor. XII.2 ('raptum eiusmodi usque ad tertium caelum'), and Isidore's wording closely follows the Vulgate: 'raptus sursum in tertium coelum' (Patrologia Latina LXXXIII,

col. 150). Aldhelm may also have been familiar with some version of the *Visio Pauli* (cf. *Prose Works*, p. 190, n. 35).

[47] For some of the details in Aldhelm's account, such as Andrew's crucifixion, cf. J. E. Cross, 'Cynewulf's Traditions about the Apostles in the *Fates of the Apostles*', *Anglo-Saxon England* VIII (1979), pp. 163–75, at 170–1.

[48] The words *sancto tegmine* ('holy roof') are ambiguous here; the line could also be translated, 'with his [St James's] holy protection'; cf. the words *sarta testudine* in *CE* IV.vi.2 (see below, n. 56).

[49] Isidore (*De ortu*, c. lxxi: Patrologia Latina LXXXIII, col. 151) says merely that St James preached in Spain: 'atque Hispaniae, et occidentalium locorum gentibus evangelium praedicavit'. Aldhelm specifically states that St James converted the Spanish peoples. It is possible that Aldhelm is the earliest securely datable source for this legend, which became one of the most widespread legends in the Middle Ages: see M. C. Diaz y Diaz, 'Die spanische Jakobuslegende bei Isidor von Sevilla', *Historisches Jahrbuch* LXXVII (1956), pp. 467–72; T. D. Kendrick, *St James in Spain* (London, 1960), esp. pp. 26–9; and J. van Herwaarden, 'The Origins of the Cult of St James of Compostela', *Journal of Medieval History* VI (1980), pp. 1–35. None of these commentators mentions Aldhelm, however.

[50] Translating *cartis ... quadratis* as 'books'; the precise implication is that they were codices, not rolls. It was through the early Christians' use of codices that rolls — hitherto omnipresent in classical culture — were eventually supplanted; see C. H. Roberts, 'The Codex', *Proceedings of the British Academy* XL (1954), pp. 169–204. This detail is not found in Isidore.

[51] Aldhelm may have taken the detail about St James's death from Isidore or directly from Act. XII.1.

[52] St John the Evangelist is also treated by Aldhelm in the prose *De Virginitate*, c. XXIII, and in the *Carmen de Virginitate*, lines 460–78.

[53] Aldhelm's account of John seems to be drawn directly from Isidore, *De ortu*, c. lxxii, but he may also have known the extensive account in Eusebius, *Ecclesiastical History*, III.xviii–xxv, in the Latin translation of Rufinus.

[54] Again, the detail of John's burial may have come from Isidore, but it is also recorded in Eusebius-Rufinus, *EH* III.xxxi.

[55] St Thomas is also treated by Aldhelm in the prose *De Virginitate*, c. XXIII, but is omitted from the *Carmen de Virginitate* (see below, p. 257, n. 12).

[56] The words *sarta testudine* ('repaired roof') are puzzling: do they mean simply 'with his protection'? Cf. the words *sancto tegmine* in *CE* IV.iv.2 (above, n. 48).

[57] In later tradition, India was evangelized by Thomas, and Isidore mentions India among many places evangelized by Thomas: 'hic evangelium praedicavit Parthis, et Medis, et Persis, Hyrcanisque, ac Bactrianis, et Indis tenentibus orientalem plagam ...' (Patrologia Latina LXXXIII, col. 152). It is probable, therefore, that Aldhelm was using a

source in addition to Isidore. This source was possibly a lost version of *Acta Thomae*: see M. R. James, *The Apocryphal New Testament* (Oxford, 1924), pp. 364–468 (cf. *Prose Works*, p. 194, n. 12).

[58] Aldhelm's wording here ('rigido transverberat ense') seems to follow that of Isidore ('lanceis enim transfixus occubuit'), but the detail of the temple-priest (*fani flamen*) is not in Isidore.

[59] The detail of James's relationship to Jesus is taken directly from Isidore, as is the general outline of this account, although Aldhelm evidently laid other sources under contribution (see following notes).

[60] The story of James's death is drawn by Aldhelm from Eusebius-Rufinus, *Ecclesiastical History* II.xxiii.4–18.

[61] That the temple was destroyed as revenge for the death of James is a detail taken from Eusebius-Rufinus, *Ecclesiastical History* II.xxiii.20.

[62] The material on Vespasian and Titus is drawn from Eusebius-Rufinus, *Ecclesiastical History* III.iv.1 and III.xiii.1. That Vespasian was born in Rome is an unwarranted inference of Aldhelm's; in fact, as we know from Suetonius (*Vesp.* c. ii), Vespasian was born in the tiny hamlet of Falacrina; but Aldhelm did not apparently know Suetonius's collection of Imperial biographies.

[63] The story of the woman butchering her son is from Eusebius-Rufinus, *Ecclesiastical History* III.vi.21–8.

[64] In his account of the apostle Philip Aldhelm departs in several significant respects from Isidore (*De ortu*, c. lxxiii). According to Isidore, Philip preached in Gaul ('Gallis praedicat Christum'), whereas in Aldhelm Philip preaches in Scythia (note that, according to Isidore, it was Andrew who converted Scythia: but Aldhelm in his account of Andrew does not mention his area of apostolic activity). Aldhelm apparently drew the detail of Philip's preaching in Scythia from pseudo-Abdias, *Historiae Apostolicae* (ed. B. Mombritius, *Sanctuarium seu Vitae Sanctorum*, 2nd ed. [Paris, 1910] II, p. 385); the same information is contained in an unprinted collection of *Passiones Apostolorum* preserved in Würzburg, Universitätsbibliothek, M. p. th. f. 78 (a manuscript in Anglo-Saxon script of eighth-century date): see J. E. Cross, 'Cynewulf's Traditions about the Apostles', p. 166.

[65] According to Isidore, Philip was both hanged and stoned ('crucifixus lapidatusque obiit').

[66] The notion that the world was divided into three parts — Europe, Asia and Africa — was probably derived by Aldhelm from Orosius, *Historiae adversum paganos* I.2: 'maiores nostri orbem totius terrae ... triquadrum statuere eiusque tres partes Asiam Europam et Africam vocaverunt'.

[67] Isidore's account of Bartholomew is very condensed (*De ortu*, c. lxxv); Aldhelm followed Isidore's outline, but teased it out with various pedantic additions (see following notes).

[68] Aldhelm here combines the etymological explanation of the name Bartholomew — which he probably derived simply from Isidore, *Etym.* VII.ix.16 ('Bartholomeus filius suspendentis aquas, vel filius

241

suspendentis me; Syrum est, non Hebraeus') or possibly from Jerome's *Liber interpretationis Hebraicorum nominum*, Isidore's source — with a hexametrical cadence from Vergil, *Aen.* IV.248 ('nubibus atris').

[69] The line 'inasmuch as ... drops' is Aldhelm's pedantic explanation of why he added the Vergilian tag to the etymology.

[70] Aldhelm here amplifies Isidore (*De ortu*, c. lxxvi) by recourse to Jerome *De viris illustribus*, c. iii: 'Matthaeus .08.. evangelium Christi Hebraeis litteris verbisque composuit'.

[70] Aldhelm here amplifies Isidore (*De ortu*, c. lxxvi) by recourse to Jerome *De viris illustribus*, c. iii: 'Matthaeus ... evangelium Christi Hebraeis litteris verbisque composuit'.

[72] The ultimate source of the evangelists' symbols is Ezech. I.10; as Jerome explains in his *Commentarii in Ezechielem* (*ad loc.*), Matthew is symbolized by Ezechiel's 'man' because the gospel of Matthew begins with the *Liber generationis, filii David, filii Abraham*, etc.

[73] This line is one which Aldhelm recycled elsewhere: see *CdV* 507 and 1636.

[74] Aldhelm clearly knew very little about Simon; his account is taken entirely from Isidore (*De ortu*, c. lxxx).

[75] Notice of the letter of Christ to Abgar derives from the extensive account of Thaddeus which makes up Eusebius-Rufinus, *Ecclesiastical History* I.xiii (Isidore does not mention the letter; but it is clear nevertheless that Aldhelm had Isidore's chapter on Thaddeus/Judas before him as he wrote: see the following notes).

[76] That Jude converted the Pontus is stated by Isidore: 'interioribus Ponti evangelizans' (*De ortu*, c. lxxviii).

[77] Isidore also states (*ibid.*) that Jude was buried in Armenia: 'sepultus est autem Berytho Armeniae urbe'.

[78] If the twelve poems which make up *CE IV* were *tituli* actually intended for inscription in a church or whatever, it is difficult to know what function was envisaged for no. xiii. In fact no. xiii rather suggests that *CE IV* was conceived as a metrical *passiones apostolorum*, not as a collection of individual *tituli*.

[79] *CE V* on Matthias clearly belongs with the preceding twelve poems which make up *CE IV*. Aldhelm apparently added it as an afterthought, to complete his treatment of the apostles. In some of the surviving manuscripts it is found with *CE IV*, nos. i–xii and preceding *CE IV.xiii* (see Ehwald, pp. 9–10). Ehwald's editorial addition of the word *ecclesia* to the title of the poem is unwarranted, therefore: no actual church is in question (cf. above, p. 232, n. 50).

[80] The number 70 is drawn from Isidore, *De ortu*, c. lxxix.

INTRODUCTION TO THE ENIGMATA (pp. 61–9)

[1] On the translation 'Mysteries', see above, p. 11.
[2] Ehwald, p. 76.

[3] *Ibid.*: 'prima ingenioli rudimenta exercitari'.

[4] The bibliography on riddles is enormous. Some beginning may be made with Archer Taylor, *A Bibliography of Riddles*, Folklore Fellows Communications CXXVI (Helsinki, 1939), and A. Santi, *Bibliografia della enigmistica* (Florence, 1952).

[5] See, for example, D. V. Hart, *Riddles in Filipino Folklore: An Anthropological Analysis* (Syracuse, N.Y., 1964); L. Harries, 'The Riddle in Africa', *Journal of American Folklore* LXXXIV (1971), pp. 377–93; and the studies listed below, n. 6–8.

[6] R. A. Georges and A. Dundes, 'Toward a Structural Definition of the Riddle', *Journal of American Folklore* LXXVI (1963), pp. 111–18, at 113.

[7] E. K. Maranda, 'Theory and Practice of Riddle Analysis', *Journal of American Folklore* LXXXIV (1971), pp. 51–61, at 54.

[8] I. Hamnett, 'Ambiguity, Classification and Change: The Function of Riddles', *Man* n.s. II (1967), pp. 379–92, at 387.

[9] See Archer Taylor, *The Literary Riddle before 1600* (Berkeley, Calif., 1948); see also D. G. Blauner, 'The Early Literary Riddle', *Folklore* LXXVIII (1967), pp. 49–58.

[10] See W. Schultz, 'Rätsel', in Pauly-Wissowa, *Realencyclopädie der classischen Altertumswissenschaft*, 34 vols. in 63 (Stuttgart, 1894–1972), suppl. ser. I.1, cols. 62–125.

[11] Aristophanes, *Wasps*, lines 20–3; Aristotle, *Rhetoric* 1412a–b.

[12] *Poetics* 1458a.

[13] Athenaeus, *Deipnosophistae* X.448b–459b (ed. C. B. Gulick, 7 vols. [London and Cambridge, Mass., 1927–41], IV, pp. 530–82).

[14] Palatine Anthology, Book XIV (ed. W. R. Paton, *The Greek Anthology*, 5 vols. [London and Cambridge, Mass., 1916–18], V, pp. 26–106).

[15] Aulus Gellius, *Noctes Atticae* XII.6 (cf. XVIII.2); Petronius, *Satyricon*, §58. In Latin poetry it is often difficult to draw a line between an epigram on an unusual but stated subject and the *enigmata* of (say) Symphosius (see below, n. 16), which were transmitted in the collection of epigrams known as the 'African Anthology'. This collection has most recently been edited by D. R. Shackleton Bailey, *Anthologia Latina I: Carmina in codicibus scripta 1, Libri Salmasiani aliorumque carmina* (Stuttgart, 1982). One might compare various poems by Florus (Shackleton Bailey, nos. 96–8) or Coronatus (*ibid.*, no. 221) with those of Symphosius.

[16] Symphosius has been edited on many occasions: see most recently F. Glorie, *Variae Collectiones Aenigmatum Merovingicae Aetatis*, 2 vols., Corpus Christianorum Series Latina CXXXIII–CXXXIII A (Turnhout, 1968), II, pp. 611–721, and Shackleton Bailey, *Anthologia Latina* I.1, no. 281. There is a translation by R. T. Ohl, *The Enigmas of Symphosius* (Philadelphia, 1928); Ohl's translation is reprinted in the edition of Glorie. Symphosius is himself an enigmatic figure. His riddles were reportedly delivered at a banquet (Greek *symposion*), and

this fact makes one suspect that his name *Symp(h)osius* is no more than a joking pseudonym, meaning 'party-boy' or the like. One might also suspect that 'Symposius' was the author of some obscene verses preserved elsewhere in the 'African Anthology' (Shackleton Bailey, no. 377); compare the first lines of these verses,

Post mille amplexus, post dulcia savia penem
confiniis laterum detortum suscipe, posco ...

with a line from Symphosius's metrical preface to his riddle-collection: 'post epulas laetas, post dulcia pocula mensae ...'

[17] 'I provide great powers from small resources: I open closed houses and again I close open ones. I keep the house open for my lord, but in turn I'm kept by him'.

[18] See the helpful analysis by P. D. Scott, 'Rhetorical and Symbolic Ambiguity: The Riddles of Symphosius and Aldhelm', in *Saints, Scholars and Heroes: Studies in Medieval Culture in Honour of Charles W. Jones*, ed. M. H. King and W. M. Stevens, 2 vols. (Collegeville, Minn., 1979), I, pp. 117–44.

[19] Ehwald, p. 75.

[20] *Ars Minor* III.6 (ed. L. Holtz, *Donat et la tradition de l'enseignement grammatical* [Paris, 1982], pp. 603–74, at 672). Donatus goes on to quote, as an example of an *enigma*, the line 'Mater me genuit eadem mox gignitur ex me' (solution: ice/water). Aldhelm quotes this very line without specifying his source (Ehwald, p. 77). Ehwald supposes (inexplicably) that Aldhelm's source was Pompeius, a commentator on Donatus who preserves the line in question. But there is no reason whatsoever to doubt that Aldhelm took the line directly from Donatus, a source which elsewhere he laid heavily under contribution.

[21] Aldhelm follows the example of Symphosius in giving the title of each *enigma* before the *enigma* itself. Like Symphosius, therefore, Aldhelm did not intend his readers to have to guess at the meaning of each *enigma*; rather, the reader was expected to perceive afresh the mystery of each object treated by Aldhelm, just as the reader of Symphosius was expected to appreciate the verbal dexterity with which he handled the object of each *enigma*.

[22] Aldhelm was not a philosopher, and it is unreasonable to expect logical coherency from his cosmological speculations. Nevertheless it is worth noting in passing that he inherited several cosmological notions (with their accompanying vocabulary) from antique philosophy. For example, that the universe consisted in opposing/warring elements held in check (*Enigm.* xlix and liv) was a tenet held by various ancient systems of thought that was repeated by Latin poets (Ovid, for example) and by cosmologically-minded Church Fathers such as Lactantius and Ambrose; on the origins of this notion, see W. Spoerri, *Späthellenistische Berichte über Welt, Kultur und Götter* (Basel, 1959); on late antique and early medieval articulations of the notion, see P. Vossen, 'Über die Elementen-Syzygien', in *Liber Floridus*, ed. B. Bischoff and S. Brechter (St Ottilien, 1950), pp. 33–46. On the notion

of the cosmic bond which held the elements in check (*Enigm.* liv.6: *foedera pacis*), see M. Lapidge, 'A Stoic Metaphor in Late Latin Poetry: The Binding of the Cosmos', *Latomus* XXXIX (1980), pp. 817–37. On *natura* as a force of moderation in the universe (*Enigm.* iv: *res nulla manet sine me* [*scil. Natura*] *moderante*), see A. Pellicer, *Natura: Étude sémantique et historique du mot latin* (Paris, 1966), esp. pp. 292–311. See also below, p. 262, n. 3.

[23] *Enigmata* nos. i, v, xvii, xxiii, xxiv, xxx, xxxii, xxxiii, xlii, xliv, xlv, l, li, lix, lxxiii, lxxvi, lxxviii, lxxix, lxxxii, lxxxiv, lxxxv, lxxxix, xc, xciii, xcvi and xcvii.

[24] *Enigmata* nos. xii, xiii, xxvii, xxxiii, xl, lii, liv, lv, lxii, lxvii, lxviii, lxxii, lxxviii, lxxx, lxxxii, lxxxix, xciv, xcvii and c.

[25] Ehwald, p. 75; *Prose Works*, p. 45.

[26] The principal source for our knowledge of Tatwine is Bede, *HE* V.23, which may be supplemented by an epitaph for Tatwine composed soon after his death (ptd. Lapidge, 'Some Remnants of Bede's Lost *Liber Epigrammatum*', pp. 811–12). In addition to the *Enigmata* (see below, n. 27), Tatwine was the author of an *Ars Grammatica* (on which see V. Law, *The Insular Latin Grammarians* [Woodbridge, 1982], pp. 64–7).

[27] Ed. F. Glorie, *Variae Collectiones Aenigmatum* (as cited above, n. 16), I, pp. 165–208.

[28] *Ibid.*, pp. 209–71.

[29] Both surviving manuscripts of the *Enigmata* name the author as 'Eusebius'. Bede, in the preface to the fourth book of his commentary *In primam partem Samuhelis* (ed. D. Hurst, Corpus Christianorum Series Latina CXIX [Turnhout, 1962], p. 212), refers to Hwætberht, a well-attested abbot of Wearmouth-Jarrow, as having the cognomen Eusebius: 'Huetberctum iuuenem cui amor studiumque pietatis iam olim Eusebii cognomen indidit'. It is usually assumed that this Northumbrian Hwætberht is the author of the *Enigmata* (see, e.g., W. F. Bolton, *A History of Anglo-Latin Literature I: 597–740* [Princeton, 1967], pp. 219–23). However, as Neil Wright has demonstrated (in the study mentioned as forthcoming above, p. 227, n. 6), the *Enigmata* share many metrical characteristics with the poetry of Aldhelm and Tatwine, and are metrically unlike that of Bede, which makes one suspect that Eusebius was an otherwise unknown Southumbrian poet.

[30] Ed. Glorie, *Variae Collectiones Aenigmatum*, I, pp. 273–343. It is not known whether Boniface composed his *Enigmata* in England or on the continent (he left England forever in 718). If the rubric in a late eleventh-century manuscript written at Salisbury could be believed, Boniface as bishop sent the collection to his *soror* (unnamed), presumably one of his female correspondents in England: 'Incipiunt enigmata Bonefatii episcopi quae misit sorori suae' (London, BL, Royal 15.B.XIX, fols. 200–5 [Salisbury, s. xi^{ex}], f. 204r). Boniface was consecrated bishop on 30 November 722; if the rubric were reliable

evidence, the *Enigmata* would *ipso facto* be later than 722. But no reliance can be placed on so late a witness.

³¹ The 'Leiden Riddle' is ed. A. H. Smith, *Three Northumbrian Poems* (London, 1933), pp. 44–6; see also pp. 7–10 and 17–19, and M. B. Parkes, 'The Manuscript of the Leiden Riddle', *Anglo-Saxon England* I (1972), pp. 207–17.

³² The 'Exeter Book' Riddles are ed. F. Tupper, *The Riddles of the Exeter Book* (Boston, 1910), and most recently by C. Williamson, *The Old English Riddles of the Exeter Book* (Chapel Hill, N.C., 1977); they have been translated by P. F. Baum, *Anglo-Saxon Riddles of the Exeter Book* (Durham, N.C., 1963) and by C. Williamson, *A Feast of Creatures: Anglo-Saxon Riddle-Songs* (Philadelphia, 1982).

³³ For Aldhelmian influence throughout the Exeter Book riddles, see Tupper, *The Riddles of the Exeter Book*, pp. xxxvii–xliv, and Williamson, *The Old English Riddles of the Exeter Book*, pp. 166, 202, 218, 243–8, 255, 265–76, 293, 323, 333 and 339–40.

³⁴ See, for example, L. N. Braswell, 'The *Dream of the Rood* and Aldhelm on Sacred Prosopopoeia', *Mediaeval Studies* XL (1978), pp. 461–7.

³⁵ The pseudo-Bede *Collectanea* are ptd. Patrologia Latina XCIV, cols. 539–62; see esp. cols. 543 (*Enigm.* iii), 546 (*Enigm.* xc) and 548 (*Enigm.* ii, iv, and ix); note that the *Collectanea* also include a number of *enigmata* of Symphosius.

³⁶ See B. Bischoff, *Lorsch im Spiegel seiner Handschriften* (Munich, 1974), p. 23 *et passim*.

³⁷ The 'Lorsch Riddles' (*Aenigmata Laureshamensia*) are ed. Glorie, *Variae Collectiones Aenigmatum*, I, pp. 345–58. Note that the so-called 'Bern Riddles' or *Aenigmata Tullii* (*ibid.*, II, pp. 541–610) are rhythmical, not metrical, and show no apparent influence of Aldhelm. It is interesting to note, nevertheless, that in two early manuscripts they are transmitted with works of Aldhelm: Leipzig, Stadtbibl. Rep. I.74 (see above, p. 16) and Berlin, Deutsche Staatsbibl. Phillipps 167 (see above, p. 39), a manuscript probably copied from an exemplar of Insular origin. The possible Anglo-Saxon origin of these 'Bern Riddles' needs careful study.

³⁸ See Ehwald, pp. 44–54, and Glorie, *Variae Collectiones Aenigmatum*, I, pp. 360–4. Refinements to the datings given by Ehwald are supplied by B. Bischoff, *Mittelalterliche Studien*, 3 vols. (Stuttgart, 1966–81), III, pp. 222–3 and n. 54. To the lists given by Ehwald and Glorie add: Leiden, Bibliotheek der Rijksuniversiteit, Voss. Q.106 (s. ix¹) and Vatican City, Biblioteca Apostolica Vaticana, Pal. lat. 1719, on which see V. M. Lagorio, 'Aldhelm's Aenigmata in Codex Vaticanus Palatinus Latinus 1719', *Manuscripta* XV (1971), pp. 23–7.

³⁹ See above, p. 220, n. 6.

⁴⁰ See M. Manitius, *Geschichte der lateinischen Literatur des Mittelalters*, 3 vols. (Munich, 1911–31), I, pp. 504–19; on the circulation of Remigius's commentaries in late Anglo-Saxon England, see M. Lapidge, 'The Study of Latin Texts in Late Anglo-Saxon England: 1. The

Evidence of Latin Glosses', in *Latin and the Vernacular Languages in Early Medieval Britain*, ed. N. Brooks (Leicester, 1982), pp. 99–140, at 104–5 and 114–16.

[41] See N. R. Ker, *Catalogue of Manuscripts containing Anglo-Saxon* (Oxford, 1957), pp. 331–2 (no. 263). The Old English glosses have been printed by A. S. Napier, *Old English Glosses, chiefly unpublished* (Oxford, 1900), no. 26. The Latin glosses have yet to receive the attention they deserve.

[42] See also the gloss to 'Pleiades' (*Enigm.* viii) on f. 84v: 'Pliades dictae a pluralitate quia pluralitatem Greci *apo to pliston* appellant. Sunt .vii. stelle ante ianuam Tauri, ex quibus sex uidentur; nam latet una. Has Latini Vergilias dicunt a temporis significatione, quod est uer quando exoriuntur; nam occasu suo hiemem ortum aestatem prime nauigationis tempus ostendunt'. This is all taken verbatim from Isidore, *Etym.* III.lxxi.13. A gloss accompanying *Enigm.* lxxix ('De sole et luna') on fol. 97r bears the source-mark: *Is. dicit.*

[43] Thus the gloss to *Enigm.* xviii ('Myrmicoleon'): 'Est enim animal paruum, formicis satis infestum, quod se in puluere abscondit et formicas interficit. Proinde autem 'leo' et 'formica' appellatur, quia animantibus aliis ut formica est, formicis autem ut leo est. Gregorius ait in Moralibus quia translatiue aput .LXX. interpretum nequaquam dicitur tigris sed mirmicaleon' (f. 85v). The reference is to Gregory, *Moralia in Iob* V.xix.40.

[44] The *Scholia Bernensia* are the source of the extensive gloss on *Enigm.* xcv ('Scylla') on f. 100v; see R. I. Page, 'The Study of Latin Texts in Late Anglo-Saxon England: 2. The Evidence of English Glosses', in *Latin and the Vernacular Languages in Early Medieval Britain*, ed. Brooks, pp. 141–65, at 160–5 and n. 35.

[45] As is clear from the glossing in three Anglo-Saxon manuscripts of that period: Oxford, Bodleian Library, Rawlinson C.697; London, BL, Royal 15.A.XVI and 12.C.XXIII. Note also that Byrhtferth of Ramsey on a number of occasions quotes from the *Enigmata*: see M. Lapidge, 'Byrhtferth of Ramsey and the Early Sections of the *Historia Regum* attributed to Symeon of Durham', *Anglo-Saxon England* X (1982), pp. 97–122, at 113.

THE ENIGMATA (pp. 70–94)

In compiling his *Enigmata* Aldhelm drew on various literary sources as well as on his own personal observation of the world around him. The literary sources — principally Pliny's *Historia Naturalis* and Isidore's *Etymologiae* (and perhaps an early recension of the Latin *Physiologus*) — were noted carefully by Ehwald, and have been discussed by Erika von Erhardt-Siebold, *Die lateinischen Rätsel der Angelsachsen* (Heidelberg, 1925) (hereafter *Rätsel*), a very valuable and full treatment of Aldhelm's sources and technique, of especial importance for its discussion of what the author calls the *Realia* of Anglo-Saxon culture. In the following notes references are given to this work wherever possible, since it is still the fullest treatment in print of Aldhelm's *Enigmata*. However, in certain respects — particularly those which pertain to Aldhelm's personal observation of the natural world — her commentary is deficient. The deficiency has now been made good by a valuable study by M. L. Cameron, 'Aldhelm as Naturalist: A Re-examination of Some of his *Enigmata*', to appear in *Peritia* IV (1985). Professor Cameron very kindly made this article available to me before publication, and the following annotation has benefited enormously therefrom.

1 The preface of the *Enigmata* (like that of the *Carmen de Virginitate*) is in the form of an acrostic. Aldhelm may possibly have learned this form from a Greek acrostic poem on the Day of Judgement, of which he may himself have produced a translation (see above, p. 16). Although the acrostic legend states that Aldhelm sang his odes in a thousand verses (ALDHELMUS CECINI MILLENIS VERSIBUS ODAS), the *Enigmata* consist of fewer than 800 verses.

2 Aldhelm is here paraphrasing Persius, *Sat.* prol. 1–3 ('Nec fonte labra prolui caballino / nec in bicipiti somniasse Parnaso / memini ...'), a passage which he quotes elsewhere (Ehwald, p. 78; see also below, p. 265, n. 3). Line 10 of Aldhelm's preface ('Castalides nimphas non clamo cantibus istuc') also bears a certain resemblance to one of the *Carmina* of Paulinus of Nola (XV.30: 'non ego Castalidas, vatum phantasmata, Musas ... ciebo'); it is worth noting that he quotes another line from this very *carmen* in his *Epistola ad Acircium* (Ehwald, p. 96: *Carm.* XV.1). See now N. Wright, 'Imitation of the Poems of Paulinus of Nola in early Anglo-Latin Verse', *Peritia* IV (1985).

3 The words 'biblical verses' correspond to *metrica carmina* in Latin (line 17). Aldhelm is referring either to the fact that some at least of the Old Testament was composed in Hebrew verse (which he will have known from Jerome), or else he is referring to the metrical *Heptateuchus* of Cyprianus Gallus, a work which he quotes elsewhere (Ehwald, pp. 80, 92, 158 and 189).

4 It is not clear what writings of the ancients Aldhelm is here referring to; but note that there is a striking resemblance between the first line of this *enigma* ('Taumantis proles priscorum famine fingor') and the first line of a poem preserved in the 'African Anthology' (A. Riese, *Anthologia Latina I: Carmina in codicibus scripta*, 2 vols. [Leipzig, 1894–1906], no. 543): 'Thaumantis proles varianti veste refulgens'. This, together with the poems of Symphosius (see above, p. 243, n. 15) may suggest that Aldhelm knew the 'African Anthology' in some form.

5 The title of the poem given in the manuscripts is *Fatum*. However, line 2 (which is quoted from Vergil, *Aen.* XII.677: 'Quo deus et quo dura uocat Fortuna, sequamur') refers specifically to *Fortuna*, and line 3 refers to her as *domina*. Unless Aldhelm thought that *Fatum* was

248

synonymous with *Fortuna* (which it certainly was not in Late Latin authors such as Boethius), the title of *Enigma* vii should be emended from *Fatum* to *Fortuna*.

6 The source of this *enigma* is Isidore, *Etym*. III.lxxi.13 (cf. above, p. 247, n. 42); according to Isidore they were called *Vergiliae* from *ver* (hence Aldhelm's otherwise incomprehensible line 5).

7 See Erhardt-Siebold, *Rätsel*, pp. 149–50.

8 *Ibid.*, pp. 173–4.

9 On the obscure word *poalum*, which probably derives from a misunderstood glossary entry, see W. M. Lindsay, *The Corpus, Epinal, Erfurt and Leyden Glossaries* (Oxford, 1921), p. 98. On the bellows themselves, see Erhardt-Siebold, *Rätsel*, pp. 13–14.

10 See Erhardt-Siebold, *Rätsel*, pp. 214–20, and 'Aldhelm in Possession of the Secrets of Sericulture', *Anglia* LX (1936), pp. 384–9. As Cameron ('Aldhelm as Naturalist') demonstrates, however, Erhardt-Siebold's supposition that Aldhelm was somehow privy to the secrets of sericulture in China is far-fetched; he shows that Aldhelm is more likely to be referring to the Oak Eggar (*Lasiocampa quercus quercus*) which is found in southern England and feeds — as here in Aldhelm — on broom.

11 See Erhardt-Siebold, *Rätsel*, pp. 120–31.

12 *Ibid.*, pp. 194–5. That the peacock's flesh never decays is a notion which Aldhelm took from Augustine (*De Civitate Dei* XXI.4); it recurs in the prose *De Virginitate*, c. IX (Ehwald, p. 237).

13 Erhardt-Siebold, *Rätsel*, p. 205. That the salamander lives in flames is a notion derived from Isidore, *Etym*. XII.iv.36; Aldhelm alludes to it in his prose *De Virginitate*, c. XXXIV (Ehwald, p. 276).

14 Erhardt-Siebold, *Rätsel*, p. 204 (referring to Isidore, *Etym*. XII.vi.47 and Pliny, *HN* IX.84). In Classical Latin *lolligo* refers unambiguously to a 'cuttle-fish' or 'squid', and Cameron ('Aldhelm as Naturalist') has shown comprehensively that the creature described by Aldhelm is a squid, not a flying fish.

15 Erhardt-Siebold, *Rätsel*, pp. 202–4. This *enigma* is drawn principally from Pliny, *HN* XXXII.54; but Aldhelm misleadingly converts Pliny's *Pontias* into *ponti*. The creature is a bivalve mollusc (shaped like a ham: hence Aldhelm's title *Perna*). Cameron ('Aldhelm as Naturalist') gives convincing reasons for thinking that the mollusc in question is that called *Pinna nobilis*. The 'tawny fleeces' produced by it are the *byssus*, which were collected and spun out into threads.

16 Erhardt-Siebold, *Rätsel*, pp. 212–13; see Isidore, *Etym*. XII.iii.10 and Gregory, *Moralia in Iob* V.xix.40 (cf. above, p. 247, n. 43). What sort of creature was envisaged by Aldhelm is not clear.

17 Erhardt-Siebold, *Rätsel*, p. 147.

18 *Ibid.*, pp. 206–8; cf. Isidore, *Etym*. XII.viii.1. The bee as a symbol of virginity ('engendered without seed') recurs in the prose *De Virginitate* cc. V–VI (Ehwald, p. 233).

19 Erhardt-Siebold, *Rätsel*, pp. 182–3.

20 *Ibid.*, pp. 21–2; Isidore, *Etym.* XVI.xxv.4.

21 Erhardt-Siebold, *Rätsel*, pp. 153–5; cf. Pliny, *HN* XXXVII.158.

22 On the difference between adamant and magnet, see Pliny, *HN* XXXVII.58.

23 Erhardt-Siebold, *Rätsel*, pp. 178–80. The cock (*gallus*) bears the name of the Gauls (*Galli*).

24 Preferring the reading *Mulciber* (= 'Vulcan', hence 'fire') in line 4 to Ehwald's *mulcifer*.

25 Erhardt-Siebold, *Rätsel*, pp. 237–8. See Isidore, *Etym.* XI.iii.38 and Servius, *In Vergilii Aen.* (*ad* VI.25) for the Cretan mythology.

26 Literally 'needle' (*acus*). Ehwald is probably correct (*pace* Pitman) in thinking that Aldhelm is here referring to a sharp, jagged rock which causes shipwreck.

27 See Isidore, *Etym.* I.iv.10 (the bastards are the letters *h*, *k*, *q*, *x*, *y* and *z*). The iron that begets them is the stylus; the 'three brothers' are the three fingers that hold the stylus.

28 Erhardt-Siebold, *Rätsel*, pp. 186–9.

29 *Ibid.*, pp. 63–7; see also W. Wattenbach, *Das Schriftwesen im Mittelalter*, 4th edn. (Leipzig, 1896), pp. 51–89, esp. 64. Wax tablets are perishable, and it is not surprising that none have survived from Anglo-Saxon England. What is surprising is that some wax tablets, containing parts of Ps. XXX–XXXII and written s. vi/vii, were recovered in good condition from a bog in Northern Ireland earlier this century; see E. C. R. Armstrong and R. A. S. Macalister, 'Wooden Book with Leaves indented and waxed found near Springmount Bog, Co. Antrim', *Journal of the Royal Society of Antiquaries of Ireland* L (1920), pp. 160–6, and E. A. Lowe, *Codices Latini Antiquiores*, 11 vols. and supp. (Oxford, 1934–72), Supp. no. 1684.

30 Erhardt-Siebold, *Rätsel*, pp. 87–8.

31 *Ibid.*, pp. 221–2.

32 *Ibid.*, pp. 190–2. Aldhelm plays on the Greek etymology of the name (which, for once, is not derived from Isidore): *nyx, nykti-* ('night') + *korax* ('raven'). The bird in question is a screech-owl.

33 *Ibid.*, p. 208; see Isidore, *Etym.* XII.viii.14 (where the insects in question are described as *muscae minutissimae*). As Cameron has shown ('Aldhelm as Naturalist'), Aldhelm is describing the tiny midge, not the larger gadfly; and in fact the word *scnifes* is glossed *mycg* in a Latin-Old English glossary contemporary with Aldhelm (see J. D. Pheifer, *Old English Glosses in the Epinal-Erfurt Glossary* [Oxford, 1974], p. 48, line 916).

34 Erhardt-Siebold, *Rätsel*, pp. 200–2. The grammarian Festus (as preserved by Paulus Diaconus) recorded that the name *nepa* was of African origin and meant 'crab' or 'scorpion' (ed. W. M. Lindsay, *Sexti Pompei Festi De Verborum Significatu* [Leipzig, 1913], p. 163: 'Nepa Afrorum lingua sidus, quod cancer appellatur, vel, ut quidam volunt, scorpios'). Aldhelm, however, is thinking of a crab. For the crab casting stones, see Isidore, *Etym.* XII.vi.51. The constellation

Cancer is 'ruddy' (*ruber*), presumably, because the crab itself is that colour.

³⁵ Erhardt-Siebold, *Rätsel*, pp. 201–11. The insect in question is not technically a spider, but a member of the class *Gerridae*, and hence the name 'pond-skater' has been preferred to 'water-spider', following the suggestion of Cameron ('Aldhelm as Naturalist'), who further points out that Aldhelm's description is based on direct observation, not on a literary source.

³⁶ Erhardt-Siebold, *Rätsel*, pp. 222–3. On the lion sleeping with its eyes open, see Isidore, *Etym.* XII.ii.5.

³⁷ Erhardt-Siebold, *Rätsel*, pp. 147–9.

³⁸ *Ibid.*, pp. 54–7. In line 4 Aldhelm refers, in a rather far-fetched, metaphorical way, to the pillow's cover or case as a 'head', so as to produce a contrived paradox: without a head the pillow flies aloft, yet it is pressed down by a head.

³⁹ *Ibid.*, pp. 195–6.

⁴⁰ *Ibid.*, p. 211. See also Isidore, *Etym.* XII.v.3 and Cameron ('Aldhelm as Naturalist') for discussion of the use of leeches in blood-letting.

⁴¹ Erhardt-Siebold, *Rätsel*, pp. 47–8. In line 3 *collum* (from *colus*, 'distaff') is so spelled *metri gratia*. The translation follows the order of verses preserved in manuscript, not Ehwald's editorial rearrangement.

⁴² Erhardt-Siebold, *Rätsel*, p. 157.

⁴³ *Ibid.*, pp. 180–2. See Isidore (*Etym.* XVII.ix.36) for the medical properties of the plant called *Chelidonia* (*chelidon* is the Greek word for 'swallow').

⁴⁴ On the retrograde motion of the planets, see Isidore, *Etym.*, III.xxxiii–xxxv and lxvii, and Bede, *De Natura Rerum*, c. xii; cf. also Aldhelm, *Epistola ad Acircium*, c. iii (Ehwald, p. 72; *Prose Works*, p. 42).

⁴⁵ Erhardt-Siebold, *Rätsel*, pp. 22–6.

⁴⁶ *Ibid.*, pp. 157–9.

⁴⁷ *Ibid.*, pp. 159–60. Cameron ('Aldhelm as Naturalist') canvasses various possibilities for this yellow flower, such as pot marigold and coltsfoot, and inclines slightly in favour of the dandelion (it is not, in any case, a sunflower, since the sunflower does not close up at night). On the Greek etymology of the name, which means 'sun-change', see Isidore, *Etym.* XVII.viii.37.

⁴⁸ Erhardt-Siebold, *Rätsel*, pp. 26–9.

⁴⁹ See Isidore, *De Natura Rerum* XXVI.3; cf. Aldhelm, *Epistola ad Acircium*, c. iii (Ehwald, p. 72; *Prose Works*, p. 42).

⁵⁰ See Erhardt-Siebold, *Rätsel*, pp. 22–6, and 'An Archaeological Find in a Riddle of the Anglo-Saxons', *Speculum* VII (1932), pp. 252–5.

⁵¹ See Erhardt-Siebold, *Rätsel*, pp. 94–104, and 'Aldhelm's Chrismal', *Speculum* X (1935), pp. 276–80 (with accompanying plates of some early chrismals). The chrismal was a vessel or coffer in which the bread or Body of Christ was kept; see the article by F. Cabrol, 'Chrismal', in *Dictionnaire d'archéologie chrétienne et de liturgie* III, cols. 1478–81,

esp. 1480 on Aldhelm. As Cabrol notes, various later Anglo-Saxon sacramentaries contain blessings of the chrismal; see F. E. Warren, *The Leofric Missal* (Oxford, 1883), p. 222.

52 Erhardt-Siebold, *Rätsel*, pp. 175–7; see also Cameron ('Aldhelm as Naturalist') on the medical uses of *castoreum*, a fluid obtained from the inquinal glands of the beaver.

53 Erhardt-Siebold, *Rätsel*, pp. 192–4. The reference to the 'deceitful poets' is in fact to Vergil, *Aen.* V.254. The word *arsantes* (line 5) does not appear to be attested elsewhere, and apparently refers to the rattling sound made by cranes (?).

54 Erhardt-Siebold, *Rätsel*, pp. 57–63; see also Wattenbach, *Das Schriftwesen im Mittelalter*, p. 227. In spite of Aldhelm's *Enigma*, one may suspect that pelican quills were not common in early England, and that the majority of the writing was done with reeds. The fields are 'whitened' here because parchment was often sprinkled with chalk before being written on.

55 See Erhardt-Siebold, *Rätsel*, pp. 229–31 and Isidore, *Etym.* XII.ii.12–13. It is not clear what is meant by the 'lofty city' to which the unicorn is led.

56 Erhardt-Siebold, *Rätsel*, pp. 77–85.

57 *Ibid.*, pp. 183–5, and Isidore, *Etym.* XII.vii.43. The reference to Caelius Sedulius is to *Carmen Paschale* I.175 (the feeding of Elijah in the wilderness). 'Let one letter be removed': and the word *corbus* ('raven') will become *orbus* ('without offspring').

58 Erhardt-Siebold, *Rätsel*, pp. 185–6; Isidore, *Etym.* VII.iii.22.

59 Erhardt-Siebold, *Rätsel*, pp. 174–5. The 'hateful race' refers to mice; the cat's name *muriceps* means literally 'mouse-catcher'.

60 *Ibid.*, pp. 17–19.

61 *Ibid.*, pp. 19–21.

62 *Ibid.*, pp. 164–5.

63 Aldhelm's Latin here reads, 'Sed me pestiferam fecerunt fata reorum'. But the phrase 'the fates of the guilty' (*reorum*) makes no sense, and it would seem that Aldhelm wrote *reorum* for the sake of the metre while thinking of *fata rerum* ('the fates of things'), a common enough phrase which would not, however, fit metrically into the last two feet of his hexameter. For a similar change made *metri gratia* see below, n. 91.

64 Erhardt-Siebold, *Rätsel*, pp. 90–3. The *enigma* contains a surprising number of words for 'shield' (*pelta, scutum, clipeus, parma*), and hence Erhardt-Siebold discusses it among the *enigmata* describing weapons. The Latin word *tortella* is of course the source of Mod. Spanish *tortilla*.

65 *Ibid.*, pp. 198–9. In line 5 ('while in the skies ...' etc.) Aldhelm is referring to the constellation Pisces.

66 *Ibid.*, p. 156. The source of Aldhelm's knowledge of this structure was evidently Pliny, *HN* XXXIV.18; cf. prose *De Virginitate*, c. XXI (Ehwald, p. 252; *Prose Works*, p. 78).

67 Erhardt-Siebold, *Rätsel*, pp. 71–5.

[68] *Ibid.*, pp. 208–10. Aldhelm's comment on the taste of the hornet's 'sweet food' may derive from personal experience.

[69] *Ibid.*, pp. 168–9.

[70] *Ibid.*, pp. 165–6.

[71] *Ibid.*, pp. 41–4.

[72] *Ibid.*, pp. 29–39 (a detailed discussion of glass-making in Anglo-Saxon England).

[73] The 'morning star' is the planet Venus, which from at least the first century B.C. was referred to as *Lucifer*, 'light-bringer' (e.g. by Cicero, *De Natura Deorum* II.53). The same epithet was used by Jerome in his Vulgate translation of the passage in Isaiah describing the vainglorious king of Babylon whose pride was brought down from heaven after he had (metaphorically) risen in the morning: 'quomodo cecidisti de caelo lucifer qui mane oriebaris' (Is. XIV.12). The verbal parallel between this passage and a passage in Luke describing the fall of Satan (Luc. X.18: 'videbam Satanan sicut fulgur de caelo cadentem') was soon noted, and from the time of Jerome onwards it became customary to refer to Satan as Lucifer, as here in Aldhelm (lines 6–8). The six companions of Lucifer, however, are the six remaining planets: see Isidore, *De Natura Rerum*, c. xxiii, and Bede, *De Natura Rerum*, c. xiii.

[74] Erhardt-Siebold, *Rätsel*, pp. 177–8. On the weasel's combat with dragons, see Pliny, *HN* XXIX.60 and Isidore, *Etym.* XII.iv.7 (where, however, it is the weasel's efficacity in killing serpents and snakes which is discussed; for Aldhelm, evidently, *draco* was equivalent to *serpens*). Concerning the weasel's unusual method of conception and birth, see Isidore, *Etym.* XII.iii.3: 'falso autem opinantur qui dicunt mustelam ore concipere, aure effundere partum'; and in the light of this passage, Ehwald (*ad loc.*) rightly wonders if Aldhelm's text should be emended from *ex aure* ('from the ear') to *ex ore* ('from the mouth').

[75] Erhardt-Siebold, *Rätsel*, pp. 169–70.

[76] On the ninety-six combined metrical feet, see Aldhelm's own discussion in *De Metris* (Ehwald, p. 150; translated above, p. 212).

[77] Erhardt-Siebold, *Rätsel*, pp. 88–90. If the fifteenth letter of the alphabet, namely *p*, stands in front of the word *aries* ('ram'), the result is *paries* ('wall').

[78] Erhardt-Siebold, *Rätsel*, pp. 85–7. On the form and size of Anglo-Saxon shields as known from surviving specimens (mostly bosses), see the discussion of D. M. Wilson, in *The Archaeology of Anglo-Saxon England*, ed. D. M. Wilson (London, 1976), pp. 18–19.

[79] Erhardt-Siebold, *Rätsel*, pp. 232–3. On the serpent's fear of encounters with stags, see Pliny *HN* VIII.118 and XXVIII.149.

[80] On the size and shape of book-cupboards in the early medieval period, see J. W. Clark, *The Care of Books*, 2nd edn. (Cambridge, 1902), pp. 40–3 and 72–4.

[81] Erhardt-Siebold, *Rätsel*, pp. 166–8. Aldhelm's knowledge of palm trees derived from Pliny, *HN* XIII.30 and Isidore, *Etym.* XVII.vii.1.

253

[82] Erhardt-Siebold, *Rätsel*, p. 155. Aldhelm's knowledge of lighthouses seems to have derived primarily from Isidore, *Etym.* XV.ii.37, although it is possible that in the late seventh century some fabric of the Roman lighthouses at Dover remained visible; on them see R. E. M. Wheeler, 'The Roman Lighthouses at Dover', *Archaeological Journal* LXXXVI (1929), pp. 29–46, and cf. Bede, *HE* I.11.

[83] Erhardt-Siebold, *Rätsel*, pp. 162–4. Cameron ('Aldhelm as Naturalist') fully discusses this *enigma* and points out that it is almost entirely based on personal observation.

[84] It is, for example, an ingredient of various remedies preserved in Bald's *Leechbook* (*Leechdoms, Wortcunning and Starcraft*, ed. O. Cockayne, 3 vols., Rolls Series [London, 1864–6], II, pp. 64, 66, 68, 86, 108, 118 and 120).

[85] The story of the beautiful maiden Scylla, who was loved by Glaucus but whose loins were turned while she was bathing into barking monsters through the ministrations of the witch Circe, who in turn was jealous of Glaucus, is told most fully by Ovid, *Metamorphoses* XIII.730–XIV.74. It is difficult to know where Aldhelm found the story, if not in Ovid: no other Latin source earlier than Aldhelm contains precisely the information which he includes. That Aldhelm knew Ovid's account may perhaps be confirmed by some verbal reminiscences: thus *Enigm.* xcv.11 ('Auscultare procul, quae latrant inguina circum') appears to be a reflex of Ovid, *Met.* XIV.60 ('Cum sua foedari latrantibus inguina monstris'). Aldhelm's statement that mariners are terrified by the barking sound issuing from Scylla's loins appears to derive from Isidore, *Etym.* XI.iii.32. It is not clear where Aldhelm found the Greek etymology whereby Scylla is said to derive from *skylax*, 'puppy': it is not found in Isidore.

[86] Erhardt-Siebold, *Rätsel*, pp. 223–4. A number of examples of exquisite ivory carving survives from Anglo-Saxon England; see D. M. Wilson, *Anglo-Saxon Art* (London, 1984), pp. 159–60 and 194–5, and pls. 165–6, 241–2, 247–8 and 266–70. In most (and perhaps all) cases, however, the ivory is walrus, not elephant.

[87] Again, the 'poets' are simply Vergil, *Aen.* XII.846.

[88] *Aen.* IV.177 and 181–4. Note that the anonymous author of the *Liber Monstrorum*, who was certainly a colleague or student of Aldhelm (see above, p. 18), makes Vergil's description of Rumour (*Fama*) — as quoted here by Aldhelm — into a marauding nocturnal monster: *Liber Monstrorum* I.42 (ed. F. Porsia [Bari, 1976], p. 196).

[89] See Erhardt-Siebold, *Rätsel*, pp. 160–2, and 'The Hellebore in Anglo-Saxon Pharmacy', *Englische Studien* LXXI (1936), pp. 161–70, who argues that the plant in question is that called Mezereon. But Cameron ('Aldhelm as Naturalist') has advanced convincing reasons against this identification, and proposed instead that Aldhelm's plant is Woody Nightshade.

[90] Erhardt-Siebold, *Rätsel* pp. 227–8. That the camel was once a consul: Aldhelm is punning on the words *camelus* and *Camillus*. His reference

is apparently to M. Furius Camillus, who was thought of as the second founder of Rome because of his activities during the period 400–370 B.C., and who is discussed at length by Livy (*Ab Urbe Condita* Bk V passim). But Aldhelm does not seem to have known Livy, and his reference to Camillus is probably derived from one of the poets, perhaps Lucan (*Phars.* I.168, II.544, V.28, VI.786 and VII.358), whom he knew well.

[91] The Latin here reads 'glandiferis iterum *referunt* dum corpora fagis', which means literally 'they return their bodies to the beech-mast', an obscure statement at best. The simplest solution is that Aldhelm wrote *referunt* in lieu of *referciunt* for the sake of metre (cf. above, p. 252, n. 63).

[92] Ancient sources observe that there are five *zonae* or *circuli* (that is, imaginary circles dividing the world up into zones); see Pliny *HN* II.68–70. The theory of five zones is followed by Isidore (*Etym.* XIII.vi) and Bede (*De Natura Rerum*, c. ix). It is not clear, therefore, why Aldhelm should have posited six (*senis*) zones; cf. the remarks of Ehwald (*app. ad loc*).

[93] On the tiny atom, see Isidore, *Etym.* XIII.ii.1–4, and perhaps cf. Lucretius, *De Rerum Natura* II.112–24.

INTRODUCTION TO THE CARMEN DE VIRGINITATE (pp. 97–101)

[1] Ehwald, p. 321; *Prose Works*, pp. 130–1.

[2] Aldhelm addresses his audience directly in line 2832 ('sed vos . . .'), but the reference is not specific.

[3] P. Godman, 'The Anglo-Latin *opus geminatum*: from Aldhelm to Alcuin', *Medium Ævum* L (1981), pp. 215–29, and M. Roberts, *Biblical Epic and Rhetorical Paraphrase in Late Antiquity* (Liverpool, 1985).

[4] G. Wieland, '*Geminus stilus*: Studies in Anglo-Latin Hagiography', in *Insular Latin Studies*, ed. M. W. Herren (Toronto, 1981), pp. 113–33.

[5] *HE* V.18 (ed. Colgrave and Mynors, p. 515).

[6] Virtually nothing is known about Caelius Sedulius. The information that he was a *Roman* poet derives from the octosyllabic poem by Aldhelm's student Æthilwald, where he is referred to as *indigena Romae* (Ehwald, p. 529). This could perhaps be dismissed as a late testimony of little value, but it is well to remember that Aldhelm had access to works by Latin poets which we no longer possess (e.g. Lucan's *Orpheus*, the poems of Paulus Quaestor), and it is possible that he had a manuscript of Caelius Sedulius in which the poet's homeland was specified, and hence that Æthilwald's statement is of high authority (recall too that the statement is made in the context of a poem describing a journey to *Rome*).

[7] Both works are edited by J. Huemer, Corpus Scriptorum Ecclesiasticorum Latinorum X (Vienna, 1885). There is an English translation

of parts of the *Carmen Paschale* by G. Sigerson, *The Easter Song being the First Epic of Christendom by Sedulius* (Dublin, 1922); Sigerson's misguided arguments that Sedulius was an Irishman, however, are best passed over in silence.

8 See the accompanying notes below, pp. 257–9.
9 In general see J. D. A. Ogilvy, *Books Known to the English, 597–1066* (Cambridge, Mass., 1967), pp. 230–2. This account must be supplemented by two sorts of evidence: that of manuscripts of Prudentius written or owned in Anglo-Saxon England (see H. Gneuss, 'A Preliminary List of Manuscripts written or owned in England up to 1100', *Anglo-Saxon England* IX [1981], pp. 1–60, nos. 38, 70, 191, 246, 285, 324, 537 and 852) and by that of booklists (see M. Lapidge, 'Surviving Booklists from Anglo-Saxon England', in *Learning and Literature in Anglo-Saxon England*, ed. M. Lapidge and H. Gneuss [Cambridge, 1985], pp. 33–89, at 88 [with refs.]).
10 On this nautical metaphor, see E. R. Curtius, *European Literature and the Latin Middle Ages*, trans. W. R. Trask (New York, 1953), pp. 128–30.
11 To the list of manuscripts of *CdV* given by Ehwald (p. 349) may be added Vatican City, Biblioteca Apostolica Vaticana, Reg. lat. 329 (Corbie, s.ix[1]) and 598 (Fleury, s. x) (fragment).
12 Alcuin's *De Laude Dei* has not been printed. It is preserved in two manuscripts, of which the best known is Bamberg, Staatsbibliothek Misc. Patr. 17 (B.II.10); the Aldhelm excerpts are on ff. 154v–155r (they include *CdV* praef. 11–18, 1–16, 32–44, 2814–28 and 2871–2904). On the *De Laude Dei* see R. Constantinescu, 'Alcuin et les "Libelli Precum" de l'époque carolingienne', *Revue d'histoire de la spiritualité* L (1974), pp. 17–56.
13 These manuscripts include: Cambridge, Corpus Christi College 285 (s. xi[in]), University Library Gg.5.35 (St Augustine's, Canterbury, s. xi[med]), Oxford, Bodleian Library, Bodley 49 (?Winchester, s. x), 577 (Christ Church, Canterbury, s.x/xi) and Rawlinson C. 697 (Francia, s. ix[2]; English provenance).

THE CARMEN DE VIRGINITATE (pp. 102–67)

The *Carmen de Virginitate* by and large adheres closely to the earlier prose *De Virginitate*; hence some points of obscurity in the poetic version may be clarified by reference to the prose work. Certain points of obscurity in the prose *De Virginitate* are discussed in *Prose Works*, pp. 193–7; a list of the sources drawn on by Aldhelm for his exemplary virgins is found *ibid.*, pp. 176–8. Significant additions to, or omissions from, the prose work are discussed below.

¹ The word *virgo* in line 2 is ambiguous: it may refer to the Virgin Mary (as rendered here), with respect to the address to *maxima ... mater* in lines 22–3, or it may simply be that *virgo* refers collectively to 'every virgin'.

² The word *puppup* is apparently a sound made only by the devil and only attested by Aldhelm (although his use of the word is followed by later poets such as Hrabanus Maurus and Dunstan).

³ This is the line on which the acrostic of the poem is based — METRICA TIRONES NUNC PROMANT CARMINA CASTOS — spelled backwards. The backwards line scans after a fashion: was Aldhelm trying to compose a *versus retrogradus*?

⁴ The promise was made in the prose *De Virginitate*, c. LX; see above, p. 97.

⁵ By 'new verse' (*novo versu*) Aldhelm is referring once again to the originality of his achievement as a composer of Anglo-Latin hexameters.

⁶ Aldhelm is referring here to God's original formation of man from mud (61: 'terrenam dignaris condere formam'); the reference is clear from Aldhelm's reminiscence of a line describing the Creation in Cyprianus Gallus, *Genesis* 31: '*inspirat brutum* diuino a pectore *pectus*'; cf. *CdV* 62: 'et *brutum inspiras* vitali flamine *pectus*', but the nuance is difficult to capture in translation.

⁷ The translation here of *libella argenti*, 'little piece of silver', is literal, but the precise meaning of Aldhelm's comparison is unclear. The general sense seems to be that even the smallest weighable piece of silver has merit.

⁸ The word *t(a)enia* literally means 'headband'; but by analogy with *infula* (cf. Ehwald, pp. 234.11, 250.10, 261.2, etc.) it comes in Aldhelm's lexicon to mean 'distinction' or the like.

⁹ The linking of Elijah with Enoch, and the mention of Antichrist, are not found in the prose *De Virginitate*. Aldhelm's source is probably Gregory's *Moralia in Iob* XIV.23 (Patrologia Latina LXXV, cols. 1053–4).

¹⁰ The following material on Jeremiah has no correlate in the prose *De Virginitate*; Aldhelm presumably added it through renewed consultation of the Bible.

¹¹ The following material on Daniel is not in the prose *De Virginitate*; it is taken by Aldhelm from the biblical Book of Daniel.

¹² The account of Didymus in the prose *De Virginitate* (c. XXIII) is omitted here.

¹³ There is some ambiguity here. From the prose *De Virginitate* (c. XXIV) it appears that the 'seat of the Augustans' was in fact Constantinople. Does *post Romae imperium* (523) mean 'after (i.e. second to) the power of Rome'?

¹⁴ Lines 534–8 have no correlate in the prose *De Virginitate*. Ehwald suggests (*app. ad loc.*) that Aldhelm's source was probably the pseudo-Clementine *Recognitiones* in Rufinus's translation.

¹⁵ There is ambiguity in the phrase *pignus mundi*, here rendered 'proofs of the pure one' (i.e. Silvester); it could also refer to the 'pledge of the world' (i.e. Christ).

¹⁶ The account of Zambrius is not found in the prose *De Virginitate*.

¹⁷ Confusingly, Ambrose's father was also called Ambrose: see Paulinus, *Vita S. Ambrosii*, c. iii: '... patre eius Ambrosio natus est Ambrosius'.

¹⁸ In the prose *De Virginitate*, a brief account of a certain Felix follows that of Basil, but it is omitted in the *Carmen de Virginitate*.

¹⁹ The grammatical incongruity here ('Those who wish' ... 'let him look') is Aldhelm's: *qui malunt ... non pigeat* (lines 766–72).

²⁰ It is not precisely clear what is meant by lines 833–4, nor how they relate to the mention of *duplam vitam* in the previous line.

²¹ Aldhelm makes numerous additions in *CdV* to his earlier prose account of Benedict, most of which are drawn from bk II of Gregory's *Dialogi* (see Ehwald's note *ad loc.*).

²² The prose *De Virginitate* does not include an account of Gervasius and Protasius. Aldhelm's source was apparently the pseudo-Ambrose letter on their *passio* which is included as *Ep.* liii in Ambrose's correspondence (Patrologia Latina XVII, cols 742–7). The account of Gervasius and Protasius replaces much of the material in the prose work, c. XXXI, as well as the account of Malchus, who is omitted here.

²³ There is some ambiguity in Aldhelm's Latin as to whether it was Alexander or Athanasius who defeated Arius. In fact it was principally Alexander (but with the support of Athanasius, then his deacon) who took an active part against the Arian heresy at the Council of Nicaea (325), and Arius was subsequently excommunicated by a synod at Alexandria convened by Alexander; cf. the account in the prose *De Virginitate*, c. XXXII (Ehwald, pp. 272–3; *Prose Works*, pp. 92–3).

²⁴ On the salamander living in fire, cf. Aldhelm's *Enigma* xv (above, p. 73).

²⁵ For some unknown reason, *quingentas* (500) in the prose *De Virginitate* (Ehwald, p. 282.16) has here become *quinquaginta* (50) (line 1325).

²⁶ Aldhelm's long excursus on classical mythology (*CdV* 1327–51 and 1372–85) has no correlate in the prose work.

²⁷ Ehwald suspected that a line had fallen out after line 1371. But more drastic editorial surgery may be necessary. It is not easy to see, for example, why the discussion of Dagon (lines 1352–70) should come in the middle of the catalogue of classical gods. The problem can be solved by transposing lines 1372–85 so that they follow immediately on after line 1351. Such a dislocation could have come about as a result of a misplaced leaf in the exemplar of the surviving manuscripts.

²⁸ The etymologizing of *Nitria/natron* is not found in the prose *De Virginitate*. Isidore (*Etym.* XVI.ii.7) derives the mineral name 'natron' (Latin *nitrum*), with its mineral function of cleansing, from the Egyptian place-name Nitria. Aldhelm, by contrast, derives the place-name from the mineral. Did Aldhelm misremember (or misunderstand) Isidore's discussion?

[29] The Latin here is *Parcae nulli parcentes*. Aldhelm is playing on the supposed connection of *parco* ('to spare') with *Parcae* ('the Fates'); cf. Isidore, *Etym.* VIII.ix.93.

[30] In the phrase *mortalis aufugit* (line 1509) Aldhelm employs the archaic acc. pl. termination *-is* instead of the far commoner *-es*. The archaic form is found frequently in Vergil, but is extremely rare in medieval Latin.

[31] There is no account of Jerome in the prose *De Virginitate*.

[32] *CdV* lines 1691–1709 correspond verbatim to *Carmina Ecclesiastica* II.13–31; see above, p. 47.

[33] Both in Aldhelm's source and in his own account the identity of Lucia's suitor is not made clear. But since Aldhelm stresses Paschasius's rage, it seems probable that Aldhelm understood the consul to have been the suitor; cf. *Prose Works*, p. 196, n. 22.

[34] If the transmitted *boves ... trusissent* ('cattle ... pressed') is taken literally, the sense seems to be that Lucia, bound, was dragged by a rope and herded along with cattle; but the sense is not clear. The prose *De Virginitate* (c. XLII) makes no mention of the *boves*.

[35] It is not clear why the two verbs here — *pateretur* (1922) and *plecteret* (1923) — should be in the subjunctive.

[36] In the prose *De Virginitate*, Scholastica is linked with Christina and Dorothea; here in the *CdV*, however, Christina and Dorothea have been omitted. One may wonder about the reason for this shift in emphasis, and it may be significant that there was a nun at Barking whose name was Scholastica and who was mentioned by Aldhelm as one of the addressees of the prose *De Virginitate* (Ehwald, p. 229; *Prose Works*, p. 59).

[37] This account of Constantina is far more extensive than that in the prose *De Virginitate*, but it is apparently based on the same source.

[38] The feast of Anastasia is 25 December. She is mentioned in the Canon of the Mass (see B. Botte and C. Mohrmann, *L'Ordinaire de la messe* [Paris and Louvain, 1953], p. 84), a fact which is adverted to by Aldhelm himself in his prose *De Virginitate*, c. XLII (Ehwald, p. 293; *Prose Works*, p. 108). However, the information given here — namely that her *passio* is read annually on her feast day — is not given at the corresponding point of the prose *De Virginitate*.

[39] The word *tigillum*, literally a 'small beam', is used here by metonymy to refer to the serpent's dwelling or habitation.

INTRODUCTION TO THE CARMEN RHYTHMICUM (pp. 171–6)

[1] Ed. Ehwald, pp. 524–8.

[2] See F. Unterkircher, *Sancti Bonifacii Epistolae. Codex Vindobonensis 751 der österreichischen Nationalbibliothek*, Codices selecti phototypice impressi XXIV (Graz, 1971), p. 25.

[3] M. Tangl, *Sancti Bonifatii et Lullii Epistolae*, Monumenta Germaniae Historica, Epistolae Selectae I (Berlin, 1916), p. 144 (*Ep.* lxxi): 'Similiter obsecro, ut mihi Aldhelmi episcopi aliqua opuscula seu prosarum seu metrorum aut rithmicorum dirigere digneris ad consolationem peregrinationis meae'. The letter is dated by Tangl to 745 x 746. See also above, p. 220, n. 3.

[4] Ehwald, pp. 520–2. Ehwald's view was anticipated by L. Traube, *Karolingische Dichtungen* (Berlin, 1888), pp. 130–5, and is accepted (with various modifications) by H. Bradley, 'On Some Poems Ascribed to Aldhelm', *English Historical Review* XV (1900), pp. 291–2, and by W. F. Bolton, *A History of Anglo-Latin Literature I: 597–740* (Princeton, 1967), pp. 100 and 188–9.

[5] The matter is treated at some length in *Prose Works*, pp. 16–18.

[6] The poem which lacks this rubric is that printed by Ehwald as no. iv, which in the Vienna manuscript runs on continuously as part of Ehwald's no. iii; in other words, the separation into two poems of Ehwald nos. iii and iv is Ehwald's editorial intervention.

[7] See W. M. Lindsay, *Notae Latinae* (Cambridge, 1915), p. 6.

[8] It might seem strange that the first poem in a series would be inscribed *carmen aliter*; but there is no means of proving that the first poem in the manuscript as it survives was indeed the first poem of the series. The first rhythmical poem begins a new quire (at f. 40r), and although written by the same scribe as wrote the preceding quires, this quire has no organic connection with the ordered sequence of Bonifatian correspondence contained in the previous five quires. Since there are no quire signatures in the manuscript, it must remain a possibility that a quire has been lost before f. 40r and that this lost quire may have contained other rhythmical poems.

[9] Ed. in facsimile by H. Omont, *Anthologie des poètes latins dite de Saumaise* (Paris, 1903); also ed. A. Riese, *Anthologia Latina: Carmina in codicibus scripta*, 2 vols. (Leipzig, 1894–1906). The word *aliter* occurs as a rubric to Riese, nos. 95, 109, 114, 120–3, 125, 134–5, 138, 140, 144, 146–7, etc.

[10] 'On Some Poems Ascribed to Aldhelm', pp. 291–2.

[11] In the so-called 'Liber Vitae of Durham', ed. H. Sweet, *The Oldest English Texts*, Early English Text Society o.s. LXXXIII (London, 1885), pp. 153–66; the name Helmgils occurs in lines 10 and 244.

[12] It is perhaps worth asking, however, whether the 'Liber Vitae of Durham' includes the names of any Southumbrians. For example, the *Nomina abbatum gradus presbyteratus* include the name *aldhelm presbyter* (Sweet, *The Oldest English Texts*, p. 155, lines 58–9). The only abbot of this name who is known in sources earlier than the date of the 'Liber Vitae of Durham' (*c.* 840) is our Aldhelm abbot of Malmesbury (it may of course be that our Northumbrian sources are too incomplete to rule out the possibility that there was an Abbot Aldhelm in an unidentified Northumbrian monastery). And if Aldhelm himself is included in the 'Liber Vitae of Durham', it is possible that his

correspondent Helmgils is included as well. But the matter could not be proved, at least not without more exhaustive examination of the names and their possible identifications than has hitherto been attempted.

[13] It is tempting to think in this connection of the Hæmgils who was abbot of nearby Glastonbury (see *Prose Works*, p. 186, n. 23); but the names Helmgils amd Hæmgils are formed from different themes and are philologically distinct.

[14] See W. G. Hoskins, *The Westward Expansion of Wessex* (Leicester, 1970), p. 4, and S. M. Pearce, *The Kingdom of Dumnonia* (Padstow, 1978), pp. 93–4.

[15] See below, p. 263, n. 11.

[16] P. Klopsch, *Einführing in die mittellateinische Verslehre* (Darmstadt, 1972), pp. 8–16.

[17] For example, three hymns in the Antiphonary of Bangor (a manuscript of late seventh-century date, so that the hymns which it contains are certain to be earlier): 'Ymnum S. Comgilli', 'Collectio ad secundam' and 'Memoria abbatum'. The hymns are ed. in *Analecta Hymnica Medii Aevi*, ed. G. M. Dreves and C. Blume, 55 vols. (Leipzig, 1886–1922), LI, pp. 321–4 (no. 244), 288–9 (no. 220) and 357–8 (no. 261). The hymns are discussed by W. Meyer, 'Die Verskunst der Iren in rythmischen lateinischen Gedichten', in his *Gesammelte Abhandlungen zur mittellateinische Rythmik*, 3 vols. (Berlin, 1905–36), III, pp. 303–28, and M. Curran, *The Antiphonary of Bangor* (Dublin, 1984), pp. 81–2 and 93–6.

[18] *Analecta Hymnica* LI, pp. 275–83 (no. 216).

[19] The terminology used here is that of D. Norberg, *Introduction à l'étude de la versification latine médiévale* (Uppsala, 1958).

[20] The question of the influence of *Altus prosator* on Aldhelm has been treated at length in a forthcoming monograph on *Altus prosator* by Miss J. B. Stevenson of Pembroke College, Cambridge.

[21] As far as can be determined from surviving evidence, all Hiberno-Latin hymns were stanzaic in form. There is, however, a poem consisting of six lines of continuous octosyllables which was addressed by Archbishop Theodore (*ob.* 690) to Hæddi, bishop of Wessex (text most easily accessible in Bolton, *History of Anglo-Latin Literature*, p. 62). It is an open question whether Aldhelm's continuous octosyllables antedate those of Theodore, or vice versa.

[22] See W. Meyer, 'Die Verskunst des Angelsachsen Aethilwald', in his *Gesammelte Abhandlungen*, III, pp. 328–46; I. Schröbler, 'Zu den Carmina Rhythmica in der Wiener HS. der Bonifatius-Briefe', *Beiträge zur Geschichte der deutschen Sprache und Literatur* LXXIX (1957), pp. 1–42; and F. W. Schulze, 'Reimkonstruktionen im Offa-Preislied Æthilwalds', *Zeitschrift für deutsches Altertum* XCII (1963), pp. 8–31.

[23] Ehwald, pp. 496–7; *Prose Works*, p. 166.

[24] Ehwald, pp. 528–37.

²⁵ There is the poem of Archbishop Theodore (mentioned above, n. 21) and a poem by Hæddi, bishop of Wessex (ed. Lapidge, 'Some Remnants of Bede's Lost *Liber Epigrammatum*', p. 817), as well as an undated epitaph for one Bealdhun (*ibid.*, p. 818).

²⁶ Tangl, *Epistolae S. Bonifatii et Lullii*, pp. 6–7 (no. 9).

²⁷ *Ibid.*, pp. 280 (no. 140: Lul) and 285–7 (nos. 147–8: Berhtgyth).

²⁸ For Lantfred's octosyllables, see E. P. Sauvage, 'Sancti Swithuni Wintoniensis episcopi Translatio et Miracula auctore Lantfredo monacho Wintoniensi', *Analecta Bollandiana* IV (1885), pp. 367–410, at 400–1. Various other Anglo-Latin continuous octosyllables, for the most part unprinted, form the subject of a forthcoming monograph by M. Lapidge.

THE CARMEN RHYTHMICUM (pp. 177–9)

¹ The English name underlying Aldhelm's Latin wordplay is *Helmgisl*, which, with customary metathesis, becomes *Helmgils*, a name well attested in early English sources (see above, p. 260, n. 11). The Helmgils in question cannot be identified, however.

² The sequence of tenses in this passage (lines 17 ff.) is confusing, as Aldhelm veers between present and preterite. For sake of accuracy, Aldhelm's tenses have been retained in the translation.

³ On the metaphor of the shattered cosmic bonds — a metaphor common in late Latin poetry and ultimately of Stoic origin — see M. Lapidge, 'A Stoic Metaphor in Late Latin Poetry: The Binding of the Cosmos', *Latomus* XXXIX (1980), pp. 817–37; see also above, p. 244, n. 22.

⁴ They are found, for example, in Isidore, *Etym.* XIII.xi.

⁵ Aldhelm mentions his astronomical studies in his letter to Leuthere (Ehwald, pp. 478–9; *Prose Works*, p. 153) and we know from Bede (*HE* IV.2) that astronomy was one of the subjects taught by Theodore and Hadrian. The astronomical lore presented here, however, is not overly complex, and was probably lifted from a source such as Isidore, *Etym.* III.lxxi, esp. 6–9 and 13–15.

⁶ On the Pliades, see Isidore, *Etym.* III.lxxi.13. Ehwald (*app. ad loc.*) notes that in line 78 the Pliades are not 'of the stock of Atlantis' (*Ab Athlantis prosapia*) but are in fact his daughters, and hence suggests reading *Ab Athlante prosapia*.

⁷ The source for the name Mazaroth is Jerome, *Ep.* lxiv.19.

⁸ The phrase *per pelagi itinera* is a metaphorical expression meaning 'over sea-roads', or the like, and it is worth asking whether Aldhelm had in mind a kenning for 'sea' such as are found frequently in Old English poetry: cf. *brimrad* (*Andreas* 1262) and *streamrad* (*Gifts of Men* 54), etc.; cf. *Prose Works*, p. 201, n. 29.

9 On the word *dodrans* used to mean 'flood-tide' in Insular Latin, see A. K. Brown, 'Bede, a Hisperic Etymology, and Early Sea Poetry', *Mediaeval Studies* XXXVII (1975), pp. 419–32.

10 The *calculus* is literally the marker used on the counting-board, rather than the board itself. The abacus was not introduced into Europe until a much later time, during the tenth and eleventh centuries; see G. R. Evans, 'Schools and Scholars: The Study of the Abacus in English Schools c. 980—c. 1150', *English Historical Review* XCIV (1979), pp. 71–89.

11 This passage is of particular interest for our knowledge of the Divine Office in early Anglo-Saxon England (see above, p. 236, n. 25). In referring to *matutinam melodiam* (line 129) Aldhelm is apparently referring to the office of 'matins' or the Night Office (which consisted of three Nocturns); this is clear from the fact that dawn breaks only after the storm has interrupted the Office and wrecked the church (lines 157–60). It should be noted that Aldhelm uses here the later medieval terminology for Matins or Nocturns, rather than that of St Benedict, who refers to what are now usually called Lauds as *Matutini* ('Matutini, qui incipiente luce agendi sunt': *Regula*, c. viii). Since the storm occurred in June, the monks will have been following the summer *horarium*, which began, presumably, around 2.00 a.m (cf. D. Knowles, *The Monastic Order in England*, 2nd edn. [Cambridge, 1963], pp. 714–15). The monks divide into two responding ranks: for chanting the antiphons and responsories (cf. *CE* III.47 and prose *De Virg.*, c. XXX). Aldhelm says nothing to imply that the congregation consisted of other than monks, but the possibility should be borne in mind that the church in question was a double house (i.e. one housing both men and women).

12 On wooden churches surviving from the Anglo-Saxon period, see C. A. Hewett, 'Anglo-Saxon Carpentry', *Anglo-Saxon England* VII (1978), pp. 205–29, esp. 206–16. None of the churches in question is as early as Aldhelm; for that reason it is worth noting what Bede says in passing about the construction of a wooden church at Lindisfarne (*HE* III.25).

13 Earlier editors suspected that the word *duobus* was corrupt (Jaffé, for example, conjectured *dubiis*). Ehwald prints *duobus* but obelizes it.

INTRODUCTION TO THE APPENDIX (pp. 183–90)

1 According to Bede (*HE* IV.2), they taught not only biblical exegesis but also astronomy, computus, and metrics: 'ita ut etiam metricae artis, astronomiae et arithmeticae ecclesiasticae disciplinam inter sacrorum apicum volumina suis auditoribus contraderent'.

2 Ehwald, p. 477: 'cuius rei studiosis lectoribus tanto inextricabilior obscuritas praetenditur, quanto rarior doctorum numerositas reperitur'.

[3] In Ehwald's edition the two final chapters of *De Pedum Regulis* are both numbered CLI; I have corrected this error.

[4] For a general introduction to this metre, see S. E. Winbolt, *Latin Hexameter Verse* (London, 1903).

[5] See, further, *ibid.*, pp. 70–105.

[6] See, for example, Donatus's discussion of metaplasms in the *Ars Maior*, ed. L. Holtz, *Donat et la tradition de l'enseignement grammatical* (Paris, 1981), pp. 660–3.

[7] He does not, however, give examples of the positions in the line most favoured for elision by hexameter poets (see Winbolt, *Latin Hexameter Verse*, pp. 174–7); indeed, the vast majority of the examples which he quotes have elision at the first long (or arsis) of the second foot (e.g. *Aeneid* XI.1: 'Ocĕanl[um] intĕrĕă surlgens Aŭrlŏră rĕllĭquit') — a position which Aldhelm employs to excess in his own poetry.

[8] Edited by H. Keil, *Grammatici Latini*, 8 vols. (Leipzig, 1857–70), VII, pp. 320–62; on the date of the *Excerpta*, see Jacques Fontaine, *Isidore de Séville et la culture classique dans l'Espagne visigothique*, 2 vols. (Paris, 1951), I, pp. 197–8.

[9] In this table a dactyl is represented as D and a spondee as S; hence a line with dactyls in the first and fifth feet appears as DSSSD.

[10] The artificiality of these lines is well illustrated by the fact that many of them necessarily have a fifth-foot spondee, a feature which Aldhelm, following Audax, had already expressly forbidden (see above, p. 196).

[11] This section, which is not found in all manuscripts of the *Epistula ad Acircium*, derives not from Audax's *Excerpta*, which do not contain it, but from the closely related *De Hexametro Versu sive Heroico* of Maximus Victorinus (Keil, *Grammatici Latini* VI, pp. 206–15). Aldhelm probably added this section to *De Metris* after its completion when a copy of Victorinus's work came into his hands; see Vivien Law, 'The Study of Latin Grammar in eighth-century Southumbria', *Anglo-Saxon England* XII (1983), pp. 43–71, at 49.

[12] For a discussion of Vergil's practice, see G. E. Duckworth, *Vergil and Classical Hexameter Poetry* (Michigan, 1969), pp. 46–62.

[13] See further p. 267, n. 31, below.

[14] See, for example, the discussions of the feet found in Audax's *Excerpta* (Keil, *Grammatici Latini* VII, pp. 33–6) and Donatus's *Ars Maior* (Holtz, *Donat*, pp. 607–9).

[15] Ehwald, p. 477: 'quomodo videlicet ipsius metricae artis clandistina instrumenta literis, logis, pedibus, poeticis figuris, versibus, tonis, temporibus conglomerentur, pathetica quoque septenae divisionis disciplina hoc est acephalos, lagaros, procilios cum ceteris qualiter varietur, qui versus monoscemi, qui pentascemi, qui decascemi certa pedum mensura trutinentur, et qualiter catalecti vel brachicatalecti versus sagaci argumentatione colligantur'.

[16] The first sections of Donatus's *Ars Maior* (Holtz, *Donat*, pp. 603–12), for example, deal with the voice, letters, syllables (including *tempora*; for a definition of this term, see below p. 266, n. 18), feet, accents, and

punctuation; Aldhelm's 'poetic figures' may correspond to Donatus's closing sections on metaplasms, schemes and tropes (*ibid.*, pp. 660–74).

[17] See *Prose Works*, pp. 8–9.

[18] See also Law, 'The Study of Latin Grammar', pp. 50–2.

[19] *Prose Works*, pp. 29–47.

APPENDIX (pp. 191–211)

[1] That is, the *Enigmata*; Aldhelm's stated intention is not, as is often held, that the *Enigmata* should exemplify the rules of the hexameter, but that *De Metris* (and *De Pedum Regulis*) should explain the metre of the *Enigmata*.

[2] Aldhelm here makes an oblique reference to Servius's *De Centum Metris* (Keil, *Grammatici Latini* IV, pp. 456–67); see also below, nn. 17, 28 and 31.

[3] 'I have not moistened my lips at the nag's fountain [Pege, created when Pegasus's hoof struck the earth] nor do I recall having dreamt on twin-peaked Parnassus'. Persius refers ironically to the dream of the epic poet Ennius in which he learnt that he was a reincarnation of Homer.

[4] See below, n. 18.

[5] Strictly speaking, *habendum (e)st* is an example of *aphaeresis*, not elision. When *est* (or *es*) is preceded by a final vowel or vowel + *m*, the initial *e* of *est* is suppressed (the original pronunciation having been *habendumst*). However, neither Aldhelm nor his models, the Late Latin grammarians, distinguish between *aphaeresis* and elision proper.

[6] This manner of scansion — the syllabic division of words into the constituent feet of the line — was the standard method employed by the grammarians.

[7] Paulus the Quaestor, whom Aldhelm quotes on three occasions (see below, nn. 23 and 25), is otherwise unknown. The line cited here is modelled on *Aeneid* VIII.667, '*Tartareas* etiam *sedes*, alta ostia Ditis', and Juvenal, *Satirae* II.120, 'gremio iacuit *nova nupta mariti*'.

[8] This is line 28 of a Latin acrostic poem which translates the Eighth Book of the *Oracula Sibyllina*, lines 217–50: see W. Bulst, 'Eine anglo-lateinische Übersetzung aus dem Griechischen um 700', *Zeitschrift für deutsches Altertum* LXXV (1938), pp. 105–11 (see above, p. 16, and also below, nn. 34 and 36). Bulst's tentative suggestion that Aldhelm may himself have been responsible for this translation is perhaps unlikely in the light of the latter's limited knowledge of Greek.

[9] This poem is in fact the work of the Visigothic king Sisebut; however, it is often, as here, ascribed to Isidore — a confusion which probably arose because the poem is frequently transmitted with his *De Rerum Natura*.

[10] Aldhelm expresses himself poorly here, but his meaning is clear: *synaloepha* is the elision of a final vowel, *ecthlipsis* the elision of a final vowel + *m*; cf. Donatus's *Ars Maior* (Holtz, *Donat*, p. 662.7–13).

¹¹ Aldhelm here quotes from a book of Cyprianus Gallus's poem which has not survived.

¹² The origin of this quotation is unknown. In one manuscript these lines form part of the *Epitaphium Lucani*, which is also quoted by Aldhelm (see below, n. 26); possibly Aldhelm drew both quotations from a similar manuscript source containing both poems, now lost.

¹³ Ehwald (p. 81.1) prints 'ex numero XXIV', but the variant reading 'XIV' must be correct, since Aldhelm is referring to the fourteen metaplasms of the grammarians (cf. above, n. 10) and not, as Ehwald thought, to the twenty-four *tempora* of the hexameter line (n. 18 below); see Law, 'The Study of Latin Grammar in eighth-century Southumbria', p. 50.

¹⁴ That is, the division into long, short, and common (or middle) syllables, although Aldhelm proceeds to discuss hexameter structure rather than prosody.

¹⁵ Aldhelm refers here to Donatus's *Ars Maior* (Holtz, *Donat*, p. 615); see Law, 'The Study of Latin Grammar', p. 48.

¹⁶ Despite his references to Augustine, Isidore, and Junilius, Aldhelm in fact adopts the question-and-answer form directly from Audax's *Excerpta*, which from this point onwards is the major source of *De Metris*.

¹⁷ See above, n. 2.

¹⁸ Metrical theory held that a short represented one *tempus* and a long, two; consequently, both a dactyl and a spondee consist of four *tempora* and a hexameter line (unless its sixth foot is a trochee of three *tempora*) of twenty-four.

¹⁹ Depending, that is, on how many feet the line contains.

²⁰ The iambic senarius or trimeter is quite irrelevant in this context; the distinction between the dactylic and heroic hexameter is one of genre, not metre.

²¹ Both quotations — the first of a line attributed to Ennius (*Annales* 603), the second from an unknown author — are drawn directly from Audax's *Excerpta* (Keil, *Grammatici Latini* VII, pp. 338–9).

²² Aldhelm is being pedantic here. All hexameters are catalectic (i.e. have their full number of syllables) by definition; see below, n. 31.

²³ See above, n. 7.

²⁴ The line is in fact what Aldhelm terms a *districtus*; see above, pp. 207–8.

²⁵ See above, n. 7.

²⁶ This is the first line of the *Epitaphium Lucani*; see *M. Annaei Lucani Belli Civilis Libri Decem*, ed. C. Hosius (Leipzig, 1913), p. 338.

²⁷ This discussion of the sixth-foot dactyl, which Aldhelm largely borrows from Audax (Keil, *Grammatici Latini* VII, pp. 339–40), is quite erroneous. A dactyl in the sixth foot is impossible. Of the two Vergilian lines quoted initially, *Georgics* III.449 is a hypermetric line, i.e. the final syllable of *sulphura* is elided by the initial word of the following line (see Winbolt, *Latin Hexameter Verse*, p. 148). In *Aeneid*

VI.33, *omnia* is scanned as a trochee (– ◡) by synezesis (i.e. the *i* is treated as consonantal) and not, as Audax maintains, by elision. The final two verses, again borrowed directly from Audax, are completely artificial, the second being a reworking of *Aeneid* IX.503 (cited above, p. 203).

28 This line, which like the previous two is totally artificial, is probably cited from Servius, *De Centum Metris* (Keil, *Grammatici Latini* IV, p. 461.14–15).

29 Aldhelm borrows the following section not from Audax's *Excerpta*, but from the related *De Hexametro Versu sive Heroico* attributed to Maximus Victorinus; see above, p. 264, n. 11.

30 This is misleading; *Aeneid* VII.634 is unique. Vergil's regular practice when employing a fifth-foot spondee was to place a dactyl in the fourth foot at least; see Winbolt, *Latin Hexameter Verse*, pp. 129–30.

31 This section, the source of which is unknown, is again misguided. Hypercatalexis is impossible in a hexameter line (unless, as very rarely occurs, the line is hypermetric; see above, n. 27). At least three of the examples adduced by Aldhelm are artificial: the first and fourth lines are derived (perhaps indirectly) from Servius's *De Centum Metris* (Keil, *Grammatici Latini* IV, p. 461.17–19 and 7–9 respectively); the second line is a reworking of *Aeneid* IX.758, 'rumpere claustra manu sociosque immittere portis'; I have not been able to trace this or the third line to any source.

32 Aldhelm borrows these terms from Audax (Keil, *Grammatici Latini* VII, p. 340), although he confuses the issue by changing their meanings.

33 The line, which is entirely artificial, is again borrowed directly from Audax.

34 This is line 14 of the acrostic discussed above, n. 8.

35 The poet is Aldhelm himself; the line reappears as *Carmen de Virginitate*, 530.

36 This is line 12 of the acrostic discussed above, n. 8.

37 See Introduction, above, pp. 187–8.

38 This is special pleading on Aldhelm's part. The initial short of *Ĭtalia* was regularly lengthened by Vergil at all points of the line by *ectasis*; see Donatus's *Ars Maior* (Holtz, *Donat*, p. 661.11–12).

39 Aldhelm's definition of the third trochaic caesura is incorrect. It may be that he was misled by a faulty manuscript of his source. For example, Audax's *Excerpta* (Keil, *Grammatici Latini* VII, p. 333) define the third trochaic as follows: 'cata triton trochaeon fit quotiens in tertia regione talis dactylus ponitur, *cui si ultimum syllabam dempseris, trochaeus, qui ex duobus reliquis constat, orationis particulum finit*'. If Aldhelm was using this passage, or a similar source, and the qualifying relative clause had fallen out, this might explain his error; but see below, n. 40.

40 Aldhelm repeats his error of the third trochaic. However, like Audax, he also confuses the fourth trochaic caesura with bucolic diaeresis, which occurs when a strong pause is found after a dactylic fourth foot,

as in *Eclogue* III.1: 'Dīc mĭhĭ, Dāmŏētă, cŭĭum pĕcŭs? | ăn Mēlĭbŏei?'
This confusion may be an alternative explanation for his false definition
of the third trochaic caesura.

[41] Again this is garbled, although it is true that the *Eclogues*, in which
Vergil is imitating Theocritus, contain a higher proportion of fourth-
foot dactyls than the *Georgics* or *Aeneid*; see Winbolt, *Latin
Hexameter Verse*, p. 115.

[42] Aldhelm here confuses the division of the foot into arsis and thesis
with the position of word-accent in his examples.

[43] The division is in terms of *tempora*. To exemplify each type, a pyrrhic
($\smile \| \smile$) is *aequa* (one *tempus* to one), an iamb ($\smile \| -$) is *dupla* (one *tempus* to
two), and a bacchius ($\smile - \| -$) is *sescupla* (three *tempora* to two); the
division of all the feet is conveniently set out in Isidore, *Etym.*
I.xvii.21–8.

[44] The source of this line was unknown to Ehwald; I have not been able
to trace it.

[45] See G. B. De Rossi, *Inscriptiones Christianae Urbis Romae Septimo
Saeculo Antiquiores*, 2 vols. (Rome, 1857–88), II, p. 71; Aldhelm
probably drew this line from an unidentified sylloge or collection of
inscriptional poems (see above, p. 36).

[46] The distinction here, although Aldhelm does not draw it explicitly, is
between the practice of Classical poets, who treated the *o* of the first
person singular as long, and that of Late Latin and Christian poets,
who regularly permitted its shortening.

[47] This pentameter line is quoted from the *De Metris* of Mallius
Theodorus (Keil, *Grammatici Latini* VI, p. 590), although Aldhelm
does not appear to use this treatise elsewhere in the *Epistola ad
Acircium*.

[48] The source from which Aldhelm drew these outlandish names — if
indeed one existed — has not been traced; these terms are the only
fantastic element in Aldhelm's otherwise sober treatise.

INDEX OF NAMES

274

Addenda to the Paperback Edition

On Aldhelm's life and writings (pp. 5–24), see now M. Lapidge, 'The Career of Aldhelm', *Anglo-Saxon England* XXXVI (2007), 15–69. On Aldhelm's reading, see M. Lapidge, *The Anglo-Saxon Library* (Oxford, 2006), pp. 178–91. Aldhelm's involvement in the production of early Anglo-Saxon glossaries is examined by M. Lapidge, 'Aldhelm and the "Epinal-Erfurt Glossary"', in *Aldhelm and Sherborne. Essays to Celebrate the Foundation of the Bishopric*, ed. K. Barker and N. Brooks (Oxford, 2009), pp. 129–63. The Lives of Aldhelm by Faricius and William of Malmesbury are now available in excellent modern editions: M. Winterbottom, 'An Edition of Faricius, *Vita S. Aldhelmi*', *The Journal of Medieval Latin* XV (2005), 93–147 [with translation by M. Winterbottom, 'Faricius of Arezzo's Life of St Aldhelm', in *Latin Learning and English Lore. Studies in Anglo-Saxon Literature for Michael Lapidge*, ed. K. O'Brien O'Keeffe and A. Orchard, 2 vols. (Toronto, 2005), I, 109–31], and M. Winterbottom, *William of Malmesbury, Gesta Pontificum Anglorum*, I. *Text and Translation* (Oxford, 2007), pp. 498–662 [with R. M. Thomson, *William of Malmesbury, Gesta Pontificum Anglorum*, II. *Introduction and Commentary* (Oxford, 2007)]. The corpus of Aldhelm's verse is treated thoroughly by A. Orchard, *The Poetic Art of Aldhelm* (Cambridge, 1994); for the later influence of his verse, see A. Orchard, 'After Aldhelm: The Teaching and Transmission of the Anglo-Latin Hexameter', *The Journal of Medieval Latin* II (1992), 1–43, and, for the influence of his verse in Visigothic Spain, A. Breeze, 'The Transmission of Aldhelm's Writings in Early Medieval Spain', *Anglo-Saxon England* XXI (1992), 5–21. For Aldhelm's debt to Old English verse, see, in addition to Orchard's book cited above, P. G. Remley, 'Aldhelm as Old English Poet: *Exodus*, Asser and the *Dicta Ælfredi*', in *Latin Learning and English Lore*, ed. O'Brien O'Keeffe and Orchard, I, 90–108.

On the *Carmina ecclesiastica*, see J. Story, 'Aldhelm and Old St Peter's, Rome', *Anglo-Saxon England* XXXIX (2010), forthcoming [important new evidence for Aldhelm's visit(s) to Rome and study there of verse inscriptions].

On the *Enigmata*, see M. L. Cameron, 'Aldhelm as Naturalist: A Re-examination of Some of his *Enigmata*', *Peritia* IV (1985), 117–33; C. Milovanović-Barham, 'Aldhelm's *Enigmata* and Byzantine Riddles', *Anglo-Saxon England* XXII (1993), 51–64; M. Herren, 'The Transmission and Reception of Graeco-Roman Mythology in Anglo-Saxon England, 670–800', *Anglo-Saxon England* XXVII (1998), 87–103; E.V. Thornbury, 'Aldhelm's Rejection of the Muses and the Mechanics of Poetic Inspiration in Early Anglo-Saxon England', *Anglo-Saxon England* XXXVI (2007), 71–92; and R. Borysławski, '*Candida sanctarum sic floret gloria rerum*: Aldhelm's *Aenigmata* as a Riddle of Interpretation', *Journal of Medieval Latin* XVIII (2008), 203–16. For glossing of the *Enigmata*, see N. P. Stork, *Through a Gloss Darkly: Aldhelm's Riddles in the British Library MS. Royal 12. C. XXIII* (Toronto, 1990).

On the *Carmen de virginitate*, see G. Wieland, 'Aldhelm's *De octo vitiis principalibus* and Prudentius' *Psychomachia*', *Medium Ævum* LV (1986), 85–92; N. Wright, 'Imitation of the Poems of Paulinus of Nola in Early Anglo-Latin Verse', *Peritia* IV (1985), 134–51 [with addenda in *Peritia* V (1986) 392–6]; C. D. Wright, 'The Blood of Abel and the Branches of Sin: *Genesis A, Maxims I* and Aldhelm's *Carmen de virginitate*', *Anglo-Saxon England* XXV (1996), 7–19.

On Aldhelm's metrical treatises, see C. Ruff, 'The Place of Metrics in Anglo-Saxon Latin Education: Aldhelm and Bede', *Journal of English and Germanic Philology* CIV (2005), 149–70.

Some corrigenda:

p. 39 line 10: *for* Paul *read* Pauli

p. 229 n. 20: note that the dedication to SS. John and Paul is to two Roman martyrs, not to the apostles of those names.

Lightning Source UK Ltd.
Milton Keynes UK
UKHW040725190722
406066UK00001B/192